AF252082

THE SCULPTURE OF JOHN DAVIS
PLACES & LOCATIONS

THE SCULPTURE OF JOHN DAVIS

PLACES & LOCATIONS

Ken Scarlett

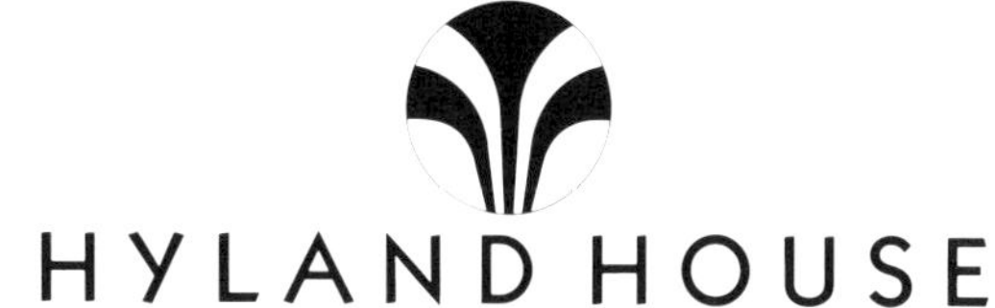

HYLAND HOUSE

First published in 1988 by
Hyland House Publishing Pty Limited
10 Hyland Street
South Yarra
Melbourne
Victoria 3141

© Ken Scarlett 1988

The author and the publishers wish to acknowledge generous
financial assistance towards the publication of this book from the
Museum of Contemporary Art, Brisbane.

This project was assisted by the Visual Arts Board of the
Australia Council, the Federal Government's arts funding and
advisory body.

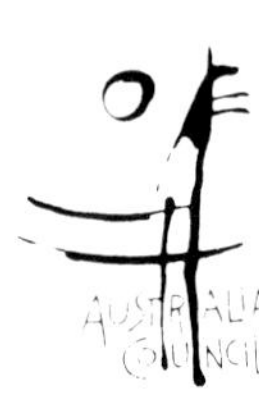

National Library of Australia
cataloguing-in-publication data:

Scarlett, Ken, 1927–
    The sculpture of John Davis.

    Bibliography.
    Includes index.
    ISBN 0 947062 26 2.

    1. Davis, John, 1936–   . 2. Sculpture, Australian.
    I. Davis, John, 1936–   . II. Title.

730′.92′4

Edited by Lee White
Index by Bettina Stevenson
Design by Rob Cowpe
Typeset by Savage Type Pty Ltd, Brisbane
Printed by Griffin Press Limited, Adelaide

BY THE SAME AUTHOR:
Australian Sculptors — Exhibition Lists (1979).
Australian Sculptors (1980).
Lenton Parr Sculptor (ed.) (1984).

Endpapers:
**John Davis: Detail of Mat
(1976). Sawn timber, twigs,
string, latex and calico. 9.5 x
81 x 69 cm. Photograph by
Mark Strizic.**

CONTENTS

ACKNOWLEDGEMENTS

The writing of this monograph would have been impossible without the co-operation of the artist, John Davis, who freely made his records available and delved into his memory, seeking answers to my apparently endless questions. A great number of private collectors, Directors and Curators of State, regional and commercial galleries also provided information on individual works as well as details of exhibitions held. I particularly wish to thank Frank Watters and Geoffrey Legge, of Watters Gallery, Sydney, for allowing me access to their files.

The publication of a book on a contemporary Australian sculptor is obviously not financially rewarding, as within Australia the market is necessarily small. It is therefore an act of courage, a dedication to the idea of promoting Australian art, that has led Hyland House to publish this book — and I thank Al Knight and Ann Godden of Hyland House for their interest and support for this project.

As far as possible, Mark Strizic has taken photographs for this book and I am grateful for his sensitive records of John Davis's work. Mark Strizic travelled interstate to Brisbane, Sydney, Hobart and Wollongong, and within Victoria to Shepparton and Geelong to photograph works in public collections, as well as to the homes of numerous private owners. Nevertheless, there proved to be many works of an ephemeral nature, installations left in the bush, or sculptures displayed overseas, where it was impossible for Mark Strizic to secure a photographic record. I am therefore indebted to John Davis and numerous photographers who made their negatives available, or provided me with prints. My thanks to James McArdle and Julie Millowick, Les Russell, Stelarc, Susan Vaughan, Peter Tyndall, Wesley Stacey, Goji Hamada, John Brash, Cindi McCain, Bill Short, Gary Shirley, Arne Folkedal, and in particular Tony Boyd who not only made some of his own photographs available, but also made innumerable prints from negatives and colour transparencies provided by John Davis and myself. Thanks also to the Herald and Weekly Times Ltd and David Syme and Co. Ltd, for permission to reproduce photographs, originally printed in the Melbourne *Herald* and *Age*, and to Ikebana Ryusei, Tokyo, for permission to use a photograph of John Davis taken in Tokoname, Japan. Daryl Jackson, Meldrum, Burrows Collaboratives Pty Ltd kindly made available photographs taken in Saudi Arabia.

Peta Pattihahuan and Kerry Paull, assisted by Nelly Bogaard coped with my illegible scrawl and typed the manuscript, plus the numerous corrections and alterations. Geoffrey Edwards and Margaret Dredge kindly read the draft of the manuscript and made a number of intelligent and sensitive suggestions.

James Baker purchased several sculptures from both the artist and author, thus adding to the collection of the Museum of Contemporary Art, Brisbane, and enabling us to put that money towards publication costs. The Visual Arts Board of the Australia Council generously gave financial assistance to Mark Strizic and me during the preparation of the manuscript and also supported the publishers, Hyland House, with a further grant.

Finally I would like to express my gratitude to my wife, Marian, whose support was of great assistance during the many years of preparation of this book, and my admiration for the professional role of Lee White as editor of *The Sculpture of John Davis*.

Ken Scarlett

BIOGRAPHY

JOHN DAVIS/SHIRLEY DAVIS

1936	**John Frederick Davis** born 16 September in Ballarat, Australia.
1938	**Shirley Heberle**, born 25 June in Wangaratta, Australia.
1955–57	**John Davis** completed Secondary Teachers Certificate (Arts & Crafts) at Melbourne Teachers College, Caulfield Institute of Technology, Melbourne University and Royal Melbourne Institute of Technology.
1956–58	**Shirley Heberle** student at Melbourne Teachers College and completed Secondary Teachers Certificate (Arts & Crafts).
1958	**John Davis** taught at Queenscliff High School.
1959–60	Both **John Davis** and **Shirley Heberle** taught at Numurkah High School — John woodwork and Shirley art.
1960	Became engaged in April.
1961	Married in January at Myrtleford.
1961–62	Both taught at Mildura High School. John Davis worked with Ernst Van Hattum on first Mildura Sculpture Exhibition in 1961.
1962	**Shirley Davis** ceased full-time teaching until 1973.
1963–66	**John Davis** transferred to Highett High School and studied part-time at Royal Melbourne Institute of Technology.
1963	Lived in rented house in Highett. First child (Penelope) born in July.
1965	Moved to rented house at 39 David Street, Hampton. Second child (Martin) born in December.
1966	**John Davis** completed Diploma of Sculpture at Royal Melbourne Institute of Technology.
c.1967	**Shirley Davis** joined Labor Party. **John Davis** also joined in early 1970s.
1967–71	**John Davis** appointed Lecturer in charge of 3D Design and Sculpture at Caulfield Institute of Technology.
1969–70	Tutor in Sculpture, Summer School, Monash University.
1972	Family travelled overseas for a year visiting California, New York, Mexico, Ireland, United Kingdom, Europe, Iran, Hong Kong and Bali. Children attended school in New York for three months and in London for two months.
1973	**Shirley Davis** recommences teaching art and craft at Westall High School. Bought weatherboard, Edwardian house at 44 Crisp Street, Hampton.
1973–74	**John Davis** appointed Lecturer in Charge of Sculpture and Lecturer in 3D Design at Prahran College of Advanced Education.
1975–80	Senior Lecturer in charge of Sculpture at Prahran College of Advanced Education.
1976	Artist in Residence, Monash University.
1978	Travelled in India, then later in year in Italy, London, Paris. Commissioner, Australian Exhibition, Indian Triennale; lecture tour of Indian Art Schools, Museums, etc.
1978–79	Family travelled for six weeks during school holidays in Mexico and USA.
1980	Family visited New Zealand.
1981	Co-ordinator, Post-graduate Studies, Victorian College of the Arts.
1982	**John Davis** visited Japan in September–October for first exhibition in Tokyo at Ina Gallery. Member of the Visual Arts Board, Australia Council.
1983	**John** and **Shirley Davis** visited Japan during 'Continuum '83' — two man exhibition with Peter Cole at Lunami Gallery, Tokyo.
1984	Visited Los Angeles. **John Davis** appointed Artist in Residence at USC (University of Southern California). Visited Los Angeles for LAICA Olympic Festival Exhibition entitled 'Australia: Nine Contemporary Artists'.
1986	Invited Resident at Djerassi Foundation, near San Francisco. Visited Emily Carr School of Art and Design in Vancouver. Visited Japan (Tokyo, Nagoya, etc.).
1987	Travelled to Saudi Arabia in January to install work in new Australian Embassy at Riyadh. During January and February Duncan MacFarland, choreographer/dancer, Clare MacFarland, dancer, and David Rosenboom, composer, visited Victorian College of the Arts, working with **John Davis.** Returned to Djerassi Foundation in April. Premiere of *Systems of Judgement* with MacFarland/Whistler Dance Art Company in San Francisco in May.

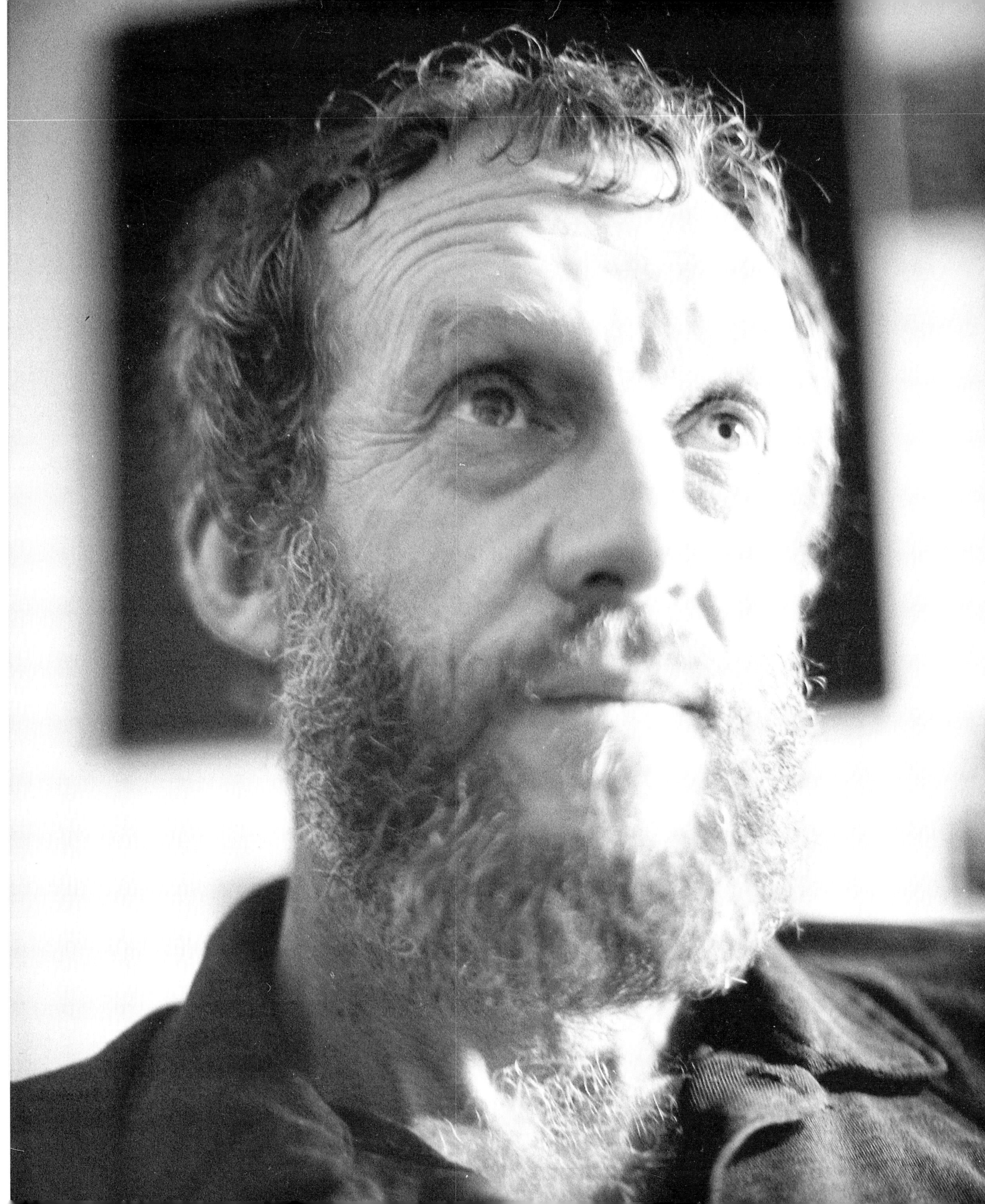

1958–88
AN OVERVIEW

1 John Davis, photographed by Mark Strizic in 1986.

This book explores the links between John Davis the young sculptor, living in the country, producing organic wood carvings, and John Davis, the mature sculptor, exhibiting in Venice, Delhi, Tokyo and Los Angeles. John Davis the secondary art teacher becomes a lecturer in sculpture at the Victorian College of the Arts. By 1986 he is an invited international guest at the prestigious Djerassi Foundation, San Francisco — and in the same year completes a major commission for the Australian Embassy in Saudi Arabia. John Davis is a new phenomenon — a contemporary Australian sculptor who is known outside Australia.

It would be reasonable to start at the beginning, with the birth of John Davis in 1936, and then discuss his life and development as an artist, but logical processes are not always the most interesting. Nor is his early work the most significant, so why not start at a later point in his career, and assess the early sculptures later?

In 1982–83, exhibitions in Tokyo, Tokoname, Kyoto, Osaka and Nagoya aroused great interest amongst a wide section of Japanese ranging from art critics to practitioners of ikebana. Yet this connection between an Australian sculptor and Japan came about almost by chance. In retrospect, one can discern tentative connections between a period of teaching at Caulfield Technical College, Stelarc (the expatriate Australian artist living in Japan), Goji Hamada (an avant-garde Japanese performance artist), and a major exhibition of contemporary Australian art in Tokyo during September 1983, entitled 'Continuum '83'.

'Continuum '83' received excellent publicity in Japanese magazines and newspapers and attracted a constant flow of spectators in the various galleries, yet it was the work of John Davis in particular that was frequently reproduced and commented on in the press. Problems of communication make it difficult to ascertain why the Japanese are so attracted to his work — one can only make some observations.

The Japanese have a profound love of nature, which is reflected in their painting, poetry, gardens, ikebana and bonsai. They show great respect for nature, yet make it clear that man is in control. The Japanese garden appears completely natural, but every tree, bush, flower and ground cover of moss is carefully placed. The practice of bonsai aims at the perfect miniature, with all the characteristics of the full scale tree carefully controlled by manipulation. The Japanese have a sympathy with the installations of John Davis, where he uses simple materials, such as sticks tied with cotton. They appreciate the fact that the sticks are used naturally. They are not broken, twisted, bent or plaited — simply used as they are found, bark and all. The fact that smaller twigs are broken off, in order to give an essentially straight stick, is an acceptable discipline imposed on nature by the artist.

John Davis has said that his work combines the broad sweep of a view to the horizon, with the detailed observation of what is directly underfoot. This is not out of character with Japanese painting, which can combine an overall simplicity of design with a love of close detail. Ikebana likewise unites a basic composition with great attention to detail.

Nevertheless, the Japanese are also aware of some differences, for John Davis has an Australian sense of scale, directly related to the scope of the Australian landscape. For the Japanese, who are accustomed to a fastidious sense of craftsmanship — made clear in everything from their wooden temple structures to wooden boxes commonly used for packaging — John Davis has the distinctive, ragged untidiness of the Australian bush. As Goji Hamada said in writing of *Journey Extended*, 'the Australian bush is grey green, without lustre, and everywhere there is peeling bark, which is twisted into irregular shapes'. He said that John Davis 'emphasises the disorderly order of nature with a kind of parallel compatability . . . art and nature become of equal value'.[1]

The early wood carvings which John Davis produced in the late 1950s had strong links with the Australian landscape, but in the many years that he has produced sculpture he has gone through a succession of styles, media and differing attitudes, some of them quite short-lived. His early career was a period of rapid change, yet, in retrospect one can see some underlying broad interests such as space, time and that elusive attribute which John Davis calls 'place'. Location has become more and more important, whether it has been shown directly in the choice of sites in the country for installations, or indirectly in the works produced in his studio, which have reflected the qualities of the Australian bush. From his early wood carvings, it has taken him more than twenty years to arrive at a new point, where he can again re-establish his links with the Australian bush.

John Davis has not been immune from overseas influences, but as a mature artist he has now absorbed and digested these influences — and added something that is distinctly Australian. It is not something as simple and direct as painting an Australian landscape with gum trees, or using early Australian history as a source of myths; it is much more subtle. The Australian elements of his work are to do with an observation of space, the character of the Australian bush, the nature of Australian towns, a sense of time and location: all made manifest with materials used in a distinctive manner.

This book is a record of John Davis's journey in search of a balance between concept, media and process; between personal expression, international influences and Australian character.

■ NOTES

[1] Goji Hamada, 'Art Focus: Performance. John Davis: *Long Journey*', *Bijutsu Techo* (Tokyo), January 1983.

ORGANIC WOOD CARVINGS

John Davis lived at Mildura near the Murray River during 1961 and 1962, and it was during this short period that he made some of his earliest sculpture. Mildura has a visual monotony, brought about by unimaginative town planning imposed on a flat and uninteresting landscape. Everything is ordered by a love of straight lines and neat right angles. The city centre, the rows of houses, the settlers' blocks with vineyards or citrus trees, all conform to orderly planning.

All except the Murray River. Most of the year the water moves slowly, but one is conscious of a great volume of water that sweeps everything before it. The earth banks of the river are eroded, exposing the twisted roots of aged red gums, some of which have collapsed into the water.

For a young artist of the early 1960s, neither the city of Mildura, nor the people of the area were a source of inspiration. Mildura lacked both the sophistication of Melbourne and the raw, abrasive interest of the dry interior. But the banks of the Murray offered endless fascination, varying from soft banks of sand to vertical cliffs, from thick forests of young saplings to twisted, gnarled roots of water-washed trees.

Predictably, the first sculptures by John Davis were wood carvings, organic in form, somewhat romantic in content. A few of the works were carved from pieces of timber he had found, exploiting the irregular, natural state, but such roots or branches present very difficult problems of control for a young wood carver. Murray pine has a straight cylindrical trunk, a regular grain and can be finished to a smooth surface, easily given a warm tactile quality with linseed oil and beeswax. In the backyard of his rented house John Davis found a stack of Murray pine logs, so he had a ready source of timber. This simple fact influenced the basic form of several early works.

The year 1961 was important to John Davis, not only as the beginning of his sculptural career, but also because it was the year of the first Mildura Triennial exhibition of sculpture. Ernst Van Hattum, the Dutch Director of the Mildura Arts Centre had organised the first national exhibition of Australian sculpture. Van Hattum analysed the local art scene and realised that most of the Regional Galleries in Victoria had failed to build up specialised collections, relying mostly on collections of Australian paintings. None of the galleries, State or Regional, had worthwhile collections of Australian sculpture. He saw sculpture as the neglected area of the visual arts, in need of promotion, which in turn would focus attention on Mildura.

In the catalogue of the 1961 exhibition Van Hattum wrote:

■ *The choice of sculpture as the subject for promotion may not be an obvious one at first thought. Yet if we consider the importance of sculpture in most of the ancient civilisations and the past periods of our western culture, against the virtual lack of good public sculpture in our cities, we must agree that no other form of arts was more deserving of assistance.*[1]

Professor Burke, also writing in the catalogue, rightly saw the first Mildura exhibition of sculpture as an historic event, for the Mildura Triennials proved to be focal points for Australian contemporary sculpture for a twenty-year period.

■ *The Mildura Art Gallery is to be congratulated on its brave proclamation of faith in perhaps the toughest of the imaginative arts and therefore one of the most influential, by its policy of collecting and exhibiting contemporary sculpture, and by launching a competition which future students of Australian art may well regard as something of a landmark in its history.*[2]

John Davis was teaching at Mildura High School, an appointment which isolated him from art galleries, libraries, other artists, theatres and films. He therefore welcomed the chance to assist Ernst

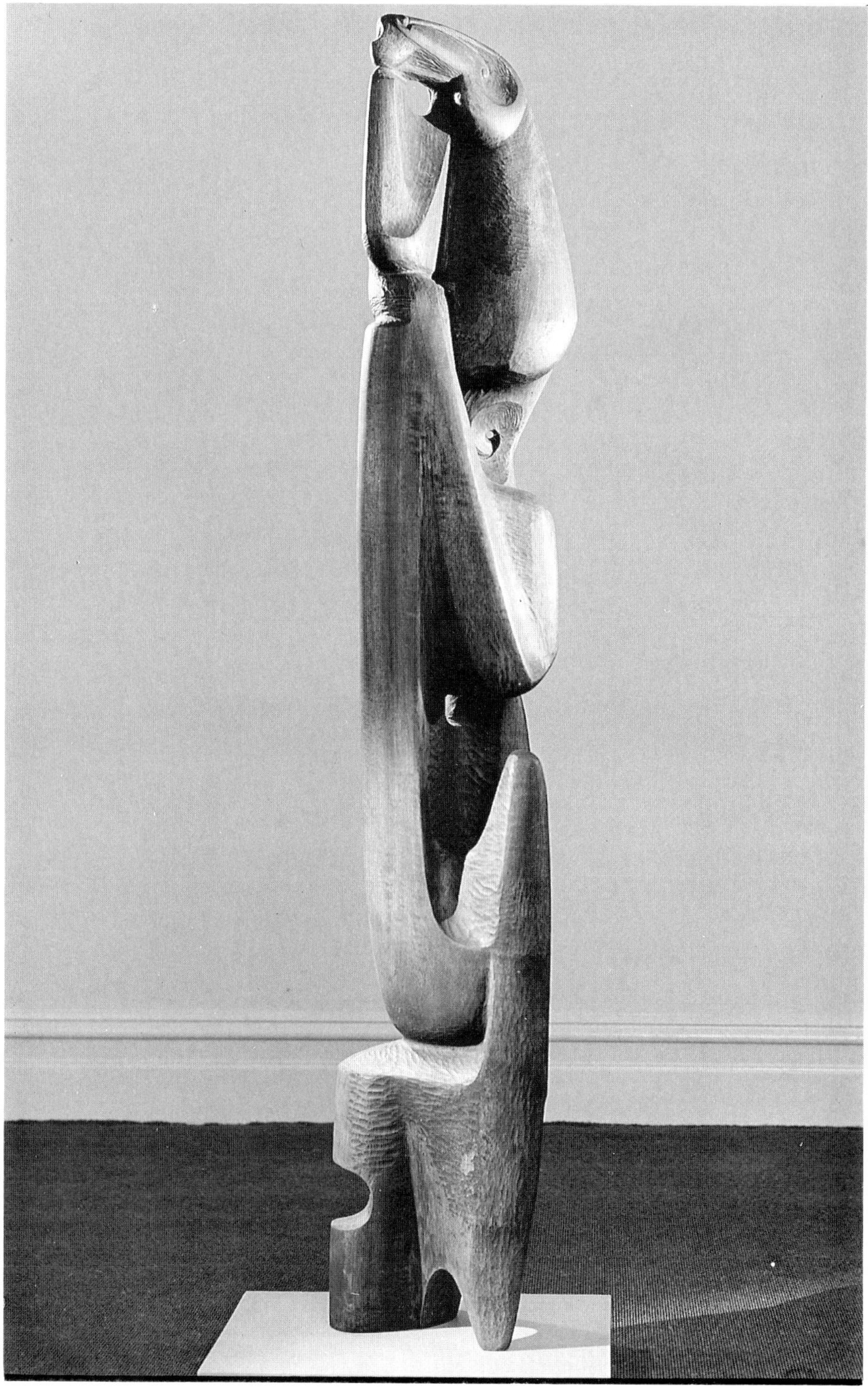

▼
2 Norma Redpath: Boy and Horse (1960). Queensland beech. Height 152.4 cm. Photograph by Mark Strizic.

Van Hattum with this major exhibition. For someone who had been a frustrated painter, the sculpture exhibition was a revelation. He was most impressed by this direct contact with contemporary sculpture, which helped to decide the direction of his own work.

In the 1961 Mildura exhibition there was a high proportion of conservative figurative sculpture. If the work was abstract, it was usually an abstraction from the human form, but there was also a significant group of artists working in an organic style: Margel Hinder, Norma Redpath (illus. 2), Stephen Walker, Lenton Parr and Julius Kane.

Julius Kane's *Group Organism* was probably the most unexpected work in the exhibition. It consisted of six vertical forms arranged in a straight line on a slab base. Each of the forms appeared to have grown out of the cylindrical shape of the tree trunks, varying in height and diameter, twisting this way and that. The composition was unorthodox and elementary, the carving was simple, sometimes even clumsy, but the whole work had a presence that could not be dismissed. Each sculpture could be viewed separately, but there was a definite similarity between all of the forms, which unified the composition. The unity was made more emphatic by an overall coat of yellow-green paint. Just as composers of contemporary music have often abandoned the classical structure with its inevitable build up to a climax, so *Group Organism* has no central point or climax.

Any young sculptor or art teacher of the early 1960s would have known the works of Henry Moore, yet John Davis says Henry Moore was not an influence on his early woodcarving. Possibly not a direct influence, but in his acceptance of 'truth to material', John Davis was working within Henry Moore's general philosophy. His concern with concavities and negative forms, with the hole piercing the sculpture, all owe a debt to Henry Moore.

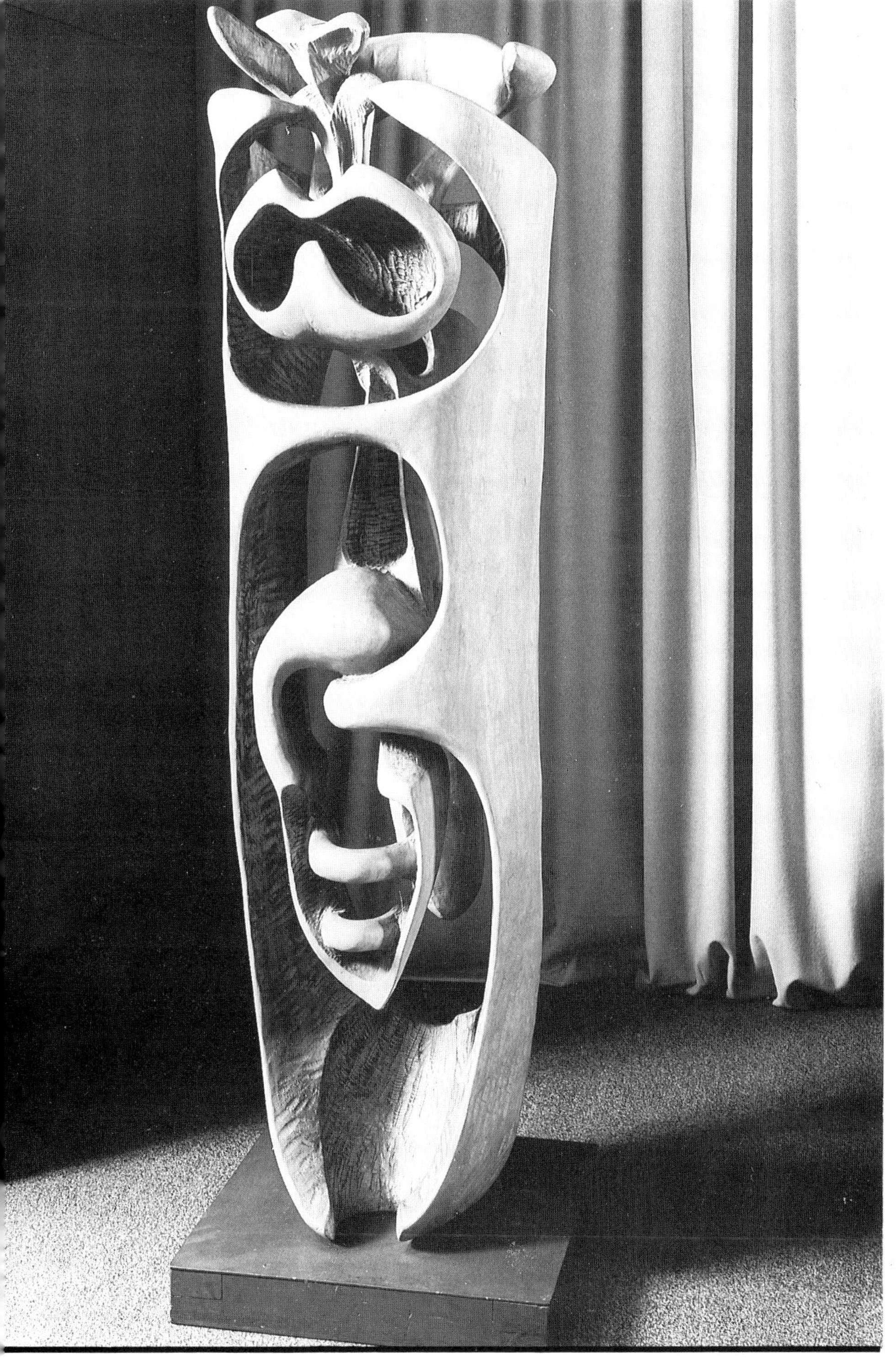

▼
3 Julius Kane: Organic Forms (1962). Wood. 193 cm excluding base x 52 cm diameter (National Gallery of Victoria). Photograph by Julie Millowick and James McArdle.

For John Davis, Julius Kane was a more direct influence. *Wood Sculpture* (or *Totem*), produced in 1965 after he moved to Melbourne, is a single, vertical organic form. Compared with Julius Kane's work it is a contrived composition without the sense of natural growth present in *Group Organism*. All of the parts relate, moving upwards to a climax at the top, unlike the unorthodox composition of Julius Kane's earlier work.

Metamorphosis, carved in 1966, consists of two vertical sculptures so in that respect it has some links with Julius Kane's row of tree trunks. But with John Davis's work the individual forms pile one on top of the other, moving vertically upwards, without the sinuous, twisting movement of Julius Kane's sculptures. Possibly the explanation is simple — Julius Kane carved from tree trunks, whereas John Davis bought a length of kauri. Originally *Metamorphosis* was displayed as one work on a slab base but later the two parts were labelled 'Metamorphosis I' and 'Metamorphosis II' (illus. 4) and sold separately.

Many years later, in 1975, John Davis paid his respects to Julius Kane by helping to organise the first retrospective exhibition of his sculpture. Clifford Last had collected the writings of Julius Kane, press reviews, catalogues and list of known works and pasted them into a scrap book, which he presented to the State Library of Victoria, after Julius Kane's death. Working with Kiffy Carter (Rubbo) and Meredith Rogers at the Ewing and George Paton Galleries, John Davis assisted in the necessary research to gather sculpture from many sources. It was a fine survey of the work of one of Australia's most original sculptors.

As Margaret Plant points out in her contribution to the catalogue, the organic style, which Julius Kane epitomised, was a style already out of fashion overseas, but it was a style that suited Australian sculptors, with their strong links with the land-

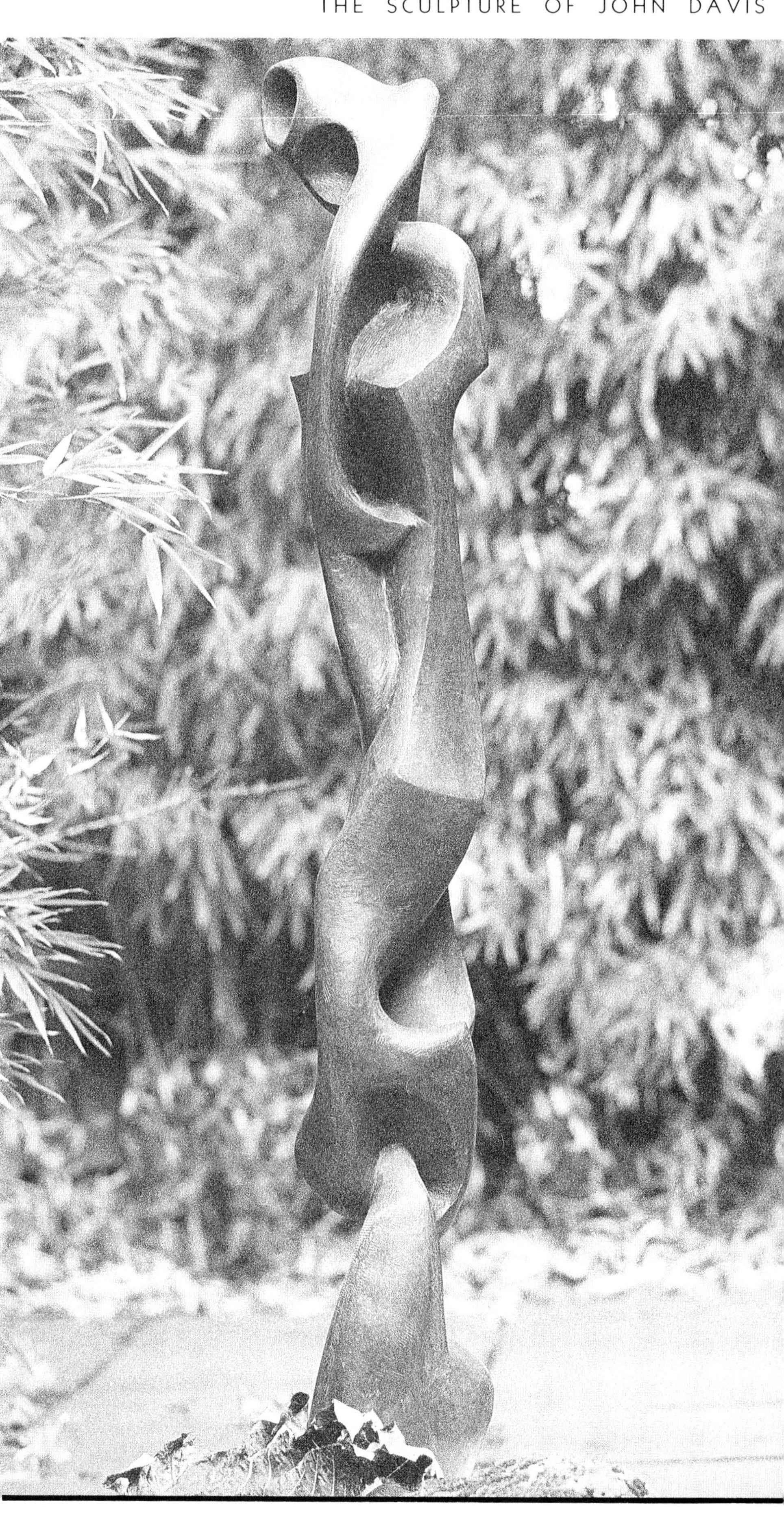

▶
4 John Davis: Metamorphosis *11 (1966). Wood, stained green. 123 x 20 x 16 cm. (In the collection of Bev. and Ian Thomas.) Photograph by Mark Strizic.*

scape. It gave them a chance to destroy the tyranny of the figure in sculpture — there *were* other subjects for sculptors. Margaret Plant refers to the 1950s as the period when organic sculpture was at its peak, but the interest in things organic was still obvious at the Mildura Sculpture Triennials in 1964 and 1967 and had only ceased to be a significant segment of the exhibitions in 1970.

■ *In retrospect the decade of the fifties will appear more and more to be dominated by the organic in sculpture: out-moded in international terms, but sympathetic to our landscape background in art, and freeing sculpture from its mediocre naturalism. It was heralded by the smooth wood-worked forms of Ola Cohn and Gerald Lewers — first essays in an Australian context sculpture. Norma Redpath carved in wood and then produced stratified bronze works simulating natural forms. The Centre Five sculptors have all been involved at some point with the organic: Inge King with her early carvings in England and her later bush creatures; Lenton Parr with his crawling creatures; Zikaras and Jomantas have worked in wood. In Clifford Last's work there has been a persistent devotion to the carving of wood and the vertical format of the organic form. In bronze, Stephen Walker's sculpture has cavities, hollow gourd-like forms and lichen frills.*

The critics in the 1950s were quick to identify the organic mode of Julius Kane's work and to pay him credit as an immigrant for vitalising the Melbourne art scene. But the appreciation of his work tended to stop with a comment on his mastery of rhythm.[3]

John Davis's *Metamorphosis* has more in common with an early work by Norma Redpath, *Boy and Horse* (shown at the first Mildura Exhibition in 1961) than with the sculpture of Julius Kane. In both cases the forms are contained within a simple vertical silhouette, there is a play of rounded, full forms against concavities and a rather static sense of balance.

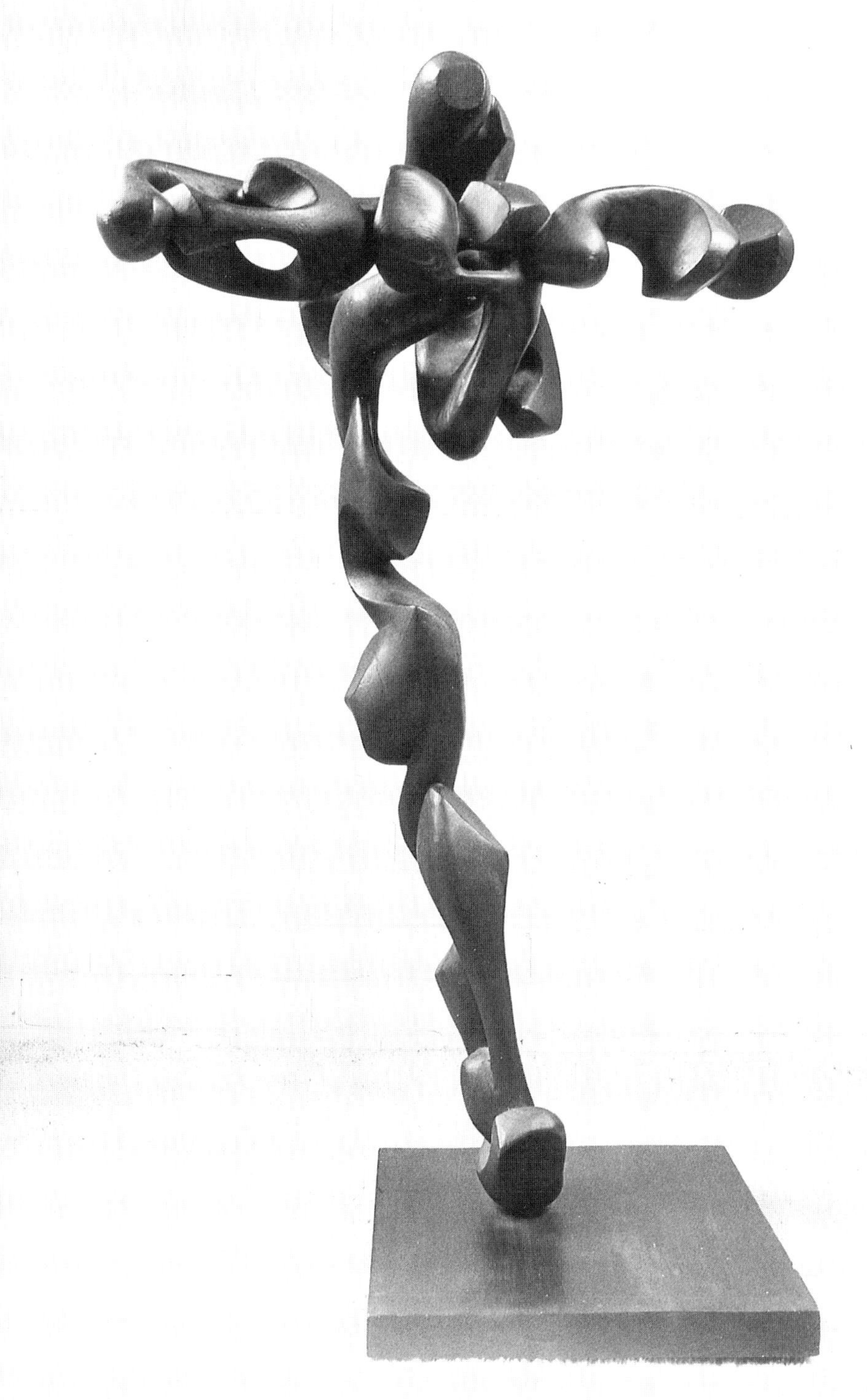

▼
5 John Davis: Abreaction (1964–66). Wood, stained black. Sculpture: 127 x 74 x 36 cm; base 4.5 x 45 x 42.5 cm. (National Gallery of Victoria.) Photograph by Mark Strizic.

Mandala, carved in 1966, has an even greater concern for concavities and voids, but is strongly held together by a cruciform composition. The deep recesses and concavities appear to outnumber the positive forms, yet the whole work has a simple strength. The cross is fragmented and parts are physically separated but all are visually linked.

Mandala and *Metamorphosis* were shown at the Annual Exhibition of the Victorian Sculptors' Society in 1966, securing almost his first brief mention in the press. 'In the Victorian Sculptors' Society show ... John Davis paying tribute to Julius Kane ...'[4] 'The Victorian Sculptors' Society annual (at the Victorian Artists' Society) is a well-presented and attractive exhibition ... and the wood carvings of the lesser known John Davis suggest a potential for possible development.'[5]

John Davis was a member of the Victorian Sculptors Society, as was virtually every sculptor in Melbourne in the mid-1960s. At that time, all Melbourne sculptors knew each other, met monthly, showed together annually. It was a small, isolated group, in need of mutual support; the annual exhibition was the highlight of the year. Expectations were low, so having a work accepted for display was rewarding, a central position within the gallery was significant and a brief mention in a review brought a warm glow of self-satisfaction.

The Victorian Sculptors Society grew out of the Victorian Artists Society, and even though the sculptors eventually had no organisational links with the older society, they never broke away from the deadening conservatism of the 'Vic Artists'. In 1968, during the last years of the existence of the Sculptors Society, the exhibitions moved from the headquarters of the VAS in East Melbourne to the Argus Gallery.[6] The annual exhibitions gave the appearance of a tolerant society, for virtually every style of sculpture being produced in Melbourne was displayed, but as the great bulk of the work was conservative, the exhibitions emphasised the past rather than illuminating any future direction. The older sculptors such as Ola Cohn, Tina Wentsher, George Allen, Victor Greenhalgh, Andor Meszaros and Stanley Hammond had battled through a lifetime of neglect with very few commissions or sales and little recognition. A younger group had formed 'Centre Five', and were quietly campaigning for professional status outside the Sculptors Society. The very young sculptors, such as Clive Murray-White, were vaguely dissatisfied, but did not have a clear alternative to the Sculptors Society. Clive Murray-White organised the 'Twenty Four Point Plug Show' in the Argus Gallery, but it was too late — the Sculptors Society was in a state of disintegration. Within a few years the new pattern had been established — a 'one man exhibition'[7] in the commercial galleries was the expected procedure and the annual mixed exhibition was professionally unacceptable.

During the 1970s the number of sculptors in Australia increased dramatically. The catalogues of the Mildura Triennials record the rapid exploration of new styles and the move towards experimental areas of performance, language, documentation, video and so on. Yet something was lost with the demise of the Victorian Sculptors Society. It is no longer easy for young sculptors to meet with older colleagues and it is unrealistic to presume that an immature sculptor should hold a one person exhibition. So where does the young sculptor start?

The Victorian Sculptors Society helped 'the lesser known John Davis . . .' and made public his 'potential for possible development'.[8] This 'potential for possible development' was gradually being realised. With *Abreaction* produced between 1964–66 (illus. 5), and *Mandala* (1966), Davis managed to free himself from the restrictions of the single log of wood, producing involved works, made up of numerous parts, mounted in high relief on white boards. For the first time, he begins to surprise with his composition. Not only do parts float in space, but a couple of forms shoot off at a tangent — and would continue outside the structure, except that they are firmly anchored. Like previous works, *Mandala* has a decorative appeal, but the dramatic impact is much stronger. There is some mystery about the object; it is a more complex work than any of the earlier sculptures.

Bent on Mayhem (illus. 6), his first major work, was a large wood carving in very high relief, produced in 1967. The wooden forms were constructed and carved, then stained black, with some areas painted bright red. The whole work was mounted on a large hardboard structure painted flat white. The change from simple wax polishes, which revealed the knots and grain of the timber, to black stain and opaque paint, was not only a slow move from the restrictions of 'truth to material', but was also a practical necessity. As the sculptures became more ambitious, larger and more complex in form, it was impossible to carve them out of one log or one length of wood. Because the sculptures were constructed out of numerous pieces of wood the black stain was needed to cover the frequent changes of grain.

Even though the basic composition of a long horizontal with three opposing diagonals is comparatively simple, *Bent on Mayhem* is quite complex. Many of the directional lines and most of the forms are broken up, so that the work has a nervous, staccato quality. The forms still have a strongly organic shape and the sculpture has an overall feeling of growth, but it appears as though some sections have been amputated. Wherever the amputation has occurred the area is left flat and painted a glossy bright red. An element of uncertainty is introduced, when one large, strong form shoots down and almost out of the composition. Another reverses direction and disappears into a

▶
6 John Davis: **Bent on Mayhem (1967). Wood, stained black, with some areas painted red, on hardboard painted white. 122 x 212 x 43 cm. (In the James Baker Collection, Museum of Contemporary Art, Brisbane.) Photograph by Mark Strizic.**

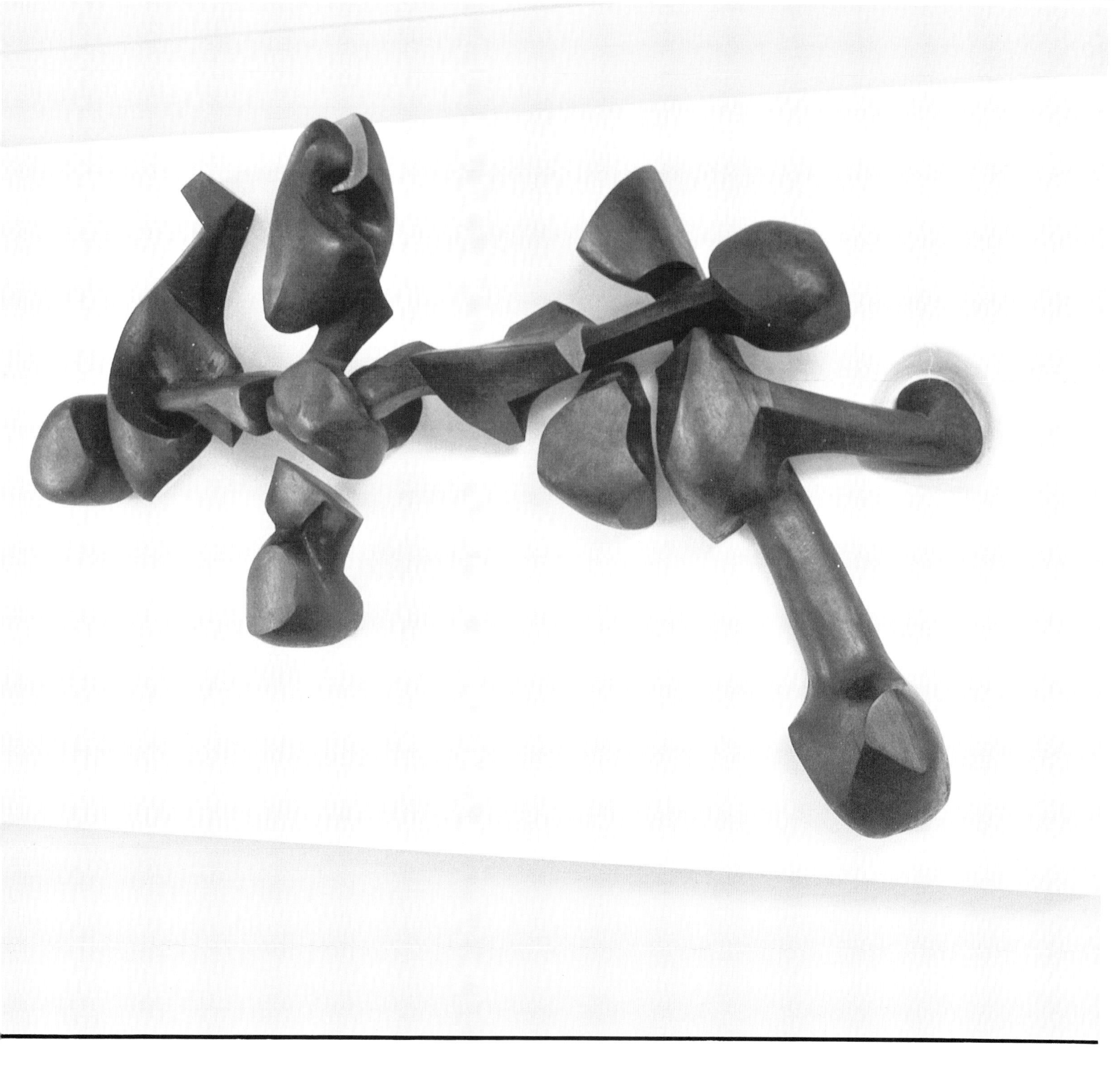

cavity of the white display board. One form is detached from the main body of the work and floats a short distance away. *Bent on Mayhem* is a forceful, dramatic work full of suppressed energy.

When shown at the Victorian Sculptors Society exhibition it was given a central position where it attracted favourable comment: '. . . John Davis's black-painted [sic] carving in kauri, "Bent on Mayhem (7)" is probably the major work in the exhibition'.[9]

In the Mildura exhibitions of 1964 and 1967 organic forms of sculpture were strongly represented by sculptors such as Norma Redpath, Clifford Last, Max Lyle, Lenton Parr, Stephen Walker, Herbert Flugelman, Robert Parr, David Tolley and Ron Upton. John Davis was part of this general interest in forms of growth and decay in nature; sometimes the eroded earth as with Norma Redpath, insects and plants with Max Lyle, horse and rider in Herbert Flugelman's *Equestrian* or forms of the forest as in Stephen Walker's *Figure* of 1964. John Davis continued to use the vocabulary of organic sculpture, but increasingly he was concerned with abstract ideas, rather than direct reference to tree trunks, rocks or landscape.

By 1963, however, John Davis had moved to the city. His early formative years in the country and his five years of teaching at Queenscliff, Numurkah and Mildura were behind him. Always strongly influenced by his environment, he was to change markedly in style and choice of materials. Further study at the Royal Melbourne Institute of Technology brought additional influences. The lecturers in the sculpture department at RMIT, Vincent Jomantas and Lenton Parr, gave a strong emphasis to knowledge of materials and processes. Wood became less relevant. In 1967 John Davis produced his last wood carving.

■ NOTES

1 Ernst Van Hattum, 'Preface', *Mildara Prize for Sculpture. Sculpture Mildura 1961*, Mildura Art Gallery, 22 April–21 May 1961.
2 Professor Joseph Burke, 'Tradition and Innovation in Western Sculpture', ibid.
3 Margaret Plant, 'Julius Kane', *Julius Kane, 1921–1962. A Retrospective Exhibition*, Ewing and George Paton Galleries, Melbourne, 6–30 May 1975.
4 Charles Bush, 'Whiteley in Depth', *The Australian*, 1 October 1966.
5 Alan McCulloch, 'Parade of Black Rhythms', *Herald*, 5 October 1966, reproduced courtesy of the Herald and Weekly Times Ltd.
6 Two exhibitions were held at the Argus Gallery in 1968: the 'Twenty Four Point Plug Show' from 6–26 May, organised by Clive Murray-White, and '16 Sculptors', from 25 November–13 December, organised by Michael Meszaros and the author.
7 'One man exhibition' was the wording used; it was before the days of 'one woman' or 'one person exhibitions'.
8 Alan McCulloch, 'Parade of Black Rhythms', *Herald*, 5 October 1966, reproduced courtesy of the Herald and Weekly Times Ltd.
9 Alan McCulloch, 'Sculpture That Can Breathe', *Herald*, 20 September 1967, reproduced courtesy of the Herald and Weekly Times Ltd.

1968–69
FIRST MAJOR EXHIBITION

After five years of teaching in country high schools, John Davis moved to Melbourne in 1963 and taught for the next four years at Highett High School. During the first year he studied at night at the Royal Melbourne Institute of Technology then for the next three years he was involved in half-time study at RMIT, completing an Associate Diploma in Sculpture at the end of 1966.

The three years at RMIT taught John Davis a great deal about materials and techniques. His sculptural repertoire grew from the limitations of wood to include bronze casting, acrylic, vinyl, aluminium, fibreglass and polyester resin. The RMIT Sculpture Department was conservatively modern, based on a strong European tradition. Abstraction was the accepted style, but an abstraction usually based on the human figure or forms found in nature. Henry Moore was the major influence. Anthony Caro was known, but had not overthrown the dominance of the older sculptor. Lenton Parr introduced oxy-acetylene welding to the Sculpture Department when he returned from England in 1957, becoming Head of the Sculpture Department in 1964 while John Davis was studying there. Parr's welded sculptures in the late 1950s were strongly organic in style (such as the welded sculpture which was commissioned for the Chadstone Shopping Centre, Melbourne, in 1959 (illus. 7)). By the early 1960s Lenton Parr's work reflected a cautious acceptance of some of the attitudes of Anthony Caro.

In spite of a few tentative experiments while studying at RMIT, John Davis did not seem to be attracted to the technique of welding and has only once exhibited any sculpture in welded steel. Nevertheless the possibilities of casting, offered by RMIT, intrigued him and many of his works of this period include sculptural forms, cast in aluminium or bronze.

Vincent Jomantas was another lecturer in the Sculpture Department. John Davis learnt to respect this impeccable craftsman who could so skilfully use a range of materials, reinforced with a strong sense of composition. Jock Clutterbuck, Gerrard White and Tom Hancy were also students in the Sculpture Department and like John Davis had all trained as secondary art teachers. For a few years in the late 1960s, Gerrard White and Tom Hancy showed their work but only Jock Clutterbuck was to continue to produce sculpture.

The change from secondary to tertiary teaching in 1967 helped to broaden the scope of John Davis's work. He arrived at Caulfield Institute of Technology (now named Chisholm Institute of Technology) in the middle of a brief period of educational experiment, when staff and students were

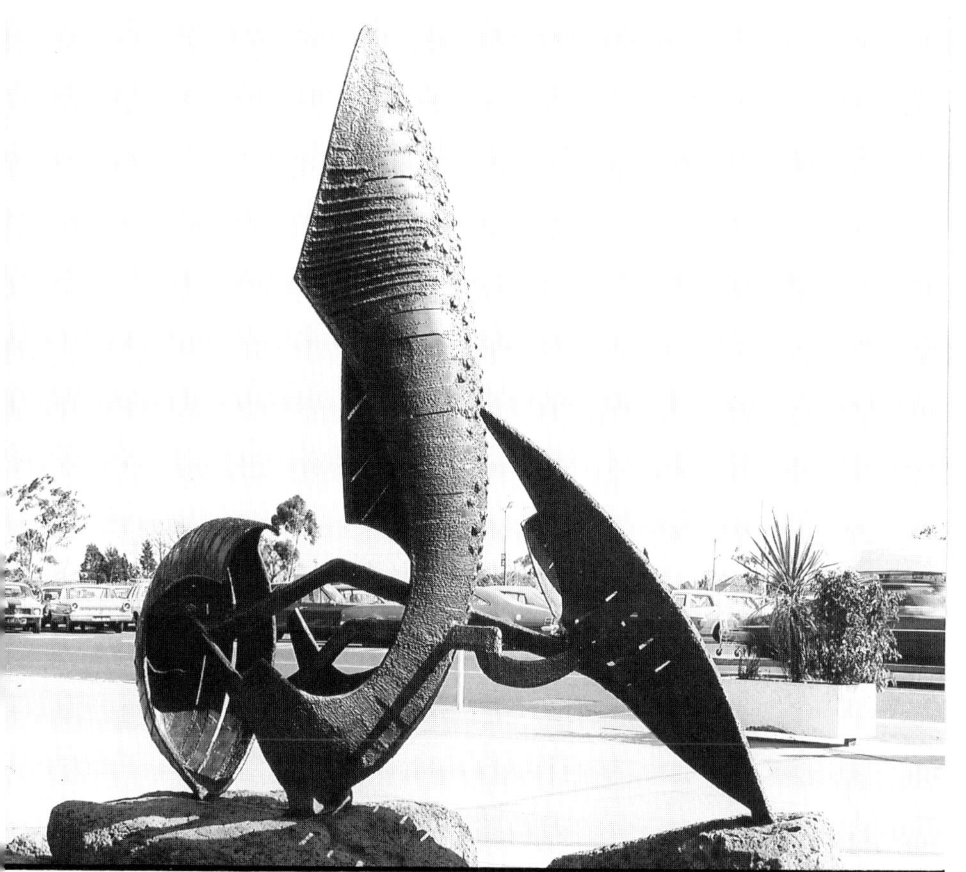

7 Lenton Parr: Untitled (1959). Welded mild steel. 259 x 259 cm. (Chadstone Shopping Centre, Melbourne.) Photograph by Julie Millowick and James McArdle.

involved in constant discussion, argument, even bitter disagreement, about the meaning of art and methods of art teaching. The painter Fred Cress had arrived back from a period in England, visiting art schools and artists, and instigated a new first year course for students. The course was welcomed by lecturers such as Vic Majzner, John Davis, David Barker and myself, but bitterly opposed by other members of staff. The course was highly experimental, encouraging students to find 2D or 3D solutions to open-ended problems using a wide variety of materials. The work produced was shown at the Argus Gallery in two 'Zetetic' exhibitions at the end of 1967 and 1968.

Nowadays there are a great number of public exhibitions of work by art students shown at the end of each year in art school galleries and in some of the commercial galleries, but in 1967 it was a radical move to show student work in a public gallery. Some lecturers were very critical, saying that students did not produce art, merely answers to problems set. They didn't wish students to get an inflated sense of their value by actually selling work. Nevertheless the two 'Zetetic Ex' shows attracted a great deal of attention and Alan McCulloch wrote a favourable review:

■ *The objective is visual and aural stimulus and the freeing of the student's imaginative and creative faculties.*

Sight and sound coalesce in this weird assemblage, and there is no doubt that the completely free reign accorded has extracted from the enthusiastic students some extraordinarily well made and inventive devices.

Zetetic means 'to proceed by inquiry', and progress here has led to madly gyrating golf balls in glass-topped boxes, colorfully whirring bicycle wheels, a croaking rotation of bucket-shaped objects, huge 'space sculptures' and finally to a darkened tent called 'Sense Compartment'[1] where one may sit on a chair surrounded by flashing lights and a brilliantly

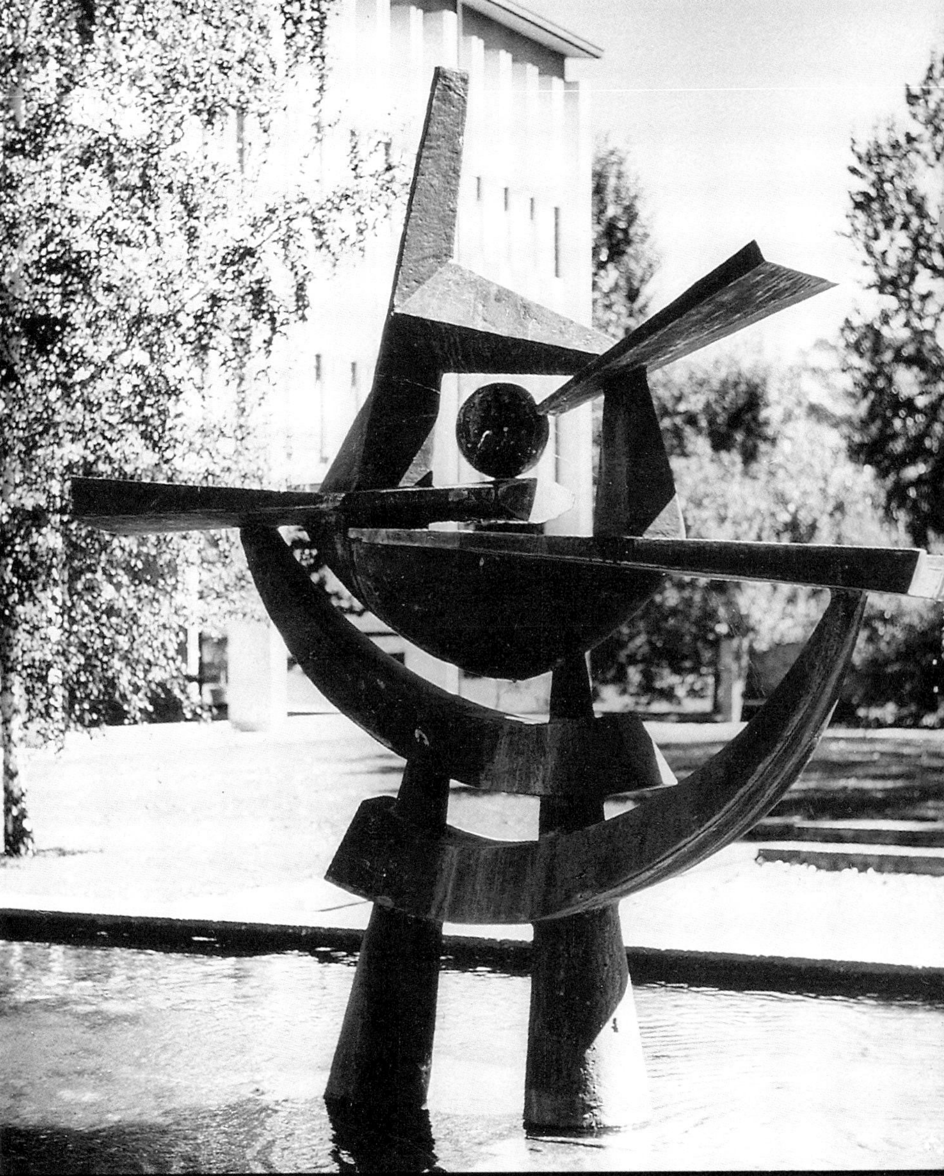

mirrored succession of images which circulate to the accompaniment of strange sounds.

The exhibition makes the college a force to be reckoned with in the art teaching profession.[2]

Twelve months later, Patrick McCaughey reviewed the last exhibition, which he described as a 'fun fair of art'.[3] Certainly there was a light-hearted atmosphere, particularly on the opening night when students gave out badges and balloons, a group played amplified music and another student intermittently read poetry to the crush of people.

■ *Zetetic 2 is the second exhibition of Caulfield Tec students' work. The emphases fall firmly and openly on the deliberate subversion of the stereotyped conception of art and the art object.*

They transform the Argus Gallery into an elabor-

ate and entertaining fun fair of art where sculptures create sounds, sway and gyrate.

The exhibition as a whole points to really lively and productive teaching.

The catalogue of 'Zetetic Ex 2, an exhibition of work by the students of the Art School at the Caulfield Institute of Technology', Argus Gallery, Melbourne, 12–29 August 1968, contained the following statement, which attempted to sum up the attitudes of staff and students involved in the course:

'Fluid situation,

plastic age,

synthetics abound.

Automation,

zybernetics,

containerisation, speed.

Absolutism seems remote.

Relativity is the

controlling factor.

Orientation through

questioning is essential.

Zetetic   to proceed by enquiry'

Fred Cress, as the main propagandist for the experimental first-year course at Caulfield, was invited to talk with art craft teachers in Melbourne. His talk was later reported in their journal:

■ *To sum up, the main points were:*

1 emphasis on criteria and methodology of creativity

2 the drive to think rather than discover

3 emphasis on answer to problem rather than personal expression, as the latter is always and automatically present

4 a contained and controlled development

5 state art area of interest and ask open-ended questions

6 do not envisage end products — leave students free to astonish both themselves and us!

7 free flow integration.[4]

◄
8 Vincas Jomantas: Fountain (1958). Bronze. Height above water level 259 cm. (Courtyard of Physics Building, Australian National University, Canberra.) Photograph by Lister Clark.

Fourteen years later I interviewed Vic Majzner and talked with him about the years we had spent at Caulfield. For me, it had been one of the most exciting periods in my teaching career, so I was interested to reminisce with him.

KS: 'Let's talk a little about the experimental first year course for which I would be prepared to give Fred Cress most of the credit. He was at Caulfield, went overseas for a couple of years, then came back to Caulfield Technical College, bringing his new-found enthusiasm into this course: point, line, shape, plane, mass etc. What do you think of that course, in retrospect?'

VM: 'I saw it as a great course because I was a student at Caulfield a year before that and went through the old course and this was like a breath of fresh air. Basically, it enabled students to be inventive in a contemporary sense, rather than in a traditional sense. I was certainly very excited — I think the whole team was also. The course was new to Australia, but it was happening in virtually every other country in the world as well, unbeknown to us at the time.

'It was basically a Bauhaus-oriented design course, which was initiated in England by people like Passmore and Hamilton.'

KS: 'At Caulfield the people involved were John Davis, yourself, Fred Cress, David Barker, myself. That was the hard core.'

VM: 'That was it at the time.'

KS: 'Ken Jack and Warwick Armstrong were the two staff members who lead the opposition to the new first-year course. Later, when Harold Farey was appointed Head of the Art Department, he also opposed the course.'

VM: 'By the time I got to Caulfield as a staff member, the major battle for the course was already won by Fred and David. My memory of that period was that it was one of continuous antagonism between ideas: the staff were split into two camps. Ours was a very close knit group, all of us: Fred, John, yourself and myself. We used to meet, take lunch together, teach together . . . socialise together and so on, so whatever antagonism there was we really didn't take any notice of it: we simply went ahead and did what we had to do. The students' response was so rewarding that it all seemed worthwhile.'

KS: 'What are your memories of John Davis at that time, as a member of that teaching team — what sort of contribution did he make?'

VM: 'I have a feeling that at the time when I arrived he was in charge of the 3D area of the course which was still new at the time. About 1968. After my arrival I was given the job to run the 2D area with Fred. So I virtually worked with John from the moment I arrived at Caulfield. In that capacity we were virtually equals at that stage. The interesting thing was that the sky was the limit. I remember we used to meet to discuss future projects or directions the course was taking. It was exciting because we were "bouncing off" each other. The course was experimental to a point where virtually all our fantasies and imaginations were given full realm. I remember John's contribution to be most inventive from a sculptor's viewpoint and as part of the creative team, like we all were.'

KS: 'What do you think was John's relationship with students? How did they see him as a teacher?'

VM: 'I've never experienced a course where such a relationship between students and lecturer occurred. The relationship between students and John was interesting. I don't think the students looked upon John or anyone in the course as lecturers with a capital 'L': we were course leaders, if you like. The students related to us virtually as young artists. The relationship of students to John was of that sort — younger artists speaking to slightly older artists about ideas which were common to all. They were also ideas that John and I were working on at the time, in our own work. I think it was a relationship concerned with the reality of making art, rather than the reality of a teaching institution. I remember works that John, Fred or myself would do, that came out of, not necessarily the projects that we would set, but out of the attitude that was implied in the course. It was really unusual and unique because the ideas we were dealing with were ideas that we were all involved in — staff and students. It was an interesting period in the history of art and art education in this country. It was perhaps the beginning of a cultural maturity in Australia.

'We were all working at a frontier which was equally new to us as it was to the students. I remember we were setting projects, not with an end in mind, but really with an opening in mind, so the possibilities were open to staff and students. In fact we never thought — or at least John and I never did — in terms of staff and students. We simply thought there's an idea that's really interesting and important now, that we felt the students should be dealing with. It was often an idea we were dealing with ourselves.'[5]

Fred Cress, essentially a painter and draughtsman, had an exhibition of works that combined both 2D and 3D in the one object. John Davis had

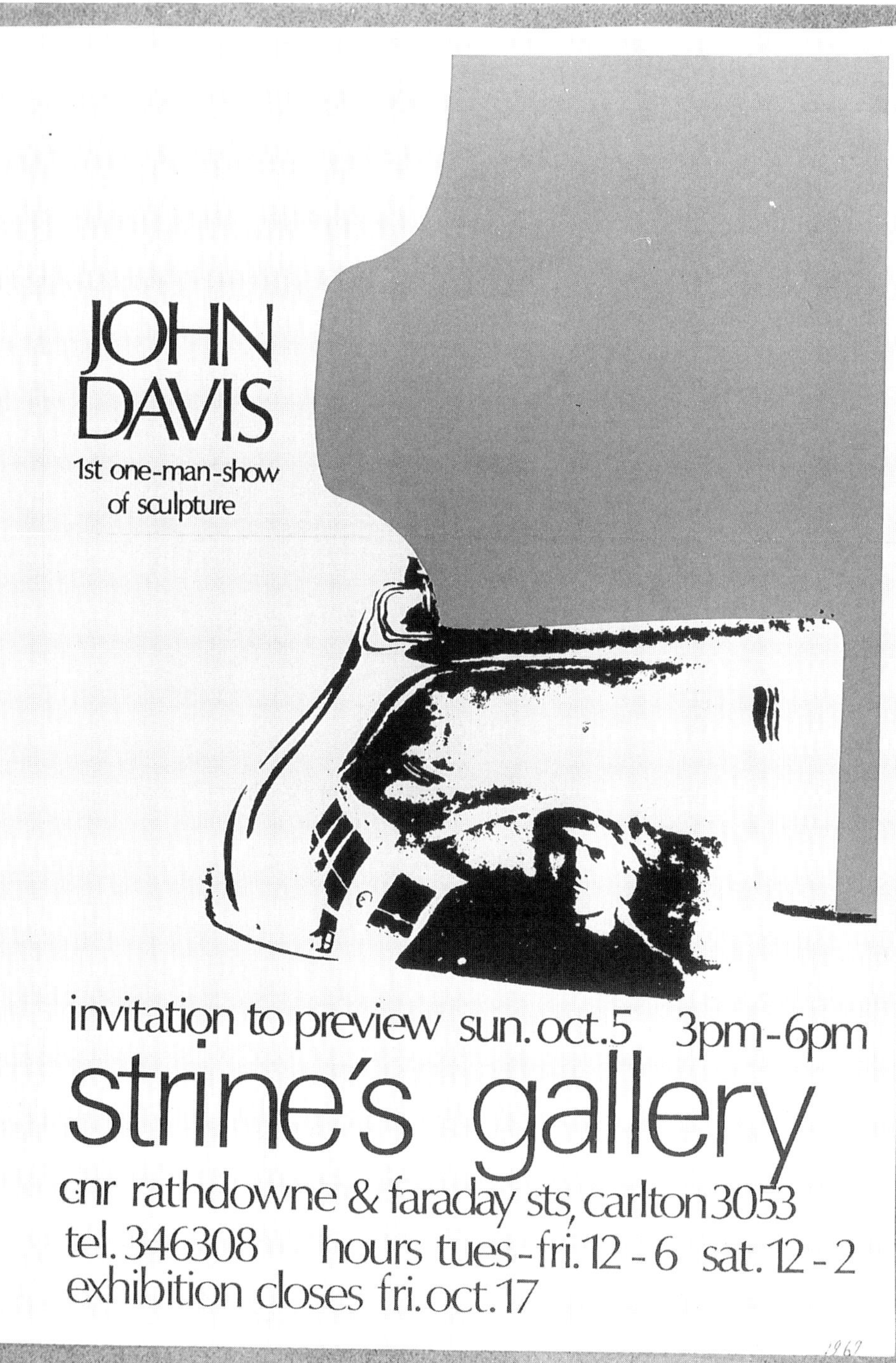

9 Invitation and poster for first one man exhibition by John Davis at Strine's Gallery, Melbourne, in October 1969. Designed by John Robinson. Printed black on white with large area of red at top right. Photograph by Tony Boyd.

his first one man exhibition at Strines Gallery, Melbourne in 1969 (illus. 9), showing sculptures that combined bronze, aluminium, vinyl, automobile duco, fibreglass and polyester resin. It was a time of experiment and enquiry when old concepts were challenged and even the most outrageous ideas were accepted. There was sense of optimism. Anything was possible.

Christo came to Australia in 1969, securing tremendous publicity for his Wrapping of Little Bay project, south of Sydney. He also carried out a less ambitious wrapping in Melbourne (illus. 10), but still needed a team of assistants. Letters of invitation were sent out to artists and art lecturers in Melbourne. John Davis accepted and worked with Christo on his 'Wool Works'.

At the time, there appeared to be no obvious influence of Christo on John Davis, they seemed to be working in unrelated areas. But in retrospect, one can realise that Christo made artists far more aware of the underlying structure, of tight skin over knuckles. He also demonstrated how the most commonplace object could be transformed into an object of great mystery by the simple process of wrapping. Looking at the work of John Davis produced ten and fifteen years later, with twigs, sticks and papier mâché, one can see that he has learned the subtle art of revealing the form by partly covering the structure.

In spite of the great impact of minimalism on Australian artists in the late 1960s, John Davis never completely embraced the mode, though works he produced after 1969 showed an influence. The first large scale exposure of minimal sculpture and hard-edge painting in Australia occurred in 1968 with the opening of the new Arts Centre, when the National Gallery of Victoria moved to the new building in St Kilda Road. The major opening exhibition was entitled 'The Field'.

To most people, in the 1960s contemporary

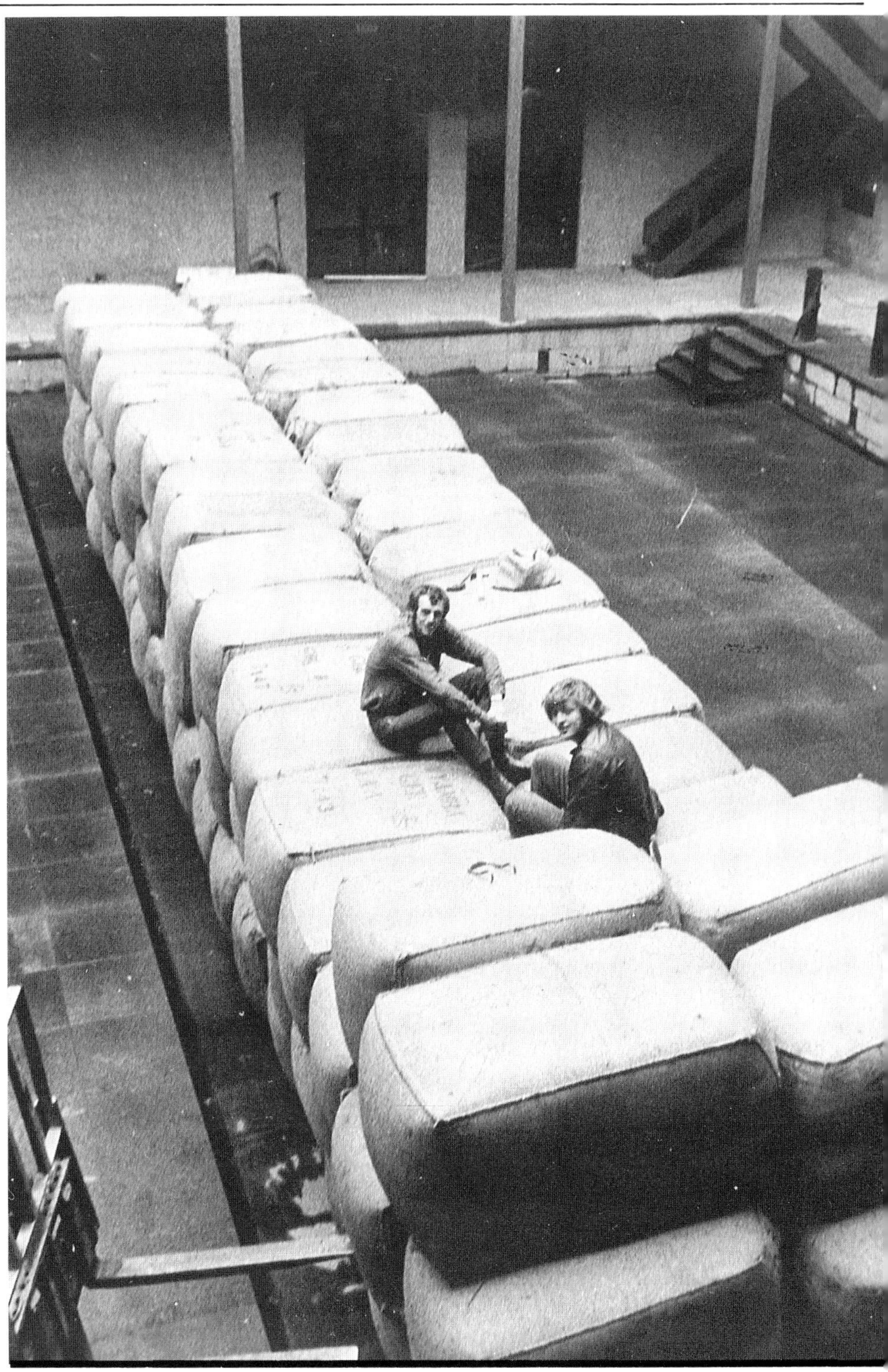

10 *John Davis seated on top of wool bales, in Murdoch Courtyard of National Gallery of Victoria, 1969, prior to the actual 'wrap up' by Christo.*

Australian art was synonymous with the mixture of personal expressionism and nationalistic myth, typified by Boyd, Nolan and Tucker. 'The Field' showed the work of a number of Australian artists who were deliberately cool, to the point of anonymity; who stressed intellect and concept, rather than emotion and personal involvement; who painted immaculately, without any impasto or texture — and more provocatively — appeared to work in an international style that had originated in New York. After the strong figuration of Boyd, Nolan and Tucker, the complete abstraction of work in 'The Field' was certain to raise controversy. Brian Finemore and John Stringer had prepared an exhibition guaranteed to arouse interest in the new Art Centre.

This exhibition also made clear the influence of Anthony Caro, the English sculptor, who had reacted against the monolithic, organic sculptures of Henry Moore. Caro and the American sculptor, David Smith, introduced the use of easily obtainable industrial steel, producing sculpture of a far greater openness of form. In order to destroy the precious quality that sculpture acquired when placed on a pedestal, they deliberately put their work on the floor where it immediately confronted the spectator.

In the late 1960s the traditional pedestal was looked on with great suspicion. Of the sculptors showing in 'The Field', Tony Coleing, Noel Dunn, Col Jordan, Mike Kitching, Wendy Paramor and Emanuel Raft all dispensed with the pedestal, while other sculptors such as Tony Bishop, Nigel Lendon and Michael Nicholson incorporated the pedestal into the composition. Strangely enough, the most dedicated of minimal sculptors, Clement Meadmore, showed two small works on traditional pedestals, though one large work sat on the floor of the gallery. Surprisingly Ron Robertson-Swann showed paintings, not sculpture.

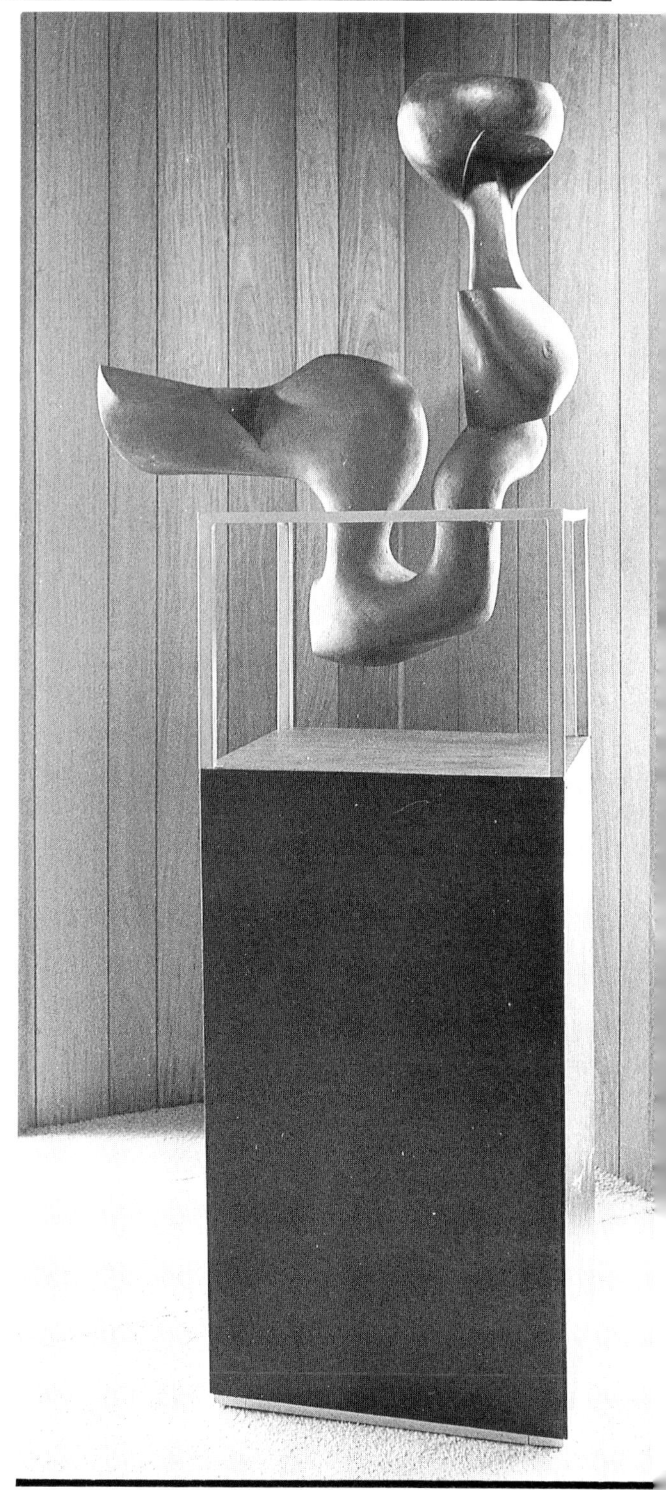

11 John Davis: Suspended (1967). Wood stained and painted, acrylic and aluminium. Total height 171 cm; pedestal 46.5 cm square. (In collection of Pat and Ray Raison.) Photograph by Mark Strizic.

Ron Robertson-Swann returned to Australia in 1968, bringing first-hand knowledge of new attitudes to sculpture, having worked closely with Anthony Caro in England. Nevertheless he was living in Sydney and did not meet John Davis until 1974. David Wilson was also strongly influenced by Anthony Caro, but after his arrival in Australia in 1965 he enrolled for more study at the National Gallery School during 1969–70. John Davis met David Wilson in 1971, but as Davis was abroad in 1972, they did not become friends until 1973, when they were both on the staff at Prahran College of Advanced Education.

John Davis has produced only one work in welded steel and has not been directly influenced by Anthony Caro, or by minimal art, nevertheless some influences can be seen. During 1967–69 John Davis produced a number of works in which he experimented with the relationship between the sculpture and the pedestal. The pedestal was cut up, reassembled, off set, extended, partly painted and changed in shape from the traditional square or rectangular prism to irregular shapes.

In *Suspended* produced in 1967 (illus. 11) John Davis used a conventional square prism as a pedestal but extended the square section by adding an aluminium outline to a transparent acrylic box. The wooden forms of the sculpture begin inside the top of the transparent acrylic sheet, then move up and outwards. There is a contrast between the contained space at the top of the structure and the solidity of the bottom of the pedestal, emphasised by staining the bottom section black. The sculptural forms are literally 'suspended' in space, not actually touching the solid black base, even though they are also stained black.

The intention was to produce a unified composition in which sculpture and pedestal were combined but in actual fact there is an interesting conflict between the two parts. It is as though the organic forms are struggling to free themselves from the rigid restrictions of the geometric structure.

The whereabouts of *Prise* is unfortunately not known, but it was also produced in 1967. In this work the pedestal was cut horizontally and reassembled with the smaller piece moved up and to one side, leaving a space between the two parts of the pedestal. In addition a wedge was cut from one side of the smaller part and added to the opposite side, increasing the sense of sideways movement. A large white circle was painted on the sides of the pedestal, but the circle was cut in half because of the separation of the two pieces of the pedestal.

Prise was not the last experiment Davis made with the problems of relating pedestal and sculpture, but it was his final wood carving. The period of organic forms carved in wood was at an end.

The abandonment of the pedestal was symbolic for John Davis, as it made clear he belonged to the period of David Smith and Anthony Caro — not Henry Moore. In actual fact his works continued to be small in scale and domestic, with a precious quality, suitable for coffee table, if not pedestal.

■

The dominant sculptural group in Melbourne during the 1960s was 'Centre Five'. Formed in 1961 its members were Clifford Last, Lenton Parr, Vincas Jomantas, Teisutis Zikaras, Inge King and Julius Kane, who had been the main driving force for the formation of the group. Norma Redpath was also associated with the group, though she lived and worked in Italy for long periods from 1962 onwards. For some years, the 'Centre Five' group existed separately from the Victorian Sculptors Society, though the seven members were also members of this society. John Davis was a member of the Sculptors Society, though like many other members, was not fully aware at the time of the existence, policies or activities of 'Centre Five'.

Clifford Last says that Julius Kane wrote the five-point programme and brought the list to the first meeting in 1961. 'Centre Five' was chosen as a title to symbolise the five-point programme of interests and concerns which were:

■ **1** *to bridge the gap between artist and public through individual and group activities, including exhibitions and lectures, radio and television appearances, newspaper and magazine articles;*
2 *to seek better representation in the National Art Galleries of Australia;*
3 *to foster a closer relationship with architects;*
4 *to publicize the need in Australia for an art development policy similar to that in other countries based on the principle of devoting a percentage of public building costs to works of art;*
5 *to seek assistance in creating more scholarships and fellowships for sculptors.*[6]

In addition, 'Centre Five' had an active programme to promote the work of its six members, who showed their work regularly in Melbourne, Sydney and Newcastle, secured architectural commissions and built a solid professional reputation for themselves.

As had been mentioned earlier, John Davis was influenced by the work of Julius Kane, though he never met him. It is unlikely that John Davis was affected by the activities of 'Centre Five' during the 1960s, though some of the professionalism may have influenced him. His work until the late 1960s was in a formative stage, whereas the 'Centre Five' were already mature sculptors.

Unlike his earlier, organic woodcarvings, the work that John Davis produced in the late 1960s, culminating in his first one man exhibition at Strines Gallery, Melbourne, in 1969, was very much the product of an urban twentieth century society. Even though the sculptures had been made by hand, there was an emphasis on man-made synthetic materials and twentieth century technology. Forms were all smooth and highly polished. Surfaces were often reflective. One was reminded of the shine of automobile bumper bars, radiator grilles, fins, tail lights and other aspects of car design. The link with the automobile was made even more direct by spraying fibreglass and resin surfaces with automobile duco, achieving the same perfect surface one expects on a new car.

When reviewing Davis's first one man exhibition, Alan McCulloch saw the link with the automobile and hinted there was a certain brashness in the highly reflective surfaces, 'that would delight the eye of any car salesman'.

■ *. . . John Davis (Strines) and Richard Stankiewicz (Arts Centre) conjure up visions of the by-products of machine technology. Davis from the automobile production line and Stankiewicz from the industrial no-man's land of rusting iron pipes and tee-sections.*

Davis's non-utilitarian objects are seductively tactile, elegantly shaped and topped off with a degree of mirror-polish that would delight the eye of any car salesman.[7]

The works produced by Davis in 1968 and 1969 were highly inventive, often consisting of a number of separate forms in metal, held together by the basic shape of the pedestal. The apparently fluid metal flowed out of the geometric pedestal, drooping as it solidified. Sometimes the metal flowed as it descended to the lower section. In *Engine*, cylindrical metal parts popped up out of the horizontal pedestal, as though the pistons of an engine had burst through the engine head.

The use of a variety of different geometric forms for the pedestals was visually exciting, but also hinted at 'good design'. In the late 1960s, 'design' was at its peak in popularity in tertiary art schools in Australia, being regarded as not just a fundamental subject, but as the basis for all art teaching. Qualifications changed name, from 'Diplomas of Art' to 'Diplomas of Art and Design'. John Davis was much influenced by the first-year course at Caulfield Institute of Technology and the basic attitudes which were at the core of the experimental course. Like the students he was teaching, he managed to avoid building on tradition and was able to examine each problem, as though he were encountering it for the first time. His three-dimensional solutions were fresh and original and quite sophisticated.

Yet one can now see that these sculptures were too sophisticated and too closely allied with technology and man-made materials to truly represent John Davis. At the time, neither John Davis, nor spectators and friends examining his work, would have realised that his sculpture was to become far more impersonal. It was to be many years before John Davis worked his way through several styles and fought his way back to simple solutions in harmony with his own personality.

At the height of the success of the first-year course at Caulfield no one imagined that the experiment was going to be very short-lived. The younger artists who were at Caulfield were overwhelmed by the conservative members of staff, who had the numbers. Harold Farey, as the new Head of Department, changed his position from cautious support to opposition, which made Fred Cress's position and my own untenable — we both left. Over the next couple of years the course was emasculated and the remaining supporters, John Davis and Vic Majzner also vacated Caulfield, joining Fred Cress at Prahran College of Advanced Education.

But at the time, particularly during 1967–68, there was a constant ferment of ideas, which is reflected in the work produced by John Davis at this period. Not that he was alone in creating highly sophisticated images, for other artists in Sydney were working in a similar manner.

'Engine' was the title of the exhibition that Sydney Ball, Col Jordan and Ken Reinhard held at Farmers' Blaxland Gallery in Sydney in May 1967. *Engine* was the title of a piece of sculpture produced by John Davis in 1968 in Melbourne. John Davis did not see the Sydney exhibition, or even the catalogue of the show, yet there are interesting parallels. Ken Reinhard had shown his work at the South Yarra Galleries, Melbourne, in August 1967 while Col Jordan had a one person exhibition at Strines Gallery, Melbourne, in May 1967 and again in December 1967.

The choice of identical titles is probably pure coincidence, but the three sculptors at that time shared a love of sophisticated forms produced in twentieth century, man-made materials. *Engine* by John Davis was a relatively small sculpture, only 25 cm high, with a maximum length of approximately 45 cm. It consisted of a horizontal T-shaped base with a rectangular prism projecting upwards from the intersection of the T. This basic structure was made from hardboard, covered in vinyl, such as one might have found on car upholstery. Five separate chrome-plated bronze forms projected from various parts of the base. As an 'engine' it had a suppressed energy. Its actual function as an engine was unknown, yet not mysterious, for the work had a conviction which did not allow for uncertainty.

Anvil was produced in 1968 and included in the Strines exhibition. The pedestal was essentially vertical, but had a projecting horizontal top, which cantilevered in one direction, giving the pedestal an inverted 'L' shape. The inside of the 'L' was curved, emphasising the flow outwards for the projecting section of the pedestal. The basic hardboard structure was covered in vinyl with the metal sculpture resting on the flat top of the pedestal, but placed well outside the centre of gravity. Normally a piece of sculpture which doesn't appear to balance produces a feeling of tension and uncertainty in the spectator. Strangely, this does not happen with *Anvil*. The placing of the chrome-plated bronze sculpture is so deliberately off centre that physical balance is just not possible — the spectator is immediately aware that he is the observer of a visual trick. For the observant, the contradiction between what is known to be possible, and what is seen and yet known to be impossible, becomes one of the sophisticated delights of the work. The sophistication of *Anvil* may have been seriously undermined if spectators had known that the pedestal could only balance with the hidden assistance of several heavy bricks in the base!

The title *Anvil* is obviously based on the shape of the pedestal, not the small sculpture resting on the pedestal. The metal sculpture consists of a number of organic forms, all strangely truncated at their extremities. The chrome-plated, highly polished forms vaguely resemble a figure lying on its back with arms and legs extended upwards and outwards. Unlike a number of works produced by John Davis at this time, the metal does not flow out from, or into the pedestal, but the small sculpture merely rests, vulnerably on top of the pedestal.

Maquette for Prise was produced in 1968, some time after *Prise* was completed in 1967, so it is not a study for the larger, earlier work. It consists of two separate pedestals, one supporting the other. Both are square prisms, but the larger of the two has a semicircular form projecting at top and bottom, making a link with the other square prism, which has a circular shape projecting from one side. The two geometric pedestals are linked with fluid aluminium forms, that flow from the higher to the lower. Basically constructed of hardboard on a wooden construction, the circular projecting parts of pedestals were made of fibreglass and polyester resin. The whole construction was painted black,

▶
12 John Davis: Loop *(1969). Polished aluminium, polyester resin and fibreglass over hardboard, sprayed with blue-green automotive duco. 21.5 x 45 x 30 cm. (In the James Baker Collection, Museum of Contemporary Art, Brisbane.) Photograph by Mark Strizic.*

▶
13 John Davis: Wrapped Around *(1969). Cardboard construction covered with fibreglass and polyester resin, sprayed with red automotive duco. Cast bronze form, chrome plated and polished. 39 x 46.1 x 25.5 cm. (Shepparton Art Gallery.) Photograph by Mark Strizic.*

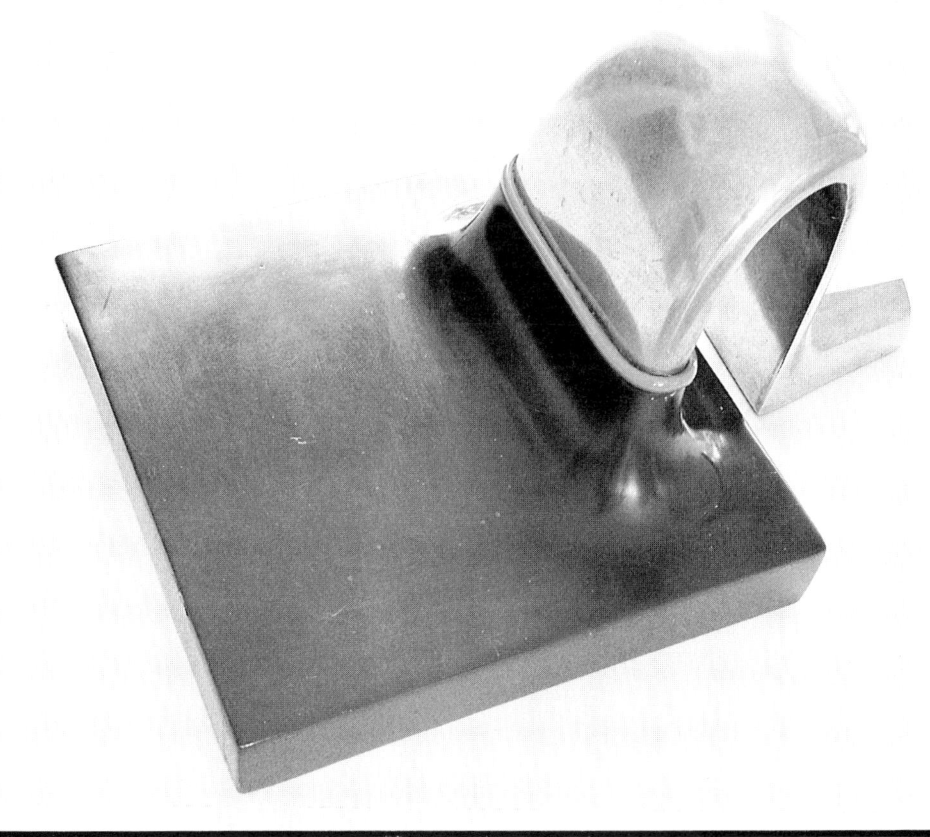

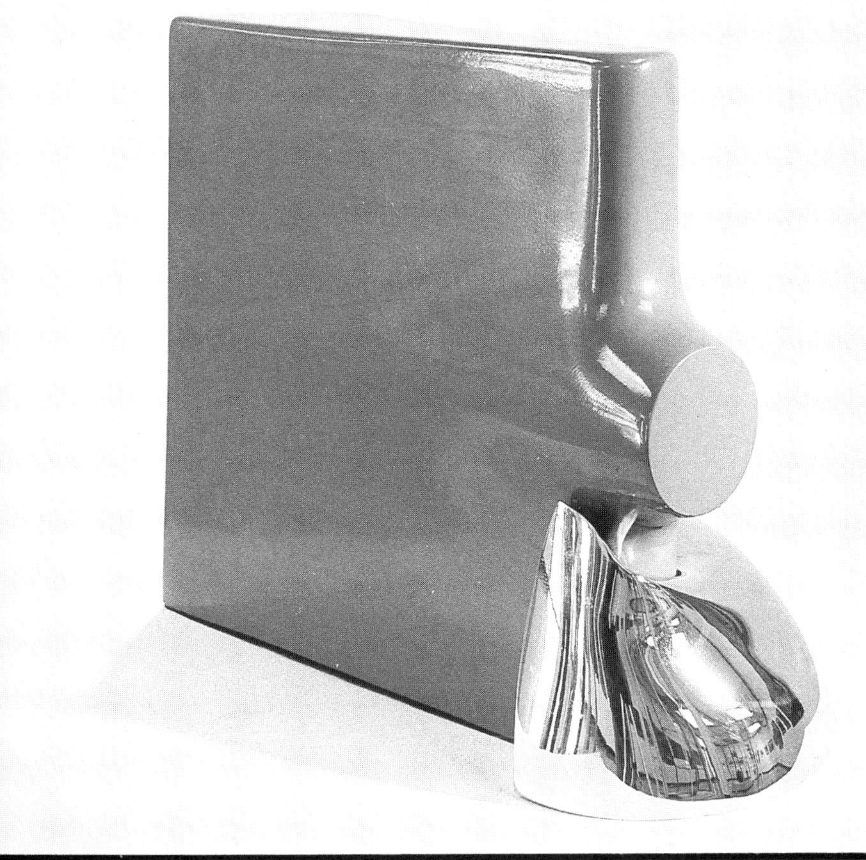

except for the red laminex on the sides. As with *Anvil*, the work defied natural balance, though visually the weight flowed from the higher, smaller section down to the larger more stable pedestal. Again, some house bricks inside the pedestal were necessary in order to establish effective balance.

Traditionally, the pedestal has always been a neutral colour. White is fashionable at present, though I can remember the pedestals at the old National Gallery of Victoria were always painted grey. I can also remember that some sculptors, in the days of the Victorian Sculptors Society, brought along pedestals covered in hessian. John Davis frequently used black and white on his pedestals. The use of black paint seems to have been a natural flow on from the use of black stain, in earlier wood carvings. His use of red laximex, red duco and red house paint also goes back to his wood carvings, such as *Bent on Mayhem*, where he introduced areas of red. Seldom was any other colour introduced, though there was the colour of the aluminium or bronze forms. A few sculptors had introduced colour into their work which was shown at the 1967 Mildura Prize for Sculpture, virtually the first time that Australian and New Zealand sculptors had shown painted sculpture. But by 1968 strong colour was frequently used by the sculptors who showed in 'The Field' exhibition at the National Gallery of Victoria. John Davis was inventive three-dimensionally, but cautious in his use of colour. Black and white, with an occasional area of red, were the most commonly used colours, which gave sufficient dramatic impact without introducing any emotional content. The emphasis was on intellectual experiment, in which colour was always subservient to the form.

Thru (or *Through*), *Loop* (illus. 12) and *Wrapped Around* (illus. 13) were three works in the Strines exhibition which shared similar characteristics. They were all relatively small sculptures, displayed

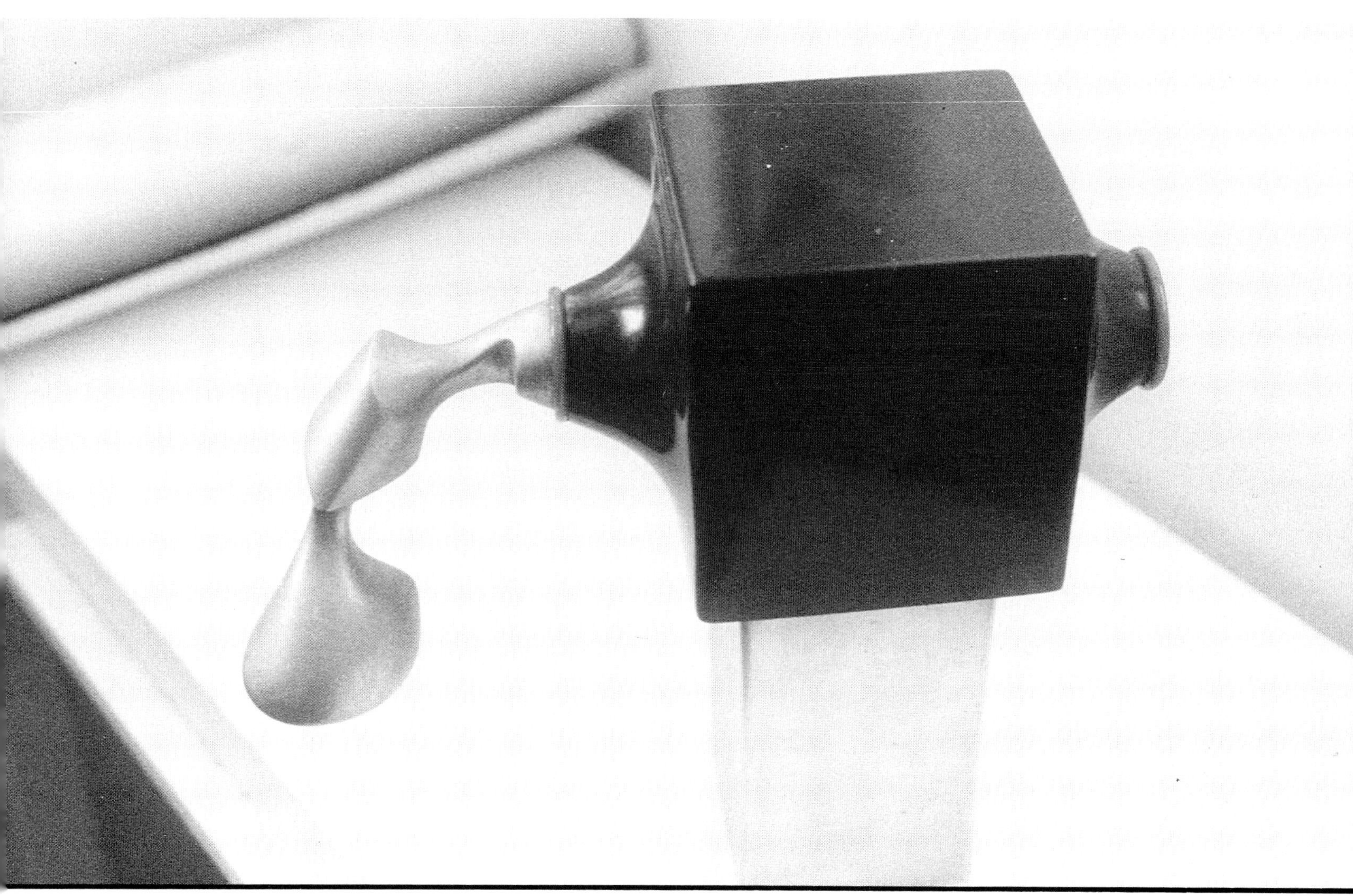

on pedestals. They all consisted of a rectangular form — placed horizontally with *Loop*, and vertically with the other two — which was pierced by a highly polished aluminium or chrome-plated form. The contrast was between the fluid form with a highly reflective surface and the geometric form constructed of cardboard or hardboard, covered in fibreglass and then sprayed with duco. The contrast was between cool metal and the colour of the duco — deep purple, green or red. They were domestic-sized works with a strong tactile appeal, ideal for a coffee table where one could easily reach out and touch.

Drop Out (illus. 14) was not the most radical of the works shown at Strines Gallery in 1969, but it is an important link between those sculptures shown at John Davis's first one man exhibition and his later works. The aluminium form used in *Drop Out* was the starting point for a series of works which occupied him until 1971 and his departure for his first overseas trip.

The pedestal for *Drop Out* consisted of a cube on top of a white square prism. The top section, covered in polyester resin and fibreglass, sprayed with blue automobile duco, supported a relatively large aluminium form which drooped groundwards. It was this flowing form, obeying gravity, emerging like water, or molten metal, that was to be the basis for another nine or ten works, such as *Sixteen, 100* and the winning work for the Comalco competition and the subsequent commission for the Hydro Electric Commission Building in Hobart, Tasmania.

In 1969, a year after 'The Field' exhibition, John Davis was exploring sculpturally some of the ideas put forward by the painters. Artists such as Dale Hickey and Robert Rooney had exhibited paintings consisting of sequential repetition of identical shapes. The titles of works produced by

◀
14 John Davis: **Drop Out** *(1968). White square prism with cube on top, covered in polyester resin and fibreglass. Top cube sprayed with blue automotive duco. Polished aluminium form emerging from circle on side of blue cube. 28 x 24 x 12.5 cm. (In possession of the artist.) Photograph by the artist.*

John Davis during 1969, 1970 and 1971 are indicative of a new interest in the repetition of forms and the use of grids: *Hanging Three, Three Thirds, Sixteen, Through 5, Multiples*, and astonishingly, *100* — a work which consisted of one hundred identical forms arranged 10 × 10 in a large square, hanging on the wall.

John Davis's first one man exhibition at Strines really showed an artist in transit. There were the works using polished aluminium and chrome-plated bronze, combined with forms spray painted with duco, and there were the later sculptures entirely in white fibreglass and resin that explored the repetition of identical forms. The first group of works represented a burst of activity over a relatively short period, 1967–69. The sculptures based on the repetition of identical spatulate forms occupied John Davis for a further two years, 1969–71. The Strines exhibition was midway and showed these two streams of thought, whereas the Watters Gallery exhibition of 1971 was a more cohesive exhibition showing works in one style, in one material, and all entirely in one colour, white.

Yet the sculptures produced during 1969–71 can be seen in retrospect to be bland, devoid of emotion and almost (but not quite) anonymous. At the time it was a logical development of forms that emerged from previous work — the drooping form of *Drop Out* mentioned earlier. Compared with the minimal sculpture that was still in favour, John Davis's work was not entirely anonymous — it was recognisable as the work of John Davis. It still had a slight organic quality, as though based on metal flowing or water pouring. But in contrast to mature works produced years later, it was cold, impersonal, logical and built entirely of synthetic, man-made materials — all qualities that were out of character with the artist. At the time John Davis probably thought his earlier wood carvings, such as *Bent on Mayhem*, were excessively emotional and

dramatic. The cool, detached attitude of artists producing minimal sculpture and hard-edge painting obviously had an effect on him and if not entirely seduced by the minimal movement, he at least was influenced by the prevailing style. But it was the current interest in grids and the deliberate repetition of identical forms that intrigued him and it was these works (some shown in Melbourne at Strines in 1969) that formed the basis of his first exhibition in Sydney at Watters Gallery in 1971.

Given time, John Davis was to prove that intuition was a more important ingredient in his work than logic, but in 1969, when reviewing his one man exhibition at Strines, Alan Warren was greatly impressed by his 'concentration upon formal relations'. Certainly his last sentence was prophetic. 'With John Davis (Strines Gallery) premeditation takes the place of instinct. It is the intense, exclusive concentration upon formal relations; the attempt to develop form out of form for form that confers on his six pieces such astonishing authority. He is someone to watch and collect.'[8]

■ NOTES

1 'Sense Compartment' was by Stelios Arcadiou who later became internationally known as Stelarc, famous for his Suspension Events.
2 Alan McCulloch, 'World Boom in Graphics' review of 'Zetetic Ex', Argus Gallery, Melbourne, 28 August–8 September 1967, in *Herald*, 30 August 1967, reproduced courtesy of the Herald and Weekly Times Ltd.
3 Patrick McCaughey, 'Art: Patrick McCaughey', *Age*, 14 August 1968.
4 Fred Cress, 'First Year Art at Caulfield Technical College', *ATAV Journal* (Art Teachers' Association of Victoria), (Melbourne), September 1968.
5 Vic Majzner interviewed by Ken Scarlett, 31 August 1982.
6 First published by Margaret Plant, 'Centre 5: A note on a decade of activity' in C. B. Christesen (ed.), *The Gallery on Eastern Hill*, Victorian Artists Society (Melbourne), 1970.
7 Alan McCulloch, 'A Sculptor's Skill', *Herald*, 15 October 1969, reproduced courtesy of the Herald and Weekly Times Ltd.
8 Alan Warren, 'Young Artists Enliven Scene', *Sun*, 8 October 1969.

REPETITION, GRIDS, MULTIPLES AND PROCESSES

The use of polyester resin and fibreglass forced John Davis to consider the process of making his sculptures. The accurate mixing of ingredients, specialised techniques of working the materials, the concern with repetitious procedures, even precise timing, were all totally different processes to the contemplative actions of a woodcarver.

Aesthetic judgements were played down in favour of the process establishing the form. Or, to put it more accurately, aesthetic judgements, based on past experience and previous works of art, were held in abeyance while a new set of aesthetics developed to cope with the new interest in processes.

During the late 1960s a number of artists were intrigued by grids, repetitious patterns and sequential serialisation in their paintings and sculpture. Dale Hickey showed his paintings at a one person exhibition at Tolarno Gallery in 1967 and his *Yellow Square* was included in 'The Field' in 1968. *Yellow Square* was in fact a long horizontal rectangle, consisting of fifty yellow squares, 5 high × 10 long, looking like an extremely accurate painting of a tiled surface. The painting of fifty identical shapes, over a large area, required considerable skill and much patience — one might say a dogged determination. The final work was immaculate and anonymous. Unlike the earlier abstract expressionism, which had been in vogue, the artist's personality was almost entirely subjugated.

Robert Rooney had several one person exhibitions in Melbourne during the 1960s, including one at Strines Gallery in 1968. From the title of his painting *Kind-Hearted Kitchen Garden V*, shown in 'The Field', one would have expected something more personal, intimate, or even amusing, but the work was as detached as Dale Hickey's painting. It was constructed on a rigid grid of horizontals and verticals, giving a pattern of 11 squares high × 11 squares wide.

One could easily conclude that a number of artists of this time were interested in mathematics, yet their work would demonstrate a very simplistic attitude towards mathematical relationships. Taking some of 'The Field' paintings and sculptures as examples it is possible to see some of the simple combinations of shape and form. Melvyn Ramsden had a *No Title* painting, consisting of one very long, narrow, horizontal rectangle, painted in one colour in gloss enamel. Emanuel Raft showed *Monolith 5* and *Monolith 8*, both sculptures in painted wood. John Peart used a square within a square for two of his paintings *Cool Corner 11* and *Corner Square Diagonal*. Symmetry and the repetition of two identical forms was commonly used, as in the paintings *Ispahan* by Sydney Ball, *Start* by Ron Robertson-Swann, and the sculptures *Untitled* by Noel Dunn and *Luke* by Wendy Paramor. Wendy Paramor had three identical forms in *Triad* and Robert Jacks had five identical rectangles in *Red Painting*. Trevor Vickers used a simple progression of 1, 2, 3 or 1, 2, 3, 4 in two untitled paintings.

The mathematics used was not of the involved Fibinacci principle as used by Bartok in some of his musical compositions. There was no suggestion of the mathematics of a Bach fugue. Rather, the progression could only go towards extreme simplicity, in which one shape or one form was the ultimate, or the logic could go towards the maximum repetition of one shape or form, in which case the greater the number, the greater the success.

John Davis tried both of these approaches. *Drop Out* consisted of one form emerging from a supporting pedestal. At the other extreme was *100*, consisting of 10 × 10 identical forms projecting from a large square board. It took three years for him to work his way through the possibilities, culminating in his one person exhibition at Watters Gallery, Sydney, in 1971.

All of the works shown at Watters Gallery were

Figure 1

39 Daria St,
Hampton 3188
Monday 15th March

Dear Frank,

Thought I'd drop you a line to let you know how things are proceeding and to inquire about one or two things. As usual I'm surrounded by bits and pieces and very soon I hope they will all come together. The show should consist of constructed pieces mainly in fibreglass and a series of photographs on some procedural work I've been experimenting with over the last couple of months.

After my phone call in January inquiring about the size of the gallery doors so that I could fit a large piece through there, one piece will be 8'2" x 8'2" and consisting of 100 multiple images.

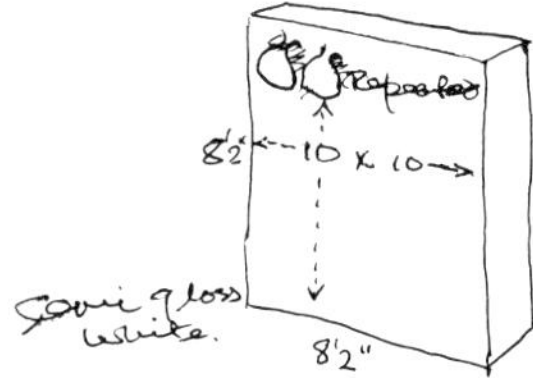

To hang this piece would it be possible to drill holes into the wall and insert ½" bolts to support it above the floor?

Another piece consists of 5 boxes (15"x12"x12") with lid and showing a process of multiple forms through these 5 stages, something like this —

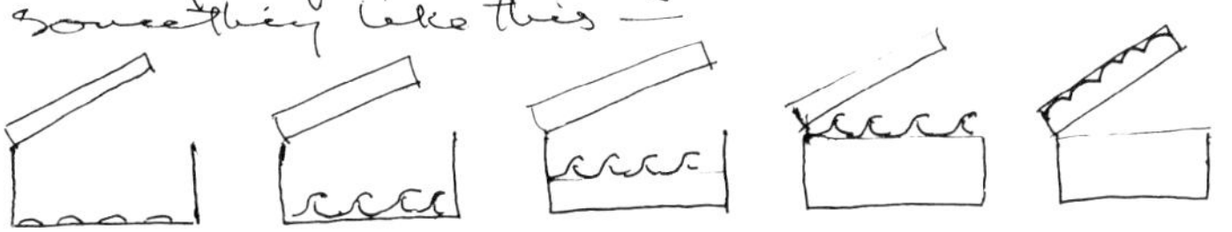

In the gallery on the lower level occupied by your desk, I've organizing 16-20 panels to line each wall so that the viewer walks between them. They'll be something like this — ➤

②

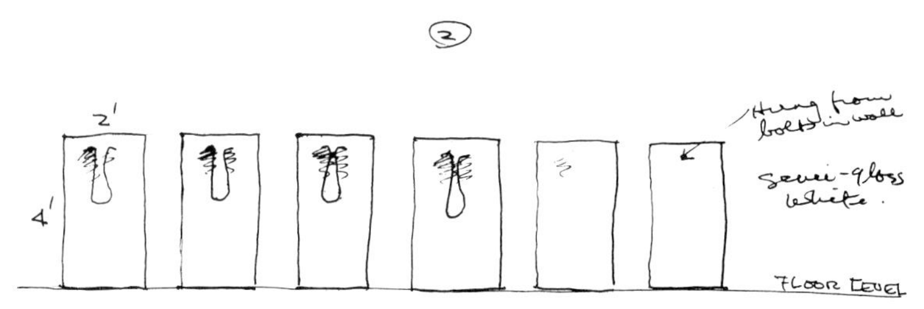

The process photographs will be filed in the order in which the procedure took place. It consisted of a pattern formed on our back lawn from the dust after sanding the scoop forms and eventuated into plastic sheeting with 100 holes cut into it and the grass bunching and growing through these holes

Another one in this series is an idea for a large area — an acre of grazing land, M.C.G, public gardens etc.

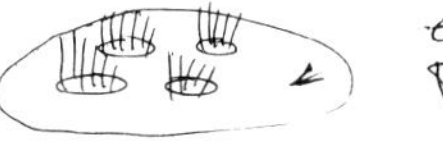

These photographs link up with my constructed work in that it is basically about a procedural approach to sculpture in its calculated formality and it seems a development from my earlier work.

Two other pieces were shown at Stines and another I'm contemplating using was shown at Mildura and the Sydney Captain Cook last year. Maybe one or even two of these won't be needed.

15 John Davis: Three Thirds *or* 3/3 *(1969). Three forms in polished aluminium, on backing of hardboard, covered in white polyester resin and fibreglass. 76.6 x 78 x 26 cm. (Brisbane College of Advanced Education.) Photographed by the artist when exhibited at Strine's Gallery, Melbourne, 5–17 October 1969.*

hanging on, or leaning against the wall. All were strictly frontal. In this respect the sculptures were similar to works produced by the painters Dale Hickey and Robert Rooney.

Just prior to his first one person exhibition in Sydney, Davis sent a letter to Frank Watters briefly outlining what work he intended showing.[1] Simple diagrammatic drawings, showing the works and methods of display were included (see Figure 1).

It would have been convenient for future art historians if John Davis had made *Drop Out* with one form and had progressed through two, three, four or more forms, until he reached his maximum of one hundred. It was not quite as direct as that, though that was the general direction. After *Drop Out* came *Three Thirds* or *3/3* (illus. 15), which was the prototype for the drooping, spatulate forms emerging from a flat background, used in a considerable number of sculptures in 1969, 1970 and 1971. In *Three Thirds* the projecting forms were polished aluminium, pouring forth but stopped in full flow by the solidity of the metal. The forms emerged from circular openings, slightly protruding from the flat background, as though the pressure from the rear was forcing out the aluminium. The three aluminium forms were attached to three separate white hardboard backgrounds through which the aluminium forms flowed down and touched.

Logically one would have expected John Davis to produce *Hanging Three* directly after completing *Three Thirds*. In *Three Thirds* the spatulate forms are arranged horizontally beside each other, whereas in *Hanging Three* the three large drooping forms are placed one beneath the other. In actual fact, *Sixteen* (illus. 16) was the next work and it has the distinction of being the first of a considerable number of sculptures cast in polyester resin and fibreglass. The traditional casting procedures, using plaster of paris moulds that John Davis had

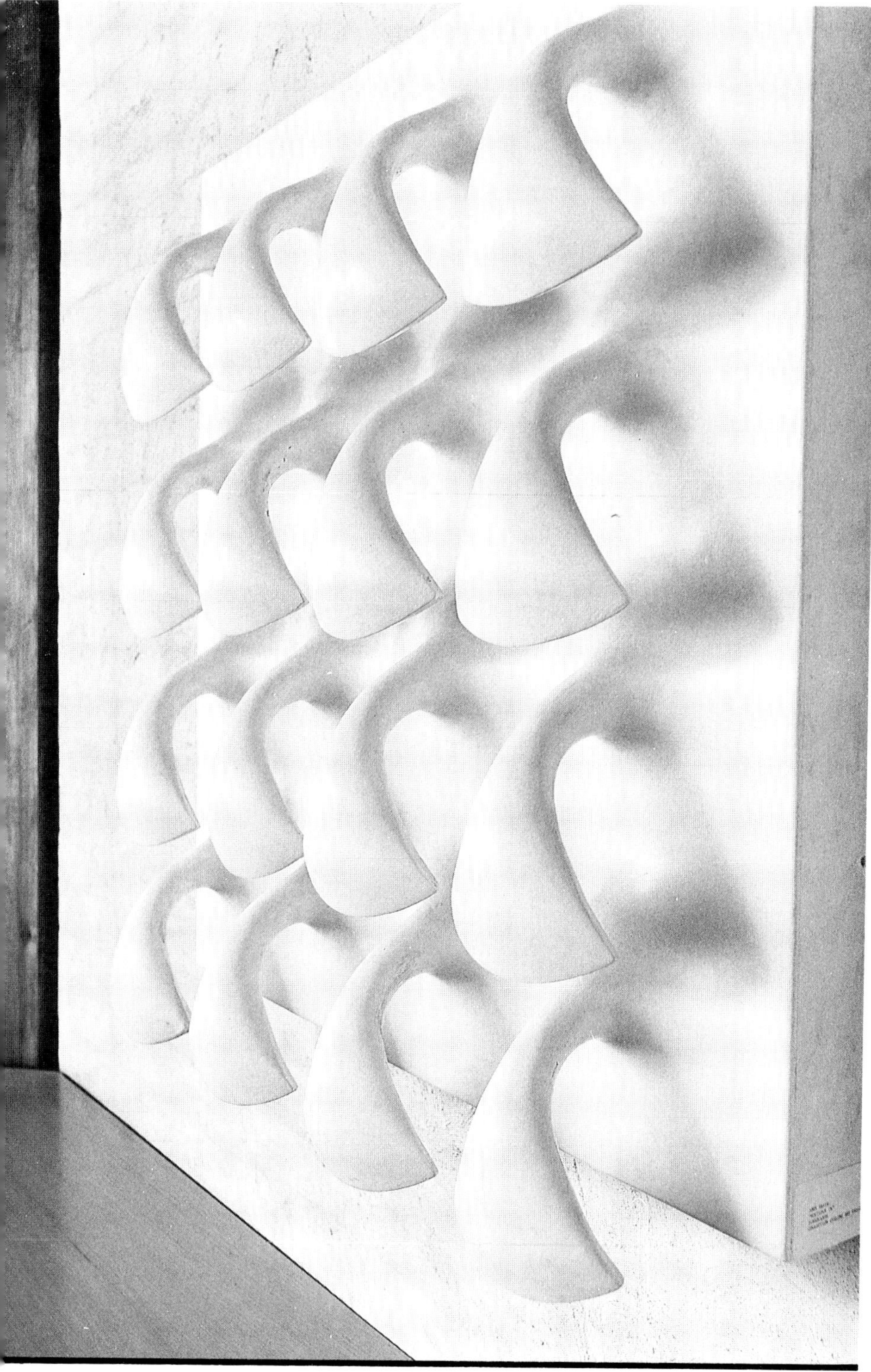

▼
16 John Davis: Sixteen or 16 (1969). Fibreglass and polyester resin on hardboard and timber structure, painted white. 103 x 99 x 25 cm. (Geelong Art Gallery.) Purchased in 1970 with funds from the Miss G. Bell and J. H. McPhillimy Bequest.) Photograph by Mark Strizic.

learnt at RMIT, proved to be very useful in making the polyester resin casts. Once the first form was made from clay and a mould made, it was then possible to cast a considerable number of identical forms in polyester resin. The procedure helped the production of sequential, repetitious forms. The philosophy of truth to material became truth to the process. Later he became interested in processes themselves.

Sixteen (or *16*) was a decisive jump from the production of single objects into serialisation and the repetition of identical forms. Each spatulate form was identical, from the same mould, placed equidistant apart, on a rigid grid of horizontals and verticals. The whole structure was 4 forms wide × 4 forms deep. The only variation to the simple repetition was brought about by the fact that the drooping forms actually curved out and down, beyond the square board to which they were attached. This gave a space at the top and a different outline at the bottom, where the forms went outside the square.

A sculpture such as *Sixteen* relied very heavily on good lighting to show up the forms (white on white background), for the pattern of light and shade and the cast shadows emphasised the repetition, though even with strong lighting and intense shadows, the works never became dramatic for the general effect was of calculated, controlled order.

If art is an expression of man's wish to impose his sense of order upon his environment, then *Sixteen* and other sequential works should have been great art — but they were not. They were extremely interesting pieces of sculpture, in which an order had been decisively imposed upon the forms, but life itself was threatened by the monotony of the order. There was no room for the accidental or the unexpected. Intuition was totally suppressed.

John Davis was not a minimal sculptor and was not included in 'The Field' exhibition in 1968 (nor would he have been widely known at this period). Nevertheless his work received similar criticism as the hard-edge painters and minimal sculptors. To many this work appeared cold and impersonal, international rather than Australian. Elwyn Lynn defended the artists of 'The Field' exhibition against these criticisms:

■ *While this splendid efflorescence of talent may be an enthusiastically cool, an eagerly detached look at the way art works, it produces an opaque art that needs no veils to be torn to reveal its metaphysics, symbolism and allegories; it needs no decoding like a Duchamp or a Kitaj. Though it is not ostensibly concerned with the human condition, it is not dehumanized or impersonal; if it were one would have to exclaim how varied were dehumanization and impersonality! It has been accused of sterility, international anonymity, anti-Australianism and so on, so let it be said that those who derive their notions of realism from Delacroix's Romanticism or European Expressionism will always think the light, tranquil and Rococo trivial and the classically severe sterile and dehumanized.[2]*

Sixteen, with its repetition of identical forms, implied that the pattern could go on forever in each direction. *100* was the logical development, in which there were ten identical forms across and ten down. They were the same spatulate forms, from the same mould. One might logically ask: 'Why stop at 100? Why not 1000?' A wall totally covered with identical forms — a room with four walls completely covered — these would have been fascinating developments.

Luckily a human factor intervened. The task of making identical fibreglass forms from a mould is a tedious and monotonous process. The resin is sticky and unpleasant to use, with a smell that can induce headaches. Fibreglass frequently causes a mild skin irritation and itch. The materials require precise control and timing, in order to mix the ingredients and remove casts from the moulds. At the time of making his fibreglass and resin sculptures, John Davis was working in an extremely small studio — an old bungalow in his backyard in the suburb of Hampton. He lacked space, light and ventilation. The boredom of the process and the technical monotony convinced him that *100* was enough.

Years later, in an interview with me, John Davis explained why he changed to materials such as twigs, sticks, string and paper:

■ *I was becoming heartily sick of working in materials such as fibreglass and metals where the process tended to be a long, drawn out affair and at the end of that process one was then concerned about the finish of the surface, and then the preservation of that finish. By working directly with materials such as twigs, one could move much faster, so that . . . the work was evolving at that point — and not having to go through a distant process . . .[3]*

Nevertheless, not all of the works produced in this period prior to the Watters Gallery exhibition in 1971, suffered from an extreme discipline of order. John Davis's innate need for freedom and genuine love of life fought through, in spite of the rigid system he attempted to impose upon his work. *9 Through 5* (illus. 17) used the same spatulate forms, in this case, nine to a box, arranged in orderly rows of three. The five boxes were identical, being painted black on the outside and white inside. The lids of the boxes could be closed, though the work was usually shown with the boxes open. In the first box, on the extreme left, the nine forms had not emerged and were only visible as nine bumps on the bottom of the box. In the second the forms were clearly visible. In the third, more prominent. By the fourth box the nine forms were close to the top so that the lid barely closed on them. The fifth and last box was empty, though the

▶
17 John Davis: 9 Through 5 or Nine Through Five *(1971). Five chipboard boxes, painted white inside and black outside. White forms of fibreglass and polyester resin inside boxes. Each box 30.8 x 33.3 x 40.3 cm. (Newcastle Region Art Gallery.) Photograph by Mark Strizic.

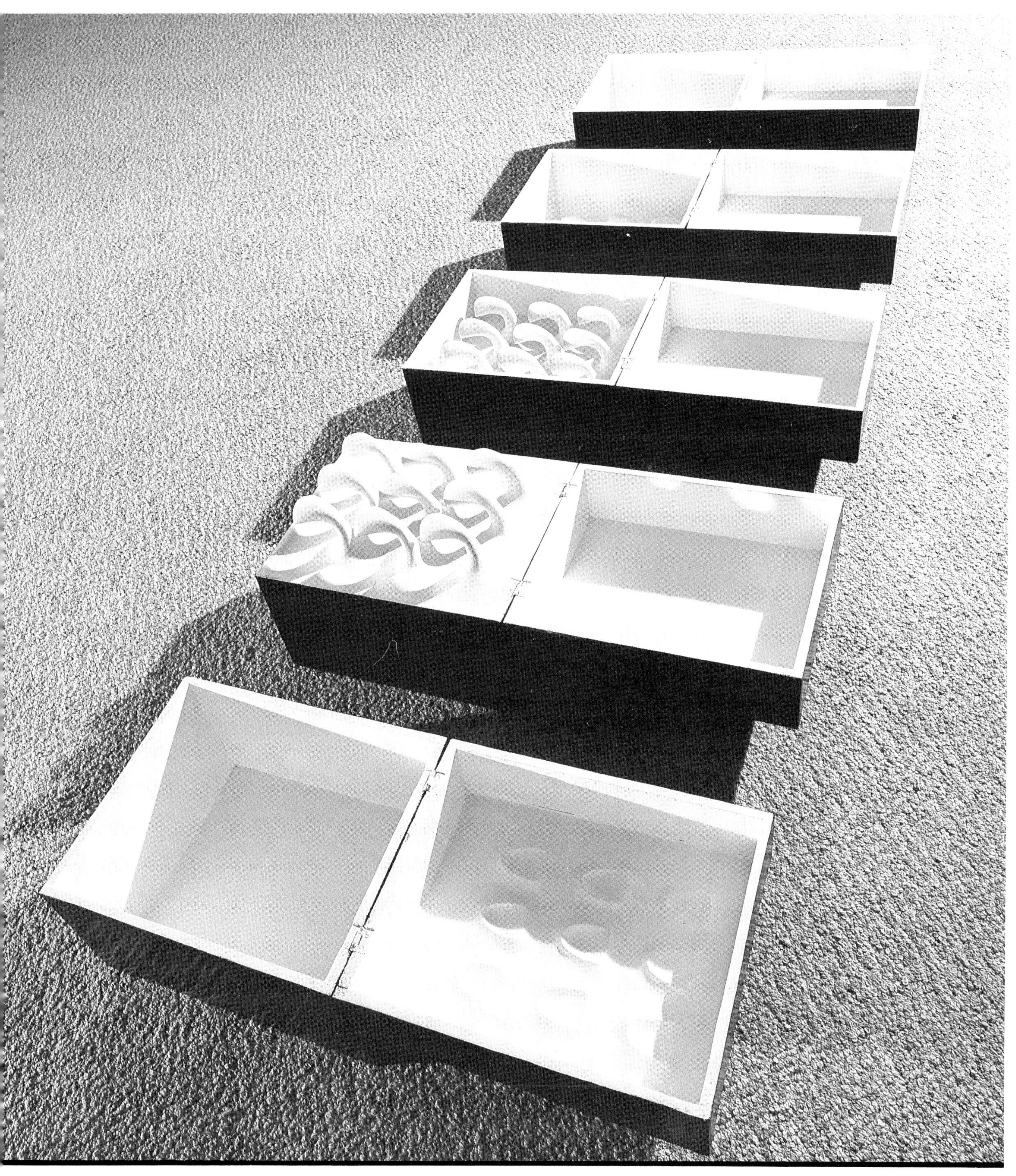

pressure of the upward movement of these strange forms had left indentations in the lid of the box. The cold, bland system had acquired an air of mystery. The spectactor was left puzzled by an incomplete system. There were numerous unanswered questions: why were the nine forms kept in boxes? what pressure forced them upwards? in what manner had they mysteriously disappeared? The identical black and white boxes were clinical in appearance, as though they contained specimens for display, but the forms had a strange sense of relentless growth which was mildly amusing, or a little alarming, according to the spectator's point of view.

Davis was later to exploit the mysterious quality of boxes and containers in a number of works in markedly different materials.

By 1970 his sculpture was sufficiently well known for him to be invited to contribute a maquette for the annual Comalco Invitation Award for Sculpture. The award had started in 1968 when Vincent Jomantas was the winner. The 1969 prize was given to Ron Robertson-Swann, though it was Margel Hinder's entry that was commissioned by the National Capital Development Commission for the Woden Town Centre in Canberra.

The 1970 catalogue, published by Comalco, stated that the terms of the award were as follows:

■ *Architecture undoubtedly provides the major source of commissioned work for sculptors. The Comalco Award is designed to foster this inter-relation. The subject of the Award, which will vary from year to year, is related to sculpture for specific architectural environments.*

The competition for the Award is by invitation to six sculptors each year. These people are selected by exhaustive reference to gallery directors, critics and others concerned professionally with the Arts in Australia. Each sculptor competing for the Award receives a fee of $750 and the winner receives, in addition, $3000.

Six sculptors were invited to design a maquette not exceeding 36 inches maximum dimension for a work of relief sculpture to be fixed to the solid wall end of a glazed foyer in a new administration building for a public authority.

The sculpture would generally be viewed from a distance of approximately 40 feet although close inspection would be possible.

As it would be seen from the side as well as from directly in front and the special emphasis is along the major axis, full scope was available for a positive three-dimensional design.

At night the foyer and sculpture would be brightly illuminated and would be seen clearly by passing traffic.

The suggested theme for the 1970 award was 'Energy'.

John Davis won the award with an untitled work (illus. 18) that was entirely appropriate in the terms of the competition, yet the sculpture was only a development of works already produced by him. He stated this in the Comalco catalogue:

■ *Simply this sculpture is about my sculptures past and future. It contains links with previous works — a continuity if you like — and indicates a direction that the next one may follow. It happens to be a work conceived in this context but in this case for a predetermined site which resolves its scale and space relationships.*

The 'foyer in a new administration building for a public authority' mentioned in the terms of the competition was actually the foyer of the Hydro Electric Commission Building in Hobart, Tasmania (illus. 19). The five verticals, with emerging spatulate forms at the bottom, were directly linked with previous sculptures, yet in terms of the competition they appeared to admirably represent the theme of 'Energy'.

The Sydney art critic, Elwyn Lynn, was one of the judges:

■ *The John Davis, unanimously selected by the*

▶

18 John Davis: Untitled (1970). Maquette for Comalco Invitation Award for Sculpture 1970, for which the theme was 'Energy'. Aluminium, cast and fabricated. 109 x 76.2 x 24 cm. (Comalco Ltd.) Photograph by Mark Strizic.

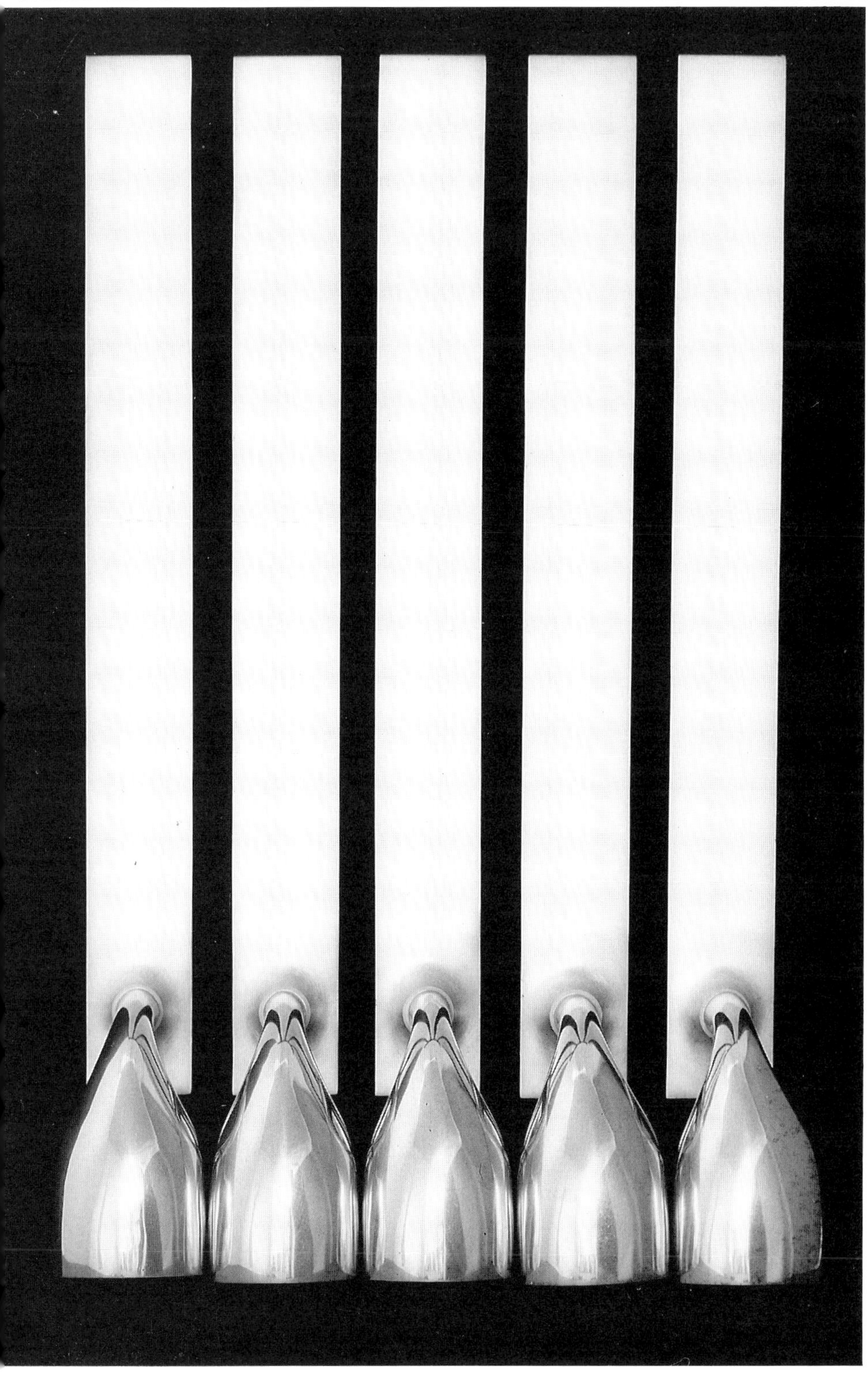

judges, Eric Westbrook, Rod MacDonald and myself, has five satiny, flat, vertical shafts which break into glistening, biomorphic nodules at the bottom. The nodules, like shorn-off pods, placed in the finished work at eye-level, will reflect and slightly distort the passerby, engage him without distraction, humour him without halting him, and the whole work, with its positive five verticals and its reflecting nodules — symbolising by accident the sweep of water and the vast mouths of pipes — will annihilate by distortion and sheer power these niggling details which, it seems, must inhabit foyers. It is a development of his square pedestals with trifid heads seen this year at Mildura and Sydney's State Office Block, and like them it is about energy, creating benign biochemical shapes.[4]

On the other hand, Ross Lansell, often a highly independent art critic, was critical of the whole competition and of John Davis's winning entry in particular:

■ *One of this year's trio of judges, Mr Elwyn Lynn (the others being one Mr R. I. MacDonald, a Carlton architect, and the ubiquitous Mr Eric Westbrook) is on record saying that some pieces were considered by the judges to be 'too formidable and dominating' and 'too disjunctive' to get the $3000. So blandness was the prime requisite. They certainly got it with Melbourne John Davis's typical quintet of faucets, a passable trade mark for a firm of vacuum cleaners or tap manufacturers. It's not as bad as expected, though such simple-minded systemisation usually means poverty of imagination. But is it anything more than just polished plumbing? Despite its technical competence, which should be taken for granted on such occasions, it seems stylistically second-hand (ie: the aftermath of minimalism) and singularly sterile.*[5]

During the 1960s in Australia there were a considerable number of exhibitions organised as awards, prizes and competitions. Most artists accepted the situation as a way of displaying their work, but gradually became disenchanted with a system in which there was only one winner and

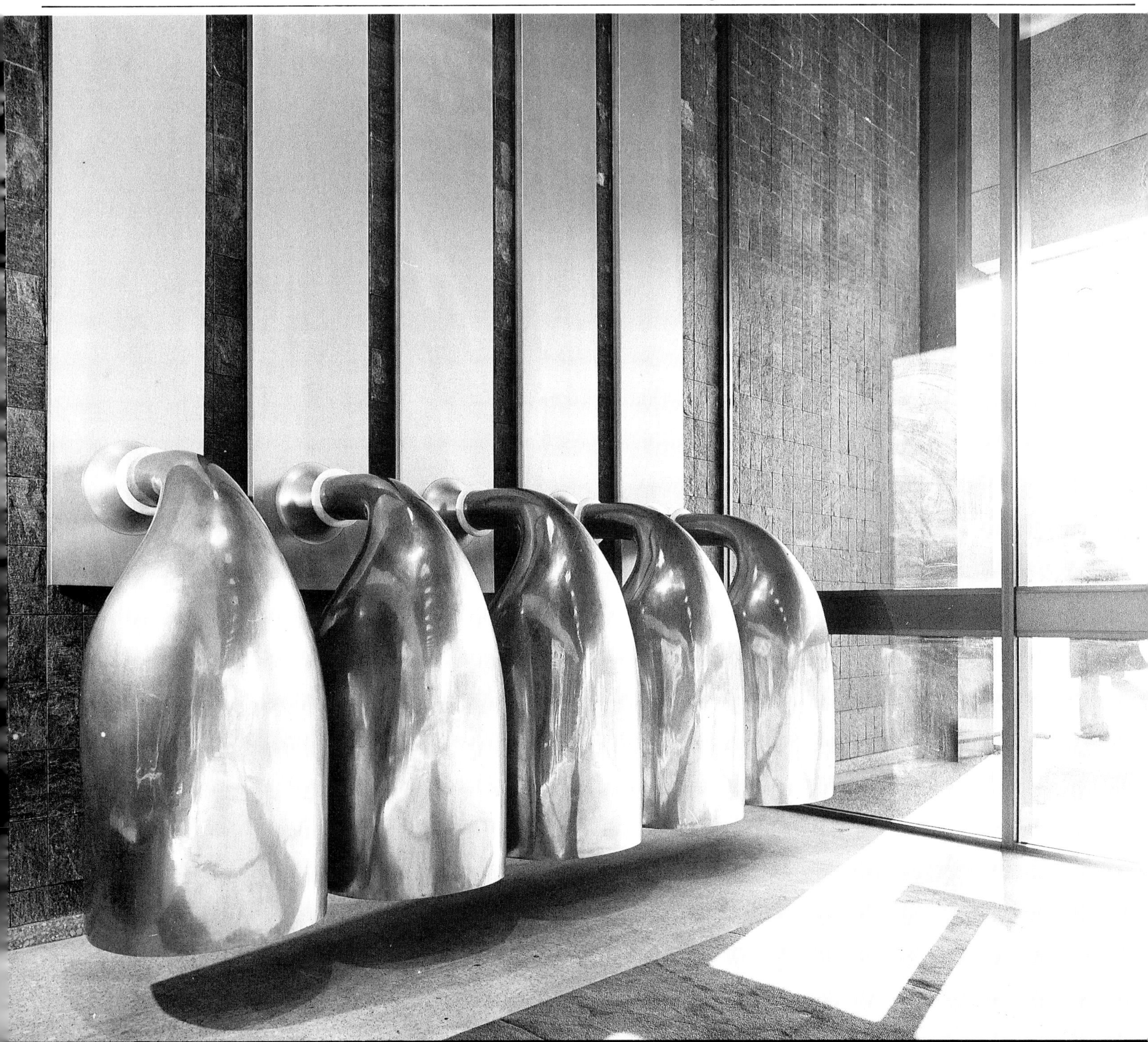

19 *John Davis: Foyer of Hydro Electric Commission Building, Hobart (1971). Commission, following Comalco Award. Aluminium, cast and fabricated. 533 x 293 x 100 cm. Photograph by Mark Strizic.*

many also-rans. By 1970, Margaret Plant was expressing an opinion that was becoming common amongst artists, bringing about the gradual cessation of such competitions.

■ *In the too-frequent situation of the art prize, we are asked to assume that all artists are equal but some, usually three, are better than others.*

To award prizes to single works in isolation without taking into account the artist's body of work and development of ideas; to see him not in relation to his own work but in relation to other competitors, fortuitous or invited, continues to falsify and confuse the community response to art. There is a mania for judging, but little accompanying mania for looking.[6]

Like many other artists of the period John Davis exhibited in a great number of competitions and art prizes. He had sculpture in the following exhibitions:

1961	Mildara Prize for Sculpture
1966	Alcorso Sekers Travelling Scholarship for Sculpture
1967	Mildura Sculpture Triennial; Doncaster and Templestowe Festival of Arts
1968	Alcorso Sekers Travelling Scholarship for Sculpture; Eltham Awards
1969	Eltham Awards
1970	Mildura Sculpture Triennial; Captain Cook Bi-centenary Sculpture Exhibition; Comalco Invitation Award for Sculpture; Monash University, Law School, Sculpture Award Exhibition
1971	Marland House Sculpture Competition; Transfield Art Prize

The Marland House Sculpture Competition, for a new building in Melbourne, was extraordinarily well organised with very generous payments to the sculptors. Nevertheless the work submitted by John Davis, which consisted of fourteen separate parts, all relatively small in relation to the site and most very low to the ground, raised the question with the adjudicators of whether 'they were much more than pedestrian hindrances'.[7]

By the end of 1971, even the once important Transfield Prize had reached a low point. The Sydney art critic Elwyn Lynn was scathing in his review: 'The Transfield at present is where the Archibald usually is. Art has simply been going on elsewhere; but you have to get out of the armchair and look, not just wait for an annual ordained event'.[8] By the terms of the competition all work had to be in steel, so John Davis produced nine identical cubes with cast steel forms inside. It was not one of his best works and was to be his only sculpture in welded steel.

The one man exhibition at the Watters Gallery in 1971 was the culmination of consistent work over a three-year period. It was also the end of a style for John Davis. During all of 1972 he was abroad, viewing new art work, meeting new people, absorbing influences and reassessing his ideas.

Although this was his first one man exhibition in Sydney, his work was known to Sydney critics who had seen his work at the Mildura Triennial exhibitions, in the Comalco exhibition which was taken to Sydney and in other competitions such as the Alcorso Sekers. The work looked consistent in style, strong and stark in the simple spaces of Watters Gallery. As with the Strines exhibition in Melbourne in 1969, the Watters exhibition did not result in any sales, but critical reviews were favourable.

Donald Brook, who was concerned with promoting post-object art, was particularly intrigued with photographic documentation of some works using growing grass which were included in the exhibition. Donald Brook related the exhibition back to the 1970 Comalco winning entry and then went on to mention 'an art of processes':

■ *At Watters Gallery, the Melbourne sculptor, John*

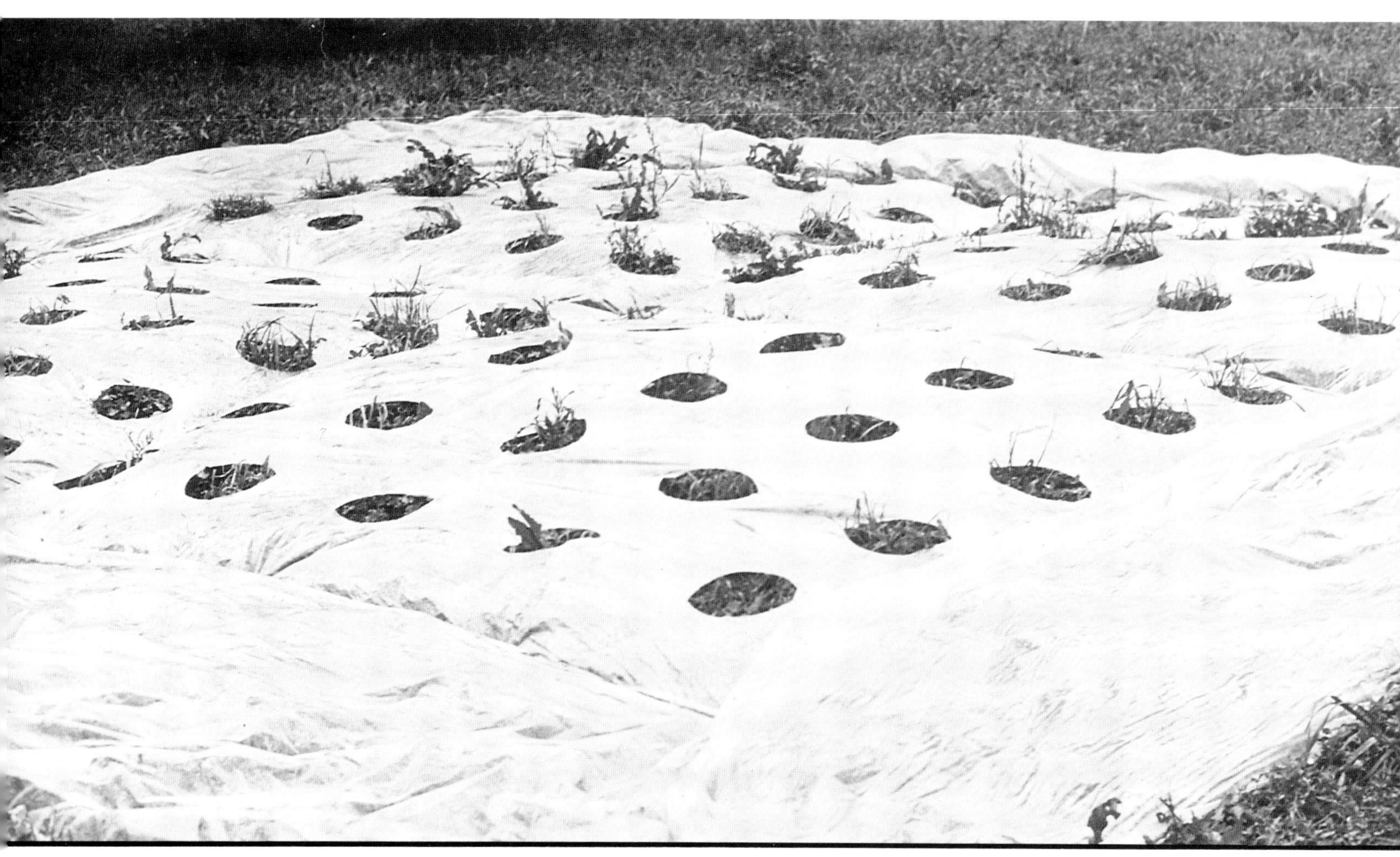

Davis shows a range of works that mostly relate in form to his 1970 Comalco prize-winner.

It is amusing to notice how interpretation follows occasions. His Comalco piece, being advertised as a design for a hydro-electric power station, was widely interpreted as representing falling columns of water, collected at the foot and brought to issue through cascading spouts.

The sculptures now at Watters, having no such place or occasion, encourage no particular interpretation. One might think, if anything (having nowhere to start), of the comical simultaneous collapse of rows of over-ambitious spatulate erections.

But it is likely that the artist would discourage all such talk, since he seems to be concerned with uninterpreted units of form in simultaneous and in sequential relations. There are also some tentative essays in controlling artificially the growth of grass, so that nature and art inter-act in both space and time without telling any tale whatsoever.

John Davis, like so many other sculptors today, is

in his own example a metaphor of transition from an art of objects to an art of processes.[9]

Donald Brook made brief reference to John Davis's 'tentative essays in controlling artificially the growth of grass'. These experiments had occurred in the artist's own backyard — photographs of the lawn appeared in the Watters Gallery exhibition.

The origin of these process works is interesting and illuminating. Because his studio was very small and the sanding of white fibreglass forms caused a great deal of dust, he had been forced to work on his back lawn. Having sanded a number of circular objects he was fascinated to see the circular patch of green grass (which had been covered by the sculptural form), surrounded by an aureole of white dust. He was intrigued by the possibilities. An element of chance had appeared to break down the rigid systems he had been using.

Two ambitious process works, using polythene sheeting over grass were carried out at John Reed's

◄
20 John Davis: 'Grass Process Work — Part 1' (1971). Square of transparent plastic with circles cut out placed on top of grass. c. 460 x 460 cm. (Temporary installation at John Reed's property, Bulleen.) Photograph by the artist.

home at Templestowe Road, Bulleen (now the Heide Park and Art Gallery). One work consisted of a large area of transparent plastic sheeting 4.5 × 4.5 m, in which a regular pattern of circular holes had been cut. The grass was covered by the plastic and allowed to grow through the holes (illus. 20).

The other work was more casual, consisting of a series of transparent plastic bags, placed over the grass and tied in position. In 1978, Robert Lindsay, in 'Survey I', was to incorrectly call the plastic bags 'shower caps'. They may have looked like shower caps, but they were merely plastic bags, strung out in a meandering line across the paddock. The following invitation was sent out to a limited number of people who could inspect the site at stated times:

■ *At present a process work has been set up by John Davis on the property of John and Sunday Reed, at 'Heide', Templestowe Road, Bulleen.*

It is a work which introduces an artificial factor to re-emphasise and re-define the natural processes.

The changing aspects of the process will be documented by photography at significant times in the work's development and presented by the artist at the Pinacotheca Gallery, at a later date...

I distinctly remember a small group of people tramping across the rough grass of the paddock in John Reed's property. Little knots of friends engaged in conversation, standing around on a pleasantly warm Saturday afternoon. The works themselves did not encourage profound discussion and as with artists at the opening of exhibitions, the conversation was about subjects other than the art. In order to gain any knowledge of the process one needed to visit the site on a number of separate occasions, checking on the growth of the grass and the effect of the plastic upon the natural environment. One wonders if anyone other than John Reed and John Davis actually made a second visit. The work looked far better in slides and black and white photographs, for the photographs contained the pattern within a limited format — and of course the photographs showed the variation that occurred over the weeks, as growth changed the nature of the work.

A dramatic change occurred when the Yarra flooded and the grassy paddocks disappeared under muddy water. After the floods subsided the plastic was revealed a little grubby, but the grass continued to grow, poking up in little tufts through the circular holes and pushing up the plastic sheeting in other areas.

John Davis showed photomontages of other possible sites, including the oval at the Melbourne Cricket Ground. The prospect of covering the entire huge oval with plastic and allowing only certain exposed areas to grow was an intriguing thought but unlikely to be viewed favourably by the Melbourne Cricket Club.

The important aspects of these process works using grass were that the rigid systems were being abandoned and the environment was being allowed to play its role. Even though the process was simple there was room for a great deal of variation and an element of chance was always present. These ideas sounded the death-knell of the sequential serialisation which had been the basis of the majority of John Davis's work at Watters Gallery in 1971.

■ NOTES

1 John Davis, letter to Frank Watters, 15 March 1971.
2 Elwyn Lynn, untitled article, 'The Field', National Gallery of Victoria, Melbourne, 21 August–28 September 1968.
3 Interview with John Davis by the author on 26 October 1982, following Davis's return from Japan.
4 Elwyn Lynn, 'How to Stimulate Sculptors', *Bulletin*, 3 October 1970.
5 Ross Lansell, 'Polished Plumbing', *Nation Review*, 17 October 1970.
6 Margaret Plant, 'The Mania for Judging', *The Australian*, 3 October 1970.
7 Gordon Thomson, John Reed & Elwyn Lynn, 'Adjudicators' Report', signed by Elwyn Lynn, 17 June 1971.
8 Elwyn Lynn, 'Monuments to Boredom', *Bulletin*, 11 December 1971.
9 Donald Brook, art review, *Sydney Morning Herald*, 20 May 1971.

Chapter 4

1972
TWELVE MONTHS OVERSEAS

A year abroad in 1972 brought a great number of influences to bear on John Davis. By the time he returned to Australia and exhibited work at the Mildura Triennial Exhibition of Sculpture in 1973 his work had changed radically.

Flying across the Pacific with his wife and two children he stopped at Los Angeles on the west coast of USA. It was his first direct confrontation with the ideas and culture of the USA. Visiting the County Museum and the various commercial galleries along La Cieniga Boulevard he became aware of a sense of region, as opposed to international art or the high art of New York. Disneyland and Forest Lawn Cemetery made him aware of another new phenomenon apparent in the USA — the acceptance of artificiality, almost a love of kitsch. He was impressed by the audacious scale of murals around the city and a general feeling that anything was possible. A number of these attitudes undermined and challenged his beliefs in the fundamentals of good art, which he had previously seen as essentially European-based.

A trip south to Mexico gave another new set of experiences. For an Australian, living within Australia, it is very difficult to acquire any conception of time in relation to man's culture. Mexico gave John Davis a sense of history, stretching from the present through the Spanish conquest back to the various pre-Columbian Indian cultures. Social tradition is not strong in Australia and only seems to survive in isolated pockets of revival medievalism in the church, the judiciary, parliament and the universities, mainly in outmoded forms of address and costume. It came as a surprise to find that social traditions were not dead amongst the people in Mexico. Support for the Roman Catholic church was obviously strong and local religious festivals, shrines and saints were respected and revered.

John Davis found the contrasts in Mexico very great. The old and the new, the poverty and the progress, the colour and vitality all seemed to come together in Mexican art and craft. Mexicans seemed to have the ability to bring together many facets of life in their art. It was an art that varied from the huge public murals and mosaics through to folk art in ceramics, papier mâché or plastic, yet always it displayed national characteristics.

Flying north, the Davises went to New York where they spent three months. John Davis said 'Three months in New York changed my life'. He was impressed by the directness of the people, basically a take-it or leave-it attitude, which was also evident in the art produced in New York. No longer was he looking at colour plates in art books but actually viewing the work of major modern painters and sculptors. He saw *Guernica* by Picasso and the first real piece of sculpture by David Smith. He visited Australian artists Bob Jacks, Mel Ramsden and Ian Burn, resident in New York. At first alarmed by tales of violence in New York, overwhelmed by the sheer quantity of art in the galleries, he quickly adapted to the tempo of life and loved the sense of energy.

In a letter to me, written from New York, he mentions galleries visited, people he has met and some of his impressions of America.

■ *We've been able to get a small apartment-type room here ($250 per month & tax), small (about a total area of your living room) but everything we want plus the advantage of being in a relatively safe area, only 1½ blocks from Greenwich Village School, 5 minutes walk from the avant-garde downtown galleries, and right on 5th Avenue for buses to uptown (15–30 minutes' trip, depending on time of day). We've only been here about 2 weeks, so not a great deal to report. It's been mostly finding our way around, settling the kids into school (security guard at the entrance) and keeping mostly to this area. However, we're enjoying New York very much — so much to see and experience, people real mixture of all sorts, most of them transient (17*

▶ *21 Wire and papier mâché skeletons on bicycle, purchased by John Davis in Mexico in 1972. Photograph by Mark Strizic.*

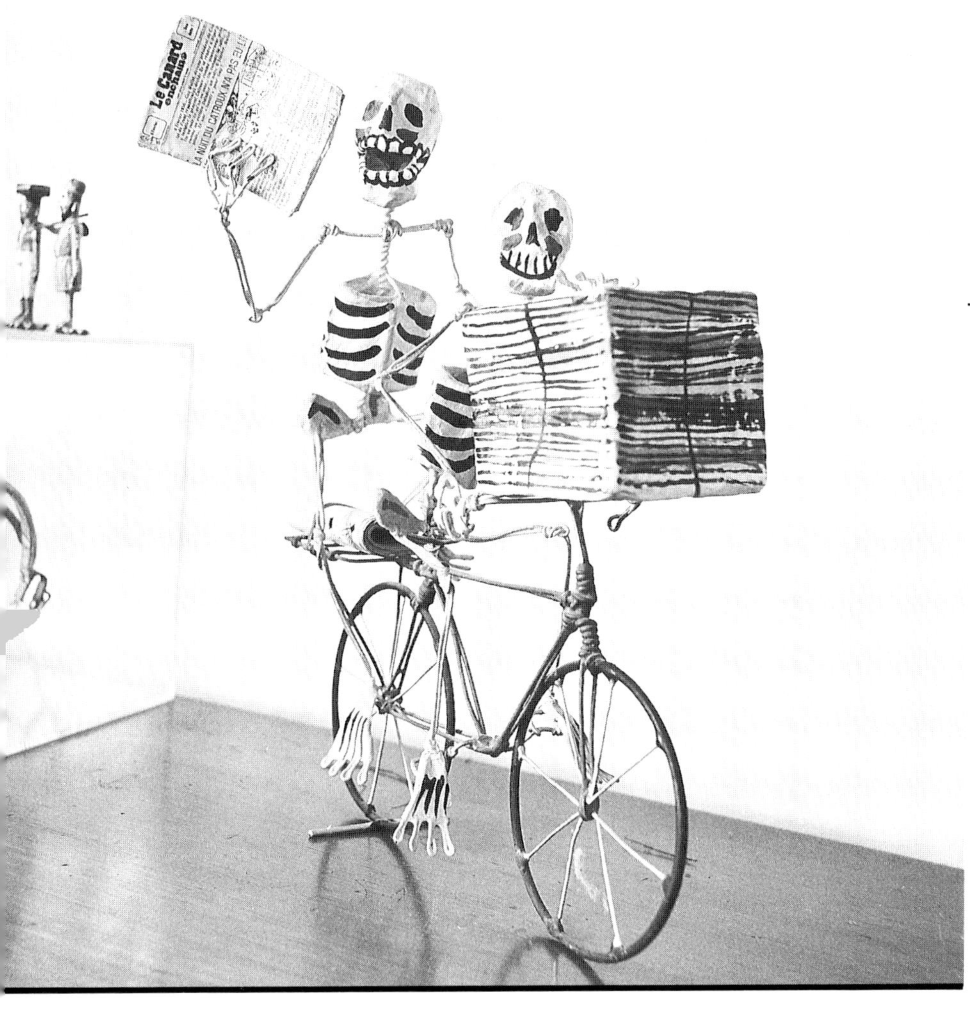

Brundage combined/Jasper Johns lithos/my first sight-ing of Smith sculpture, an old favourite Noguchi piece, plus US recent painting. Then drove down coast road, spectacular beautiful views of Pacific and rugged coast for about 300 miles, and passed through beautiful and interesting places like Carmel, Monterey, San Luis Obispo, Santa Barbara (old mission towns with very interesting old Spanish Missions) to Los Angeles. It's a marvellous place if you like everything on a large scale and get turned on by chaotic architectural arrangement, extroverted signs and car parks. We loved it. No building really gives you any idea architecturally of what happens inside — your only guide is a huge, colourful, kinky sign outside, we never know what to expect next. The freeways are incredible and certainly move the traffic (60–70 mph) 4–6 lanes wide with lead off or on ramps and side tracks moving in one direction while the same thing is happening in the other direction as you pass under or over similar systems. Hollywood has built the place so the reflecting philosophy of fantasy is everywhere, nothing is really real. 2 great museums, LA County, good collections of everything, Pasadena — marvellous exhibition of Oldenburgs' sculptures and drawings. Private galleries mostly commercial decoration but a few inter-ested in serious art. Were lucky to make friends with a girl who runs 'Ace' gallery — show sculpture and people like Serra, and her husband who organises mul-tiples at Gemini G.E.L. with Johns, Rauschenberg, Price, Albers etc. Also met Guy Dill and Ron Cooper — prominent young sculptors and made contact with Market Street Program gallery which is organising the year's exhibitions by surveys and computers. Jim Doolin was very helpful and we spent some time together — really nice people . . .[1]

On such a short visit it was difficult to establish a studio, yet he felt the need to make something. He had noticed that many New York artists had frequently used ordinary materials, often objects and materials found in the streets, yet had finished

million live here at the moment) etc. etc. Bob Jacks [ex-Melbourne painter] lives very close by and we see he [sic] and Kerry quite frequently. They've been a great help. John Stringer and June have had us over to their place in Brooklyn and John took me to the opening of the Matisse sculptures at the Museum of Modern Art the other night. It's the only show of Matisse's sculp-tures that has ever been assembled and it was marvel-lous to be able to see his development, and form one's own judgement instead of reading about it. There is also a Picasso show on covering all his periods, and initially I had this strange feeling of seeing pages from Art History Books and not concentrating on the paint-ings themselves. It's really hard work over here, but of course most exciting. I've seen most of the private galleries, but not many shows to get excited about, all very competent and ambitious in scale but obvious extensions of say Caro or the American Decade. How-ever it's too early to form judgements yet . . .

Saw lots of art at museums and private galleries — marvellous oriental collection of Museum & Avery

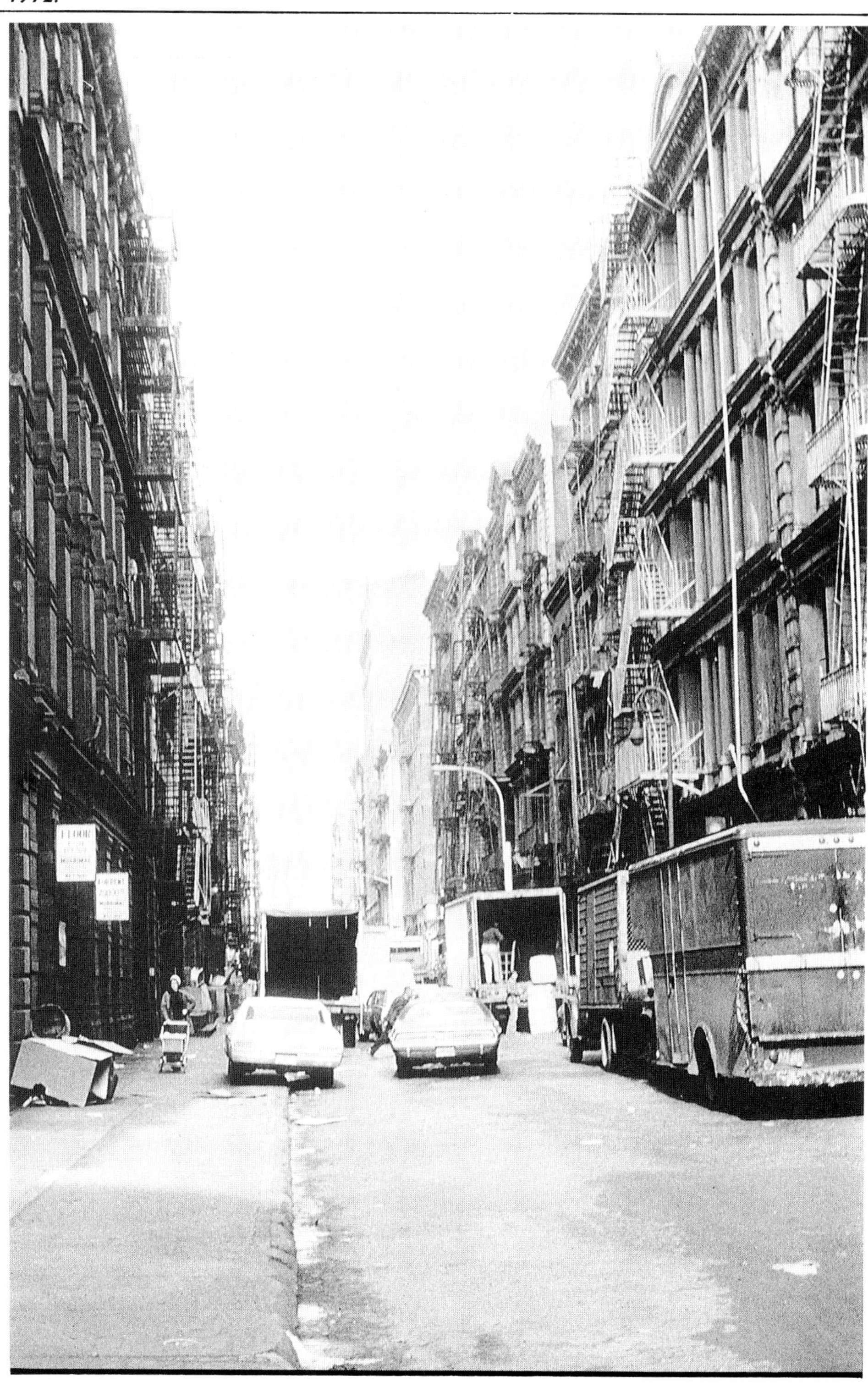

22 *Greene Street, New York.*
Photographed by the artist in
1972.

up with works that were intelligent and sophisticated. He found some very commonplace cardboard cylinders, covered the surface with papier mâché made from newspapers, and started a whole chain of objects that were to occupy his interest for the next two or three years. The simple cylinder was the basic form used in his sculpture on his return to Australia. 'During 1972, in New York, I had little money and no studio', Davis remembers. 'So I started using cardboard tubing that was just lying around in the streets, either setting it up in the streets or in the tiny apartment.'[2]

Having covered nine cardboard cylinders with papier mâché he then proceeded to work on the surface with a pencil, building up tone and texture. The simple cylindrical forms were as anonymous as twentieth century urban architecture, but the pencil marks added character. The nine cylinders, cryptically entitled *Drawing — New York*, were photographed and then given to Bob Jacks.

The only other work produced in New York was 'Greene Street Piece' (illus. 22, 23), which remarkably few people would see as humourous. It only exists as photographic documentation, yet it proves that John Davis exhibited in the prestigious Greene Street, where the American superstars of the 1960s had their studios. Artistically it was the most famous street in New York.

'Greene Street Piece' was very simple, consisting of three cardboard cylinders covered in papier mâché. The three cylinders were placed down the centre of the road, looking somewhat like traffic lines painted in the middle of the road — except it was a one-way street and they were unnecessary. The cylinders were chosen to both heighten and contradict conventional perspective. The three cylinders became rapidly shorter as they went away from the spectator but they also became fatter, wider in diameter. John Davis had noted how the buildings of New York seemed to emphasise the

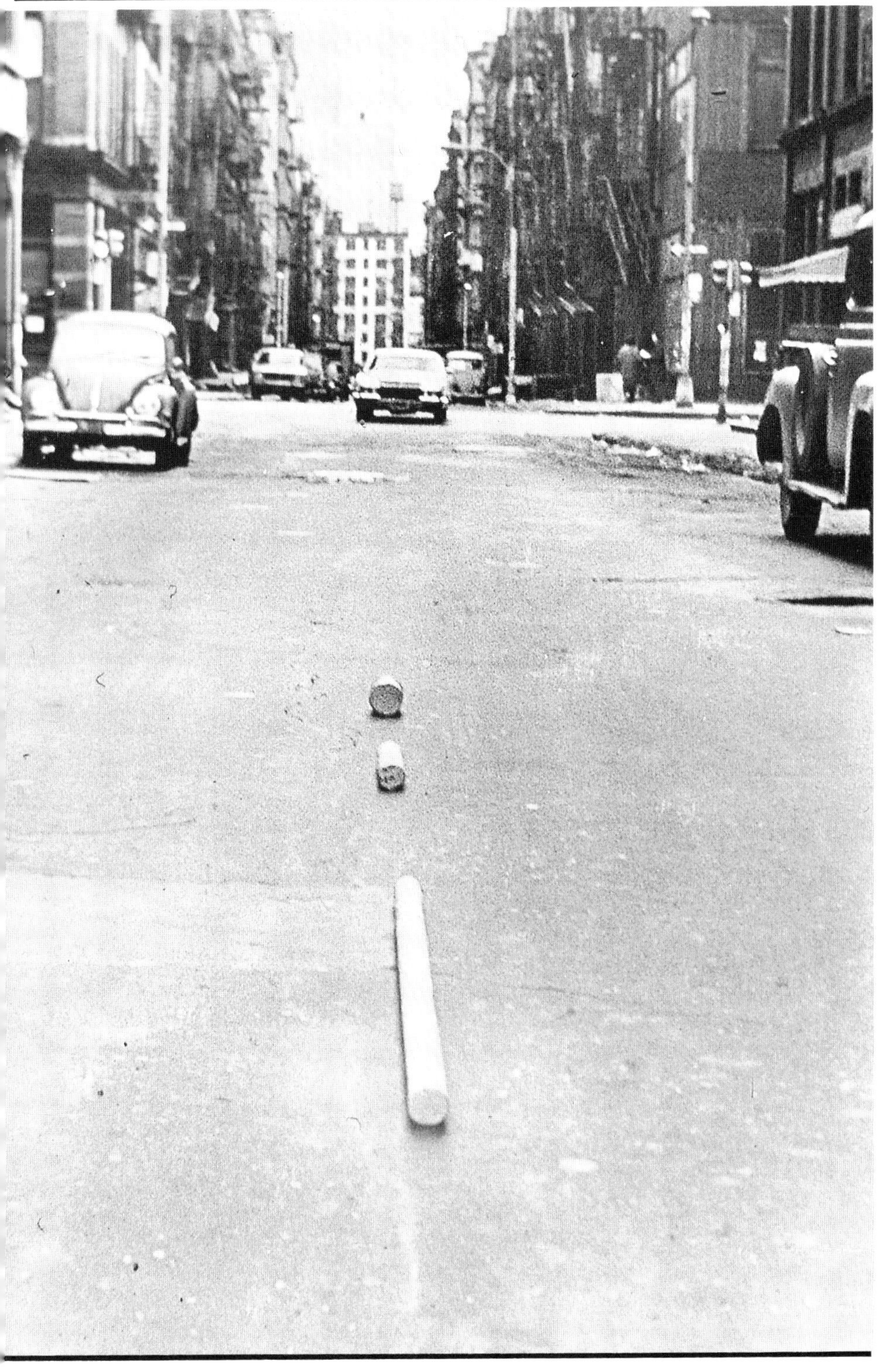

23 John Davis: 'Greene Street Piece' (1972). Three cardboard cylinders placed in Greene Street, New York. John Davis later used four photographs of this work, each 47.5 x 32.5 cm, and added pencil marks in 1973. *The photographs are now in the collection of the National Gallery of Victoria. This photograph, of Greene Street, when the cardboard cylinders were in place, was taken by the artist.*

perspective of the street and he wanted to use perspective as part of his work. It was not a very successful work. One feels that Uccello used his broken cylindrical lances, strewn on the ground, in his paintings of *The Rout of San Romano*, with far greater success in the fifteenth century than John Davis did in 1972. Nevertheless Carl Andre used humble materials and John Davis was exploring similar possibilities.

After three months in New York the Davis family flew to Ireland, then proceeded to London, which was a base from which to explore areas of England and Scotland. On one trip they travelled in the Scottish Highlands, sleeping in a hired campervan at nights. The weather was extremely cold. While waiting for his wife to prepare an evening meal, he and the two children gathered rocks, pieces of timber and with some string, made a structure — which, in retrospect, may be thought of as art. At the time it served two purposes: it helped to keep the two children amused while tea was prepared and the activity kept the three people warm. After returning to Australia, he was to make many more structures from the materials found in a landscape.

The campervan group travelled through the continent: France, Belgium, Holland, West Germany, Austria, Switzerland, Italy, ferry to Greece, then back via Yugoslavia, Italy, France and Spain to London. The whole trip took 3–4 months.

The most direct influence Davis experienced during his travels was the huge exhibition 'Casel Documenta' at Casel (W. Germany), prepared by Harald Szeeman, whom he had met in Australia in 1971. Patrick McCaughey as art critic for the Melbourne *Age* was a strong influence on art in the 1960s in Melbourne. He espoused a cause based on the ideas of the American critic Greenberg. It appeared that there was mainstream art, the official art propounded by the art critics in America and

Australia. Casel Documenta proved visually that artists were engaged in a wide range of activities outside the limits of McCaughey and Greenberg. This experience confirmed John Davis's reaction to the American art scene — anything is possible.

On the return journey from Europe, Davis visited Iran, Hong Kong and Bali. In spite of the vast increase in the tourist trade at places such as Sanur and Kuta Beach, Balinese culture still exists in the hundreds of small villages. The Hindu religion and the social organisation of the people appears to go on with little change except in the tourist-dominated areas, where western influences have destroyed traditional Balinese life.

Many aspects of Balinese culture appealed to John Davis and helped to shape ideas forming in his mind in relation to his own work. The Balinese used the materials they found in their own environment, everything from the semi-permanent soft volcanic stone for carving, to stalks of rice plants for making ceremonial figures. The women prepared elaborate offerings of food, multi-coloured layers arranged in tiers to be carried on their heads to the temple. Many offerings at the temples or shrines were very simple, a small arrangement of flowers or a symbolic grouping of foodstuffs. In a climate that was hot, wet and humid, most things had a very limited life. The Balinese accepted the fact that art could be made from impermanent materials. It was a fundamental yet very simple idea that was to become basic in later work produced by John Davis.

During 1972 he was subject to influences from places as diverse as London, Mexico, New York or Bali. He spent the next year absorbing ideas, digesting the relevant and disregarding the inappropriate. Early in 1973 he produced a number of small-scale experimental works, mostly untitled and unshown, made from ceramic cylinders and wrapped in sheet latex. These works led to a group

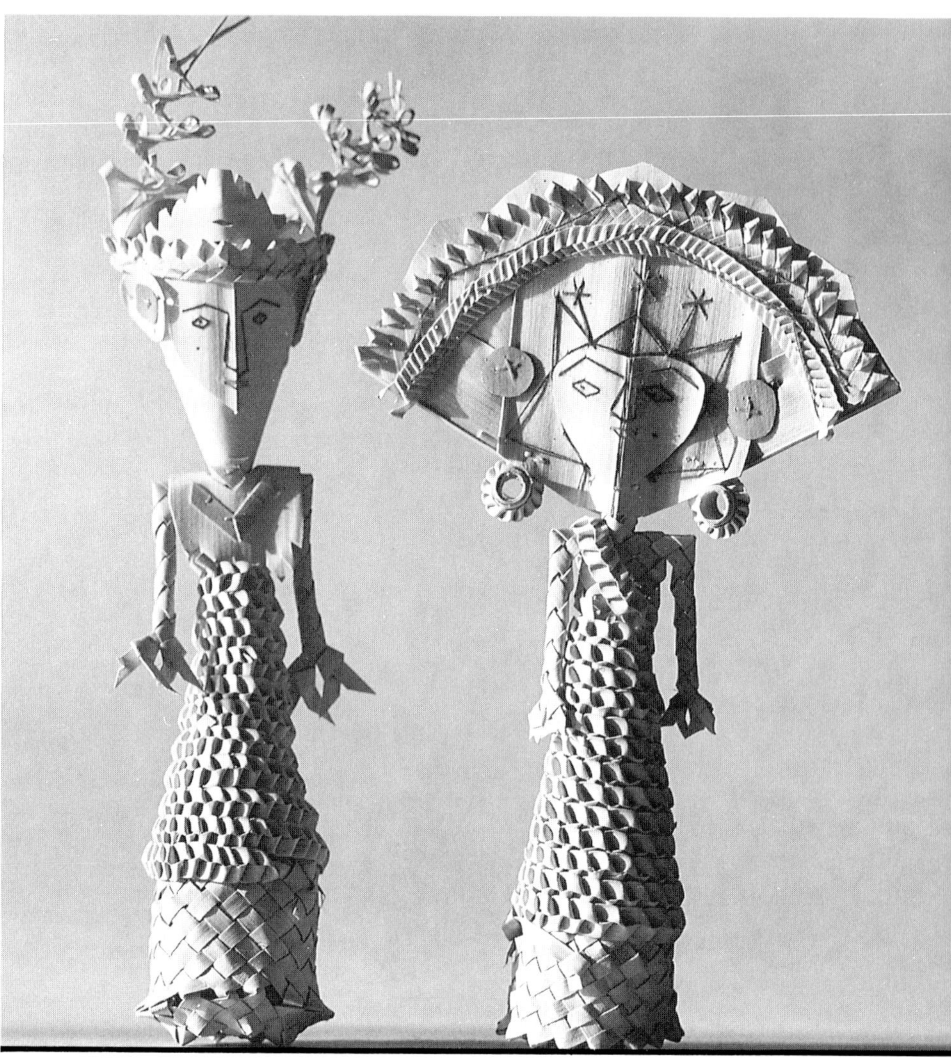

24 *Rice goddesses made from straw and dried leaves. Collected in Bali by the author. Photograph by Mark Strizic.*

of sculptures, produced in 1973, shown at the Pinacotheca Gallery in 1974, in which rows of cylinders were used.

The first sculpture John Davis displayed publicly on his return to Australia combined the cylindrical form of his two works produced in New York with very simple materials, the whole work located in the scrubby landscape of the Mildura 'Sculpturscape '73', organised by Tom McCullough. The Mildura Triennial Exhibitions of Sculpture, begun in 1961, had been basically centred on the gallery and the lawns in front, but for 'Sculpturscape '73' an additional area was used. Sculpture was shown over a large 8 ha area of scrubby land, down hill from the gallery and adjoining the Murray River. It was rough land, covered in salt bush, containing a few scattered clumps of trees with patches of bare earth and cliffs of clay. The big advantage was that sculptors were able to get away from the well-

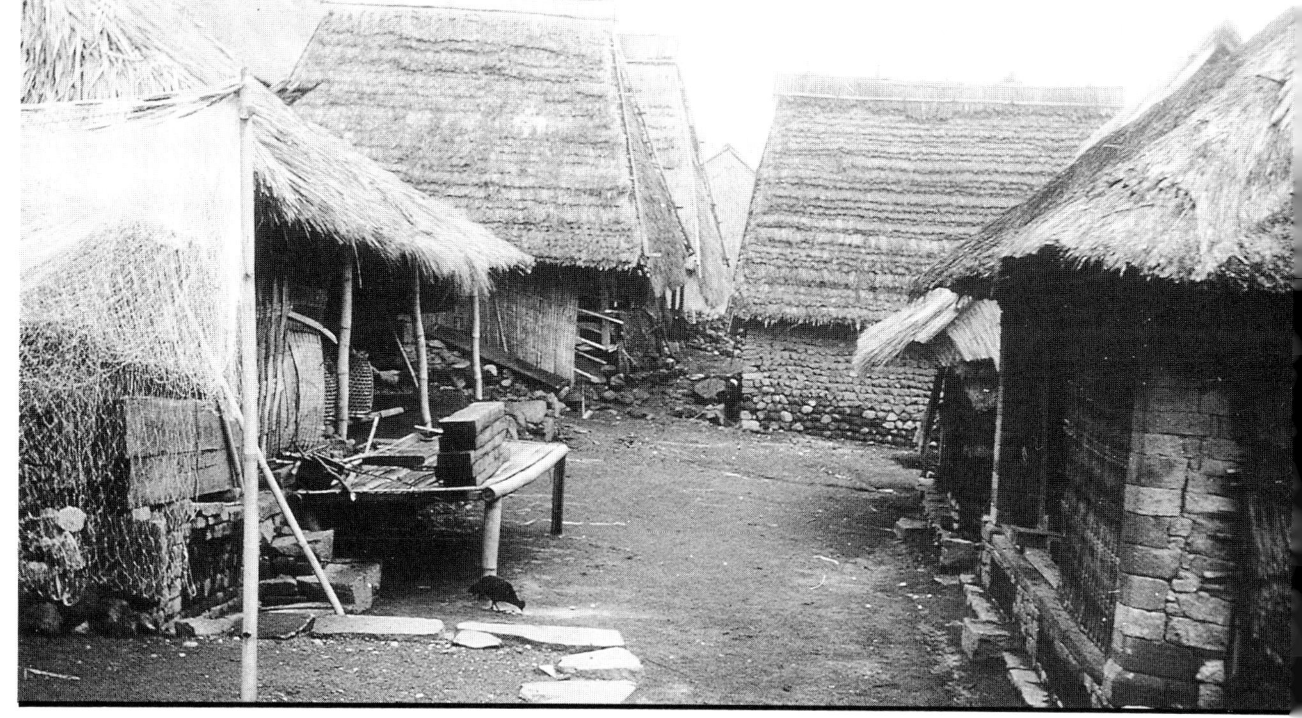

▶ 25 Stone buildings with thatched roofs at Trunjan, a small village on the edge of Lake Batur (the lake is within the crater of Mount Batur), photographed by the artist when in Bali, 1972.

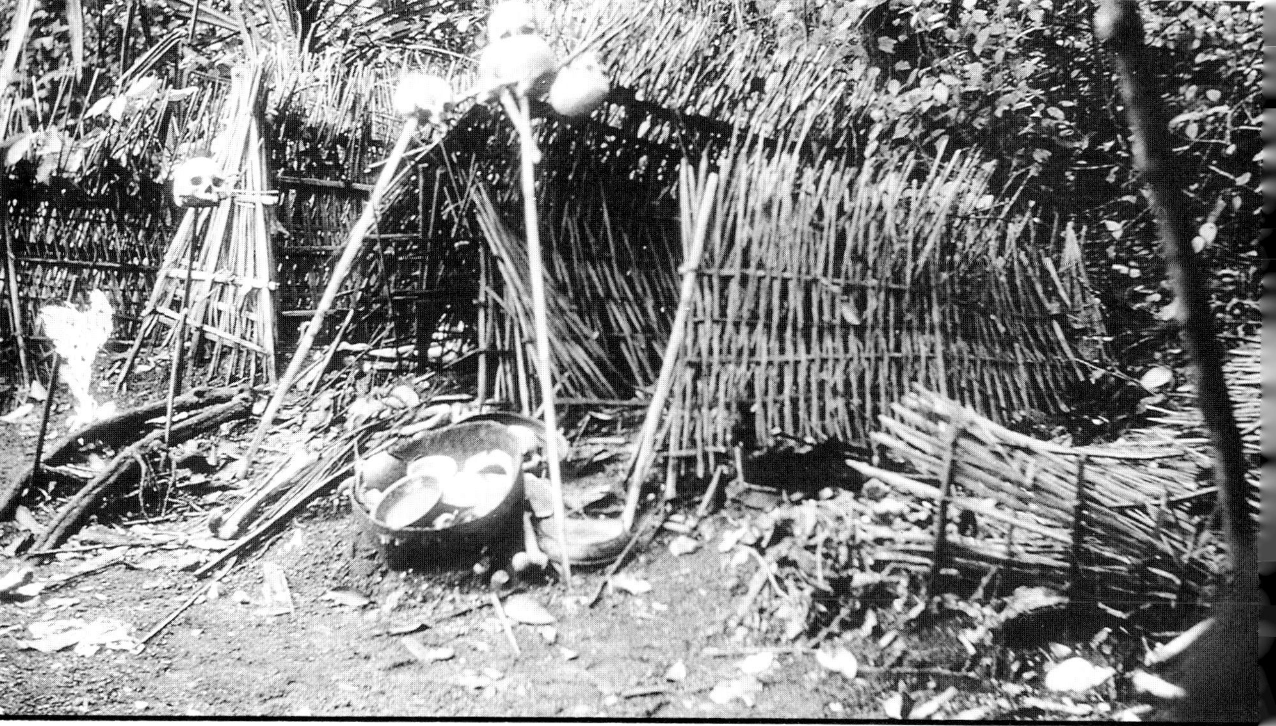

▶ 26 Above-ground burial sites at Trunjan, Lake Batur, Bali. Photographed by the artist in 1972.

manicured green lawns outside the gallery and place their works in an Australian environment. This was a totally new experience for most Australian sculptors, which some used to great advantage but others were not able to cope with. In some cases work produced was out of context with the raw environment.

There had been very few outdoor exhibitions of Australian sculpture and they had been in parks and gardens. 'Sculpturscape '73' was unique in that a large area of Australian bush was used for the exhibition. The *Age* art critic commented on the site:

■ *The '73 exhibition has expanded the scope of this event greatly. Abandoning the gallery and its well watered and planted lawns the 130 sculptors were spread across 20 acres of a sandy, saltbush-covered bank of the River Murray.*

It was a splendid natural arena, a sculpturescape for a remarkable and exciting event.

The site itself is so beautiful in a dry, sparse and slightly scruffy way that it threatened at times to overwhelm the sculpture itself.

Presently, however, much sculpture is seeking a new identity for itself — informal and literally at home with the environment.[3]

The Director of the Mildura Arts Centre and organiser of 'Sculpturscape '73', Tom McCullough, wrote about the innovative move out of the gallery into the Australian bush: 'It has been a major experiment for a public Art Gallery to move a serious, selective exhibition completely away from a museum-bound atmosphere as much as possible. In itself, the exercise is bringing many artists, their works and this landscape into an unusual kind of rapport.'[4]

The new setting provided some memorable works such as Ti Parks's *Chainone*, a simple placing of heavy metal chains on the ground, to which rags and fragments of clothing were attached. The

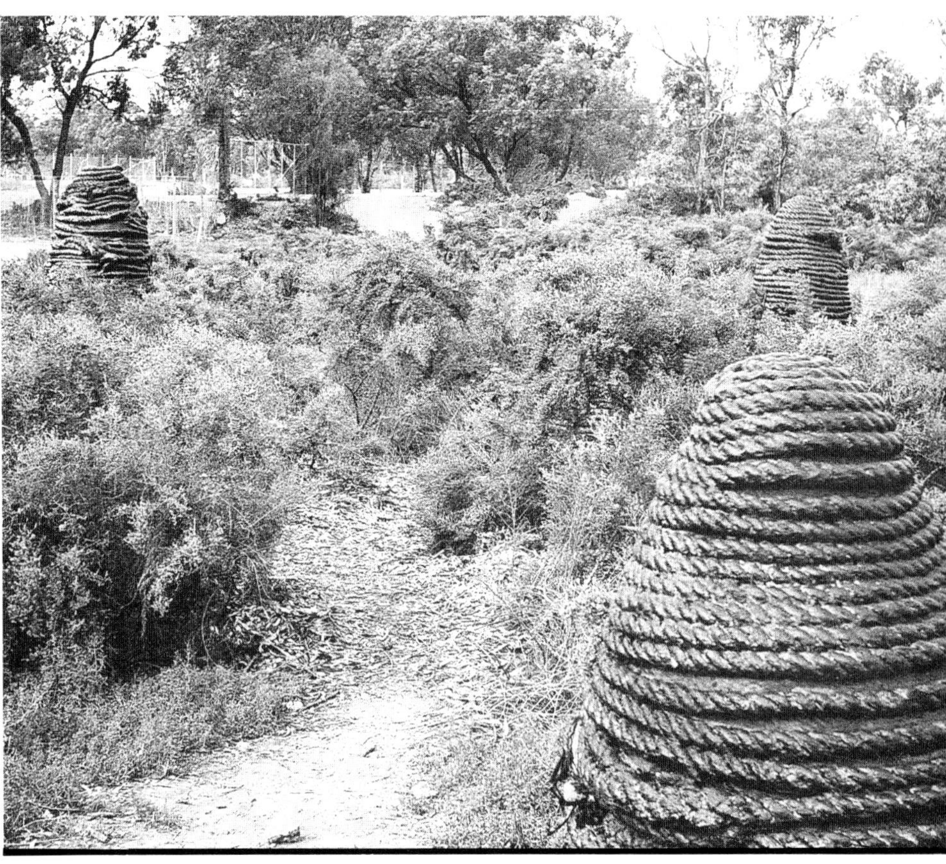

▲
27 Kevin Mortensen: Objects in a Landscape, Mildura 'Sculpturscape, '73'. Rope and bitumen. Four units 213.5 x 91.5 cm, 187 x 91.5 cm, 122 x 122 cm, 91.5 x 152 cm. (Mildura Arts Centre).

▶
28 John Davis: Tree Piece and Unrolled Piece (in foreground) (1973). Tree Piece consisted of six eucalypt trees with trunks covered with (from left to right) papier mâché from newspapers; green binder twine; canvas tied on with binder twine; polythene sheeting with pockets containing grass clippings; sheet of latex; four rows of small sticks tied together. Spectators at Mildura 'Sculpturscape '73'. Photograph by the author.

work hinted at torture, even massacre. Kevin Mortensen made four, large beehive-shaped, conical structures from very heavy rope, covered in bitumen. They related extraordinarily well to the area of low bushes where they were placed, looking like huge dollops of dung from some monstrous beast (illus. 27).

The exhibition brought some new sculptors to light, and one, Ross Grounds produced an environmental structure which used the site to great advantage. He excavated a large circular hole in the sandy soil until he reached the water level of the nearby Murray River. The circular shape was surrounded inside with sand bags and the sand removed from the site was used to build a low conical mound over the top. Spectators could descend a rough staircase to the bottom of the pit where they could look up to a small patch of sky. The top was covered with a rope net. Several pigeons were imprisoned in the limited space.

Michael Nicholson organised *Saxhorn Variations*, a three-dimensional intellectual game for a number of participants, using an area of bushland, sheet plastic, ropes and large balloons filled with helium gas. Peter Cole produced *Pool*, a totally use-

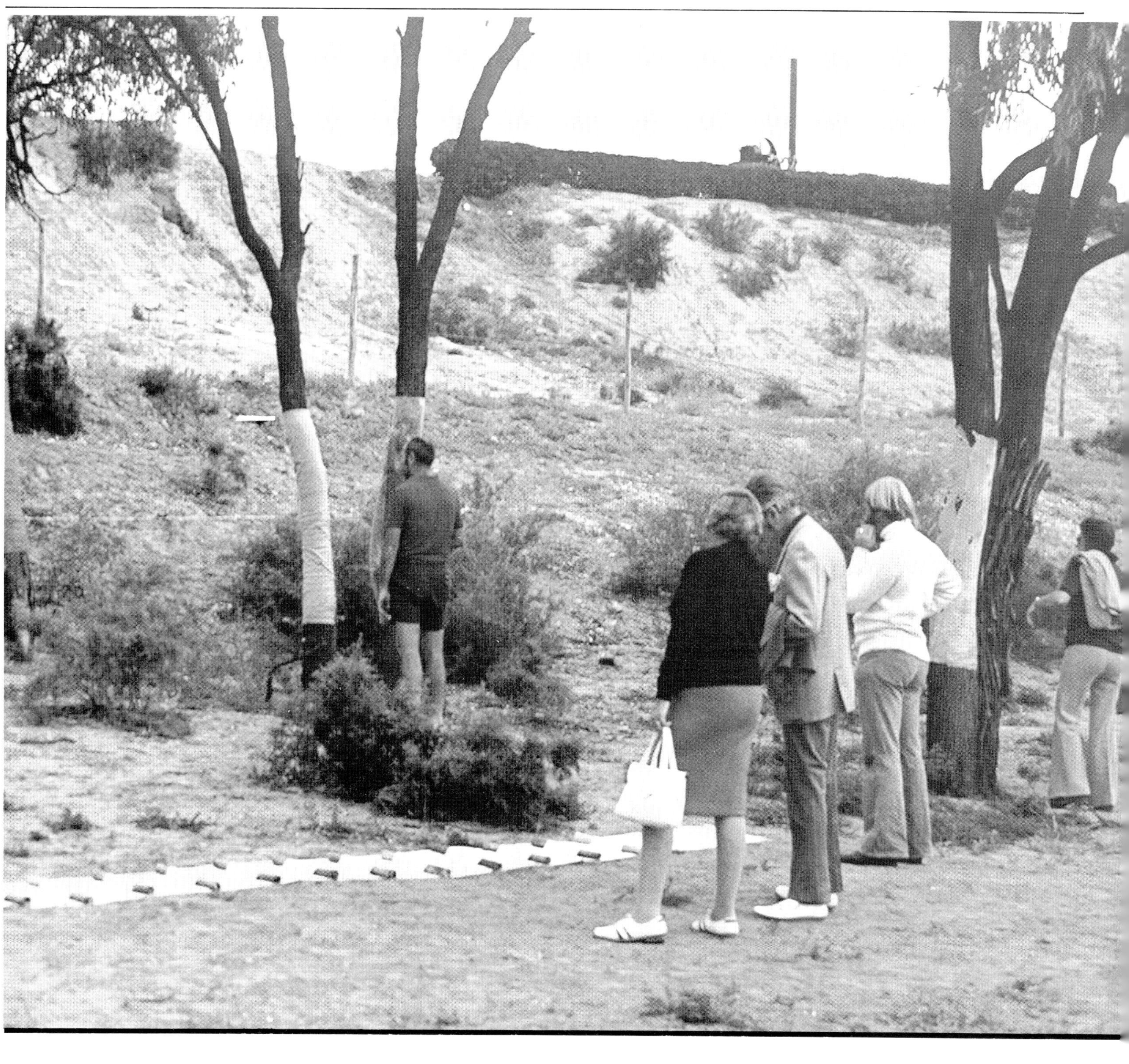

less miniature swimming pool, accurate in every way with light blue tiles, stainless steel tubing, water, water filter system, chloride tablets, grass and sprinklers all completely surrounded by a high cyclone wire fence. Tony Coleing cast a concrete letter 'T' and chained it to a small eucalyptus tree, calling the result *T-Tree*.

Other sculptors were less successful. David Wilson's two untitled works, about a metre square and built of steel and perspex, would have looked convincing on an art gallery floor, but outside became covered in dust and dirt and lost their essential character. Clive Murray-White's three sculptures in steel were so low to the ground that they were in danger of being completely camouflaged by growing vegetation.

John Davis showed two works, *Tree Piece* and *Unrolled Piece* (illus. 28). They both used the repetition of the cylinder as the basic unifying form — a simple form which had its origins in the two works which he had made in New York.

Tree Piece used the trunks of six trees, each one bound for a distance of about 1½ metres above the ground with the following materials: papier mâché made from newspapers, green baling twine, polythene sheeting with pockets containing grass clippings, a latex rubber sheet, canvas, and four rows of small sticks tied together. It was a situation that was consistent and yet variable, for each of the cylindrical tree trunks were about 38 cm in diameter, but the materials used were different for each tree. It was a tentative relationship between sculpture and landscape that wasn't entirely satisfactory. The formal qualities were fairly basic — six cylindrical surfaces of approximately equal size, but with very little three-dimensional relationship between the six tree trunks. Some of the materials had been gathered on the site (twigs), others had been brought from Melbourne ready-made (latex), and other surfaces were made from compatible

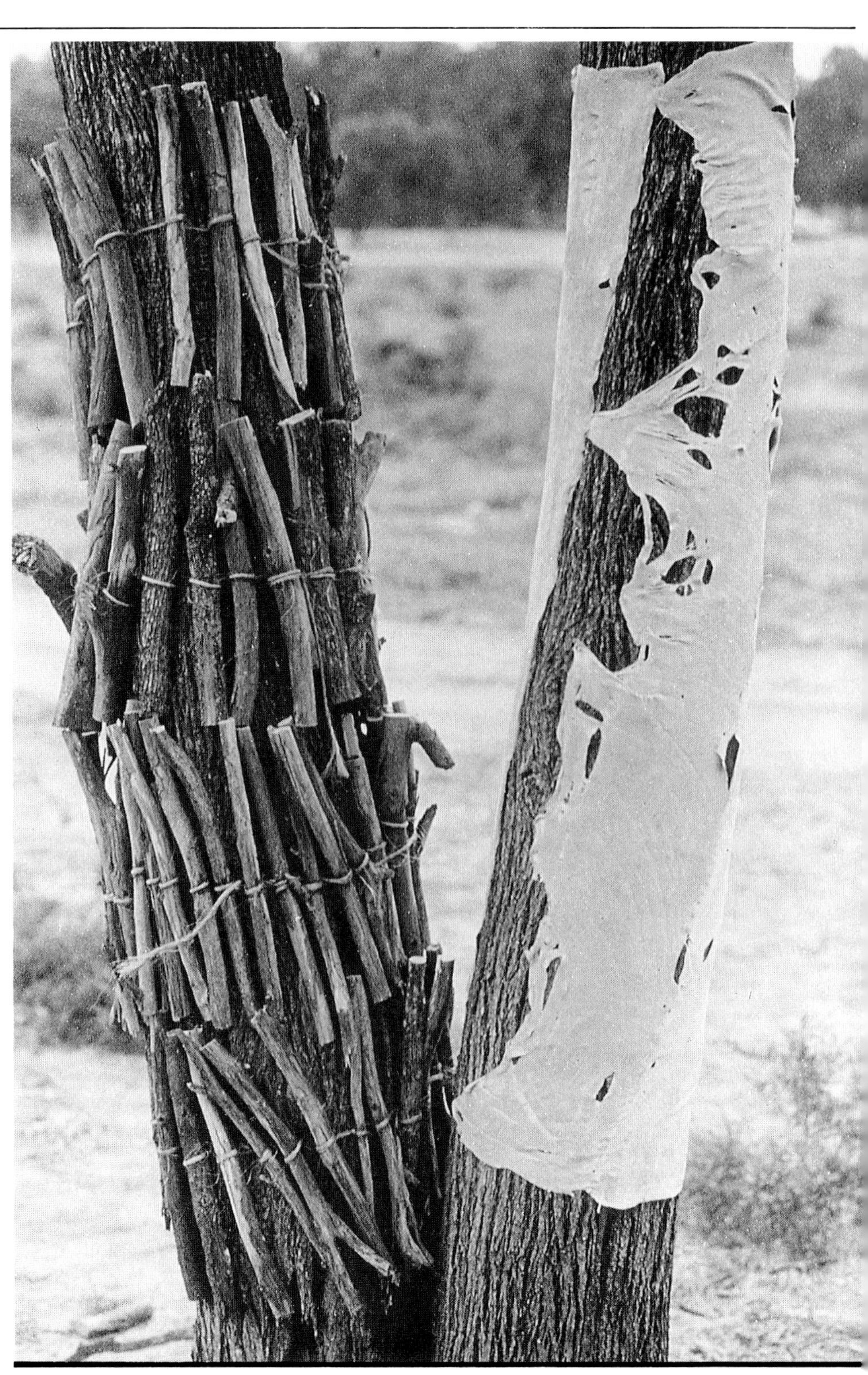

materials such as green binder twine used on the spot. The visual result of the combination of these various materials lacked a sense of mystery and looked more like experiments in tree surgery.

Nevertheless the underlying attitude was important, showing a new sensitivity towards nature, a willingness to work without disturbing the ecology, and an interest in materials found in the bush. When photographs of *Tree Piece* were shown as part of the exhibition 'Recent Australian Art', Frances McCarthy and Daniel Thomas made comments in the catalogue linking John Davis with other artists of similar interests.

■ *Not surprisingly in Australia, where landscape art has a long, continuous tradition, it is the earth and ecology aspects of the new art — Grounds, Davis, Burns, Coleing, Kirkman — which seem more dominant than urbanism. The new art included here is typical of its time in its attempt to show us the reality of the world, often in ephemeral installations of humble materials made especially for this exhibition. It is an art which proposes that all objects can be experienced as art, and that all people can be, to some extent, artists; it is an art which dislikes the idea of the artist-as-genius or freak, of art as a precious object or expensive capitalist commodity. It is probably, like all ambitious art, impossible, but it is an art which would like to destroy the distinction between art and life.*[5]

His other work, called *Unrolled Piece*, was more convincing. It had a strange authority, in spite of the fact that there was no apparent logical reason for its existence. The sculpture consisted of a long white canvas strip, with 49 pockets, in which were placed 49 ceramic rods. The rods were of terracotta, with a limited amount of opaque white glaze, put on irregularly. It was shown completely unrolled on the sandy ground, though it could be rolled up into a large and rather heavy bundle — there was provision for tying it up. The ceramic rods were intentionally limited to 49 as John Davis

◀

29 John Davis: Tree Piece (1973). Detail of two of the six eucalypt trees. Left, four rows of small sticks tied together; right, sheet of latex. Mildura 'Sculpturscape '73'. Photograph by the author.

felt that 49 was incomplete, suggesting that the work may continue, whereas 50 would have been complete and final.

Unrolled Piece lay on the ground, fragile ceramic rods in perishable, easily stained canvas, resting on an uneven surface of sand and small vegetation. Some fragile things survive, because people respect the fragility, but many people have little respect for experimental contemporary sculpture. The resultant damage to *Unrolled Piece* was almost inevitable. The story is told that some teenagers rode their bikes the full length of the piece. As the sculpture had been acquired by the Mildura Arts Centre a number of new ceramic rods had to be fired and the canvas was remade.

Even though it was to be a few years before John Davis again constructed sculpture in the Australian bush or displayed the objects he had made in an outdoor environment, 'Sculpturscape '73' was an important step. He re-established a working arrangement with the Australian landscape, though markedly different from his early wood carvings. He also collected a basic vocabulary of materials that he was to use again and again over future years: papier mâché, newspaper, string, twine, canvas, latex, twigs and the recurring cylindrical forms which reappeared in fired clay, papier mâché or even polyester resin.

■

After his return to Australia, John Davis was offered a position as Lecturer in Charge of Sculpture at Prahran College of Advanced Education, which he took up early in 1973. The philosophical attitudes of the staff at Prahran in relation to teaching were fundamentally different from the staff at Caulfield Institute of Technology. I discussed this point with Vic Majzner, who like John Davis, had been at Caulfield, then moved to Prahran.[6]

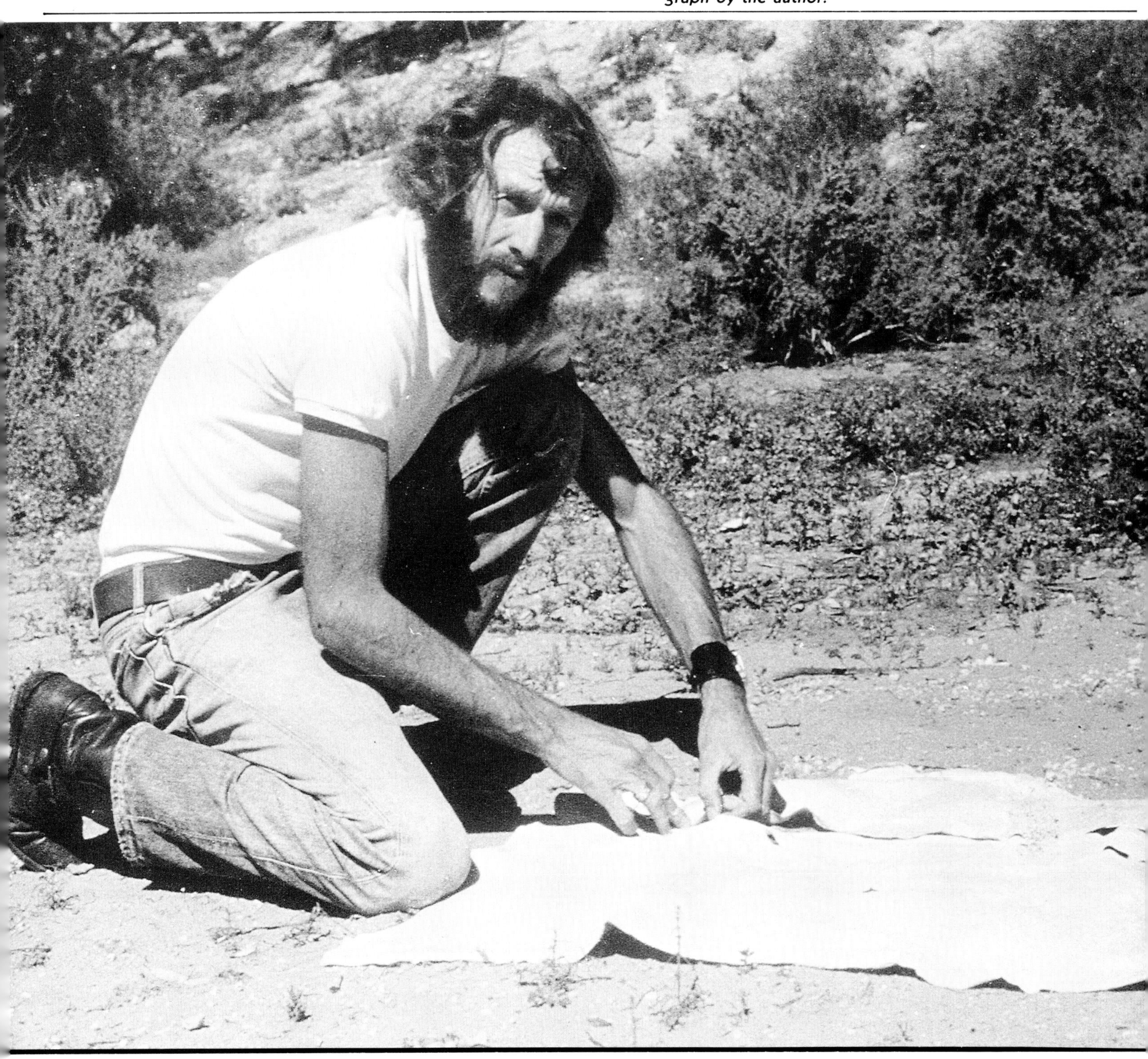

30 *John Davis preparing latex sheets for Tree Piece, Mildura 'Sculpturscape '73'. Photograph by the author.*

KS: 'Interesting that Fred Cress, John Davis and yourself all ended up at Prahran. John Davis went to Prahran in 1973 and you arrived some months later. At the same time David Wilson was appointed to the staff. A vigorous sculpture department developed with John Davis, David Wilson and Caroline May. As Director of the Gryphon Gallery I helped stage a number of exhibitions of student work from the Sculpture Department at Prahran. It seemed to me that students in some cases were fairly strongly influenced by these dominant people — I would think the heavy metal related to David Wilson, the twigs, sticks, string and rope to John Davis, and maybe, to a lesser extent, the casting in bronze and aluminium to Caroline May. Is my observation too critical? What is your assessment?'

VM: 'I think it's very realistic. Prahran creates its tradition of teaching by the staff that it employs. It does not really involve itself with any particular teaching theory, but more with the reality of art practice. I think the sculpture department in the ways that you're describing it, is very much symptomatic of that. It employed certain people, because of their standing as artists, and they taught from their experience, as artists, rather than teachers. It is inevitable that the students are going to be influenced. I guess that the underlying attitude is for students to be influenced by what artists do rather than by how teachers teach. It also so happens that the best artists happen to be the best teachers for younger artists.'

The art school at Prahran CAE was run on traditional lines, almost like the European academy, employing well known artists, rather than teachers who were also artists. The emphasis was on the relationship between the student and particular members of staff, in the areas in which the students had an interest, rather than a concern for a theoretical course of study. This was a basically different attitude from the underlying philosophy of the first-year course at Caulfield, in which Davis had been involved. At Prahran, Davis chose staff of diverse, even diametrically opposed points of view, in order to expose students to the excitement of heated discussion and engagement with many forms of sculpture.

In contrast to Davis's attitudes, David Wilson was a formalist working in welded steel and Simon Klose was a conceptualist. Students were obviously influenced by these artists, each of whom had strong personalities and firmly held beliefs, but given time, the students outgrew the obvious influences and a considerable number went on to establish reputations as sculptors.

Fiona Orr was in sympathy with Davis's growing interest in natural images and his use of simple materials. Over the years her work has become more symbolic, and even though the fascination for twigs and branches remains, she has also moved towards more permanent materials, such as ciment fondu and bronze. Marcus Shannahan was a student at Prahran and also worked as an assistant with David Wilson, but his use of welded steel developed quite differently from Wilson's work. His sculpture was often aggressive, but also witty, with a sophisticated re-use of Cubist forms. One could also list Linda Fish who worked in papier mâché, with brightly painted semi-organic forms; Jane Saunders who produced sculptures in steel, wood and various mixed media; Annie Testro who used natural materials and barbed wire; and George Christofakis who was intrigued by political concepts. The list could go on to include Damian Curtain, Kevin Alder, John Appleton, Barry Malcom,

Peter Neville and others. Only time will tell which of these young sculptors will continue to produce work in the difficult area of sculpture.

Ten years after his appointment to the Sculpture Department at Prahran in 1973, the Melbourne art critic, Memory Holloway, assessed John Davis's influence on young sculptors in Australia as a very positive force. 'John Davis has taught a generation of Australian sculptors how to shake off the heavy armour of welded steel sculpture and to look to the Australian environment as a resource for their work.'[7]

There is a widely held belief that artists are artists, but lecturers in art schools are artists who haven't quite made the grade. Teaching is not held in the same high repute in Australia that it is in Europe. John Davis has been actively involved in teaching and at the same time has been deeply committed to his own work. It has been a two-way process, whereby teaching has given a sense of security and a constant income which has enabled him to produce sculpture. Being an artist actively engaged in his own work has no doubt made him a more stimulating teacher. Teaching has its own subtle rewards for the constant contact with young artists is always challenging — when ideas are constantly questioned, flexibility is essential. The enthusiasm and energy of young people is contagious and a good protection against middle-aged conservatism and lethargy. Students may be lacking in experience, but this enables them to believe that anything is possible, which in turn generates an optimistic drive.

Whether as a result of his own basically optimistic attitude, or the contact with students, John Davis has retained a youthful approach and a continuing belief that anything is possible. Here is just one example: while he was Lecturer in Charge of Sculpture at Prahran College of Advanced Education he sent the following letter to the Honourable D. J. Killen, then the Minister for Defence.

■ *Dear Sir,*
Some months ago I was visiting Sydney and during a tour of the Harbour, noticed an aged aircraft carrier anchored in one of the inlets. On enquiring I was informed that it was out of service and idle.

Since then I have devised a means by which the vessel could be productively and imaginatively used in the service of Australian art or more specifically, Australian sculpture, at the same time capturing international notice and prestige.

Very simply, my plan is as follows:

1 The vessel should be converted into studio and workshop space below decks where the aircraft are normally housed. This would be relatively inexpensive and easily done. The upper deck could be used in fine weather after appropriate safety features had been added. Further space would be allocated for the storing of materials and a number of kombi camper vans or buses for land transport and overnight accommodation. Existing crew accommodation would be used for crew, students and lecturing staff.

2 The vessel would then depart for an excursion to various countries where important art is to be found, such as Egypt, Greece, Italy or large cities with great museums such as New York, London, Tokyo, San Francisco, in the meantime stopping off at islands in the Pacific area to study crafts and primitive arts. The camper vans would be used to travel across country where applicable, eg: from the Suez Canal where the ship would proceed, to visit the pyramids etc. While at sea, the students would make sculpture in the studios and workshops and attend lectures, preparing them for the next port of call. While travelling overland they would also make works from the landscape materials, eg: timber from jungles, forests; stones from deserts etc.

3 Students would be predominantly Australian, chosen on their ability to cope with such an adventure and to take full advantage of the situations which shall arise. Some students should come from other countries to expand the educational and social values.

I am writing therefore to propose that you give this project your serious consideration in any decision which is to be made on this vessel's future, and I hope the ambition, imagination and romance of this project will overcome any economical or logistical difficulties which you will obviously foresee.

Sincerely,

John Davis *(Senior Lecturer in Charge, Sculpture)*

As a member of parliament Jim Killen was noted for his skilful use of the English language and his scathing tongue. What a pity that we haven't a copy of his reply to this madly impossible proposal! Only Don Quixote would have understood!

■ NOTES

1 John Davis, letter to the author, 26 February 1972.
2 Alycia Watson, 'Monash Sculptor Experiments with Latex and Fibreglass', *Monash Reporter*, Monash University, 7 July 1976.
3 Patrick McCaughey, 'Natural Setting for Exciting Sculpture', *Age*, 10 April 1973.
4 Thomas McCullough, Introduction to 'Sculpturscape '73', *Sculpturscape '73, The 1973 Mildura Sculpture Triennial*, 7 April–7 July 1973.
5 Frances McCarthy & Daniel Thomas, Introduction, *Recent Australian Art*, Art Gallery of New South Wales, Sydney, 18 October–18 November 1973. (John Davis showed 'Three documentary photographs, each 61 × 50.8 cm, of *Tree Piece 1973*'.)
6 Vic Majzner, interviewed by the author, 31 August 1982.
7 Memory Holloway, 'The Mid-Career Backroom Boys', *Age*, 23 June 1983.

LOW TECHNOLOGY AND CHEAP MATERIALS

The works shown at Pinacotheca Gallery in 1974 illustrated a big advance in John Davis's search for a personal means of expressing his ideas. Except for one large work constructed at the far end of the gallery, the sculptures were in two main groups. The works were either related to rectangular boxes or to white canvas structures that folded or rolled up.

The exhibition space at Pinacotheca is very large and the objects made by John Davis were dwarfed by the size of the old warehouse. Most of the sculptures were laid out on simple trestle tables, some on the walls — none were displayed on pedestals. The general atmosphere was very cool, almost remote, yet the objects had a mysterious quality that compelled the spectator to take them seriously. The conviction of the work forced one to re-examine the objects in an endeavour to discover the meaning. There seemed to be a private logic, a play with the significance of numbers, a repetition of forms and materials in a particular sequence. I found myself counting the number of cylinders in a row or the number of objects in a box. There didn't appear to be any mathematical sequence, but rather an implied suggestion that a group of nine objects was not necessarily complete.

Looking at the various boxes, some in wood, others made by hand from cardboard, as well as the canvas structures with their pockets and pouches, one seemed to be examining the private collection of a strangely obsessed collector. Yet in line with the current philosophy there were no precious objects. One work, *Ingots* (illus. 31), had a long, narrow wooden box with 27 wooden divisions, 9 filled with papier mâché forms cast into an ingot mould, 9 filled with forms of an identical shape made from terracotta and 9 filled with lead ingots. There was an inbuilt contradiction, the media — papier mâché, terracotta and lead — were not precious materials, but the final object assumed precious qualities. The precious object had been dethroned from the pedestal but the strange quality of the object asserted itself. John Davis made use of commonplace, cheap materials such as newspaper, clay, canvas and lead, in an attempt to make art democratic. He was saying at the time that his work was not a precious object, and anyone who wished could make art from similar cheap, throw-away materials. Yet the contradiction was that only John Davis could make the objects he was producing. His sculptures transcended his materials.

As early as 1971, while still teaching at Caulfield Institute of Technology, John Davis had sought the advice of Eugene Kupsch in the Ceramics Department and had fired a series of partly glazed terracotta cylinders. After his return from

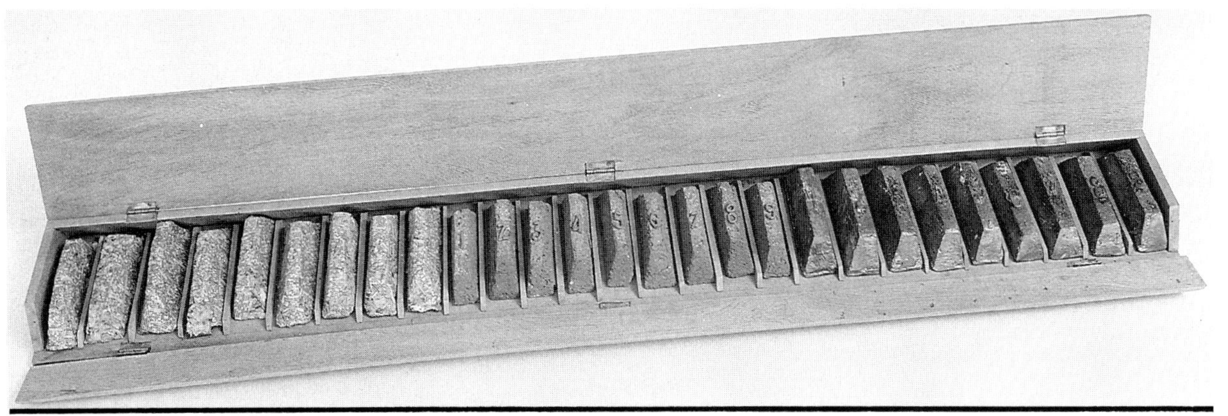

31 John Davis: Ingots *(1974). Long narrow wooden box with hinged lid and twenty-seven divisions, nine filled with papier mâché ingots, nine with terracotta and nine with lead. Box: 5.5 x 103 x 14.5 cm. (In the James Baker Collection, Museum of Contemporary Art, Brisbane.) Photograph by Mark Strizic.*

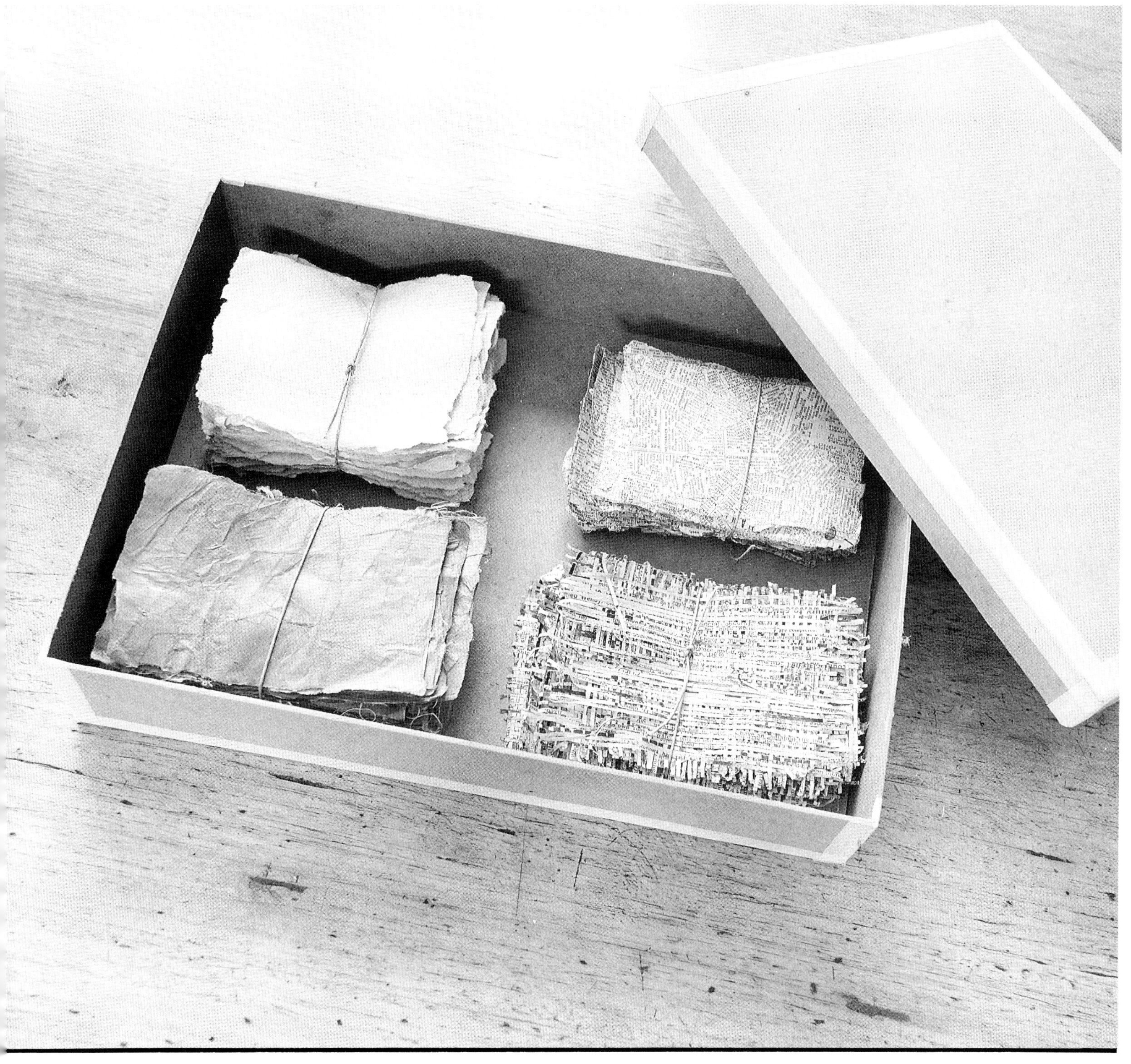

32 John Davis: Asyntatic or Asyntactic (1973). Cardboard box containing four paper bundles with each bundle consisting of twenty-seven paper sheets of torn newsprint, cut newsprint, torn paper towel, torn wrapping paper. Each bundle tied with string. Box: 7 x 28 x 38 cm. (In the James Baker Collection, Museum of Contemporary Art, Brisbane.) Photograph by Mark Strizic.

▶

the United States in 1973, he remembered that students at Caulfield had used latex, obtained from a small backyard factory in Malvern. The ceramic tubes were wrapped in sheets of latex, which was stitched by hand to hold it in place. Nine cylinders with latex became *Tubes and Box* at the Pinacotheca exhibition of 1974.

Latex became a recurring material in John Davis's work, which in some ways was strangely out of character. In 1974 he was concerned with simple, cheap materials of commonplace origins. Later he was to move towards found materials retrieved from the bush, twigs, sticks, stones, but in both instances the latex was the odd material out, being the product of a highly sophisticated technology. Yet it suited his needs as it was a versatile material that could be poured as a liquid into a plaster mould to adopt any form, or could be poured onto a flat slab to give a sheet. The neutral, almost anonymous colour, the soft yet resilient texture, and its ability to relate to other materials he used made it a familiar medium in his repertoire.

Another work produced in 1971, before the visit to USA, was *Transfield Sculpture*, shown at the Transfield Sculpture Competition in Sydney. It consisted of nine small sheet-steel boxes, each 12 × 12 × 12 cm, containing some forms in cast iron. *Nine Through Five* was made in 1971 and also used the box form, but by 1974 the box became quite a strong element in the Pinacotheca exhibition. *Drawing Piece*, *Four Paper Bundles* and *Five Paper Pieces* were all conveniently packed and displayed in shallow cardboard boxes. The boxes suggested specimens that had been stored and were temporarily on display. The curator of this collection was obviously fascinated by the infinite varieties of paper mâché made mainly from newspaper, cut, torn, pulped, drawn upon, tied into bundles or arranged into sheets. The boxes were simply, but well made and gave an orderly, systematic air to the exhibition,

contradicted by the contents, which were irregular in shape, often twisted and warped during the drying process of the papier mâché. Neatly typed labels in the lids of the boxes identified the work, the materials and the process.

Cylinders, boxes, papier mâché sheets and canvas containers were the recurrent forms at Pinacotheca. At the time John Davis was proud of the fact that he had made the canvas pockets and canvas bags on his wife's sewing machine. The craftsmanship was adequate and appropriate if not professional.

Asyntactic Part I (illus. 33) was a smaller version of *Unrolled* shown at Mildura 'Sculpturscape' in 1973. The long canvas container had a series of small pockets at right angles to the length of the canvas, each pocket to contain a ceramic rod. *Asyntactic Part III* consisted of a rectangular piece of canvas with nine pockets, each one containing a small sheet of dark grey papier mâché made from newspapers. The sculpture could be folded up into

▼

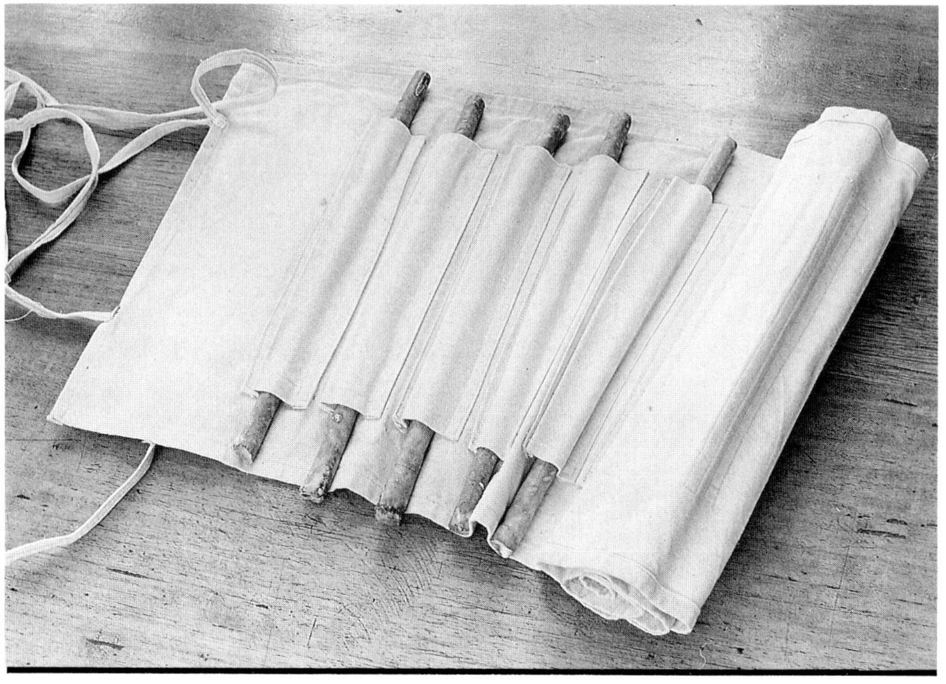

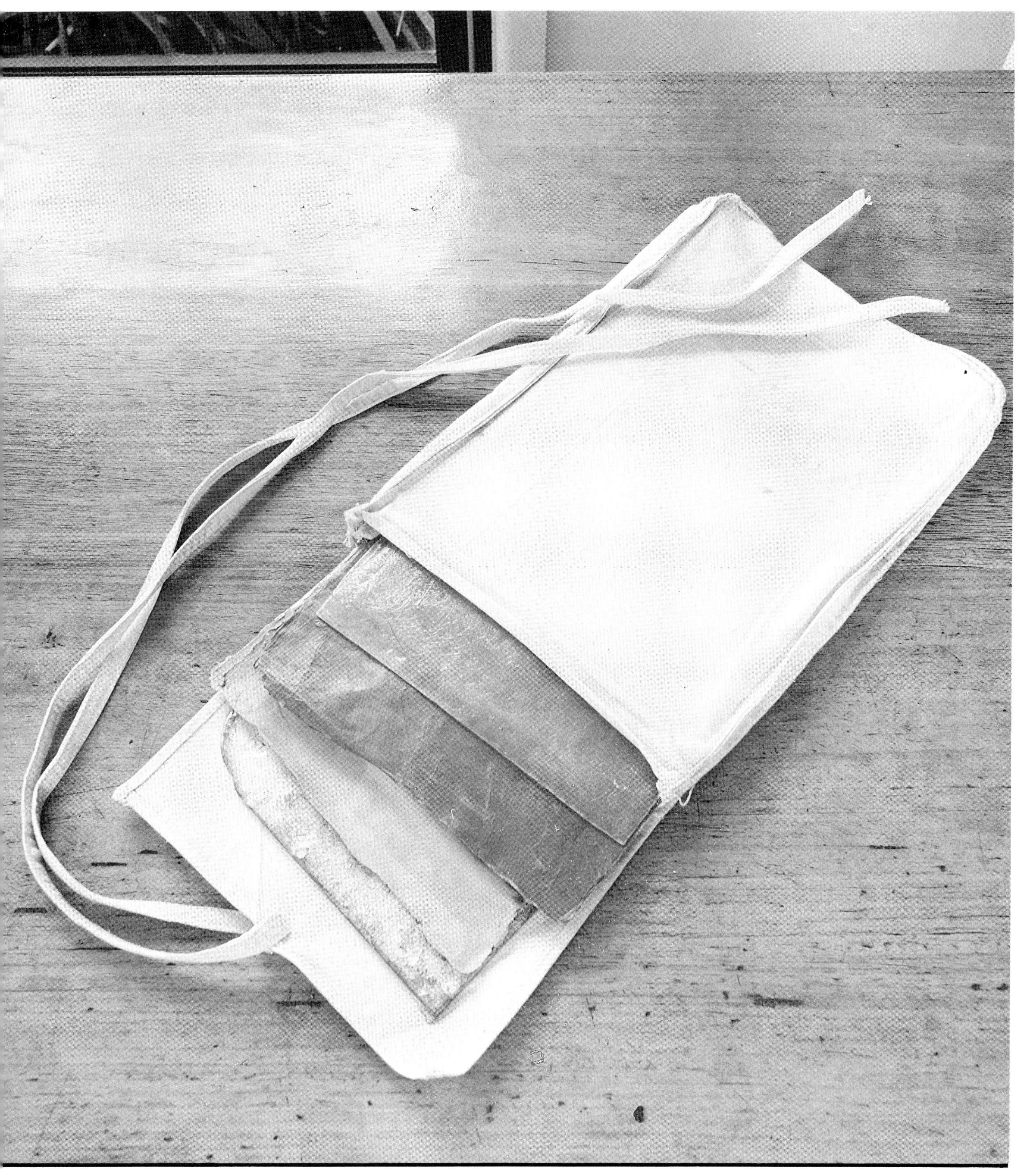

a square bundle. There were cords attached with which to tie up the work which made it quite portable. The non-precious object became a strangely mysterious object, like a modern-day version of icons which Christians took with them in an earlier age. *Asyntactic Part III* could be unwrapped simply and hung on a wall. One wondered at the significance of the nine pockets and nine sheets of papier mâché — was it a game of chance, could it foretell the future like Chinese sticks, was there some superstitious ritual?

Another work *Asyntactic Part II* (illus. 34) exploited the portability of the object. It consisted of a simple canvas bag, complete with straps for tying. The bag was deep, in order to take four sheets, but was shallow, as the four sheets were quite thin. The range of materials was strangely extreme — lead, latex, orange paper and polyester resin (a translucent casting resin without any fibreglass reinforcing). The lead sheet contradicted the portability and threatened the fragility of the papier mâché.

At the far end of the Pinacotheca Gallery was a construction which was demolished at the close of the exhibition. In the centre was a large, shallow, rectangular container of sheet lead. On either side were vertical poles of papier mâché, in two lines of five. They were held up by coarse string, tied down to two long rods of plaster of paris on either side. Leaning casually against the white brick wall of the gallery was a large canvas container with 'spare' papier mâché rods. There was also a square canvas bag with additional string. Again, as with some of the other works in the exhibition, the suggestion was that the work was not necessarily complete, it was capable of enlargement or change. It was as though one had caught the artist at work. He had gone to lunch, but would be back to assess the construction and decide upon the next move. It emphasised structure more than anything else in the show; a structure that defined space — which accounts for the title, *About Space*. The shallow lead container was a container of space in a definite fashion, whereas the papier mâché poles probed space in a more tentative manner. The strings defined the space in a linear way, like a drawing for an imaginary tent. It was strangely reminiscent of Ti Park's *Tent II* now in the collection of the National Gallery of Victoria, which was produced in 1968 and shown in the Argus Gallery, Melbourne.

It can now be seen that the 1974 exhibition at Pinacotheca was a significant one for John Davis. He had absorbed ideas and influences from his 1972 year abroad and had evolved new combinations of materials and new techniques to help him express his concepts. The Melbourne art critic, Maureen Gilchrist, reviewed the exhibition perceptively:

■ *John Davis' exhibition at Pinacotheca (10 Waltham Place, Richmond) is an encouraging occasion.*

So often the transposition of ideas into new materials is all there is of interest in ostensibly adventurous art. Often conventional form shows through quickly once the surprise of its new location has worn off.

But Davis employs new materials — particularly latex — with old — wax, clay and paper — in such a way that he transmutes common materials, investing the banal with eerie and inexplicable significance.

This is not an exhibition where either object or idea dominates, but one which seeks a new aesthetic that goes beyond formal qualities to explore the problems and relationships between ideas and materials.

What the work attempts to solve in this regard is as important as what it looks like.

The only imperative of this exhibition is a continual probing of the premises of sculpture. Davis refuses to become doctrinaire about the proper functions and directions in art.[1]

At the time John Davis was very much concerned with intellectual concepts, making this clear by placing eight pages of typed material on the gallery wall, using Jung to define the concept of number, Freud to analyse the use of systems and Koestler to explain the creative act.

A brief statement by John Davis followed by a quotation from the writings of Marcel Duchamp makes clear the significance of the numbers one, two and three:

■ *1 implies unity*
2 is duality
3 implies multiplicity

John Davis

For me it is a kind of magic number, but not magic in the ordinary sense. Twenty millions or three is the same for me.

At the conscious level, the number three expresses the anonymity of a crowd, a concept that relates perfectly to a nondogmatic attitude which abolishes categories, whether they be physical (male/female), aesthetic (art/non-art), or moral (suspension of judgment).

Duchamp

John Davis added a further comment of his own:

■ *To present an alternative proposition, the number two presents a theatrical situation in which 'one' endeavours to assert some authority over the other 'one', whereas three establishes a duality of 'one to one' thus presenting a type of closed circuit in a controlled dimension, and where an emphasis is still placed evenly. Three is the limit where an integral relationship can be established.*

Alan McCulloch also reviewed the 1974 Pinacotheca exhibition, starting with a criticism of Marcel Duchamp and referring to his 'sinister influence', but by the end of his review McCulloch had warmed to the appearance of the sculpture if not to the ideas expressed.

■ *One of the very few artists to try conclusions with this sinister influence and get away with it is John Davis.*

In his new work at Pinacotheca Davis selects for experiment Duchamp's theory about numbers.

The number one implies unity, two is duality and three implies multiplicity. 'Three is the limit where an integral relationship can be established' wrote Duchamp as quoted by Davis.

Davis quotes also Robert Irwin, Barnett Newman and Carl Jung, but Duchamp is the main motivation for most of what follows.

In playing his numbers game Davis gives us in one work a shallow, cedar box containing nine ingots, three made of papier mâché, three of clay and three of lead.

There is something quite beautiful about these immaculately boxed little units.

But the beauty resides more in the making and the finish than in the theory and thus brings the end result into conflict with the iconoclastic ideas on which it is based.

The same goes for the bars of similar materials arranged on the floor and for the nine papier mâché units slotted into canvas pockets on the wall.[2]

Alan McCulloch had referred to John Davis's quotes from Marcel Duchamp, in relation to numbers 1, 2 and 3. I was fascinated by the recurrent combinations of nine in many of the works on display in the 1974 Pinacotheca exhibition: *Asyntatic Part III* — nine pockets with nine sheets of papier mâché; *Redaction* — nine divisions and nine ceramic cylinders; *Ingots* — twenty-seven divisions with nine papier mâché, nine terracotta and nine lead ingots; *Asyntatic* — contained twenty-seven paper sheets. What is the fascination of the number 9?

Sydney sculptor, Marlee Creaser, gives her opinion on the significance of the number nine: 'Nine is the complete and ultimate number and contains *all* the other numbers. After nine one starts again. This is the encompassing number'.[3]

Perhaps Carl Jung should have the last word on the use of numbers and mathematical concepts, for he points out that anything made by man goes

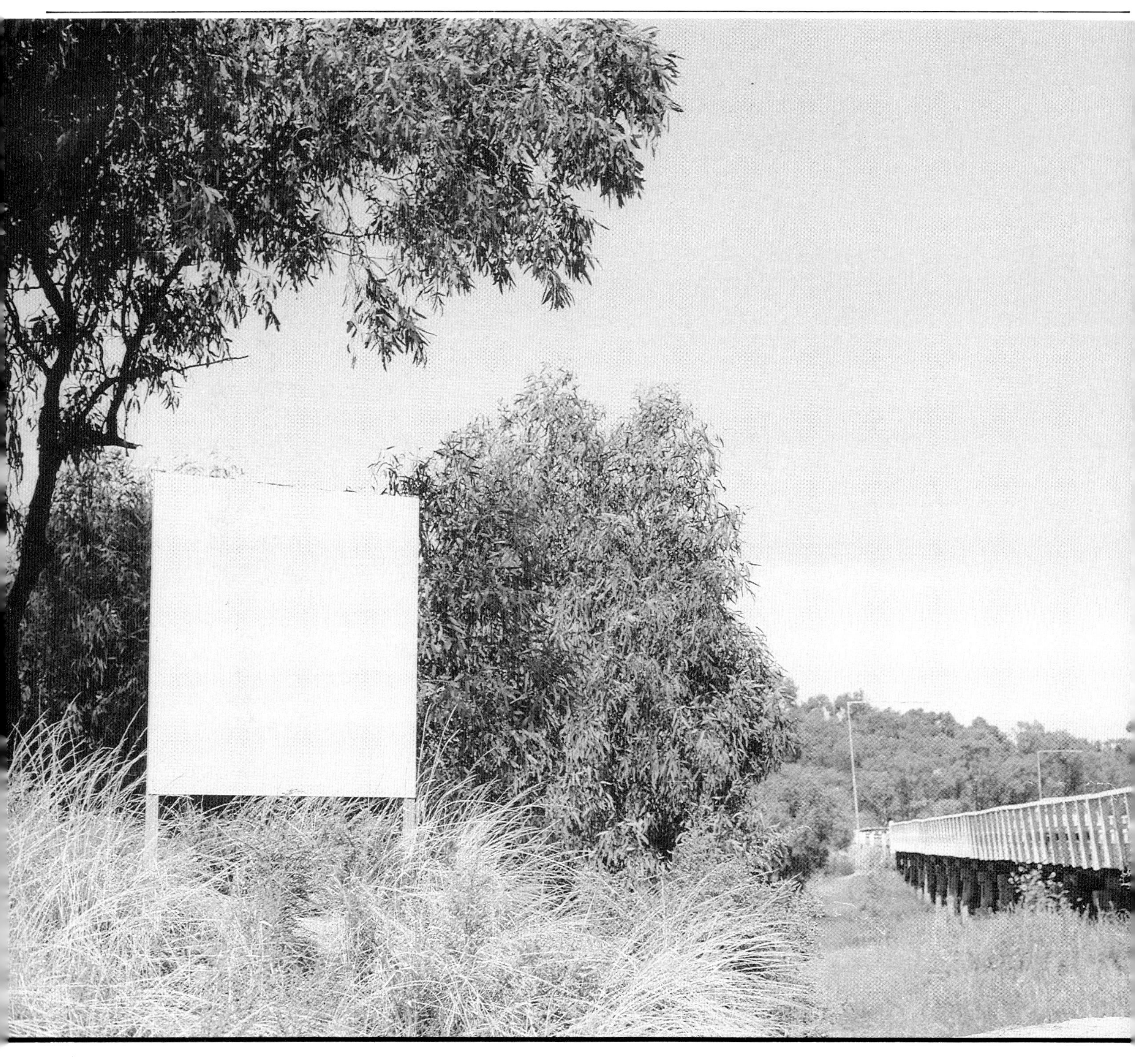

beyond the intellectual system into the 'unknowable'. The last quotation used by John Davis at his Pinacotheca exhibition explains why the mysterious images have remained firmly in my mind while the systems he used seem unimportant. 'Even the most carefully defined philosophical or mathematical concept which we are sure does not contain more than we have put into it, is nevertheless more than we assume. It is a psychic event and as such, partly unknowable.'[4]

In the long section of Pinacotheca, at the most extreme point and round the corner of the last screen was a continuous video screening of *Tearing*, made in 1974. The video only loosely related to the rest of the works. Paper was a material used frequently in the exhibition by John Davis, usually cheap newspaper and paper towelling transformed into papier mâché. *Tearing* documented the process of actually tearing up sheets of newspaper, but the visually tedious video contradicted the mysterious conviction of the exhibition as a whole.

Basically John Davis is an intuitive artist, but periodically in the past he has seemed to suspect his own judgement and attempted to become intellectual. Sometimes the results did not have an intellectual conviction.

He gave the impression of being highly intellectual, when he showed *Place* at Mildura in March 1975, at the sixth Mildura Sculpture Exhibition. Number 31 in the catalogue, it was listed as 'Video, photographs and mixed media'. The catalogue also grandly gave the location as 'Interior of room, environment of Mildura'. Within the small room on the first floor of the gallery were a TV monitor showing black and white video, three black and white photographs of the outskirts of Mildura (illus. 35) and ten black and white photographs of John Davis tying together numerous lengths of plaited string. There was also a piece of chipboard, about 1.2 m square, leaning against the wall. Except for the check pattern on the carpet, which attracted undue attention, the whole room was painted white, with black and white photographs and black and white video. Devoid of furniture and without any windows the room appeared austere and clinical.

The catalogue also contained a photograph of the artist tying lengths of string together. Beneath the photograph were four cryptic lines:

PLACE
PERIPHERY — reference/extension
PROCESS — procedure/structure
OBJECTNESS — material/inertia

To some spectators *Place* gave the impression of being profound, because it was not easy to understand. Alternatively, other visitors found it easy to understand, but then felt they must have missed the meaning — the work could not be so simple. But it was! Simple in content and execution, yet essentially esoteric.

PLACE. As Noel Hutchison said, 'Place' is a '. . . locality and its modification by an artwork'.[5] In this work, 'place' was the room in the gallery and the area enclosed within the reference points, as defined by four square white boards. One white board was within the room as a central marker, and three other identical boards were placed on the outskirts of Mildura on main roads leading to other cities — Sydney, Melbourne and Adelaide.

PERIPHERY. By implication, all contained within the periphery of this large area, the gallery, the city of Mildura, the homes, shops and the people, all annexed and made part of 'Place'. This was the 'reference/extension'.

PROCESS. This was the 'procedure' that gave 'structure'. By the simple act of plaiting string, which was shown on a 45-minute long video, a cheap material and a homely process was elevated to a statement on time.

OBJECTNESS. At a time when the expression

35 John Davis: **Place** (Mildura 1975). Consisted of: 'Video, photographs and mixed media', 'Interior of room, environment of Mildura' (from catalogue of Sixth Mildura Sculpture Exhibition). There were four identical white boards, one within room at the Gallery, and the other three on the outskirts of Mildura, on main roads leading to other cities — Sydney, Melbourne and Adelaide. Photograph by the artist.

'post-Object Art' was in vogue, it is interesting that John Davis is stressing the 'Objectness', the particular qualities of the object — a new version of truth to material? The 'material' is itself contained within its own 'inertia'.

When the work was reshown at Monash University Exhibition Gallery in September 1975, the order of things was altered in the catalogue, becoming:

PROCESS
TIME
SPACE
PERIPHERY
FUNCTION

Which can be briefly interpreted as:

PROCESS	—	Plaiting
TIME	—	Plaiting for 45 minutes. Shown on video. The lapse of time is made clear to the spectator.
SPACE	—	Ten lengths of plaited string, each 10 feet long, knotted together, occupying and defining space.
PERIPHERY	—	The gallery and the area enclosed within the reference points, as defined by the four square white boards, one within the gallery, the other three on roads leading out of Monash University.
FUNCTION	—	That is a difficult aspect to interpret, for as the artist says in the catalogue: 'The work may be approached quite arbitrarily'.

It may be of interest to quote the words of John Davis as printed in the Monash catalogue:

■   *PLACE*

Process
A procedure of organizing material and gesture.
An investigation into the nature of raw material, meaning and structure.
A measurement of the time factors which are constituted in the work.
Secondary considerations — development of manual/ intellectual skills, and subjective responses.
An indication of the 'on-going' nature of the artist's procedures by presenting possibilities for future projects, through some form of internal link.
A means of possibly eliminating 'style' if this elimination is considered important to the work.

TIME — in which thirty feet of string is plaited over a period of forty-five minutes.
site: Ewing Gallery, Melbourne University.

SPACE — in which ten lengths of plaited string, each ten feet in length, are knotted together.

Periphery
Indicating a limit to how far the work may extend from the gallery installation.
A means of establishing a lineal device to define relative positions in space.
The inclusion of any events, visual aspects, life patterns, cultural activities, dialogue, which may occur in the space which exists between the reference points.
Sites to function as a time indicator when the viewer confronts the gallery installation, or when the site is located away from the gallery installation.

Function
Within a framework of prior works.
Within an art context, using generally accepted sculptural means.
As a diagnosis of the means employed to construct the work.

That no one part of the total work is to be considered more important than the other, although the viewer may have preferences.
Presenting an environmental format extending beyond the gallery and an attempt to incorporate social structures within the work.
Within the spacial confines of the gallery.
As a means of presenting empirical considerations.
Does not depend on any authoritative statement in order to read the work.
The work may be approached quite arbitrarily.
As a statement about the qualities of materials, and the lesser or greater degree that 'materialness' plays in the meaning of the work.

The question of function is raised. As an art work, in an art gallery, 'using generally accepted sculptural means,[6] what did the artist say through his work and to whom was he saying it? It would seem that John Davis was endeavouring to involve the whole of Mildura or all of Monash University in his sculptural statement by staking his claim, by visibly defining the limits with the three boards on the outskirts of Mildura or around Monash University. Was he hoping that the work of art would affect all of those people within the stated limits? Did he presume that the people of Mildura would be conscious of the significance of the three white boards and see themselves within that defined space? Would they then have a new concept of space?

Yet, *Place* was of such an esoteric nature that only an artistic élite would grasp its philosophical meaning. It took the work of art outside the confines of the élitist art gallery, but was in no way democratic. Far from being democratic it actually alienated the average person, for the public was accustomed to a TV commercial that gave its elementary message in 30 seconds. Gallery visitors found it totally unacceptable to stand and watch a home-made video depicting a person in an empty room plaiting string for 45 minutes.

Maureen Gilchrist wrote a review of *Place* at Monash University which was partly descriptive and partly analytical. She had no difficulty in comprehending the work, though she left her personal statement to the end of the article, when she referred to the video.

■ *Davis is engrossed with concepts and processes at very basic, easily demonstrable levels. He is concerned with ideas as they affect materials, meaning and structure. He is concerned also with measurement, cause and relation and questions of context: both physical and cultural.*

'Place' is essentially a diagnostic exhibition, probing classification and relationship within the raw data of the artist's experience and procedures.

In the catalogue which encapsulates the entire show (excluding the factor of duration on the video screen), Davis says that the work may be approached arbitrarily.

Approaching it in this fashion I detect a parody of our soporific television viewing in the monotonous plaiting of string. It seems to me also that Davis is interested in the way video follows the contours of experience rather than making and structuring it in the way film does.[7]

When I rewatched 'Plaiting' in 1982, seven years after it was first shown at Mildura, I was even more bored than when I first saw it! Possibly I am amongst a very small group of people who have watched the entire 45 minutes. One sees merely hands, hands methodically plaiting. Even when John Davis bent down to pick up another piece of string, his face never came into view — the work was totally anonymous.

One wonders who John Davis thought of as his audience, for he certainly was thinking of this fundamental question, which he mentions in a letter to Frank Watters:

■ *Over the last few months out at Monash, I've been able to work uninterrupted and consequently able to apply myself more fully to my two major concerns, my art and to whom my art seems to communicate and effect some sort of response. As to the former, a lot of ideas I've been involved in, though disparate and seemingly at times unrelated, seem to have certain links such as space and time and material, very much the stuff of sculpture. I can now see an overview of where I think I'm heading for the next year or so, — taking the form of installations and occasional individual pieces, sometimes objects, drawings, or video tapes as a kind of extension of parts of the installation. I suppose what is happening is that all the information and activity I've been involved in since we got back from overseas in '72 is now becoming evident, and the subtlety I've always been after is now happening in a really relaxed way. That's what pleases me most about my activity this year.*[8]

The fascinating aspect of this letter is it reveals that in 1976 John Davis was concerned with 'space and time and material, very much the stuff of sculpture'. These were used in a dry theoretical manner in *Place* in 1975, but in *Nomad*, a work which he made at Monash, only a year later while artist in residence, space, time and the material become magical ingredients in a subtle work.

During 1975 the National Gallery of Victoria organised a series of intriguing exhibitions entitled 'Artists' Artists'. The rather clumsy title signified that the exhibiting artists had been chosen by their fellow artists. The idea originated with Graeme Sturgeon, who was then Temporary Exhibitions Officer. He sent circular letters to many artists in Melbourne asking them to nominate who should be invited to exhibit. Those whose names were listed by a number of artists were then invited to show their work at the gallery. There were separate exhibitions for paintings, drawings, and sculpture. Whereas the first two were held in the temporary exhibitions gallery, the sculpture was displayed at various sites within the gallery over a period of several months, two or three sculptors at a time.

John Davis chose a long corridor-like area for his exhibition space — an area with a lot of through-traffic to the Great Hall. Unfortunately the wall surface was of large, terracotta bricks, placed vertically. The bricks had a series of vertical lines incised on the surface. This busy surface was subdued by building a long, white, chipboard wall for the full length of the area, up to a height of about 2.4 metres.

Against this white wall were arranged a series of disparate objects, loosely linked visually by the repetition of a square or rectangular shape. The whole effect was very casual, even arbitrary, in the placing of the objects. It appeared as though the artist had put the various parts on the floor, or leaned them against the wall and could easily come back later and rearrange them in a different sequence. There was a logic behind the arrangement — horizontal square beside vertical square, solid square against a square of space, tied up square bundle beside stack of rectangular sheets, big contrasted with small, line compared with solid form — but the logic was elusive.

As a sculpture, *On the need for a proper delineation in a moment* (illus. 36) didn't have any classical precedents. One could hardly compare it with a low relief on a wall, though it had a narrative quality to be read from left to right (or right to left?). One proceeded from the rectangle to transparent plastic sheeting on the floor, at the far left, to the shallow, square tray of sheet-lead leaning against the wall. The opaque heaviness of the lead was contrasted with a large open square of space, defined by two vertical cardboard cylinders, covered in white canvas. The eye then came down to the floor again to a series of four, square or rectangular forms, in latex, canvas, solid papier mâché or sheets of papier mâché.

On the wall, at eye level, at the far left, were a

▶
36 John Davis: On the need for a proper delineation in a moment (1975). From far left (barely visible) thirty-six small photographs, rectangle of transparent plastic sheeting on floor, square shallow tray of lead leaning against wall, two vertical cardboard cylinders covered with canvas, filled with sand and linked with string, a small square latex form, with four ceramic cylinders attached to top, square bundle covered in white canvas, a square of cast papier mâché and on right, a stack of large sheets of papier mâché with drawing on top sheet. Temporary installation at National Gallery of Victoria in 1975. Photograph by the artist.

▶
37 John Davis: Ewing Work (1975). Ceramic rods, latex sheet with eyelet holes, string. Cardboard cylinder covered with canvas strips and ceramic rods (tied on with string). Grid: c. 70 cm square; latex hung down c. 22 cm. Temporary installation at Ewing Gallery, University of Melbourne, 'The Grid Show. A Structured Space', 11–22 August 1975. Photograph by the artist.

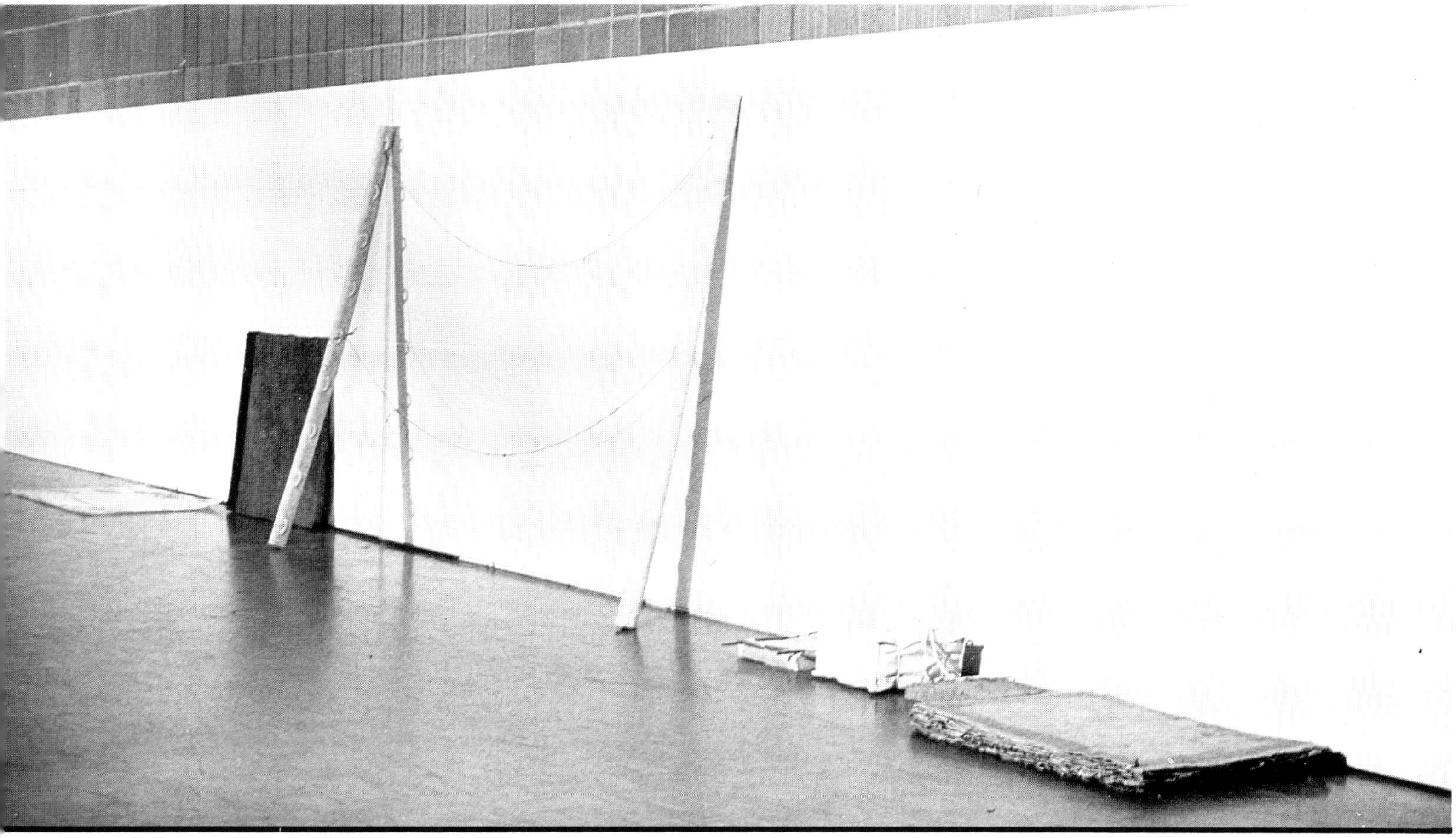

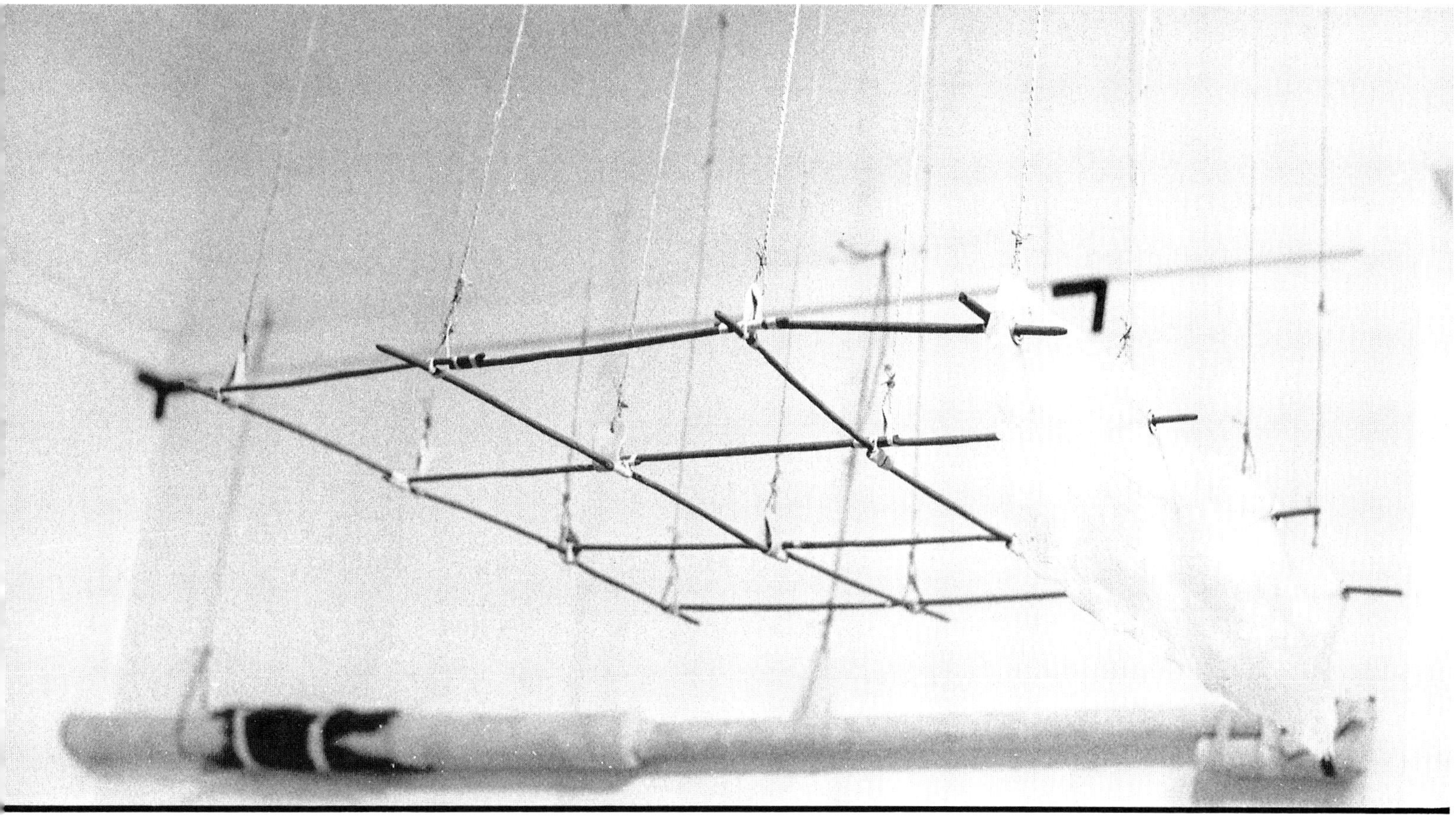

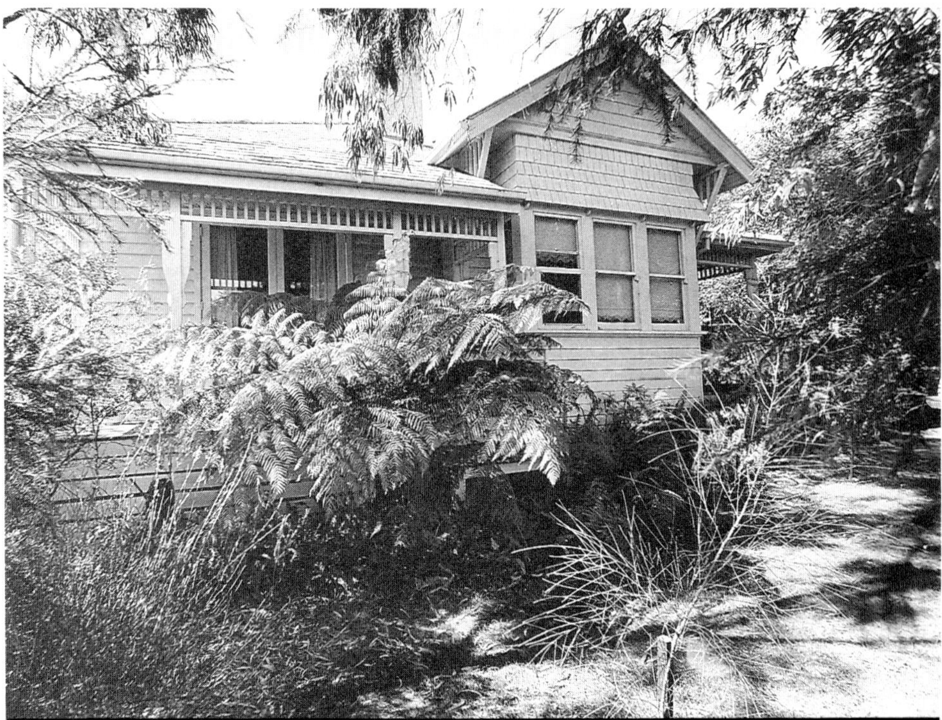

38 Exterior of John Davis's house at 41 Crisp Street, Hampton (1986). Photograph by Mark Strizic.

39 The artist in his study. Photograph by Mark Strizic.

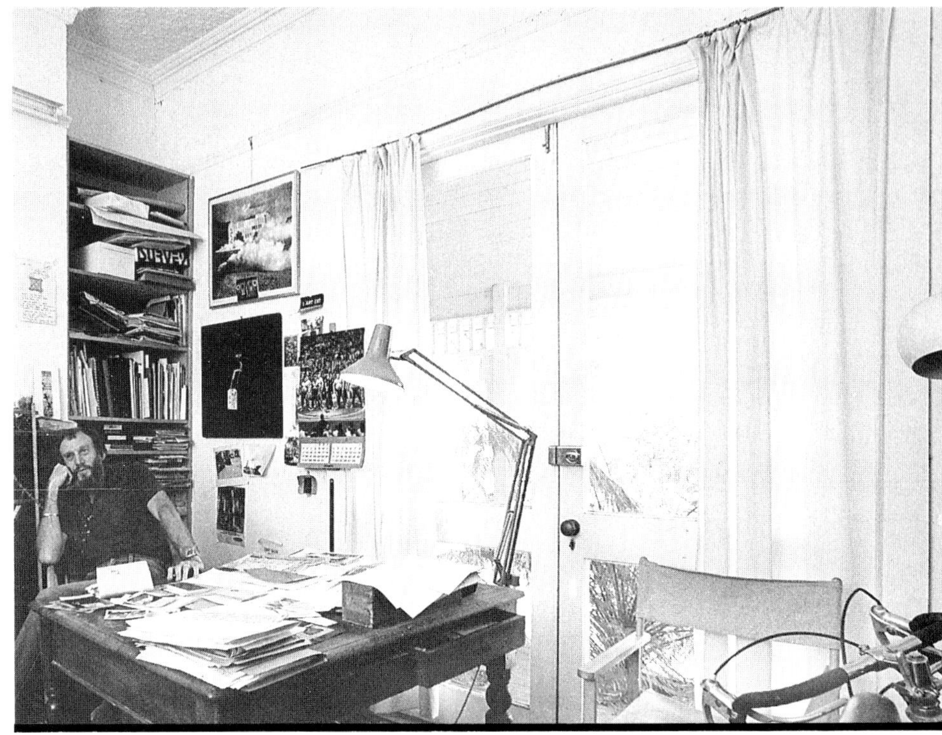

series of 36 small photographs showing a latex cube getting progressively smaller and smaller. The photographs seemed to confuse the issue, for even though they were also to do with the repetition of a square, the logic seemed too obvious and didn't have the mysterious and intriguing quality of the work as a whole.

The classical notion of the essential unity of a piece of sculpture was not a fundamental base for the work. The relative independence of the parts is illustrated by the fact that the sculptor kept some elements himself, gave the square bundle covered in white canvas to the sculptor, Marlee Creaser in Sydney, and at Marcia Gunn's request gave the stack of papier mâché sheets to the Monash University Collection.

Under Kiffy Carter's (Rubbo) guidance the Ewing Gallery ran a series of theme exhibitions: 'The Letter Show', 'The Box Show' and, in 1975, 'The Grid Show'. The work which John Davis showed in one of the small bays of the Ewing Gallery for 'The Grid Show' (illus. 37) was hung from the ceiling just above head level. It consisted of a structure of thin ceramic rods, tied together with string to form a grid of 3 × 3 squares. The whole fragile construction was supported by loops of latex, which in turn were suspended from the ceiling by plaited string. At one side of the grid there was a sheet of latex. Hanging on the wall was a long thin cardboard cylinder, covered in canvas, to which was bound with string a group of ceramic rods.

The work was a perfect answer to the theme 'The Grid Show — A Structured Space'. It was also a forerunner to the major work *Nomad*, which John Davis made in 1976 and exhibited in the Art Gallery of New South Wales during the Second Biennale in 1976.

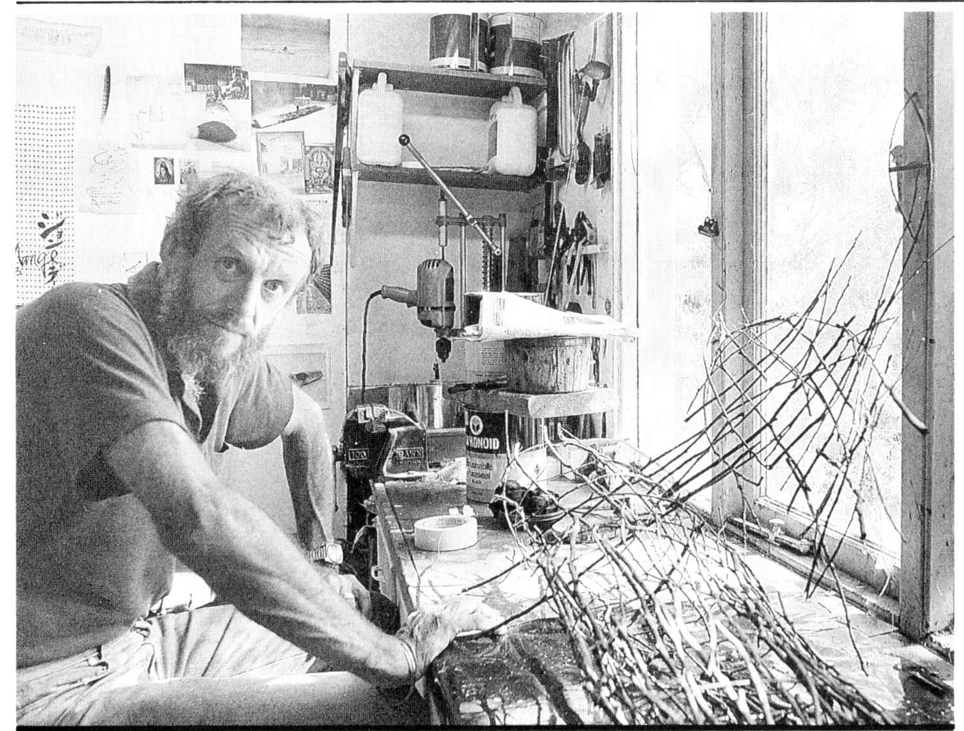

▼ *40 The artist in his studio. Photograph by Mark Strizic.*

▼ *41 John Davis's studio in backyard at 41 Crisp Street. Photograph by Mark Strizic.*

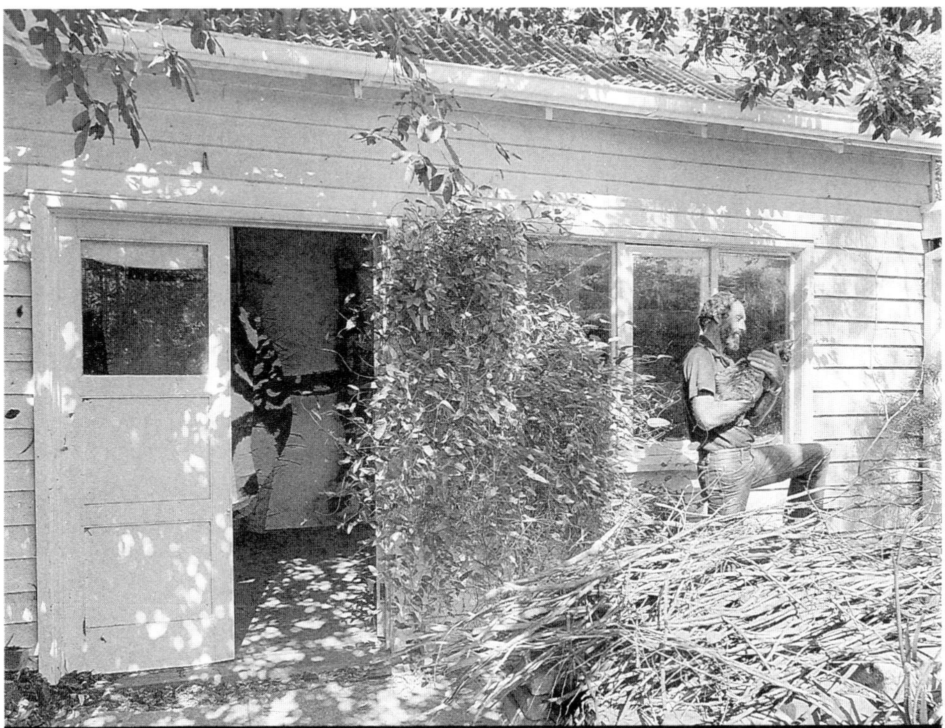

Most sculptors like to work in a large space, not only because they need a considerable area for storage of materials, but also because they need the space in order to view their work. Strangely, John Davis has always worked within very limited space. His studio from 1966–71 was an extremely small shed in the backyard of his home in David Street, Hampton, no bigger than a child's cubby house. Yet in that limited space he produced all of the polyester resin and fibreglass works, culminating in *100*. The space was so limited that he was forced to move out to the lawn to assemble parts. He complained of the lack of studio space but never sought an alternative.

While abroad in 1972 he was restricted by the lack of a studio, but produced small-scale works in cardboard and papier mâché. On his return to Australia John purchased a house in Crisp Street, Hampton (illus. 38), which did not have any studio space. He obtained a grant from the Visual Arts Board in 1974 to help set up a studio and purchase equipment, but he used the money to modify one of the front rooms of his house. The verandah was extended and he built a long bench in the room, but it remained basically a small room (illus. 39), which a previous owner had used as a bedroom. Eventually another room at the rear of the backyard garage was also used as a studio (illus. 40, 41), but again it was a small space. When he took up his position in 1981, as Co-ordinator of Post-Graduate Studies at the Victorian College of the Arts he had the choice of a number of rooms for his studio and office. He chose two very small rooms. Just prior to his 1981 exhibition at Watters Gallery his studio space at the Victorian College of the Arts had narrowed to a passageway between the entrance door and his very limited office space in the second room. The first room was almost filled with works stacked on the floor and leaning against the wall. One could presume that he liked working within a limited space, a factor which has influenced his choice of materials and the size of the sculpture produced. Alternatively one could say that materials such as papier mâché, latex, twigs and string do not need a large amount of space. More correctly the choice of working space, the materials used, and the scale of the works produced, all reflect the personality of the sculptor. John Davis appears to work best on a modest scale, though of later years he has arranged objects in large-scale installations.[9]

To varying degrees, sculptors have the qualities of craftsmen, the love of materials, the interest in things made by hand and a fascination in the processes of working. Davis's early organic wood carvings had a quality that was brought about by patient work by hand, though this attitude did not exclude the use of hand-held power tools. The early exhibition at Strines Gallery in 1969 demonstrated his ability to make objects that were quite precious in appearance and immaculately crafted. The tedious, repetitious procedures necessary for casting in polyester resin and fibreglass tested his patience (yet he is a patient man) and caused him to take short cuts. Some of the forms really needed an additional layer of fibreglass and were cast rather thinly. The transition from one form to another, or areas out of the spectator's view, were sometimes treated cursorily. Resin and fibreglass seemed to be one process that he did not enjoy. The strict sequential procedure necessary for casting seemed out of character with his intuitive approach.

After his return from Europe, John developed an interest in a range of materials such as papier mâché, latex, clay and metals, which were all easy to manipulate with simple technical procedures. Cheap materials and low technology made it appear that he was no longer interested in craftsmanship, but this was not the case. For a sculptor, craftsmanship or technical skill can never be an end in itself. Craftsmanship should never be more than appropriate to the ideas, the materials and the processes. If it is any more than that it attracts too much attention. The best craftsmanship goes unnoticed.

■ NOTES

1 Maureen Gilchrist, art review, *Age*, 4 September 1974.
2 Alan McCulloch, 'The Inspired Larrikin', *Herald*, 11 September 1974, reproduced courtesy of the Herald and Weekly Times Ltd.
3 Marlee Creaser in letter to the author dated 'Wednesday, early February 1983'. At the time of writing Marlee Creaser was working in Sydney, but has subsequently lived in Italy and USA.
4 Carl Jung, *Man and His Symbols*, Aldus Books in association with Allan (London), 1964.
5 Noel Hutchison, 'Introduction', *Place*, when shown at Monash University Exhibition Gallery, 2–26 September 1975.
6 John Davis in *Place* catalogue, ibid.
7 Maureen Gilchrist, 'Prints Move into The Limelight', *Age*, 19 September 1975.
8 John Davis, letter to Frank Watters, 16 June 1976.
9 In a conversation with the author, 6 June 1987, John Davis raised the possibility of acquiring a disused factory as studio space, which he subsequently purchased.

Chapter 6

1976–77
TWIGS, PAPER AND STRING

For six months during 1976 John Davis was artist in residence at Monash University in the Department of Visual Arts. The appointment, which had been brought about by Patrick McCaughey's admiration for recent work by John Davis, carried considerable prestige.[1] Yet in some notes made in 1976, Davis realised he had a variety of roles within the university — 'entertainer, personality, information giver, catalyst for activity, freak'. Probably the greatest benefit for him was the freedom from timetable commitments of teaching and the chance to concentrate on his sculpture full-time. 'Best of all, I just work through day after day non-stop uninterrupted on my thing, not having to help solve somebody else's problems.'[2] While he had this luxury of time John decided to revisit the Hattah Lakes in northern Victoria. He had first visited the area when he was living in Mildura and he felt the need to go back and re-examine the Mallee. By the time he drove from Melbourne it was only a four-day visit, but the impact of the environment had a strong effect upon him (illus 42).

He camped at the Hattah Lakes by himself, enjoying the quiet days, building structures of twigs, branches, leaves, bark and string. Sometimes he incorporated standing dead trees (illus. 43, 44), stumps of trees and roots. It was simply a matter of making sculpture with whatever materials were available, so branches and twigs were the most commonly available media.

This was a big change for John Davis. Even though he had used mainly cheap, commonplace materials, they were all man-made materials such as papier mâché, latex, fired clay, bronze, lead etc.

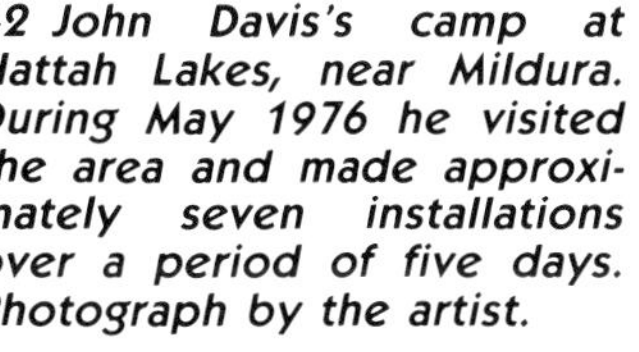

42 John Davis's camp at Hattah Lakes, near Mildura. During May 1976 he visited the area and made approximately seven installations over a period of five days. Photograph by the artist.

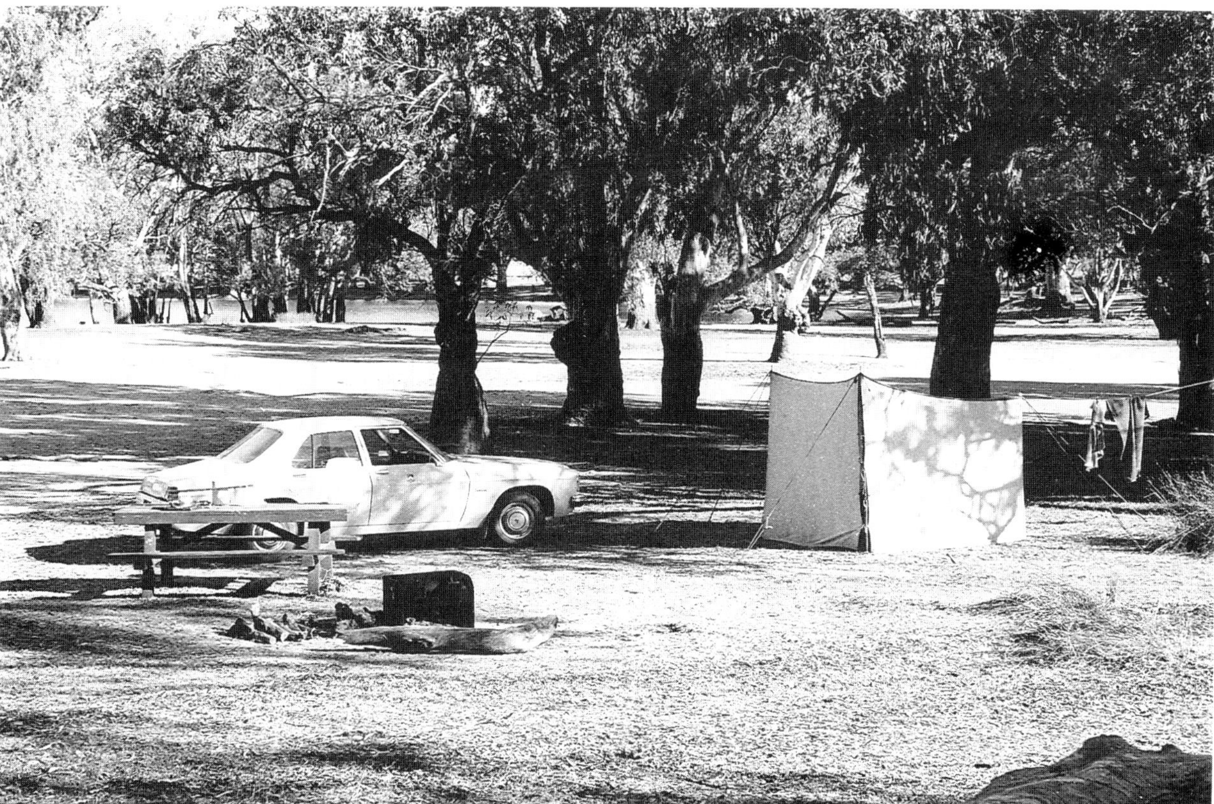

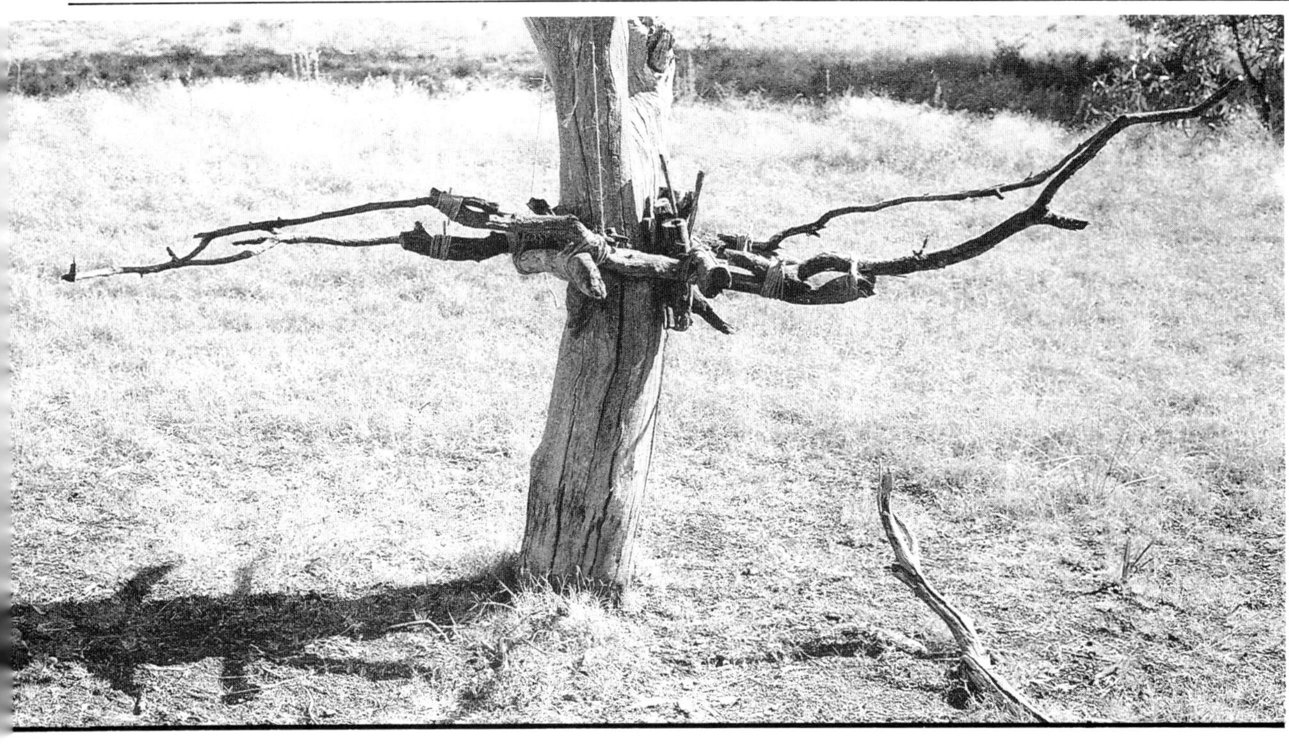

◀
43 John Davis: Installation using branches and a dead tree at Hattah Lakes (May 1976). Photograph by the artist.

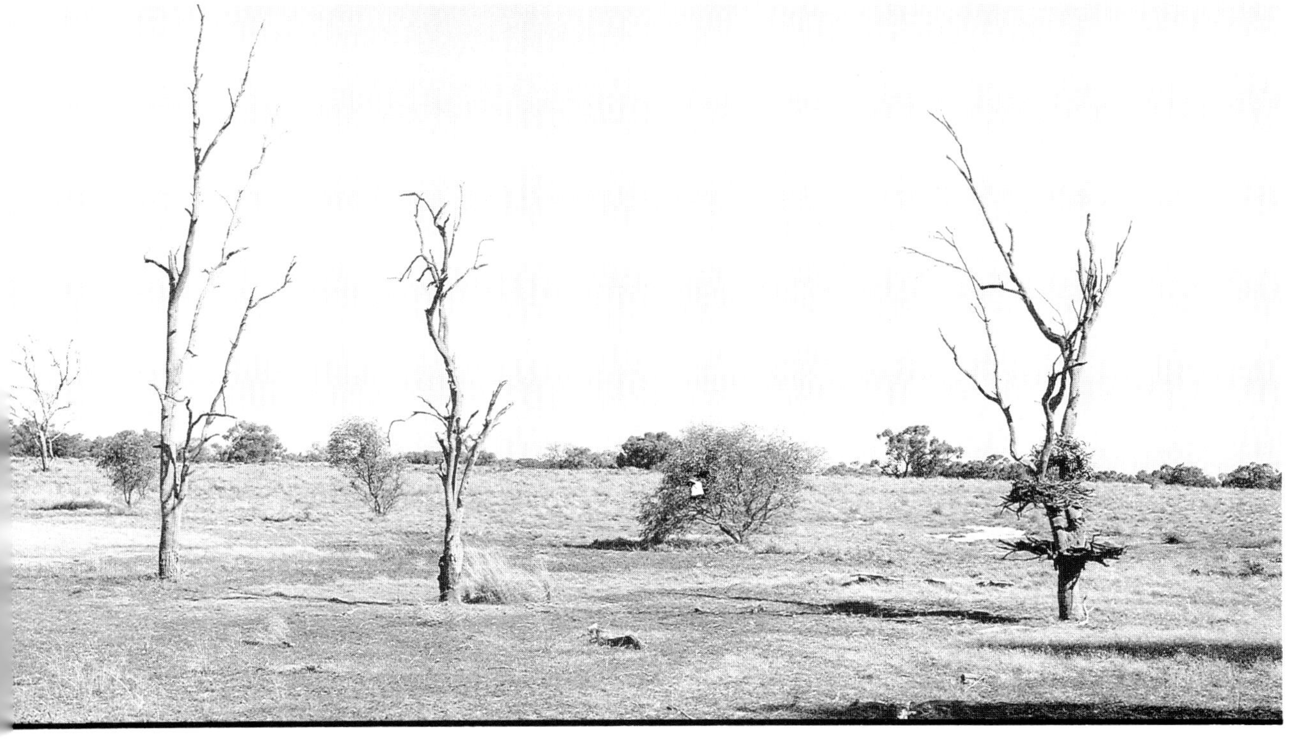

◀
44 General view of the country at Hattah Lakes. The tree on the right was used as the starting point for an installation by John Davis. Photograph by the artist.

This nostalgic return to the Mallee made him aware of an endless supply of very cheap (cost free) materials such as branches and twigs, which he was to use for a considerable number of works from 1976 onwards.

John Davis was not the only contemporary artist in the world to use natural materials, such as sticks and stones, but this is not to say that his work derived from overseas sources. The materials and work produced were a direct result of his basic interest in nature and obviously link with his early organic wood carvings. Whereas his interest had been in the gnarled roots, the twisted branches or the solid trunk of the trees along the Murray, he now looked at the smaller branches and the fine twigs of trees in the Mallee. Such materials were impossible to carve, but ideal for construction. Using sticks, twigs and stones combined with papier mâché, John Davis had to develop a series of techniques for tying with cotton and string, for pasting with paper, for joining structures, for giving strength to fragile materials. The materials and the techniques were a perfect combination, ideal for the processes of working that he enjoyed for they allowed an intuitive growth by the slow, patient tying of string and the addition of torn papier mâché.

In his early wood carvings he had accepted the growth of the tree and had used the forms as the basis of his sculpture. In his works after the Hattah Lakes installations he allowed the sculptures to develop with a natural sense of growth and structure. The order grew naturally from the materials and the process.

Any sculpture, by definition, is man-made, but sometimes man's sense of order is dominant and the materials are relegated to a secondary position. John Davis not only achieved a fine balance between his sense of structure and the use of the materials, but he also brought about a delicate relationship between concept and the means of expression of his ideas. It was a lesson learnt from modern attitudes towards ecology — in nature all things are related, interdependent. Destroy one type of plant and the birds or insects are affected. Bring in cattle or sheep and the pattern is irrevocably altered. John Davis brought about a finely balanced relationship between his ideas, materials, processes of construction, logic and intuition.

There was one apparent contradiction in this attitude towards conservation, ecology, low technology, cheap materials and fundamental interest in the Australian bush — John Davis lives in the heart of suburbia. Hampton is a typical seaside suburb of Melbourne with wide streets and endless rows of modest houses. If the vast majority of Australians live in very large cities and only drive into the country on Sunday afternoons, should the art of Australia be based on the life of the city dweller, or can the bush still be a valid source of inspiration? Is the average Australian, who lives and works in a totally man-made environment, still aware of the vast continent? When he drives his caravan from Melbourne to Surfers Paradise, or takes the train across the Nullarbor Plains to Perth, does he become aware of some of the characteristics of the Australian landscape?

Sidney Nolan has continued to use the vast Australian landscape, yet his cosmopolitan attitude and sophistication is not thought contradictory. He has strengthened the conviction of Australians in the legends of our early explorers so that their exploits are still remembered. Except for some early paintings of St Kilda 1941–45 and a few of Sydney in 1978, Sidney Nolan has barely painted the cities of Australia.

Fred Williams is now accepted as being one of Australia's greatest landscape painters, yet he lived in a busy section of suburbia surrounded by the blatant signs of man's invasion. The most dominant objects on Fred Williams' horizon were traffic lights, a huge screen for a drive-in theatre, a shopping complex, a freeway, a railway line and a series of huge gasometers. It is ironical that Fred Williams never drove a car and relied on someone else to drive him into the country.

If John Davis feels so much in tune with the bush, why does he live in the heart of a big city? When asked the question he replied: 'Living away from the "source" gives a clearer perception, less chance of producing illustration and a chance to concentrate on *art*'. The factors that bind one to a particular place are complex and cannot be dismissed simply as inertia. John moved to Highett after his first appointment to a city school, Highett High School, in 1963. Three years later he moved to the adjoining suburb of Hampton, and except for changing houses, has lived there ever since. At one stage a considerable number of artists lived in the locality: Alun Leach Jones, Clive Murray-White, Geoff La Gerche, Fred Cress, Lenton Parr, Lesley Dumbrell, Victor Majzner, Ken Leveson, Sandra Leveson. Both John and his wife Shirley were, and still are, members of the Labor Party and have been active in local issues, helping to give out 'How to Vote' cards at election time, organising fund raising events. John Davis has been interested in sailing, so Hampton's proximity to the sea has given him more chance to get out on to Port Phillip Bay.

Very few Australian sculptors earn their living by producing sculpture. The handful of sculptors supporting themselves from sales of their work are either unmarried, living very frugally, or are prepared to work in a variety of conservative styles in order to gain commissions. A high proportion of Australian sculptors are teachers, often starting as secondary school teachers and moving into tertiary art schools as their careers and reputations rise. John Davis is a teacher and his employment at Highett High School, Caulfield Institute of Technology, Prahran College of Advanced Education,

and lately at the Victorian College of the Arts has all been within a reasonable distance from Hampton.

An artist's reputation is often directly linked to the frequency of his exhibitions and the relative status of the gallery where he exhibits. In our society, an artist risks extinction if he fails to exhibit. It is essential that the artist's name be noted, works be seen, so that gallery directors, curators, dealers, art critics and gallery visitors are all familiar with his name and his work. The artist who frequents gallery openings and is on first-name terms with gallery directors and curators has a tremendous advantage over the artist who is living anonymously in the country.

John Davis is tied to Hampton and Melbourne by hundreds of invisible strings, most of which he doesn't see or feel himself. But so it is with all of us.

The sculptures Davis produced in 1976 continued to emphasise his bush associations. The simple grid structure suspended from the ceiling in the Ewing Gallery in 1975 was the obvious precursor for *Nomad* (illus. 45), a large work, produced while John was artist in residence at Monash University.

Nomad consisted of three parts. The grid of delicate fibreglass rods was tied together with cotton, held by loops of latex, then suspended from the ceiling by string. The grid of 5×5 rods was erected just above head level. On one side a sheet of latex hung downwards. On the floor was a square of knitted string to which a thin cylindrical bundle of twigs was attached. Displayed on the wall were groups of photographs, twenty-six in number, showing various installations at the Hattah Lakes. Beneath the photographs, sitting on the floor, were three small structures, one mainly constructed from twigs, the other two of partially carved wood, but also containing fibreglass and latex.

When *Nomad* was shown at the Art Gallery of

▶

45 John Davis: Nomad *(1976). Grid of fibreglass and polyester resin rods, tied together with cotton, held by loops of latex, suspended by string from the ceiling. One sheet of latex attached and hanging from rods. Square of knitted string on the floor. Thin bundle of twigs on floor attached to knitting. Three small structures on floor made from twigs, carved wood, fibreglass and latex. Twenty-six photographs on the wall of installations at Hattah Lakes. Grid approximately 215 cm above floor, 183 x 250 x 30 cm. Shown at 'Second Biennale', Art Gallery of New South Wales, 13 November–4 December 1976. Temporary installation, since destroyed. Photograph by the artist.*

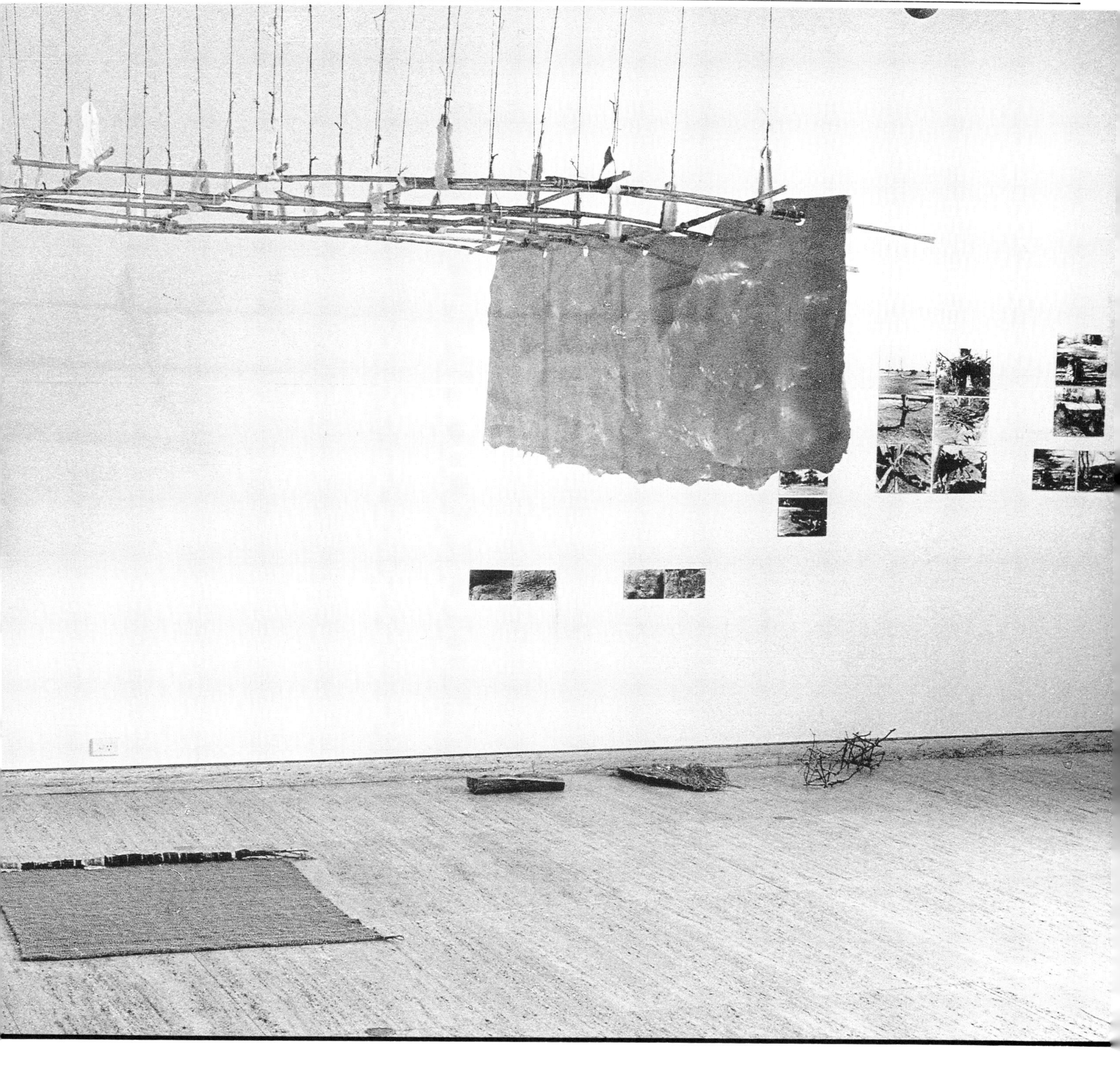

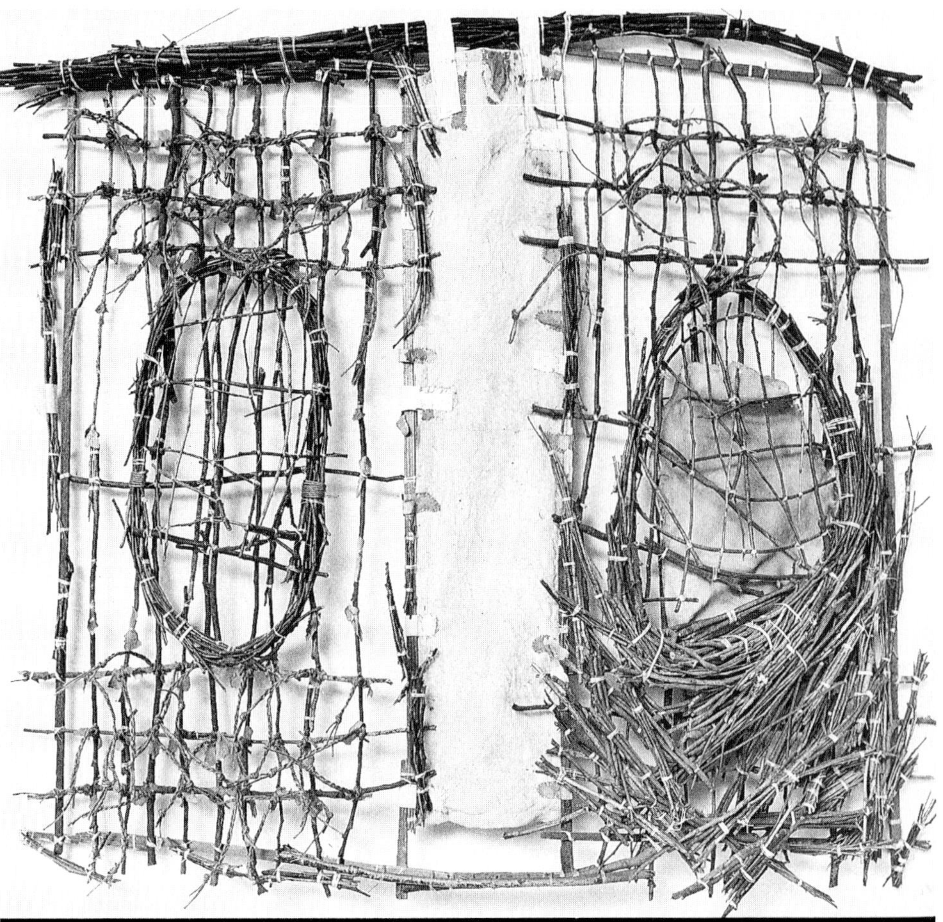

46 John Davis: Mat (1976). Sawn timber, twigs, string, latex and calico. 9.5 x 81 x 69 cm. Originally designed to be viewed on the floor (in collection of Dr and Mrs Douglas Callister). Photograph by Mark Strizic.

New South Wales during the Second Biennale in 1976, it was well-located in a corner of the gallery, but it was almost impossible to photograph. Only details could be adequately recorded. The structure was light and delicate. The parts were separate and casually placed on floor, wall and ceiling.

The title *Nomad* and the work itself made reference to nomadic, tribal people. One wondered whether the main structure was a form of shelter, partially constructed. The knitted square of string on the floor suggested the presence of people, the site of a camp. The three small sculptures on the floor were evidence that people had stayed in the area for some time, making their simple artefacts before moving on. The photographs appeared to be the records of an anthropologist who had visited the area, not contacted the people, but photographed the signs of their presence. What were actually the structures made by John Davis, at the Hattah Lakes, appeared to be simple ritual constructions of a departed nomadic people.

Nomad was a subtle, elusive work that could easily be missed in the company of the avant-garde sculpture of the Sydney Biennale. Whereas other works demanded attention, setting out to shock or delight, fighting aggressively for public viewing, *Nomad* was quietly understated. It was at its best when the gallery was nearly empty and slow contemplation was possible, for when the gallery was crowded with visitors its meaning was lost.

Mat (illus. 46) was another sculpture produced during 1976 that helped establish the direction of later work. The initial structure of light, sawn timber, was approximately 1 metre square, establishing a grid of three rectangles. The two larger rectangles were of the same size, on either side of a smaller, central rectangle. This simple geometric structure was overlaid with a pattern of twigs tied with string, so that the general effect was of intertwining complexity. Small bundles of twigs were tied together, reinforcing the structure and visually emphasising the pattern of rectangles and two ovals. The two ovals, within the larger rectangles and the central smaller rectangle were filled in with canvas, stressing their shape against the linear pattern of the twigs.

The composition of *Mat* was simple, direct and tightly knit, whereas *Bicycle II* (illus. 47), also produced during 1976, was a very loose relationship of two disparate forms. On the left was a small shelf-like construction of essentially rectangular forms, of twigs and papier mâché, whereas on the right was a long thin form made up of innumerable twigs bound together. The form on the left hung on the wall, whereas the bundle of twigs was held in three latex slings, which were suspended from the ceiling. The two separate forms were tied together by a loosely sagging piece of string.

The year 1976 was an important one. John Davis not only consolidated his new use of materials such as twigs, branches, string, and papier mâché, he also developed a personal style which became clearly recognisable and identifiable.

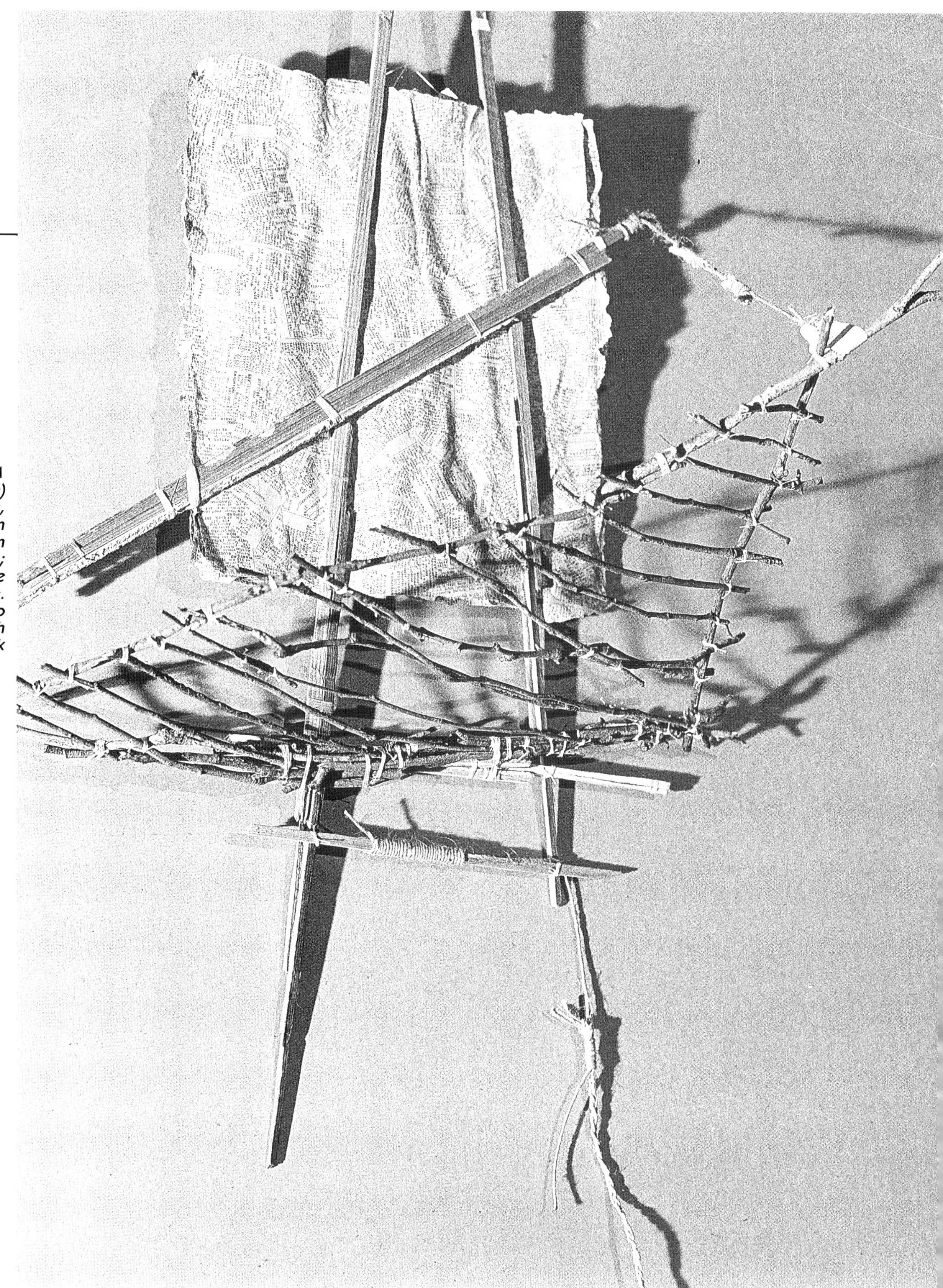

47 John Davis: Bicycle 1 (detail of left-hand side) (1976). Sawn timber, sticks, papier mâché, string, cotton thread and knitted string. In two parts: left, 77 x 51 x 2 cm; right, 24 x 62 x 3 cm; distance between two parts variable. (Donated by Marr Grounds to the Art Gallery of New South Wales.) Photograph by Mark Strizic.

His exhibition at Watters Gallery, Sydney, in 1977 showed the public a body of work in this new style. Yet as an exhibition it was not a totally cohesive whole, for it was an exhibition of individual parts, some hanging, some leaning against the wall, a few on the floor and one large work hanging from the ceiling. They were exploratory works from an artist who had evolved a new style and was enjoying a sense of discovery.

Some works were a direct result of considered development — from the simple grid structure at the Ewing Gallery in 1975, to *Nomad* in 1976 and then *Journey II* in 1977. In fact, John Davis had used rigid grids of horizontal and vertical lines in many works of 1970–71, but the emphasis had been on geometric shapes and strict repetition of identical forms. *Journey II* also had a pattern of horizontal and vertical lines, but the structure and materials were organic — sticks and string with some small quantities of latex, paper and underfelt. The horizontals were never quite horizontal, the verticals never really straight, the rectangles all of differing sizes, the right angles approximate. It looked as though it had grown casually, spasmodically, without ever really coming to a final point of completion.

Hanging by string from fifteen points along the top edge, *Journey II* hung as a delicate screen from the ceiling. It stirred memories of sights from plane windows: views of fields in irregular rectangles, the regular plan of a surveyor thwarted by the vagaries of nature, fence lines forced to alter because of outcrops of rocks, small fields intensely cultivated in rich land, large paddocks lying fallow. *Journey II* was like a sensitive drawing. The string was the basic line, thickened here and there, given emphasis in some parts by the addition of sticks and twigs.

The writer, Patrick White, was most impressed by *Journey II*, which he purchased and later donated to the Art Gallery of New South Wales.

A few years later, in 1981, the Art Gallery of New South Wales organised an exhibition entitled 'Patrick White's Choice', which included *Journey II*. When interviewed concerning his choice of works in the show, Patrick White gave his own personal reaction to the fragile work. '. . . John Davis in his *Journey II* (1977) assembles the twigs and silences of the Australian bush as we know it, along with the smells and cobwebs of old barns and humble goatyards.'[3]

One can never judge the success of a work of art by the ease with which the spectator can come to the same conclusion as the artist himself. Each human being approaches a work of art from a personal point of view, based on previous experiences, ideas, prejudices, knowledge — or lack of knowledge. It is fascinating that John Davis has never referred to the smells of the farmyard, as Patrick White does, but sees the work quite differently.

'*Journey II* reads like a road map with areas of interest at the intersections. Some "roads" are major, some merely wandering tracks. The lines define the space within the work and the entire piece is engulfed in the space within the room.'[4]

A number of works were presented at Watters Gallery almost as though they were museum specimens in shallow wooden boxes, displayed behind transparent acrylic, or laid out on a table. *Collection A Collection B* consisted of two groups of apparently identical objects: three real rocks and a small branch, with a label; three paper casts from the actual rocks and a facsimile of the real branch, made from matches tied together and covered in papier mâché, plus a typed label. All of the items were attached to a white display board, surrounded by a simple pinewood frame, protected by transparent acrylic and hung on the wall. The commonplace objects took on an air of authority. They became rare and worthy of preservation and display.

▶ *48 John Davis:* Table, Journey 1, Kite. *All one work, though produced in 1977, 1976 and 1976 respectively. Each of three works contain some materials in common — twigs or sawn timber, papier mâché, cotton thread — and in addition, canvas, latex, knitted string, pencil marks, all mounted on acrylic, inside wooden frame. Each of three sections 122 x 122 x 6 cm. (In collection of Chandler Coventry.) Photograph by the artist.*

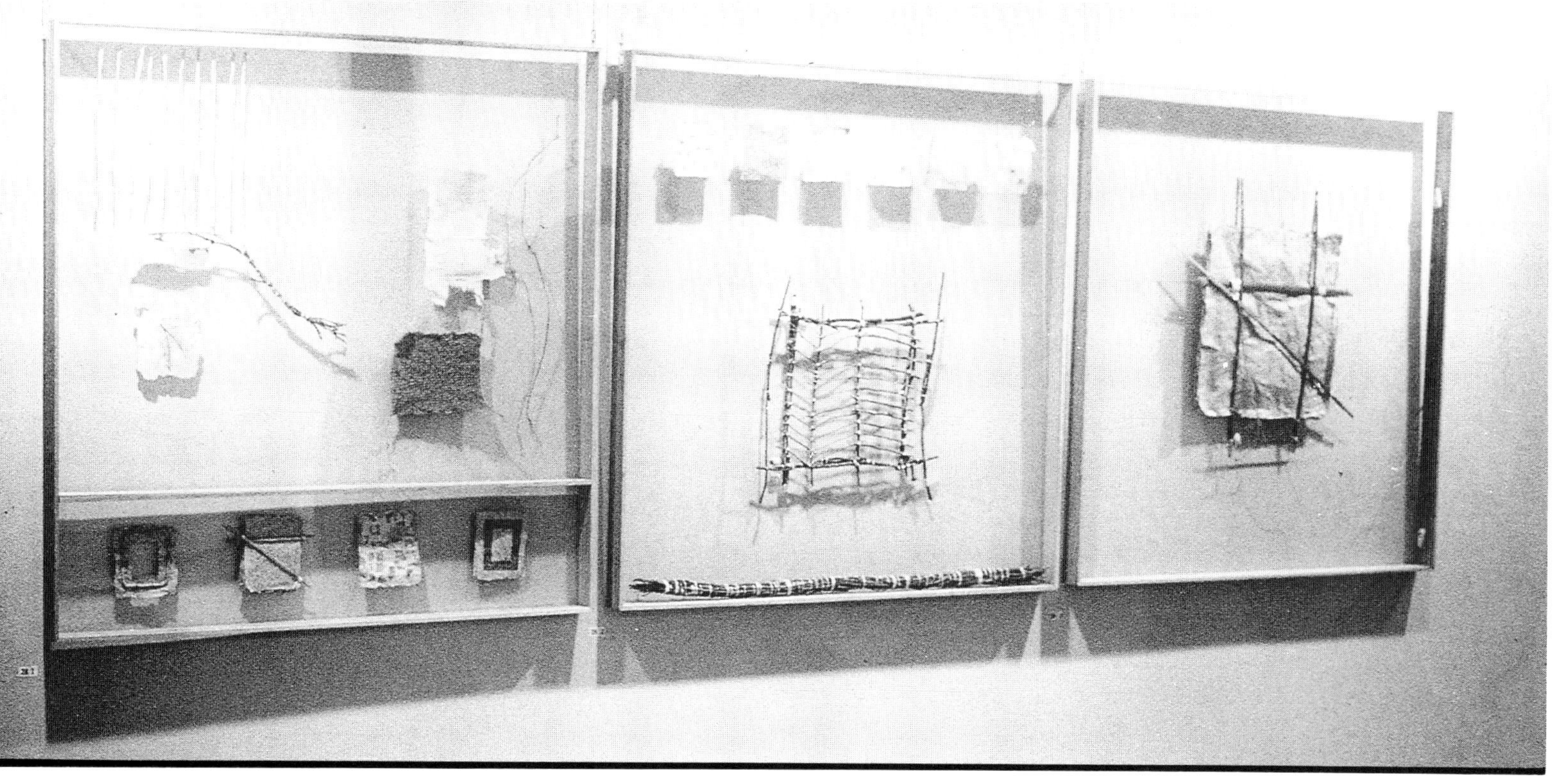

Table, *Journey I* and *Kite* (illus. 48) were displayed in a similar fashion, in three shallow wooden boxes with all of the objects attached to acrylic sheets. In spite of three separate titles they were actually one work, hung very close together, the three squares forming one long rectangle just inside the door of Watters Gallery. The repetition of the square shape was the compositional device that held all of the numerous parts together — often a series of squares were arranged in a line to give a long rectangle, echoing the basic arrangement of the three boxes on the wall. The display was orderly, as one would expect in a museum displaying fossils or shards of pottery from an archaeological dig. The basic layout was symmetrical in each box, but with sufficient subtle variations to break the monotony of complete symmetry.

Just as the museum spectator looks at the fossil remains or the pottery shards with a puzzled fascination, so one viewed *Table*, *Journey I*, *Kite*. The materials were simple and commonplace — twigs, papier mâché, string — though sometimes in odd combinations such as knitted string, or matches bound together and covered in papier mâché. But the total effect was not commonplace. One's mind was satisfied by the logical sense of order, but also puzzled by the objects. Why were they significant?

What made that square of papier mâché worth displaying? What did the pencil marks on the papier mâché mean? If the display had no scientific basis, what was the symbolic or mystical meaning? After consideration one is satisfied by the sense of order and enjoys a quiet delight in the fundamental beauty of simple objects made with a sense of dedication.

Another series of works exhibited a different attitude towards our continuing exploration of man's sense of order. *Wood/Stone*, *Lean-to*, *Sack* and *Marker* (called *Icon* in the catalogue) didn't display any of the easily distinguishable attributes of good design. They were casually put together, in a similar way that children would build a cubby house in a tree. They were built with whatever materials were available, with a sense of ingenuity, and a willingness to improvise. They were not major works in themselves but were evidence of a new attitude, which was to be developed very successfully by John Davis in later exhibitions in New Delhi, Venice and subsequent shows in Australia.

The Sydney critic, Nancy Borlase, reviewed the 1977 Watters exhibition very favourably, listing it as 'one of the most satisfying exhibitions of the year'. Her review raises a considerable number of interesting points such as Davis's quiet, restrained

49 John Davis: Exchange works from Installation and Exchange Work No 3 (1978). Twigs, papier mâché and some pigment. These ten works were shown at Act One, Canberra, 4–12 November 1978 and were exchanged for a variety of goods and services. Photographer not known.

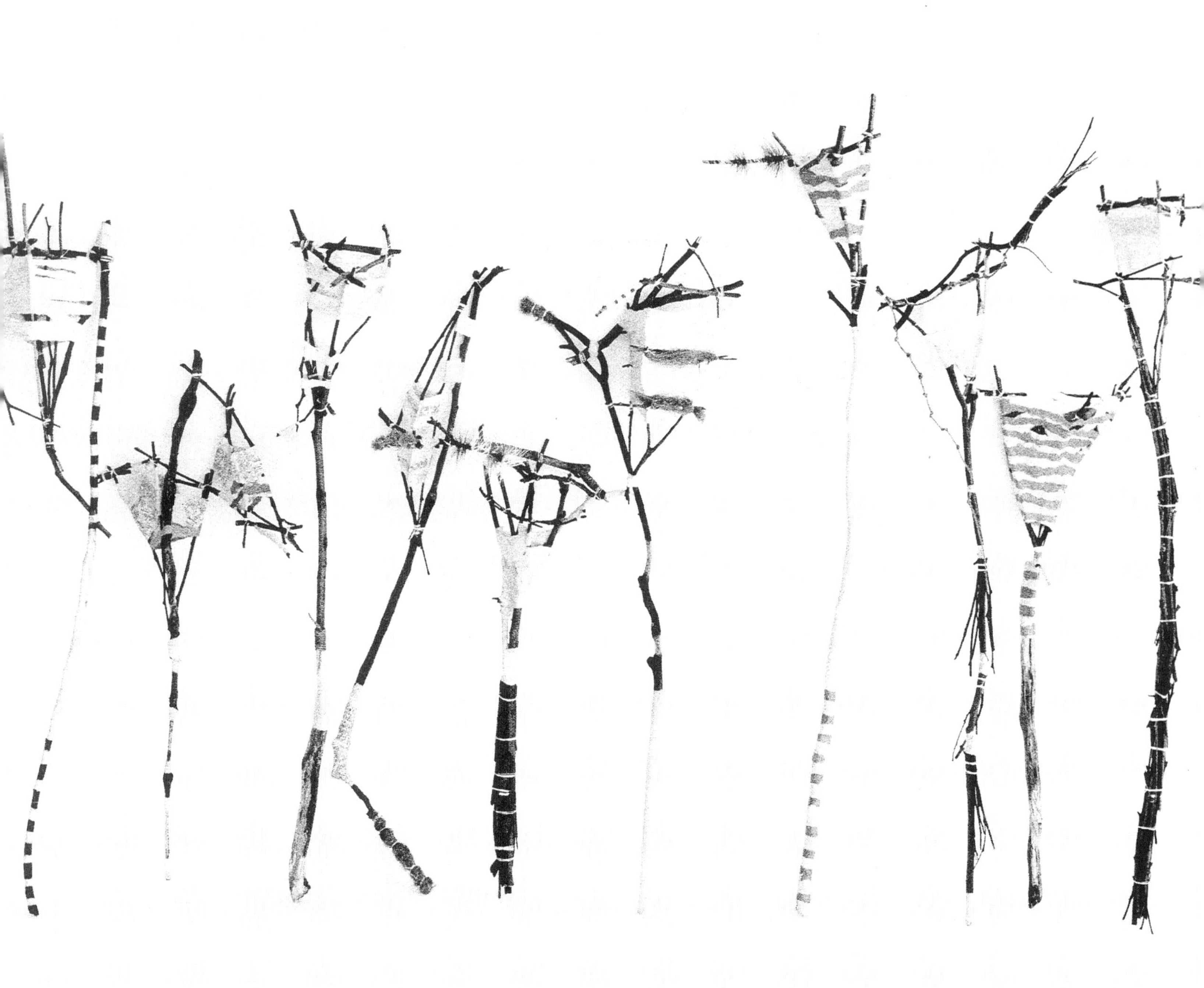

romanticism, his links with the art and ritual of primitive tribal societies, his patient craftsmanship.

■ ... *John Davis works with her [nature] in harmonious, pliant accord, in one of the most satisfying exhibitions of the year.*

One of a new breed of neo-romantic, ecology-conscious artists, Davis obviously finds fulfilment in emulating the ritualised, communal, art-in-life activities of tribal, primitive societies.

He teaches at Prahran College of Advanced Education and lives in suburban Hampton, which rather belies the persistent impression, in his exhibits, of a man remote from all contact with urban living, an eccentric, perhaps, content to while away his time working with natural fibres, binding twigs, tying knots, balancing stones in slings, making small ceremonial exchange offerings, with infinite fastidiousness, and fabricating kites and icons from the detritus of Western civilisation.[5]

Another innovative aspect of the 1977 exhibition at Watters were the *Exchange Works*, twenty-two in number, hanging in an irregular line on the wall at the far end of the gallery. They were not for sale but could be swapped. It was up to each person to decide upon a suitable offer, which John Davis could either accept or reject, before completing the exchange. The idea had grown out of discussions with students in a 'Post-Object Art Unit', a class that John took at Prahran CAE in 1976. The thought had a number of interesting components for the exchange process circumvented the commercial galleries and enabled artist and collector to form a direct and personal relationship, and since neither party exchanged money it was a return to simple barter. John and the students sent exchange works to the heads of sculpture departments at a number of tertiary art schools in Melbourne: Royal Melbourne Institute of Technology, Preston Institute of Technology, Melbourne State College, Victorian College of the Arts, and Gippsland Insti-

tute of Advanced Education. Only one tertiary institution accepted the gesture and sent works back. Paul Hayes, then a student at Melbourne State College, returned small works incorporating mouse traps. John Davis had more luck at Watters Gallery. All of the twenty-four works were swapped. The exchangees offered everything from expertise in the stock market to other works of art (from Geoff Proud and Alun Leach Jones), to a necklace of paper clips and a garden rake!

The Watters Gallery exhibition of 1977 proved to be very successful. A number of important works were purchased and went into major collections. *Journey II* was purchased by Patrick White and donated to the Art Gallery of New South Wales; *Table*, *Journey I* and *Kite* (actually regarded as one work) were purchased by Chandler Coventry; *Bicycle II*[6] was acquired for the Australian National Gallery, Canberra, and *Marker* went to Alun Leach Jones.

The timing was propitious. The exhibition, the nature of the work, the comments of critics, the sales to important institutions, were all noted amongst artists, gallery directors, curators at State Galleries and members of the Visual Arts Board. These factors all helped to make the following year, 1978, highly significant in John Davis's career.

■ NOTES

[1] Patrick McCaughey was Professor of Visual Arts at Monash University 1974–81.
[2] John Davis, letter to Frank Watters, 16 June 1976.
[3] Patrick White, quoted by Janet Hawley in 'Art Patrick White Admires', *Age*, 22 December 1981.
[4] John Davis, 'Some Brief Notes on Issues Which I Think are Raised in My Art', written in answer to questions from Kimio Akiyama, Editorial Department, *SOKA Ikebana Ohara*, November 1982.
[5] Nancy Borlase, 'Two Aspects of Nature', *Sydney Morning Herald*, 23 July 1977.
[6] There is some confusion over numbering. The 1977 Watters Gallery exhibition catalogue lists *Bicycle I*, but *Bicycle I* was actually shown at the Watters Gallery November–December 1976, purchased by Marr Grounds and donated to the Art Gallery of New South Wales. Therefore the work of the 1977 exhibition has been listed as *Bicycle II*.

 1974–77
DOCUMENTATION, PHOTOGRAPHY, VIDEO

The interest in documentation, which became evident in Australia in the late 1960s and early 1970s, was a wonderful development for future art historians, who will have material on many ephemeral works which would otherwise have disappeared for all time, but there are restrictions. The video or still photograph of the installation, event or performance can be compared with a film of an opera or photograph of a ballet dancer. Only a part is recorded. The totality of a three-dimensional structure, the relationship to the environment, the lapse of time, mood, atmosphere, space and scale are all impossible to record adequately.

Sometimes documentation means no more than the artist taking photographs of his work, as evidence that he had actually made a particular object — as with the records John Davis made of his *Grass Process Works* at John Reed's property 'Heide' in 1971. At other times the photographic documentation almost surplanted the actual object or performance, as with the records of Stelarc's many suspension events (illus. 50). Most of his earlier events were witnessed by only a small group of people, a few friends and assistants, whereas the detailed, photographic records have been exhibited and published world-wide. Sometimes artists have taken the current fashion for photographic documentation too seriously. To merely record the object is apparently a guarantee of its immortality — it is recorded for all time. No doubt posterity will ultimately decide what is immortal.

The Mildura Triennial Exhibitions of Sculpture have been a mirror of the various fashions, interests and developments in contemporary sculpture in Australia. The 1970 exhibition had only one artist showing examples of documentation; a black and white photograph entitled 'Package' and 'Three signed photographs and Collage of Little Bay', all by the visiting artist Christo. The 1973 exhibition had six photographs by the English sculptor,

George Hostler, but by 1975 nine artists included photographs, maps or video tapes. Photographs and video were part of *Place*, shown by John Davis at Mildura in 1975. For the 1978 exhibition he showed black and white photographs of his *Solar Piece, You Yangs* instead of an actual sculpture or installation.

In 1977, John Davis visited the You Yangs with two students from Prahran College — George Christofakis and Shawn Murphy — specifically to make an installation in the rocky, barren hills. As the Mildura exhibition of 1978 coincided with John's visit to India and 'Survey I — John Davis' at the National Gallery of Victoria, the documentation of *Solar Piece* showed current work when lack of time made it impossible to produce a sculptural work. The one large photograph was accompanied by typed explanatory notes.

By 1981 the catalogue of 'The Australian Sculptural Triennial', held in Melbourne and organised by Tom McCullough, the ex-Director of the Mildura Arts Centre, had a special section 'Documentation/Media/Technology'. Nevertheless, changes had occurred. Over the years video became more popular than still photography and by 1981 'Technology' (a wide, all-embracing term) was the section with the most exhibits. 'Technology' appeared to cover cassette tapes, video, synthesiser, solar cells, holograms, amplifiers, speakers, oscillators, neon tubes and so on.

During 1971 John Davis first developed an interest in documenting his process works, so when he held his first exhibition in Sydney at Watters Gallery in May–June of 1971, he included a group of eleven black and white photographs. The invitation to the exhibition showed a detail of plastic sheeting, with grass coming through circular holes. The concept was simple, the materials commonplace and the result may have been no more than mildly intriguing, except that the artist introduced a note of surrealist whimsy. What appeared to be

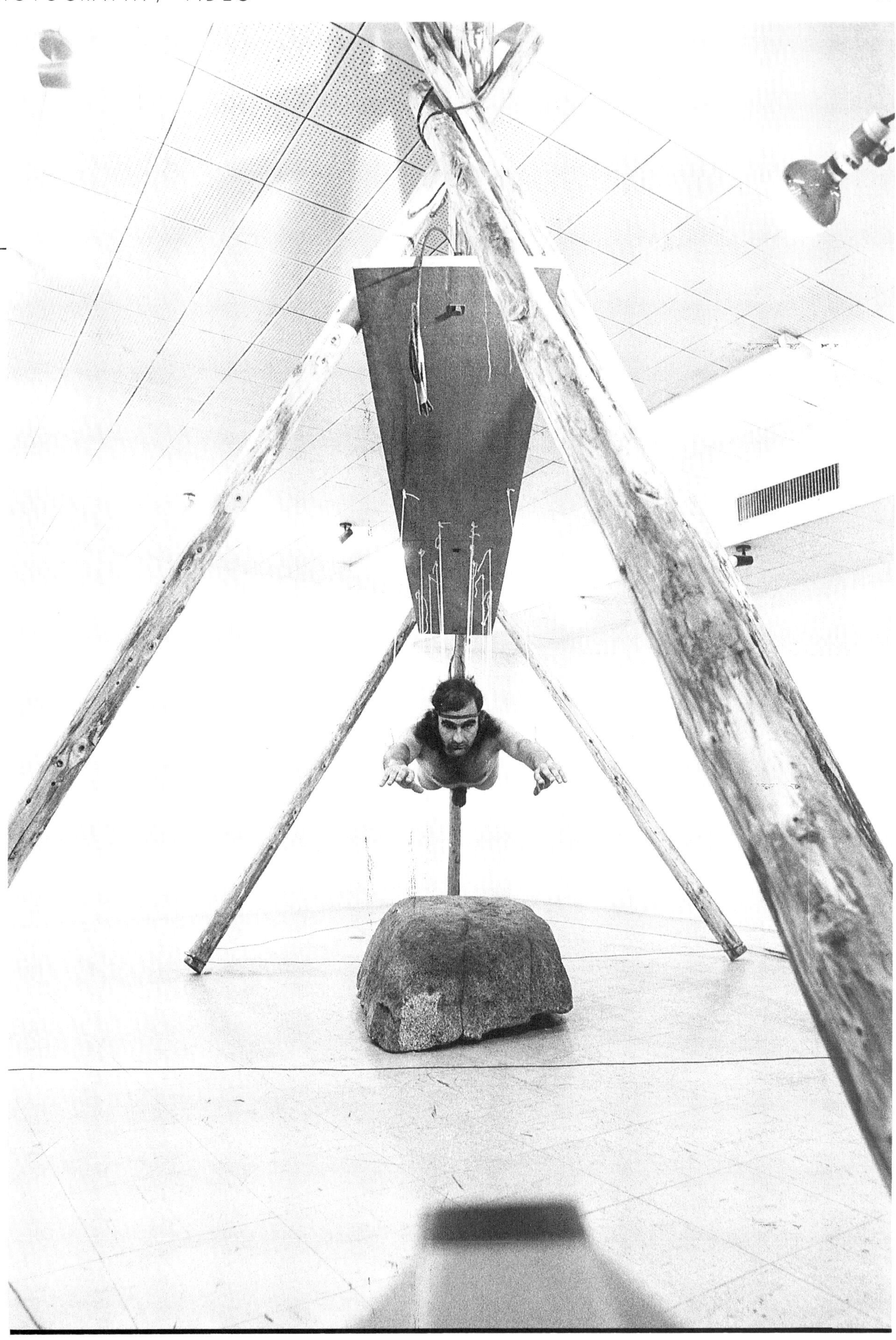

50 Stelarc: Event for Stretched Skin, *16 May 1976, Maki Gallery, Tokyo, Japan. 'The body was suspended over a 1 ton rock by the insertion of 18 hooks into the skin. The insertion took 1½ hours. The actual suspension time was 15 minutes. A laser beam bisected the space between the body and the rock. All elements were aligned east-west'. (As described on postcard of the event printed and distributed by Stelarc.) Photograph by Shigeo Anzai.*

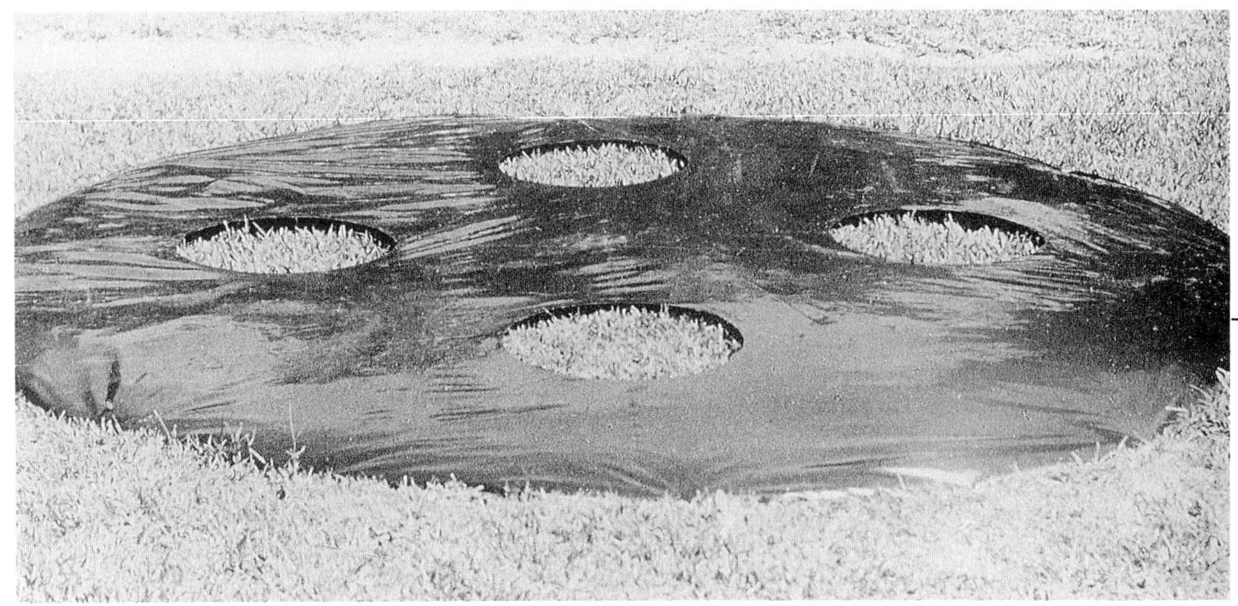

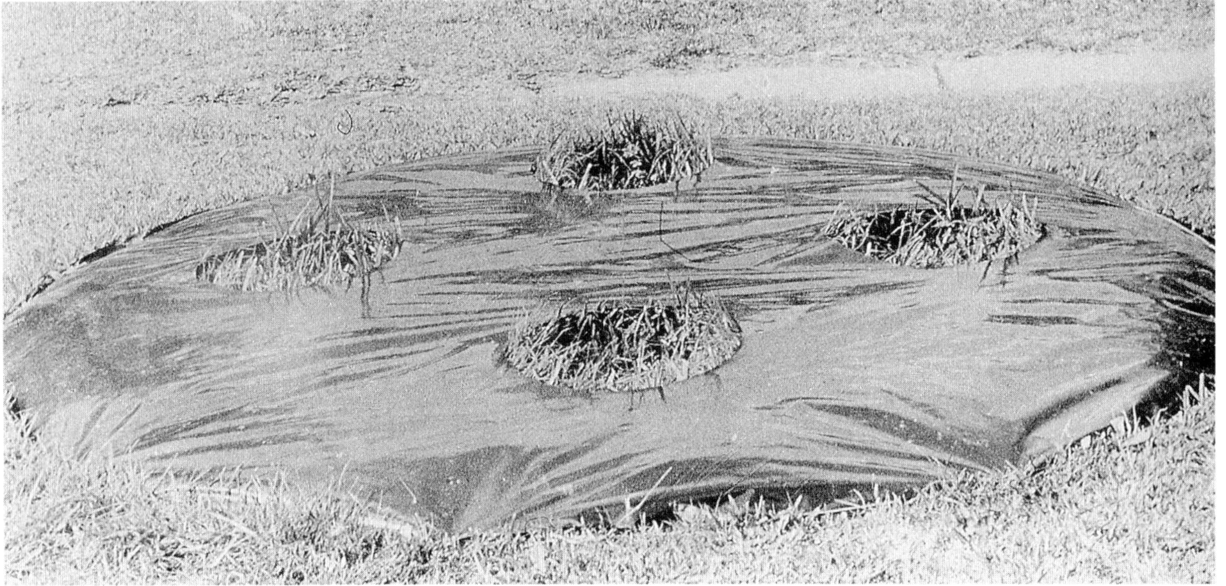

◀
51 John Davis: Photographs 2, 3 and 4 from set of 11 photographs in 'Grass Process Work — Part 1' (1971). (2) Black polythene sheeting, 1.8 m in diameter, holes 22.8 cm in diameter, fixed to grass surface by wire circle and pegs. (3) Grass develops and rises through holes. Pressure of growth causes polythene to dome upwards. (4) Polythene disc removed, covered grass bleached yellow, uncovered grass long and green. Process evolved at the home of the artist between 13 March and 2 May 1971. Photographs by the artist.

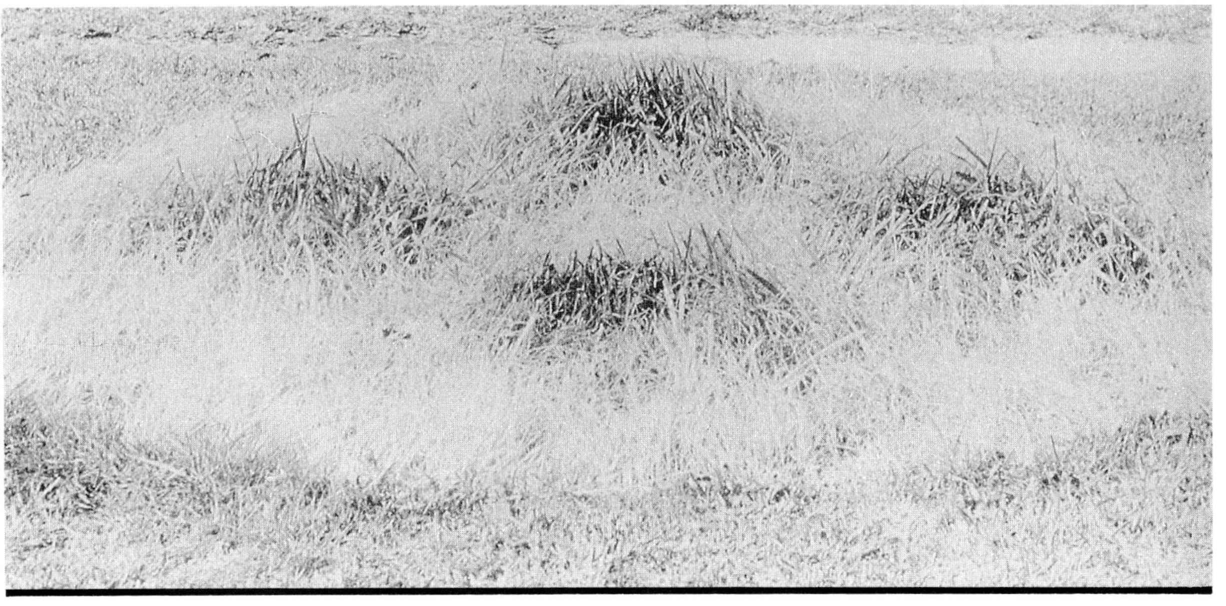

a serious investigation of a currently fashionable form of process art became amusing and satirical.

A typed sheet attached to the photographs gave a simple explanation:

■ *A process which evolved at the home of the artist between 13th March, 1971 and 2nd May, 1971.*

1. Grass selected for site of process (illus. 51 a b c):

2. Black polythene sheeting, 6 feet in diameter, holes 9 inches in diameter, fixed to grass surface by wire circle and pegs.

3. Grass develops and rises through holes. Pressure of growth causes polythene to dome.

4. Polythene disk removed. Covered grass bleached yellow, uncovered grass long and green.

Suggested sites for process with good spectator viewing potential.

5. Melbourne Cricket Ground, from the Members' stand.

6. Botanical Gardens, Melbourne.

7. The Beach, Hampton.

8. Near Woodend, Calder Highway, Victoria.

9. The Shrine of Remembrance, Melbourne.

10. Near Hanging Rock, Victoria.

11. The Eighteenth Hole East, Royal Melbourne Golf Club.

Artist/Photographer: JOHN DAVIS.

During his absence overseas in 1972, a one man exhibition was held at Gallery 1 Eleven, in Brisbane, which included three examples of documentation: 'John Reed's Process' (illus. 20), 'Black Disc Process' and 'Boxed Process'. Similar black and white photographs were shown at Geelong Art Gallery, in the stimulating 'Victorian Contemporary Sculpture Exhibition', organised by Katrina Rumley. Patrick McCaughey found it an exciting exhibition and gave it a long review in the *Age*,[1] although he did not specifically mention the only example of documentation.

Photographic documentation seemed the perfect solution for John Davis while he was living temporarily in New York in 1972. With no studio facilities, yet with a need to make something, he gathered a few cardboard cylinders and experimented with them, using his camera to record *Drawing — New York* and *Greene Street Piece* (illus. 22, 23).

During 1973 John made photographic records of his *Tree Piece* and *Unrolled*, at the Mildura 'Sculpturscape', and of an installation in St Paul's Cathedral with Kevin Mortensen. These works were documented, as any commercial photographer might do the job; the objects were shown at their best or most characteristic positions.

However, works of 1974, such as 'Inching' (illus. 52) and 'A Tearing Work' displayed a basically different attitude. These were not merely records of ephemeral works, they were the works themselves. 'Inching' was a series of sixteen black and white photographs which showed the artist's fingers measuring the approximate distance of an inch. It was shown at Pinacotheca Gallery in 1974 and purchased by Dr Donald Brook for the Visual Arts Study Collection, Flinders University (now Flinders University Art Museum).

'A Tearing Work' was the first black and white video made by John Davis. It was a logical development of his previous interest in processes, his new interest in cheap material such as newspaper, and his basic pleasure of working with materials. Personally, I found 'A Tearing Work' very boring visually. The image merely shows a pair of hands at work on the table top, methodically tearing up newspaper. Even the newspaper is anonymous, appearing to be the continuous grey columns of the *Age* classified advertisements, without the joy of recognition of a banner headline or a sensational photograph. The hands work steadily, at the same pace throughout the 27 minutes of the video, relentlessly tearing newspaper and accumulating a neat pile of torn up paper. After 27 minutes of tear-

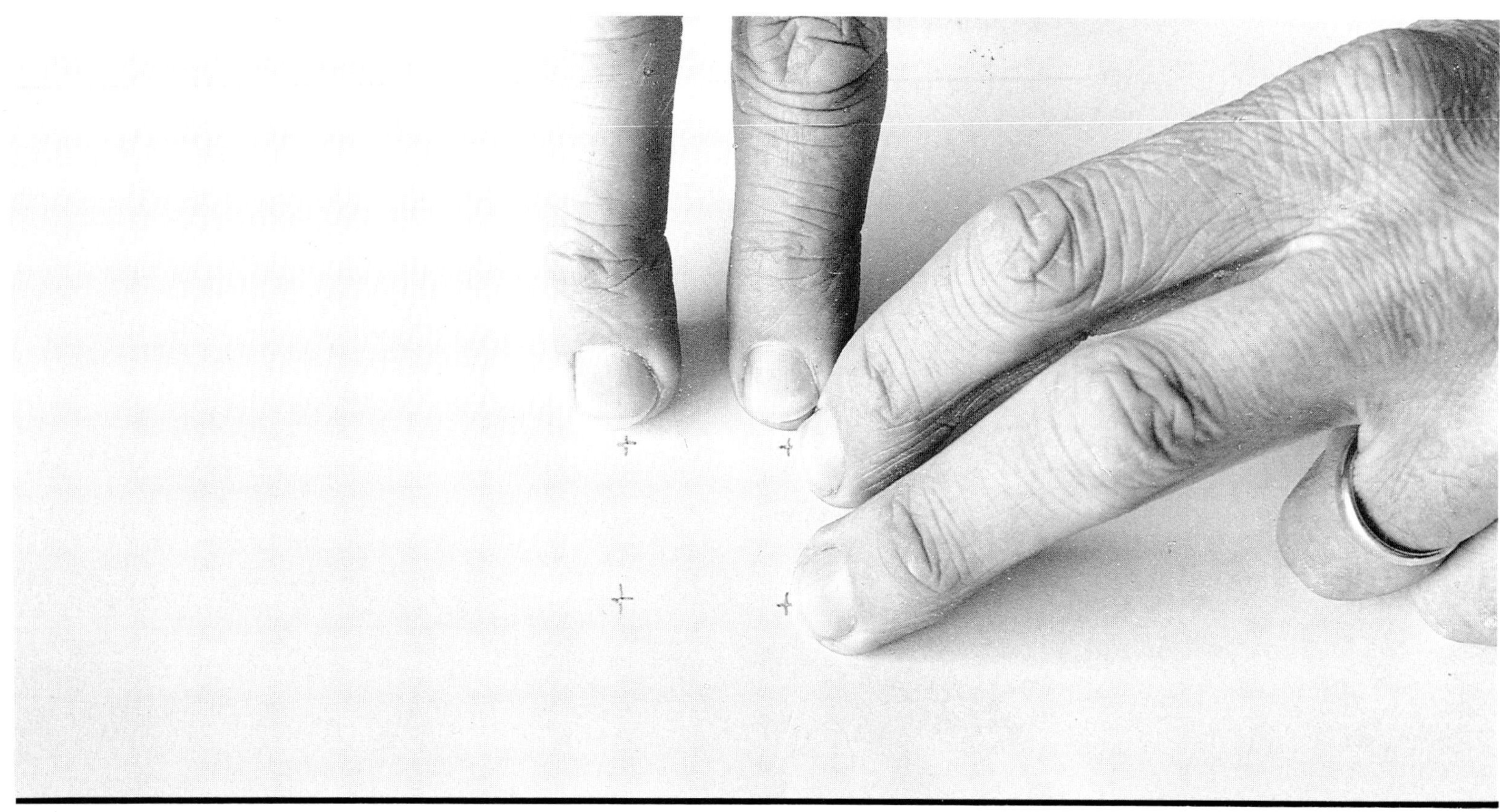

ing this way then that, of tearing large and tearing small, John Davis comes to the final sheet of newspaper. In the last few seconds of the video he shows a human nervousness and uncertainty — he folds his arms, unfolds them, his face almost comes into view (accidentally I am sure), he puts his hand to his chin, removes it — and seems at a loss, not knowing what to do after half an hour of repetitious activity.

Intellectually the work was thin. Visually it was boring. Yet boredom was an audience reaction that he seemed to welcome at the time, as though it proved that the work had real value, simply because the average person could not understand it.

In August 1974, at a conference of art and craft teachers at La Trobe University, I jointly planned an interview with John Davis, in which we showed a great number of slides of his work, slides of the environments in which he had lived and worked, and finally, simultaneously, two silent black and white videos. One video was 'A Tearing Work' and the other was a video by Joan Grounds entitled 'Seventh Burning', which had been shown at Mildura in 1973. The latter video was basically concerned with the burning of a sculptural structure

that Joan Grounds had built of papier mâché on the beach in New South Wales.

The audience reaction was predictable. At first they watched attentively and appreciatively, but as the videos went on and on, they became more and more restless. First there was intermittent coughing, then conversation began. One gentleman in a front row ostentatiously opened his newspaper and tried to read in the darkened lecture theatre. John was pleased with the result, as he felt he had really stirred and upset the audience. Certainly discussion raged endlessly during the lunchtime break.

This attitude of deliberate alienation of the spectactor was essentially out of character for John and it was only a few years later that he was talking of the democratisation of art, and having exchange pieces in his exhibitions, which were not for sale and could only be exchanged. Alienation of the audience was often carried to an extreme by performance artists, such as Mike Parr, who provoked his audiences by acts of masochism inflicted upon his own flesh, or publicly exhibited photographs of himself vomiting. As Mary Eagle wrote: 'Through the 1960s and '70s European performance art was overwhelmingly about bodies, mostly nude, usually

52 John Davis: 'Inching' (1974). This is one of sixteen black and white photographs, each 18 x 28 cm. (Flinders University Art Museum.) Photographer not known.

rude, and involving stress both for artists and audience'.[2] Later in the same article, she points out that boredom, as a calculated audience reaction, was still being deliberately used by artists in 1981.

One tries to analyse the significance of 'boredom' as an ingredient in a work of art. How can boredom be deliberately planned, when audience or spectator boredom in the past would have brought about the death of a play, musical composition or visual work of art? Alienation of an audience appears to be both an act of arrogance and élitism. Arrogant in that the basic attitude of the artist who belittles the audience, in a sense, wastes their time. Élitist, in that the artist knows what he is doing and presumes that a small group of fellow artists, gallery directors and art critics also know what is happening — and they all know that the audience will be irritated and frustrated.

Because of the ease with which video can be made, and as a deliberate reaction against the sophistication of Hollywood films and TV commercials, videos are often technically poor, the equivalent of home movies. It seems very difficult to use video with great simplicity, when we have all learned to cope with the tremendous visual speed and extraordinary technical sophistication of TV commercials.

John Davis was to make two more black and white videos, 'Plaiting' in 1975 and 'Passage' in 1976. In 'Plaiting' the viewer can only see his waist and hands, with anonymous hands engaged in the apparently endless task of plaiting string. As he moved back, plaiting continuously, the camera followed, so the hands were always the same distance away from the camera. Therefore, there was little suggestion of depth, distance or space, as the image on the screen was roughly similar for 45 minutes viewing time. Visually the images were fairly poor quality — a general, lack-lustre grey.

The third (and last) video made by John Davis

in 1976 had a long title: 'Passage. Part One. Scan. The You Yangs'. It was not made in the rocky, mountainous part of the You Yangs, but in the adjoining flat land, in the visually boring landscape that links Melbourne and Geelong. Travelling fast on the dual highway one sees little of the actual landscape, as large banks of trees have been planted beside the road. But move off the highway and a flat, dry, windswept landscape is revealed.

'Passage' opens with a view of flat land without any significant features. After a few seconds a truck is seen going along a distant road — at the time the spectator doesn't realise that he has just seen all of the action for the entire 23 minutes! The truck's appearance was probably sheer accident, and is totally irrelevant to the content of 'Passage'. The viewer becomes aware of a white rectangle, lying on the ground — is it a sheet of hardboard or a sheet of corrugated iron painted white? The next 23 minutes are occupied with varying views of the flat land, always with the white rectangle in sight. The camera moves slowly to left or right, the lens zooms imperceptibly on the white rectangle. The ubiquitous white rectangle is moved unseen to new sites and the process continues. About half way through the video one hears the sound of wind blowing on the microphone. After 23 minutes, 'Passage' ends abruptly.

'Passage. Part One. Scan. The You Yangs' may have appeared slight, or even boring to the spectator, yet John Davis had given considerable thought and planning to the making of the video. His notes reveal an intellectual approach which endeavoured to explore a wide range of possibilities, from arbitrary to obvious to obscure, from psychological to formalist (as he listed in his notes). Perhaps there were two main faults — he attempted too much and he relied on his intellect. In later years John Davis learned to know himself, his abilities and limitations. In 'Passage' we have a

▼
53 John Davis: Place included 'Plaiting', which was shown on a 45 minute video and also in ten black and white photographs of John Davis tying nine lengths of plaited string together. Photographed at Pinacotheca in 1975. Photographs by Susan Vaughan, video photographer not known.

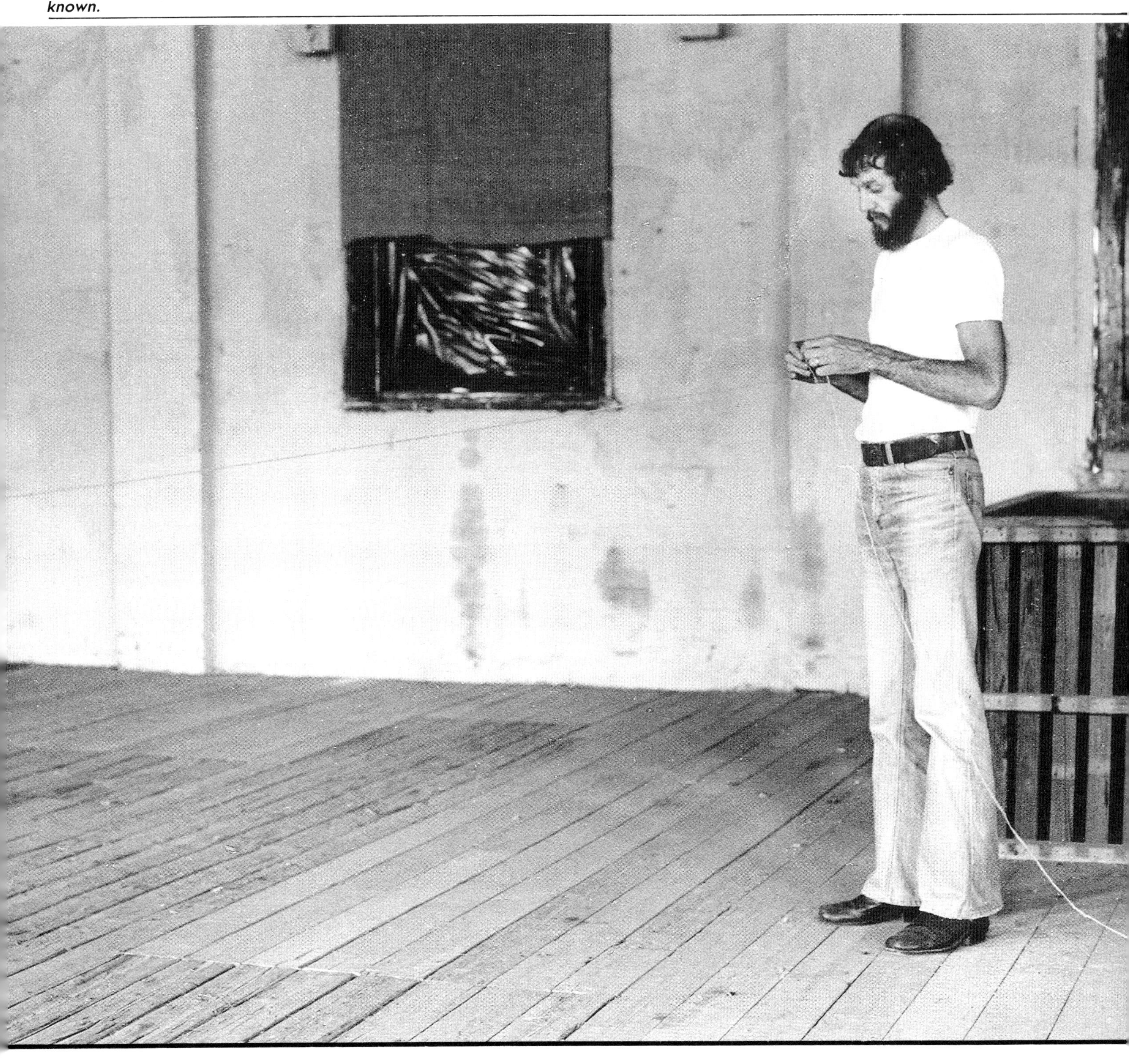

work which is within the concerns of the period, but outside the character of the artist.

Writing in 1983, Geoffrey Legge saw the situation somewhat differently. He did not think that John Davis was any less cerebral in his mature works than he was in 1976, but there was less cerebral control.

■ *I don't think John Davis is less cerebral than he used to be, but now he lets his inspiration have wider scope: it informs his conscious mind of all sorts of intricacies of life. The more open you allow your work to be the more you discover; the greater your cerebral control the less the result.*[3]

The video was shown at the Experimental Art Foundation in Adelaide, in May 1976, as part of an exhibition entitled 'Australian Post Object Art'. For this occasion the artist prepared pages of typed notes which revealed his thoughts — in fact the notes state the case much more clearly than does the video itself. Twenty possibilities are listed:

■   *Part One.*

SCAN.

A formalist work composed of sixty-two views of an area east of the You Yangs, Victoria, and in which the work —

1. (i) *Includes an element of chance in the placement of the artificial form, and in the situation of the natural phenomenon within the format presented.*

   (ii) *Includes a determined structure in that the site was consciously selected for the placement of the natural phenomenon.*

2. (i) *Presents space as effectively measured by the arbitrary distribution of natural phenomena in the landscape.*

   (ii) *Presents space as controlled by the juxtaposition of the artificial element and the natural phenomena.*

3. (i) *Established direction by the natural contours of the landscape and the growth development of the natural phenomena.*

   (ii) *Established direction by emphasis through a procedure of sequential placement of the artificial element.*

4. (i) *Implies a sense of horizontal expansion at the edge of the viewing frame.*

   (ii) *May consciously restrict a sense of evenly distributed horizontality by the intrusion of the artificial element moving along that edge of the viewing frame.*

5. (i) *Presents a visual of compressed time through conscious camera technique on each 'page' of the piece.*

   (ii) *Presents an indication of extended time through arbitrary natural forces on each 'page' of the piece.*

6. (i) *Indicates the artificial element may be observed as 'posed' subject for the camera.*

   (ii) *Indicates the artificial element may be regarded as observer of the 'posed' camera.*

7. (i) *Sometimes includes an artificial element moving dynamically forward and back while the camera moves horizontally.*

   (ii) *Sometimes includes an artificial element remaining stable while the camera moves horizontally.*

8. (i) *Contains continuity established by the recurrence of the artificial element or constant.*

   (ii) *Contains continuity established by the introduction of natural phenomena over three 'pages', and sequentially relocated from right to left across the screen.*

9. (i) *Incorporates the flatness of the screen as opposed to the perspective, determined by the location of natural phenomena through the landscape space.*

   (ii) *Incorporates the flatness of the screen as opposed to the depth of space established by the positioning of the artificial element over a series of 'pages'.*

10. *(i) Presents a format of a series of 'pages', fragmenting the broad statement inherent in a continuous time span.*

(ii) Presents the piece as a series of 'pages', introducing anticipation as an integral part of the piece.

John Davis.
Experimental Art Foundation,
Adelaide, S.A.
May, 1976.

In addition John Davis prepared notes entitled 'Part Two. Time-Table', which included the spectator in the gallery watching the video of 'Passage'. This raised a series of five additional possibilities, listed in his notes. He had asked that photographs be taken in the gallery of visitors watching the video, but it seems that this was not done.

There was one common factor in 'A Tearing Work', 'Plaiting', 'Passage' and 'Place' (the latter which was shown at Mildura Sculpture Triennial, included a screening of 'Plaiting'): they all denied traditional aesthetics. The usual components of a film — such as plot, development, conclusion, the expected technical level of photography, with a range of tone from white to grey to black — were all ignored. In the same way, previously used techniques for gaining spectator interest, such as dramatic opening, contrast of visual images, and unexpected endings were also negated as the spectator was almost ignored.

In 1975 John Davis had an exhibition at the Contemporary Art Society Gallery in Adelaide which had the puzzling title 'Substance — cause — number — relation'.[4] The exhibition was not shown in Melbourne and only some black and white transparencies, used as an automatic slide show are still in existence. Stephanie Britton wrote a review which helps one to understand the artist's intention.

■ *'Substance — cause — number — relation' is the title of a show at the Contemporary Art Society.*

It is a series of observations of a more or less detached kind, about space and time.

The reason that it is not called 'towards a definition of space and time', which, in one sense, is what it is, is very simply because there is no such thing as a definition of space or time.

The selection of philosophical comment on this subject that the artist John Davis has collected and included in the exhibition makes this exceptionally clear.

Analysis
His title, rather, indicates an attempted analysis of the relationship between four different and inter-relating factors.

He takes four photographic prints of a street, alters each by drawing on it, and sets up a series of affirmations and contradictions.

He introduces a constant — a pole stuck into the ground — into a series of photographic landscapes, so that the pole, because it always appears in the same position in relation to the picture's edge, quickly reads as a symbol of stability against a randomly changing background.

He photographs a small log leaning against a series of closed art gallery doors — a constant of a classificatory type.

The cause is a matter of conjecture. Substance, number and relation are explained.

Contrast
But, in case one imagines one has discovered some sort of a key to the meaning of these works, Davis creeps up with four or five enigmatic objects whose contribution to matters of time and space is by no means explicit.[5]

Stephanie Britton refers to 'four photographic prints of a street', which would have been 'Greene Street Piece' (illus. 22, 23), originally photographed in New York in 1972 and worked on with pencil in

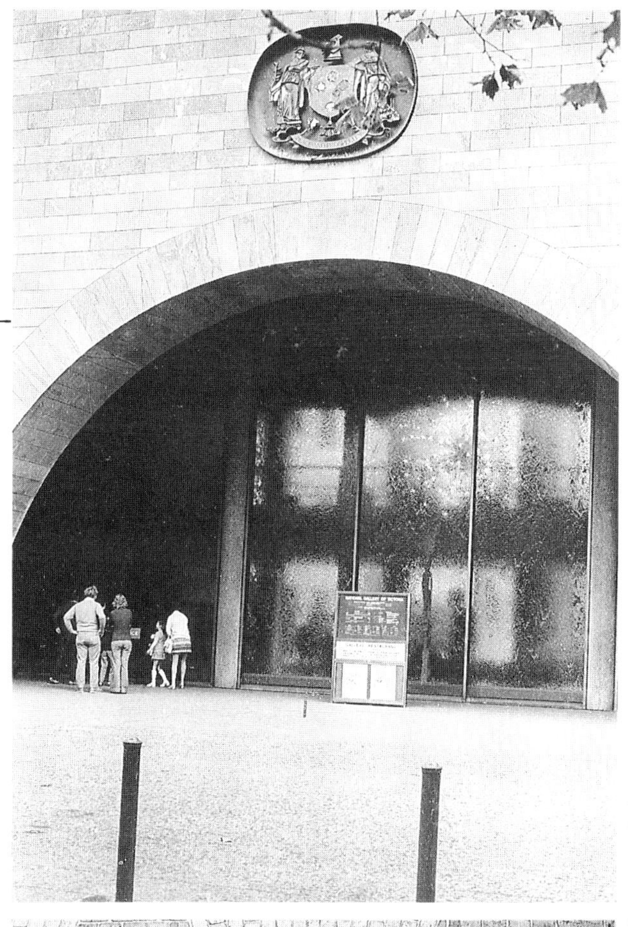

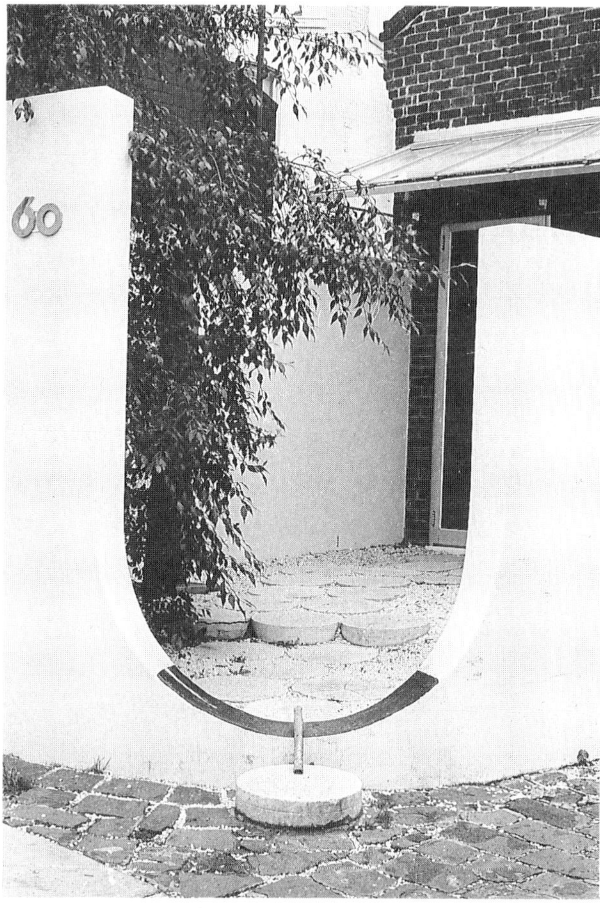

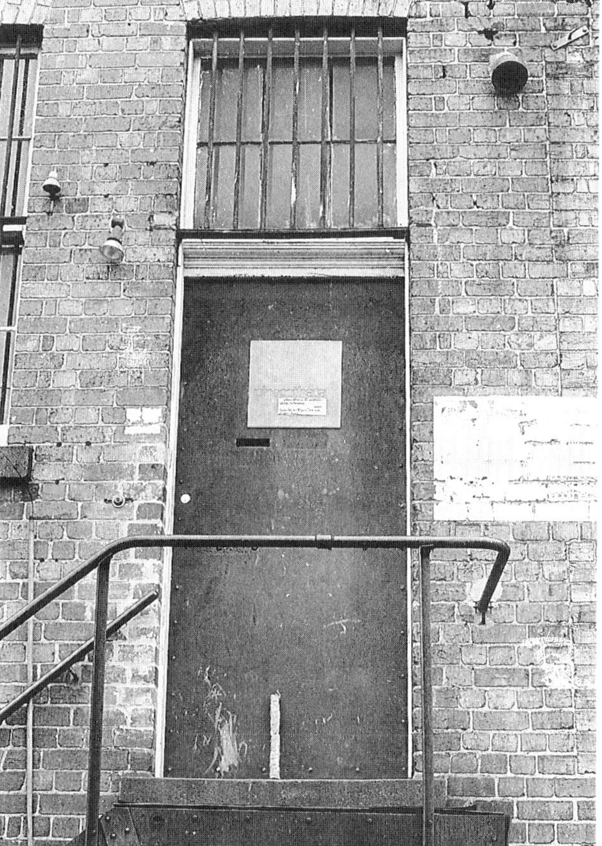

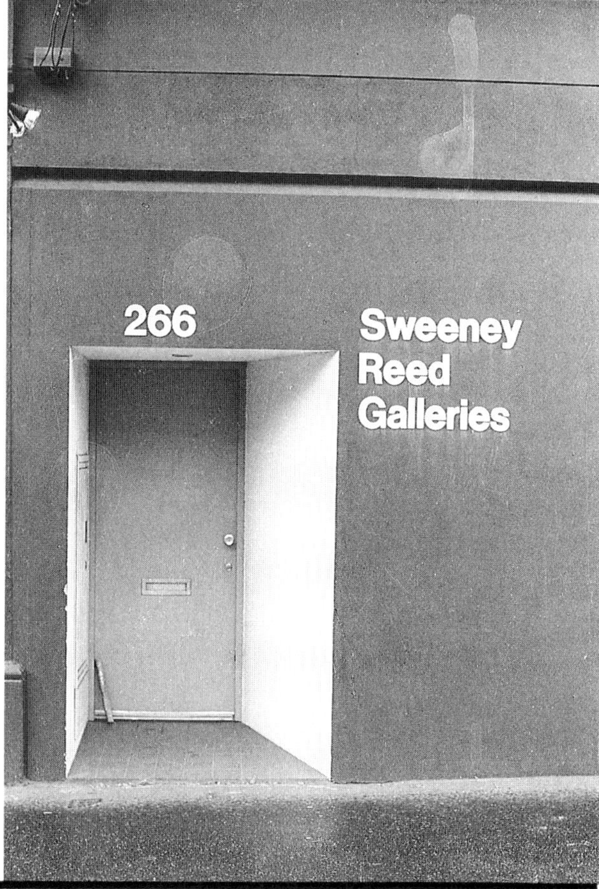

▶ *54 John Davis: 'The Artist's Dream' (1974). Fourteen ceramic cylinders placed outside fourteen galleries and one bronze cylinder outside National Gallery of Victoria. Fifteen black and white photographs taken by John Davis. Top left: National Gallery of Victoria; top right: Realities Gallery (when situated in Ross Street); lower left: Pinacotheca; lower right: Sweeney Reed Galleries.*

1973. As photographs they did not have much to do with the title of the exhibition in Adelaide, unless the contradictory perspective proved the ambiguity of 'substance'.

The 'pole stuck into the ground' refers to twelve of the eighty black and white slides, shown automatically and constantly in the exhibition. John Davis had a rough label on the two boxes of slides, which read 'Space Definition', which seems simply and immediately understandable compared with the titles that were screened for the various sections within the eighty slides. The slides gave a visual 'Space Definition', ranging from a series of views of the Cadbury Schweppes Building at St Kilda Junction, Melbourne, emphasising the bulk of the building and the surrounding space, to slides of empty suburban streets, views of flat, anonymous countryside (with 'pole stuck into the ground'), a series of slides showing groups of students defining three-dimensional forms by using their own bodies, a series of apparently irrelevant advertising signs in Melbourne, and finished with the series of slides showing one ceramic cylinder outside eleven art galleries in Melbourne. The latter was part of the humorous 'The Artist's Dream' (illus. 54 a b c d), which originally consisted of fifteen black and white photographs recording the fact that John Davis had exhibited in fifteen galleries in Melbourne concurrently.

In addition to the continuous screening of the eighty slides, Stephanie Britton refers to 'four or five enigmatic objects' which would have been some of the works from the Pinacotheca exhibition of the previous year, in which John Davis used a series of cylinders in various materials, combined with sheets of papier mâché, often displayed in boxes or canvas containers.

In retrospect it seems a somewhat confused exhibition, which was partly concerned with sculptural objects and partly to do with a conceptual atti-

tude towards art. As Stephanie Britton summed up in the last paragraph of her review: 'The contrast between over-simplistic observation and total enigma seems to me to contradict the apparent intention of the show, which is to describe inter-relating systems with some sort of internal logic.'[6]

But 'conceptual art' was of great interest to many artists at this time and the next year John Davis was invited to exhibit in an exhibition entitled 'Post Object Art: a Survey in Australia and New Zealand', which was gathered by Dr Donald Brook and Noel Sheridan and shown at the Experimental Art Foundation in Adelaide in May 1976. John used his video 'Passage. Part One. Scan. The You Yangs'. In the catalogue John succinctly expressed his ideas in this essentially conceptual work. As an ex-teacher of sculpture I found reading his ten points fascinating. I immediately tried to imagine how I would cope with such ideas if I was the sculptor, or how students would respond if given such problems to solve. The first point contrasted 'A determined structure' with 'An element of choice'. Point 6 contradicted 'A posed subject' with 'An introduced observer'. The ideas were intellectually stimulating, but the visual boredom of the video acted like a soporific, so that the spectator probably had difficulty getting past the visuals to the hidden ideas.

The ten points in the catalogue were:

1. A determined structure.
   An element of chance.

2. Space measured by arbitrary means.
   Space controlled by juxtaposition of elements.

3. Established direction by natural phenomena.
   Established direction by procedure.

4. Implies horizontal extension.
   Restricts horizontal extension.

5. Presents compressed time.
   Presents extended time.
6. A posed subject.
   An introduced observer.
7. Dynamic movement.
   Stability.
8. Continuity of repetition of placement.
   Continuity of recurrence.
9. Flatness of the screen.
   Development of perspective.
10. A series of separate 'pages'.
    An element of anticipation.[7]

Looking back one can view this play of ideas like a game of chess, an intellectual pursuit. The exploration of concepts had the great advantage of freeing sculptors from their previous restrictions and greatly widening the range of possibilities.

In spite of these radical tendencies, there was still a link with later sculpture of the 1980s. In the video John Davis broke down an art work into the processes of making — paper was torn ready for papier mâché, string was plaited ready for tying. In 'Passage' it was as though an unseen spectator walked around, viewing an unseen sculptural object, seeing it from every possible point of view, judging it in relation to innumerable possible positions within the environment. The connection with his earlier interest in process works is clear. The link with later sculptural constructions made from twigs and sticks tied with cotton and string, is less obvious. But the processes of tearing, plaiting, tying, applying papier mâché, and viewing the new object constantly from various points of view are all part of the present works. In the videos the process was the object of attention. In his mature structures the object is a result of the processes.

In a discussion with Vic Majzner I was interested in the points he raised relating materials, processes and intellectual concepts. Vic Majzner felt that the intellectual ideas grew from the business of working with materials — in fact he went further, suggesting that the development of intellectual ideas <u>after</u> physical contact with materials and processes may be a characteristic of Australian artists.

■ *The one continuity I've found in John, one of the things students always admired at both Prahran and Caulfield was a sense of pride in making. Whatever John did, be it carving or working in fibreglass, in fact whatever material he worked in, there was a sense of pride in the craft.*

Not only things being well made, but a sense of enjoyment in the process of making.

I have a hunch that often the sort of ideas that he deals with come from the process of working with the material, rather than from an idea as an isolated, precursor to the work. I think the intellectualising occurs through the process of making. In fact, the most conceptual pieces that John has made, like the things of space . . . or the torn bits of paper that he did videos of and so on — they're all very much to do with space, with the most conceptual ideas in a very tactile sense, a very real, touchable, tactile sense, and it's just a hunch that the intellectual contact came through the possibilities that he found in the direct touch sensation. I have a feeling that that is also something very Australian because I've found it with quite a number of artists in this country — where the intellectual ideas come through the process of realising the body contact with a particular material.[8]

Clement Greenberg once stated at a lecture that he had 'never met an artist who was not self-educated'. Perhaps Vic Majzner is wrong in making it an Australian trait: Greenberg was suggesting this intellectualisation occurred through the actual working process.

Most of the documentation by John Davis, whether photography or video, was to do with processes, or concepts of time and space. They were big issues, meant to be taken seriously, but occasionally he produced works that were humorous or even hinted at the satirical. The 'Grass Process Work — Part I' not only showed the process work in the fields at 'Heide', there were also additional photographs suggesting that a similar process could be applied to other sites — such as the Melbourne Cricket Ground.

His 'Greene Street Piece' proved that John Davis had exhibited in Greene Street, New York. 'The Artist's Dream'[9] of 1974 was an extension of this idea. John Davis exhibited his work in fifteen galleries in Melbourne all at the one time. They ranged from the most prestigious, such as Joseph Brown Galleries (then in Collins Street) or Realities in Toorak, to a popular commercial gallery like the Munster Arms, a traditional institution such as the Victorian Artists Society, and even included the time-honoured National Gallery of Victoria. John simply placed a ceramic cylinder outside the particular gallery (with a bronze cylinder for the National Gallery of Victoria) then photographed it, recording the fact that he had exhibited at that gallery. The fifteen photographs were shown at Pinacotheca where they were for sale at $1 each. Maybe the humour was missed by the serious-minded cognoscenti of Pinacotheca for only one was sold — to sculptor Noel Hutchison.

■ NOTES

1 Patrick McCaughey, 'Sculptors Given Full Reign', *Age*, 16 September 1972.
2 Mary Eagle, 'The Failings of Public Performance', *Age*, 11 March 1981.
3 Geoffrey Legge, letter to the author, 16 March 1983.
4 Contemporary Art Society Gallery, Adelaide, 14 September–2 October 1975.
5 Stephanie Britton, 'In Search of a Key to Time and Space', *News*, 18 September 1975.
6 Ibid.
7 John Davis, *Post Object Art: A Survey of Australia and New Zealand*, Experimental Art Foundation, Adelaide, May 1976.
8 Vic Majzner, interview with author, 31 August 1982.
9 Title given by John Davis in 1983, which may or may not be the same as the title in the exhibition at Pinacotheca in 1974.

Chapter 8

THE 1960s AND 1970s
POLITICAL ACTIVITY

The situation in the mid-1950s for young Victorians interested in a career in the visual arts was difficult. A full-time course of training at the Royal Melbourne Institute of Technology Art School, the National Gallery Art School, or other art schools in the country, was a big financial drain on a family that had already supported children through high school. The alternative was to train as a secondary art craft teacher. Until the early 1980s, students could only start the course of training if they had a studentship with the Education Department. This automatically gave a small income while training and a guaranteed job as a high school teacher at the completion of training. To many, this was the only way of gaining art training. Even though they disliked the three-year bond to the Education Department, which was a compulsory feature of the scheme, they accepted this as a necessary restriction in repayment for the chance to learn something about art, though by 'art' they usually meant painting. Along with many other students John Davis first thought of himself as a painter and it was not until 1961–62, a few years after he completed his course of training, that he began seriously to produce sculpture.

John Davis was born in Ballarat but moved to a number of country areas, as his father was a banker and was transferred from town to town within Victoria. Like her husband, Shirley Davis was also a secondary art teacher. Born in Wangaratta, her father later ran a furniture shop in Myrtleford. Both John and Shirley Davis had similar backgrounds in small country towns and similar training in the city.

In the early 1940s, the Victorian Teachers' Union was campaigning vigorously for the establishment of a Teachers' Tribunal to control wages and conditions, rather than teachers' wages being decided by the political party in power. The VTU helped bring about the downfall of the State Government and the election of the John Cain Labor Government of 1945–47. The Labor Government established the Teachers' Tribunal in 1946, an act which reaped the Labor Party praise by teachers for many years.

In the 1950s most State secondary teachers belonged to the all-embracing Victorian Teachers' Union. It was not until the late 1950s and early 1960s that the Victorian Secondary Teachers' Association began to gather supporters, but by the mid-1960s it had become a much more militant organisation, actually daring to organise strikes for teachers.

The student takeovers, riots and demands for political power that hit European and American universities and art schools in the 1960s, arrived in a much milder form in Australia. Students were very vocal at Monash University and took some strong action at Melbourne University, but in general art students were more concerned with their own personal freedom rather than any co-operative political action. When John Davis was at Caulfield Technical College in 1967–71 there was more likely to be disagreement between staff and students over the display of a painting with red genitalia than conflict with student politicians of a red persuasion. The growing sexual freedom was reflected in more daring subject matter, which presented problems when exhibited publicly. John Davis was 31 when he went to Caulfield, only about ten years older than most of the students — their ideas and attitudes were similar to his and they often took part in the same marches and demonstrations.

It was a time when students were being called up for compulsory service in the army, when some of them were being drafted to fight in Vietnam. Victoria's opposition to Australia's involvement in Vietnam reached its peak in the Moratorium March through the streets of Melbourne on Wednesday 30 June 1971. John Davis and myself, other staff and students took part in the march, led by Dr Jim

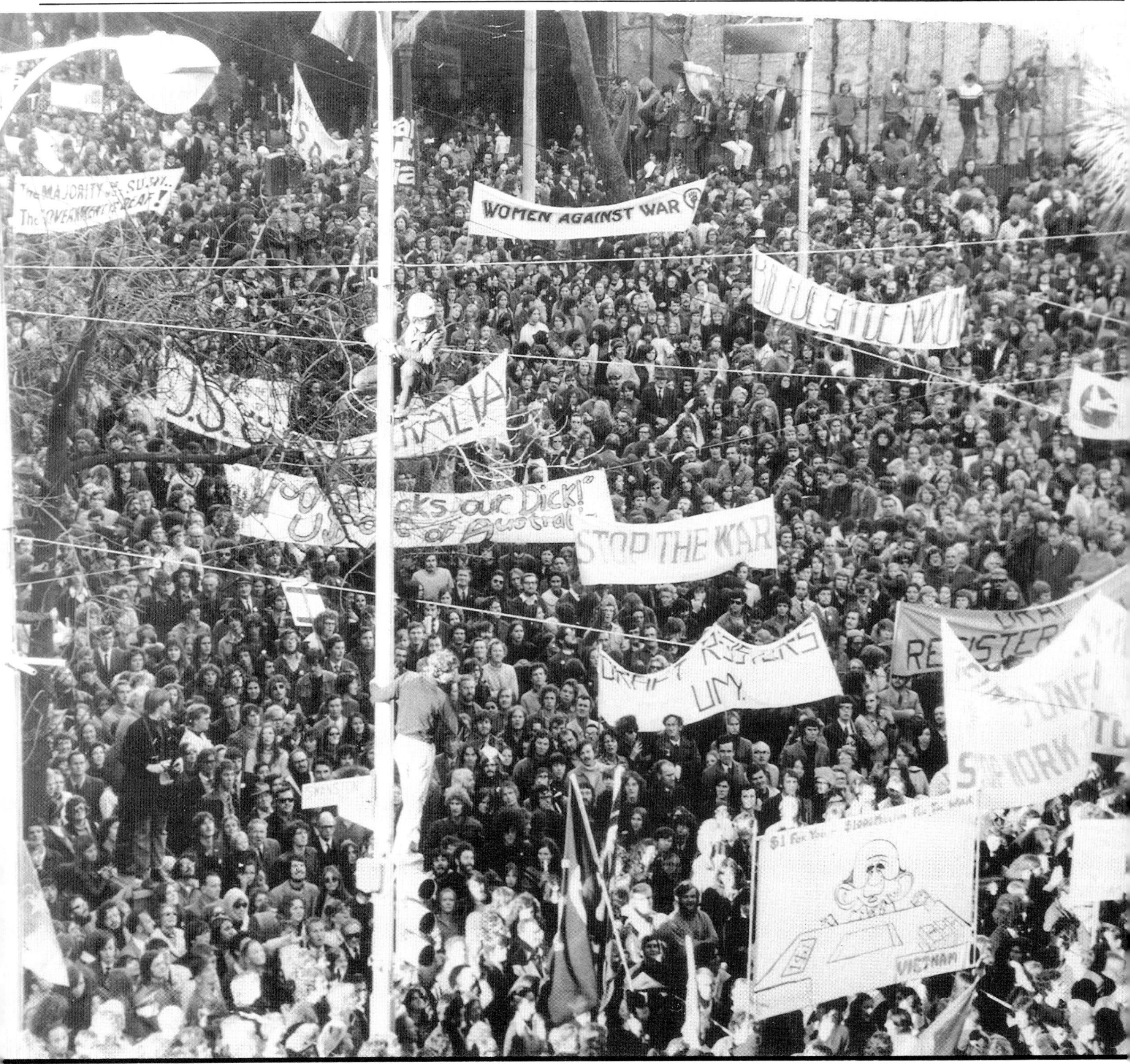

55 'Thousands Rally. Flags, banners fly in M-Day march', was the front page headline above this photograph in the Melbourne Herald, on Wednesday 30 June 1971. The photograph shows the crowd massed at the corner of Collins and Swanston Streets. Photograph reproduced courtesy of the Herald and Weekly Times Ltd.

Cairns, MHR. The event captured the entire front page of the Melbourne *Herald* which had the banner headline 'Thousands Rally'. It was the biggest demonstration ever seen in Melbourne, and it was entirely peaceful (illus. 55).

It was therefore a great shock to another group of protestors, only a few days later, when a peaceful demonstration against the visit of the South African Springbok Rugby Team became extremely violent. The anti-apartheid demonstrators, outside the Olympic Park suddenly found themselves attacked by the police. John Davis, Vic Majzner and Geoff La Gerche witnessed police horses charging into the ranks of the protestors, saw people being dragged off by the hair — Geoff La Gerche was so angered by the police action that he had to be forcibly restrained by John Davis and Vic Majzner.

In the 1950s, petitions against the use of atomic weapons were circulated, but the whole peace movement was regarded by the majority of Australians as a communist plot, a means of weakening our defences against an imminent communist take-over. By the early 1970s public opinion had changed markedly. The Moratorium March in Melbourne had proved there was a large body of people strongly against war, preparations for war, atomic weapons and later, against the mining and use of uranium.

Tom McCullough, Director of Mildura Arts Centre, organiser of the Triennial Exhibitions of sculpture, had imaginative and ambitious plans for 'Sculpturscape '73'. Not only was it going to be the biggest and most comprehensive exhibition of contemporary Australian sculpture ever held, it was also going to include an exhibition of contemporary French sculpture. But Tom McCullough had failed to anticipate the reaction of Australian sculptors. The French Government was carrying out testing of atomic weapons in the Pacific and the French Government was officially supporting the exhibition of sculpture by the French artists.

Noel Hutchison was one of the adjudicators for the 1973 Mildura Triennial who felt he could not give any support to the exhibition if the French were included. He contacted Ron Robertson-Swann and then phoned Tom McCullough in Mildura. A meeting was held in Sydney at Marr Ground's home, at which fifteen sculptors were present. Tom McCullough flew to Sydney to talk with the sculptors. After the meeting of sculptors in Sydney, Noel Hutchison posted the following letter to John Davis with a copy of the telegram that had been sent to the French Embassy, protesting against French nuclear testing and the inclusion of an exhibition of French sculpture at the Mildura Triennial.

■ *22/2/73*

Dear John,

Enclosed is a copy of the note sent to the French Embassy and the release to the Herald *that we decided on at the meeting. Tom McCullough has accepted our protest (as well as yours etc.) and has notified me that the French exhibition will <u>not go on</u> (or be associated with the Mildura Triennial in any way), <u>at the same time as the Triennial</u>. So the point has been made. Things can return to their course. We have dissociated ourselves from the French exhibition. Should it be shown in Mildura or Melbourne etc. at a later date then the appropriate action can be taken.*

Not much to tell you about the meeting except that it was a bit bloody, and went from 8 to 1. On my way home after the meeting I smashed the station wagon up, so I'm not feeling the most brilliant fella in school at the moment. The whole Mildura has cost me an awful lot. I'm sick of the whole bloody thing. I understand from Tom that virtually Ti, Clive and yourself, represented the only really committed protesters against the French show in Victoria. Apparently Tom had quite a batch of pro-French letters and telegrams. This means that as I have made my stand quite apparent and could not be regarded as an uncommitted person, I shall have to withdraw from being one of the assessors so that justice is seen to be done as well as being done. So that is about it for me. The smash has put payed to me getting my stuff ready in time I think. So all the best for the show. Please let Ti and Clive know all the details. Tom will send around a circular announcing his decision in due course.

Regards,
(Signed) Noel [Hutchison]

■

CULTURAL COUNSELLOR
FRENCH EMBASSY
CANBERRA ACT

THE FOLLOWING TWO MOTIONS WERE CARRIED AT A MEETING BY FIFTEEN NSW SCULPTORS INVITED TO EXHIBIT AT THE MILDURA TRIENNALE IN APRIL 1973.

THE SCULPTORS WERE CONCERNED AT THE POLITICAL IMPLICATIONS OF THE PRESENCE OF AN EXHIBITION OF FRENCH SCULPTURE SPONSORED BY THE FRENCH GOVERNMENT AT THE TRIENNALE — COINCIDENT WITH FRENCH NUCLEAR TESTING IN THE PACIFIC.

MOTION 1.
THE MEETING RESOLVED THAT: THESE SCULPTORS DO NOT ACCEPT THE EXHIBITION OF FRENCH SCULPTURE AT THE MILDURA TRIENNALE [SIC], PROPOSE TO VOICE A PROTEST AND RESOLVE TO DETERMINE, BEFORE THE MEETING BREAKS UP WHAT THE NATURE OF THE PROTEST SHOULD BE.

MOTION 2.
THE MEETING FURTHER RESOLVED THAT: IF THE FRENCH ARE IN WE ARE OUT.

RON ROBERTSON-SWANN
ROBERT BROWN
MICHEAL NICHOLSON[1]
TIM BURNS
DAVE MORRISEY
JOAN GROUNDS

MICHAEL BUZACOTT
RICHARD BRECKNOCK
IAN MCKAY
IMMINTS TILLERS[1]
ALEX TZANNES
MARLEEN CREASER[1]
NOEL HUTCHISON
MARR GROUNDS

. . . NOEL HUTCHISON — RON ROBERTSON-SWANN 31.7436.

In Melbourne, John Davis had phoned a few sculptors to gauge reaction, then a brief telegram was sent to Mildura:

■ WE ARE STRONGLY AGAINST EXHIBITING OUR WORK WITH SCULPTURES SPONSORED BY FRENCH GOVERNMENT. BECAUSE OF FRENCH NUCLEAR TESTING IN THE PACIFIC. UNLESS FRENCH EXHIBITS WITHDRAWN BY FEBRUARY 22 WE SHALL NOT SHOW. AWAITING YOUR DECISION.
DAVIS MURRAY-WHITE PARKS

Tom McCullough had always made a point of talking with sculptors prior to the planning of the sculpture triennials. In this case he did not agree with their decision, nevertheless, he stated: 'we will now have to change our plans for the triennial in accordance with the Australian sculptors' wishes'.[2] The French sculpture was not shown until after the Mildura Triennial was finished.

To Tom McCullough's credit he always endeavoured to be familiar with current attitudes of artists and was willing to accommodate their wishes. In the catalogue of 'Sculpturscape '73' he referred to the possible boycott by sculptors and then summed up by saying.

■ *This contentious matter has been partly aired in the national press, but the Mildura boycott threat can be seen fairly clearly as a new political awareness and rising militance amongst most artists in Australia. Art gallery professionals must face this today with*

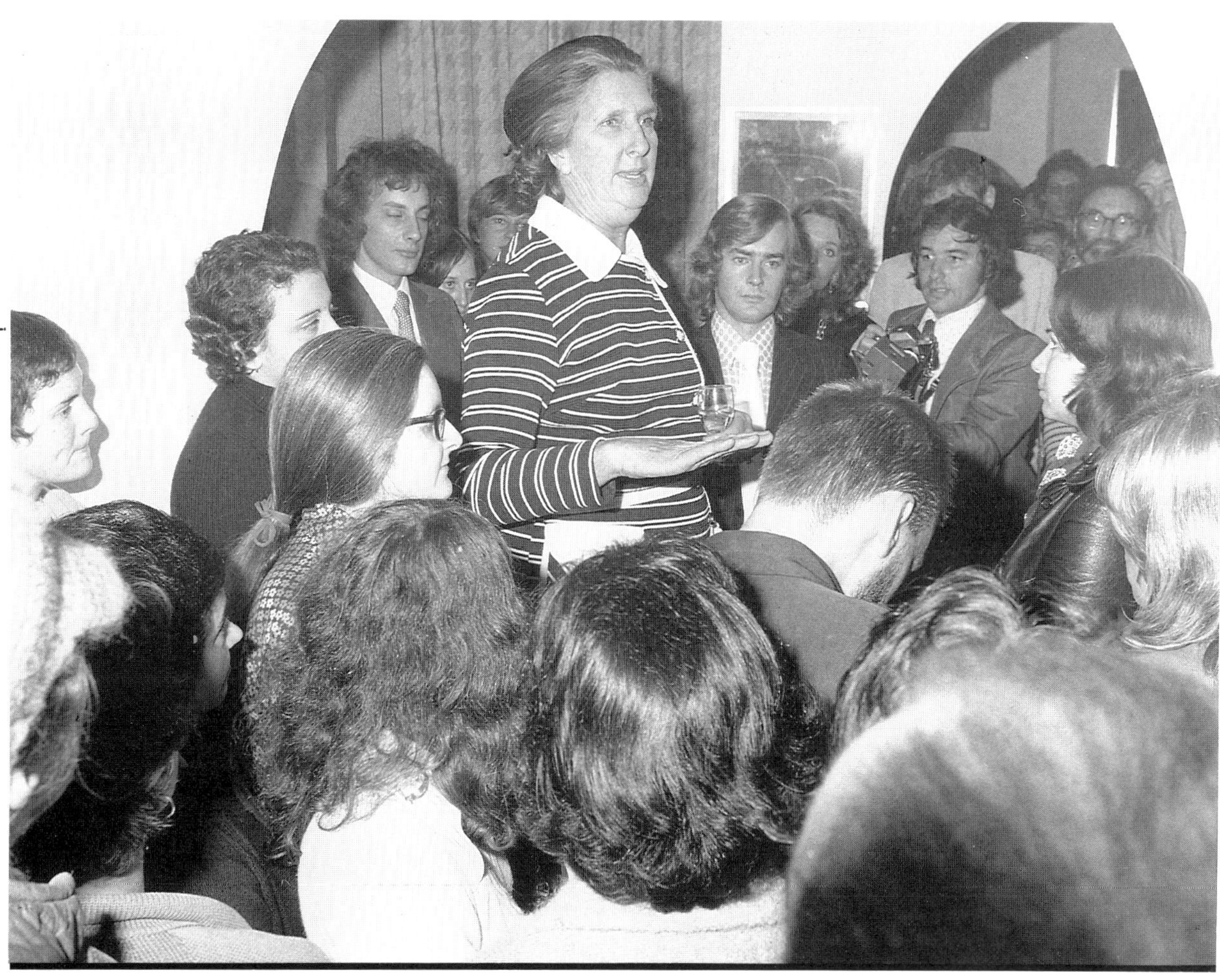

56 'Mrs Whitlam speaks at Artists for Labor exhibition', was the caption to this photograph in the Melbourne Age, on 14 May 1974. Sweeney Reed, Director of the Sweeney Reed Gallery, is shown to the right of Margaret Whitlam. Photograph reproduced courtesy of David Syme and Co. Ltd.

some sensitivity if good faith and confidence is to be maintained among their colleagues and artists alike.[3]

In 1973, 1974, 1975 and again in 1979 exhibitions were organised in Melbourne, usually with a title such as 'Artists for Labor', which was the exhibition held at Sweeney Reed's Gallery in 1974. John Davis exhibited in all of these exhibitions. Shirley Davis had joined the Labor Party in the late 1960s and John joined in the early 1970s. It was a time when many artists wished to assist the Labor Party. Artists gave generously of their works — paintings, drawings, sculpture, prints were all for sale cheaply and supporters came in their hundreds to the openings. For example, the official opening at Sweeney Reed's Gallery on 14 May 1974 was a tight mass of people packed into the gallery and flowing out on to the street. Margaret Whitlam made the opening speech (illus. 56). There was a great feeling of optimism, friendliness and a new feeling of trust between artists and politicians.

Surprisingly the exhibitions often raised considerable sums of money for Labor Party funds. In a letter to artists and musicians who had donated works to the 1975 exhibition at the Paddington Town Hall, Sydney, Clive Evatt wrote: 'Altogether $25,000 was raised for the ALP election campaign from the purchase of works of art, manuscript and musical scores by sale and by auction.'[4]

The exhibitions served a symbolic purpose as well as being a means of raising finance. They were times when artists publicly demonstrated their alliance to the Labor Party. Their names were on the catalogue, on the invitations and in advertisements. Just prior to the federal elections in 1974 a large advertisement appeared in the *Age* with the heading 'I will vote to return the Whitlam Government because . . .'[5] Then followed nearly seventy statements by painters, sculptors, print makers, art collectors, critics and gallery directors, giving their personal reasons for supporting the Labor Government.

■ *'They have created so many new possibilities for the arts.'*— *Leonard French*

'The continuation of their programme is vital to Australia.' —Roger Kemp

'They must be allowed to continue their brilliant initiatives in foreign policy, social justice and the arts.' —Alun Leach Jones

'In heart and mind I am a liberal; that is why I will vote Labor this time.' —George Mora

'I began my artistic life at a time when governments despised artists; now we have a chance to be heard.' —John Perceval

'They have made it possible to think in terms of peace rather than war, and of promoting man's creative spirit rather than his immense destructive capabilities.' —John Reed
Sunday Reed

'They stand for the new Australia, the coalition parties for the old.' —Patrick McCaughey

When the Whitlam Labor Government was thrown out of office in 1975, both the new Prime Minister, Malcolm Fraser, and the office of the Governor-General came in for strong opposition and visible protest. When Malcolm Fraser opened the Biennale of Sydney, at the Art Gallery of New South Wales, on 13 November 1976, John Davis, along with many other artists and invited guests walked out of the art gallery and staged a protest on the steps outside. When Sir Zelman Cowan, Governor-General of Australia, arrived to officially open the Australian Sculpture Triennial in 1981, organised by Tom McCullough at La Trobe University, the audience was expected to stand. John Davis along with some other artists remained seated on the grass of the outdoor amphitheatre.

Once a policy has been implemented by a political party, it can be very difficult for the opposition party to abandon that commitment when it comes to power. The Australian Labor Party initiated some important developments for the visual arts in Australia. For instance the Australia Council, established in March 1975, has done a great deal to stimulate the arts. After the downfall of the Whitlam Government, the Fraser Government continued support for the Australia Council, and set up Art Bank in 1980. John Davis has been interested in helping define Labor Party policy and was on the 'Policy Committee for Arts, Information and the Media' during 1980 and 1981. He also served on the Visual Arts Board from 1981 until December 1982 when he realised that the demands of committee work were taking time needed for his own sculpture, so he resigned. This illustrates a dilemma for artists. Do they join various organisations and cut down on precious time needed for their own work, or do they refuse to take part in these time-consuming community activities, leaving decisions on the arts to non-artists?

In 1975 there was a contentious issue concerning the banning from public showing at the National Gallery of Victoria of an installation by Domenico de Clario. An installation by Domenico de Clario was included in the sculpture exhibition which was part of the series 'Artists' Artists'. Unlike the other exhibitions in the series, the sculpture exhibition was a series of displays, three or more sculptors at a time, over the whole of 1975. After being invited to show his work and after installation at the gallery, it was removed from display without any prior discussion with the artist. In retrospect, it was a minor work and totally out of context in the area where it was shown — amongst the Australian colonial paintings. The scatter of letters, postcards and other debris from de Clario's home looked rather forlorn on the carpeted floor of the gallery. Nevertheless, it was unfortunate that Gordon Thomson, then Director of the gallery, failed to consult with de Clario, and his letter of explanation reached the artist many days after the event.

Artists saw it as an act of artistic censorship and reacted strongly in support of de Clario. Kiffy Rubbo and Meredith Rogers of the Ewing and George Paton Galleries called a meeting at the Ewing Gallery on 18 August 1975 at which about sixty artists were present. John Davis nominated me as chairman of the protest meeting. The meeting not only discussed the issue of the removal of Domenico de Clario's work, but went on to air a considerable number of criticisms of the National Gallery of Victoria. The meeting was orderly but determined to take strong action. A series of motions were passed, which were printed in a leaflet headed 'Protest. National Gallery of Victoria'. Four of the six points in the leaflet began 'We demand . . .' The notice ended with a statement: 'People will be gathering to discuss these issues in the Australian Section, 2nd floor of the National Gallery of Victoria at 4 pm on Thursday, 21st August.'

The authorities at the gallery must have feared riots and arson, for, with one exception, the hundreds of paintings in the Australian area of the gallery were all taken down. The good-humoured crowd of about 200 artists and art students met in the gallery and, though it moved down to the entrance foyer, the crowd showed no signs of leaving when the gallery closed at 5 pm. Terry Smith chaired the meeting, Eric Westbrook, Director of the Victorian Ministry of the Arts spoke (illus. 57) but received a poor reception from the audience. An Artists' Steering Committee was elected to continue to fight and to negotiate with the Trustees of the National Gallery of Victoria and the Victorian Ministry for the Arts. John Davis and myself were elected to that committee.[6]

Committee meetings went on for months in an endeavour to clarify demands. The committee was numerically almost equally divided between Labor Party supporters, putting forward relatively realistic demands and a group of the far left demanding fundamental changes. The situation was complicated by the Trustees' refusal to reply to letters or meet a delegation — a deadlock that was eventually broken by the good offices of Lenton Parr and Brian Stonier, trustees of the gallery.

Representatives of the Steering Committee met with Eric Rowlison after his appointment as the new Director of the National Gallery of Victoria. Eric Rowlison's letter of 12 March 1976 recording the discussion listed such major issues as:

    Curator of Contemporary Australian Art
    Extension Gallery for Contemporary
      Australian Art
    Present Exhibition Programme
    Acquisitions Policy
    Relationship of the Gallery to the Community

Several of these points have been dealt with, if slowly. Robert Lindsay was appointed Associate Curator of Australian Art — Contemporary in March 1977. He instigated the 'Survey' exhibitions of contemporary Australian art, shown in the corridor-like area outside the offices of the National Gallery Society. 'Survey 1' dealt with the work of John Davis and 'Survey 15' of July–September 1981 ('Relics and Rituals'), included John Davis as one of the sixteen artists. Unfortunately the 'Survey' exhibitions have ceased and the area used for those shows has been given permanently to the display of the gallery's collection of pre-Columbian art. When asked why the 'Survey' exhibitions had ceased Robert Lindsay said there were many reasons, but the major reason was simply pressure of work. He had been responsible for six 'Survey'

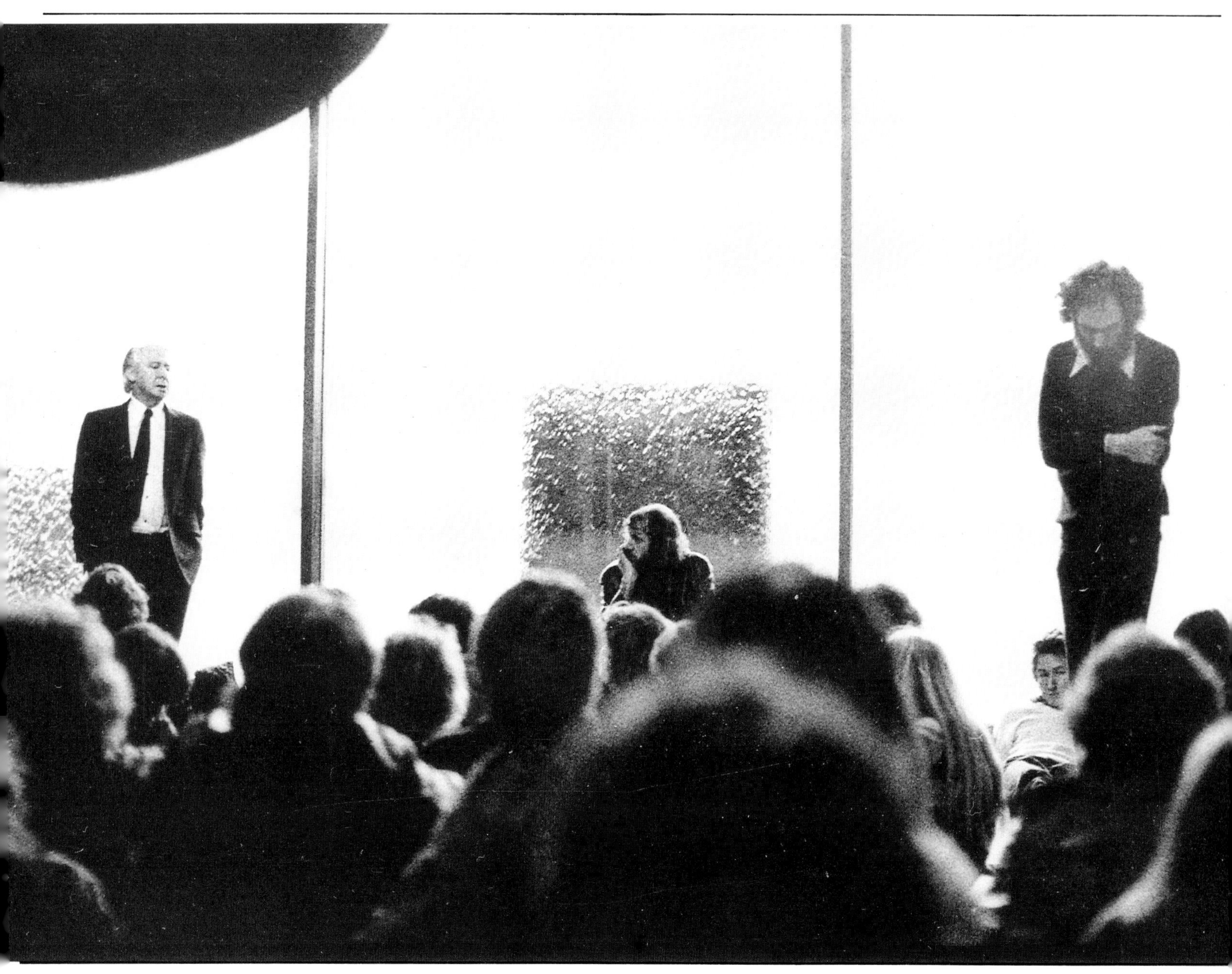

exhibitions in his first year, or a total of thirty-four diverse exhibitions in three years.

The idea of an Extension Gallery for Contemporary Australian Art prompted some discussion. Reporting on the protest meeting a few days after it occurred, Maureen Gilchrist wrote: 'Several sites are being considered, including the YMCA building in City Road, not far from the Gallery, and also the Lower Town Hall. The present plan is that after two to five years of experimenting with a temporary venue, a permanent hall will be provided.'[7]

Writing three years later, Janine Burke recalled the protest meeting, when '200 artists, students and supporters crowded into the gallery'. She went on to say: 'The projected extension gallery as a centre for contemporary art is still mooted. It must become a reality if the gallery is to expand and strengthen its commitment to recent art and not fall back into its previous doldrums'.[8]

Nothing came of the idea for some years. Then in December 1982 an advertisement appeared in the *Age* calling for applicants for the position of Director of the 'Domain Gallery: Centre for Contemporary Art'. A disused building near the Shrine of Remembrance had at last been chosen as the site for a contemporary gallery, showing mainly, but not entirely, Australian art. John Davis was one of the members of the interim management committee to interview applicants. The Australian Centre for Contemporary Art has now been operating for some years, and with the addition of new gallery space behind the original gardener's cottage has become a vigorous centre for the display of contemporary art.

The relationship of the gallery to the community was the last point listed in Eric Rowlison's letter of 1976. One must give credit to Eric Westbrook who established a new image for the gallery, particularly after moving to the new building in St Kilda Road in 1968. The gallery became public and almost popular. The great 'block buster' exhibitions such as 'Modern Masters' in 1975, 'The Chinese Exhibition' of 1977 and 'Pompeii' in 1981, seemed to prove that the public could be enticed by mass advertising to visit the gallery in great numbers. Yet a survey of attendances at the National Gallery of Victoria was carried out in 1982 because attendances in the period 1968–80 had fallen by 50 per cent.[9] One of the interesting findings of the survey was that most people visiting the gallery felt intimidated and were not at ease within the precincts of the National Gallery of Victoria.

The fourth point on the original leaflet produced at the protest meeting had been: 'We demand the right to contribute to policy-making at all levels within the Gallery, in particular, the Board of Trustees, the Director's Office, the Department of Australian Art and the Exhibitions Department'. The gallery did hold a function one Saturday afternoon in 1977, to which artists were invited.[10] The invitation said: 'The Trustees of the National Gallery of Victoria believe that strong links between the gallery and the artistic community are very important and they have decided to invite artists, craftsmen, dealers, art teachers, critics and others to the gallery to meet members of the Council and staff informally'.

John Davis has not been deeply involved in political activity but his democratic attitude has been apparent in a variety of ways, from his attitudes towards students and teaching, his support for particular causes such as the Vietnam Moratorium, fund raising for the Labor Party, or support for the Aborigines. His political views have also had an influence on his choice of materials with which he has made his sculpture. He has chosen cheap, commonplace materials, believing that this would make it easier for people to relate to the works. John Davis explains his attitude:

■ *Some materials used in sculpture create barriers*

◀
57 Protest meeting, which became a 'sit-in' at the National Gallery of Victoria on the evening of 21 August 1975. The first protest meeting, held at the Ewing Gallery (chaired by Ken Scarlett), was called to support Domenico de Clario, whose installation had been removed from the National Gallery of Victoria. The second meeting (chaired by Terry Smith), put forward a wide range of demands for change at the National Gallery. From left to right: Dr Eric Westbrook, ex-Director National Gallery of Victoria, at the time, Director of the Victorian Ministry for the Arts; Terry Smith; John Davis. Photograph originally reproduced in 'The Art Almanac', published by Ewing Gallery, Sept-Dec 1975. Photograph by Peter Tyndall.

for people to overcome when viewing the art. They have been given a mystique through association with certain art contexts, and therefore will always remain outside of some viewers' close relationship. I hope my materials will encourage the viewer to approach the work with some confidence through their familiarity with the material, even to the extent of encouraging them to make art from materials they know and understand, and not to be dissuaded from making art by their lack of knowledge of 'prestige' art process and material. Therefore my choice of materials is also socio/political.[11]

One must sympathise with his democratic intention, yet the realistic facts are that the general public probably still thinks of sculpture in terms of bronze and marble, something solid and lasting, and actually may be more alienated by his choice of materials than they would be by traditional materials. John Davis would be reluctant to admit it, but he is making art for a relatively small élite who know something about contemporary art. His predicament is only different in degree from Vladimir Tatlin, the Constructivist artist of the early days of the Soviet Union who designed a *Monument to the IIIrd International*. The work was built in 1919–20 of steel and glass and was totally abstract in form. 'Tatlin's monument was to be twice the height of the Empire State Building.'[12] John Davis, being a genuinely modest man, works on a much smaller scale, but probably has no greater contact with the masses than did Tatlin. The alienation of the artist from the community is one of the great tragedies of the twentieth century.

■ NOTES

1 Michael Nicholson and Imants Tillers names have been spelt incorrectly, though Marlee Creaser was Marleen at that time.
2 Tom McCullough, quoted in 'Sculptors Boycott Mildura Triennial Over N-Tests', *Sunraysia Daily*, 21 February 1973, p. 2.
3 Thomas McCullough, Introduction to 'Sculpturscape '73' *Sculpturscape '73. The 1973 Mildura Sculpture Triennial*, 7 April–7 July 1973.
4 Clive Evatt, letter to John Davis, 'On behalf of the Committee of Artists for Parliamentary Democracy', 7 December 1975.
5 *Age*, 11 May 1974, p. 14.
6 Report in *Art Almanac*, Ewing Gallery, Melbourne, September–December 1975.
7 Maureen Gilchrist, 'Local Artists Call for a Better Deal', *Age*, 25 August 1975.
8 Janine Burke, 'Survey Spotlights the New Faces in Art', *National Times*, 14 October 1978.
9 The survey was made by Mike Hurrel who was employed as a marketing consultant for the National Gallery of Victoria.
10 26 November 1977 in the Great Hall, National Gallery of Victoria.
11 John Davis, 'Some Brief Notes on Issues Which I Think are Raised in My Art', written in answer to questions from Kimio Akiyama, Editorial Department, *Ikebana Ohara*, November 1982.
12 Camilla Gray, *The Russian Experiment in Art: 1863–1922*, Abrams (New York), 1971.

INSTALLATIONS

Many new words have come into the art vocabulary over recent years — or old words have acquired new meanings: Happenings, Environments, Events, Performances, and Installations. In the sense that John Davis uses the word 'installation' it means a sculptural work, or group of works, that have a total cohesion and relate to each other within a given space — though he uses the term loosely. The first time the word appeared in one of his catalogues was for the 1977 exhibition at Watters Gallery, Sydney. Items 31.1–31.7 were listed as an 'Installation', with a total price for the group, but they were also catalogued individually and could be purchased separately. There were four other major works in the exhibition, plus a considerable number of Exchange Pieces, which were not part of the Installation.

In terms of exhibitions within a gallery space, the work at Venice Biennale in July 1978 was probably the closest to an ideal situation for a gallery installation. The space was a very simple room with only two doors, no windows and soft diffused natural light coming through the ceiling. The measurements had been sent from Italy, so John Davis was able to make works specifically for the exhibition.

The situation is not always so ideal but as John Davis said in discussion with me in February 1983: 'I attempt to include the entire space of the gallery within the relationship established between the objects, rather than individual objects occupying their own discrete space'.

Davis had earlier made the following statement about the traditional pedestal for sculpture and his own reason for preferring an installation:

■ *My exhibitions must be laid out as installations. A pedestal 'locks' the piece into its parameters and excludes the space of the room. I want to include the space of the room into the objects, so that it is a linking device between them as it flows from the interior of the objects to exterior space, very much like marks on a page working formally and psychologically.*[1]

The 1981 exhibition at Watters worked well, as all the parts had a link in concept and materials. The invitation listed 'First Expedition — Region, Long Journey, The Crossing. Three installations...' The three major works did indeed relate to 'the entire space of the gallery', as the artist had intended. Even the seven small works *Regional Extension 1–7* were part of the whole control of space within the gallery.

The word installation seems to have a less ambiguous meaning when used to describe works that have been placed in the natural environment, such as those made at Hattah Lakes, the You Yangs, Barmah Forest, etc. Because the materials have been gathered on the site and the resultant object constructed for the specific environment, the word 'installation' accurately describes something that has been installed in a particular place, whereas the gallery installations can be and were moved to other gallery sites. John Davis has also used the word installation in retrospect, to describe works such as *Tree Piece*, which was produced for the Mildura 'Sculpturscape' in 1973.

It was not until 1980, in the catalogue of the Wollongong City Gallery exhibition, that John Davis actually listed 'Solo Exhibitions, Installations and Selected Group Exhibitions'.[2] In this list of installations he restricts the group to those works constructed in country rather than gallery environments.

The first work which could be labelled an installation was a casual piece, built by John Davis and his two children, in the Scottish Highlands in 1972. It was built from found rocks and timber plus string.

One of the experiments of 1973 was an aside, a cul-de-sac, interesting at the time, but not to be explored any more. John Davis and Kevin Mortensen co-operated in an installation at St Paul's Cathedral, Melbourne, as part of the Spring Festival. Possibly the title 'Spring Festival' revived

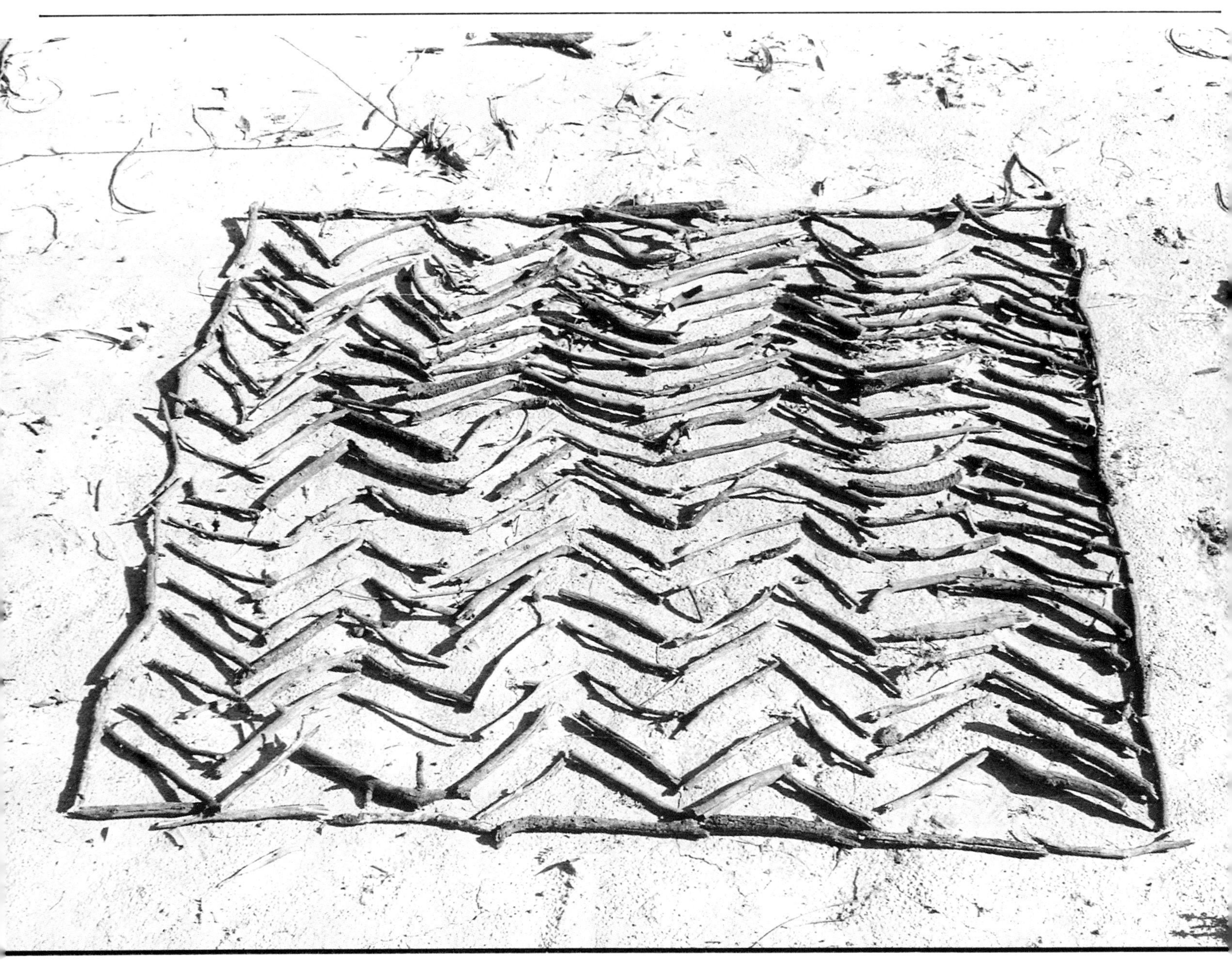

memories of old pagan rites — certainly there was no evidence of Christian symbolism. The area used was at the southern end of the cathedral, opposite the main entrance. The elaborate, Gothic baptism font and the sunken baptismal area for total immersion were both incorporated into the installation. The range of materials was strangely out of character with a revival gothic cathedral — sheets of latex, canvas bags filled with sand, polyurethane, vertical posts wrapped in white fabric topped with four stuffed animal heads — all at odds with solemn stone columns, patterned Victorian tiled floor and religious stained glass.

The installation was not able to compete with the strong atmosphere of the cathedral, which overwhelmed and enveloped the strange structures in one isolated area of the church. The only part of the installation which commanded attention, achieved by a certain shock value, was a figure seated in the rear pews. The real male figure, naked from the waist up, wore a large goat's head as a mask. The goat's head, complete with long horns, sat quite convincingly on the shoulders of the model and introduced a decidedly pagan note. The presence of this unmoving figure, seated at the rear of the cathedral, was quite disturbing.

Four years after his work in the Scottish Highlands, during his visit to Hattah Lakes, 68 km south of Mildura, John Davis revived the simple notion of choosing local materials and building temporary structures within the environment.

The installations which John Davis made at Hattah Lakes in May 1976 now only exist as documentary photographs, as the works themselves were ephemeral. One consisted of two, long, thin bundles of twigs, placed parallel, but some distance apart. The two slender constructions sat on the sandy earth in a large flat area of landscape almost completely devoid of vegetation. Another installation was made from short sticks, broken to similar lengths, arranged in a zigzag pattern within a rectangular frame — again lying directly on the sand (illus. 58).

Neither of the works made any profound statement, but they were of interest in that they showed John Davis making the equivalent of sketches, trying out ideas, sorting out possibilities. They represented a fairly decisive step away from man-made materials and twentieth century technology, to a statement that was in sympathy with the natural environment. They merely said 'Man has been here'. Nothing was done that might be harmful to nature in any way.

Another structure was built in a large dead tree, with an arrangement of found timber placed in the branches at two levels. The horizontal arrangement was in opposition to the vertical and diagonal movement of the tree, and even though only one tree was used as the basis of the installation, in the photograph of the scene, one cannot avoid viewing the other nearby trees. As with his *Tree Piece* at Mildura in 1973, it is difficult to define boundaries, the work relates loosely to the surroundings. The stacked branches resembled the debris left behind after a flood, detritus caught in the fork of a tree after the water has receded.

Twenty-six photographs of the various installations at the Hattah Lakes were incorporated in *Nomad*, shown at the 1976 Biennale of Sydney.

In September 1976 John Davis visited the Ovens River area of Victoria and again made some small installations. One work was a cairn of water-washed rocks from the river surmounted by a bundle of reeds. The pyramidal form was emphasised by the linear definition of four straight branches, making a steep-sided pyramid. At the apex of the branches was a small horizontal bundle of reeds (illus. 59).

In later years John Davis was to use the pyramidal form in such works as the two shown at the

◀
58 John Davis, Installation using sticks on the ground at Hattah Lakes, May 1976. Photograph by the artist.

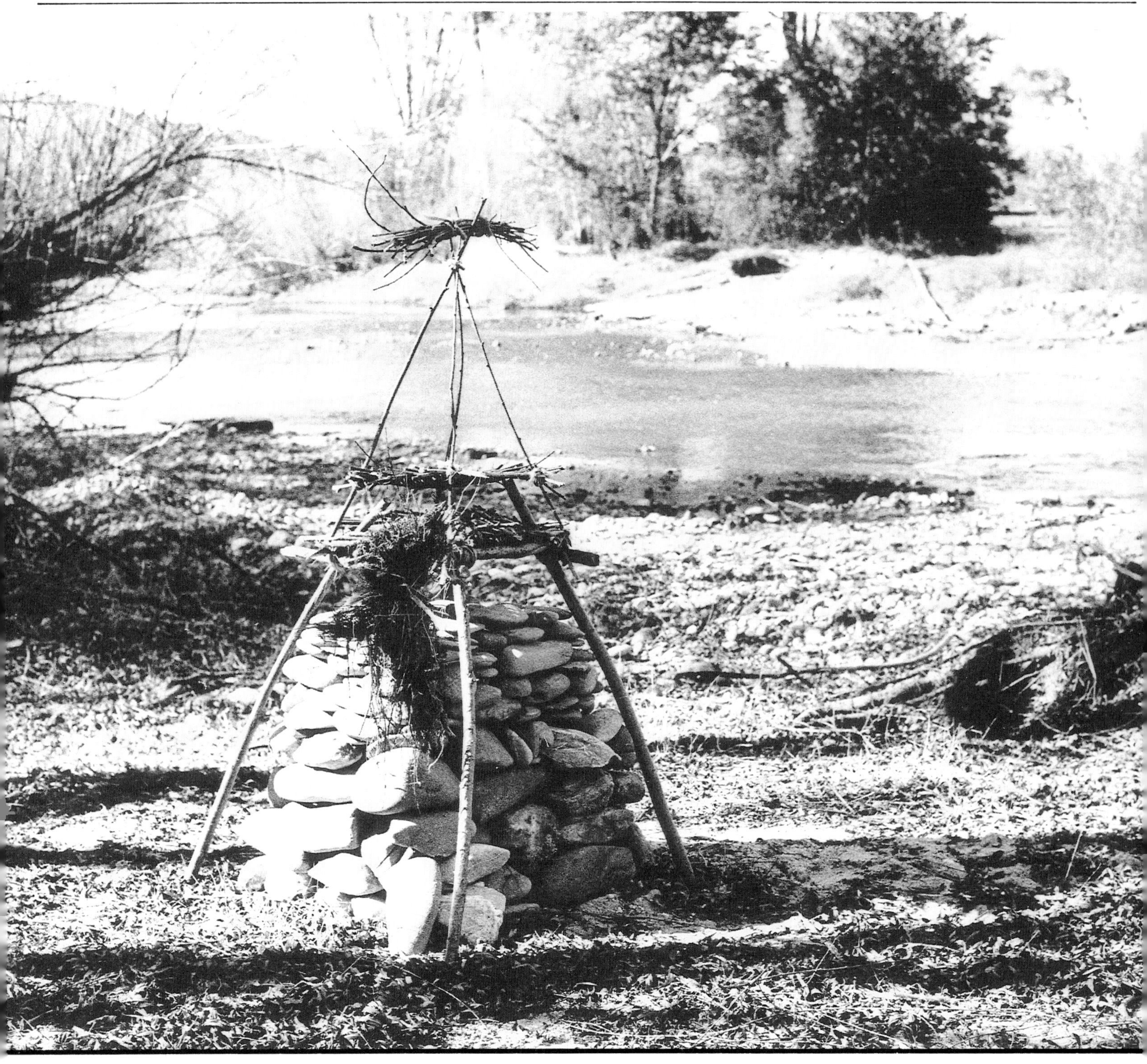

▼
59 John Davis, Installation beside the Ovens River, near Myrtleford, using materials found at the site — rocks, branches, twigs, reeds, c. 120 cm high. September 1976. Photograph by the artist.

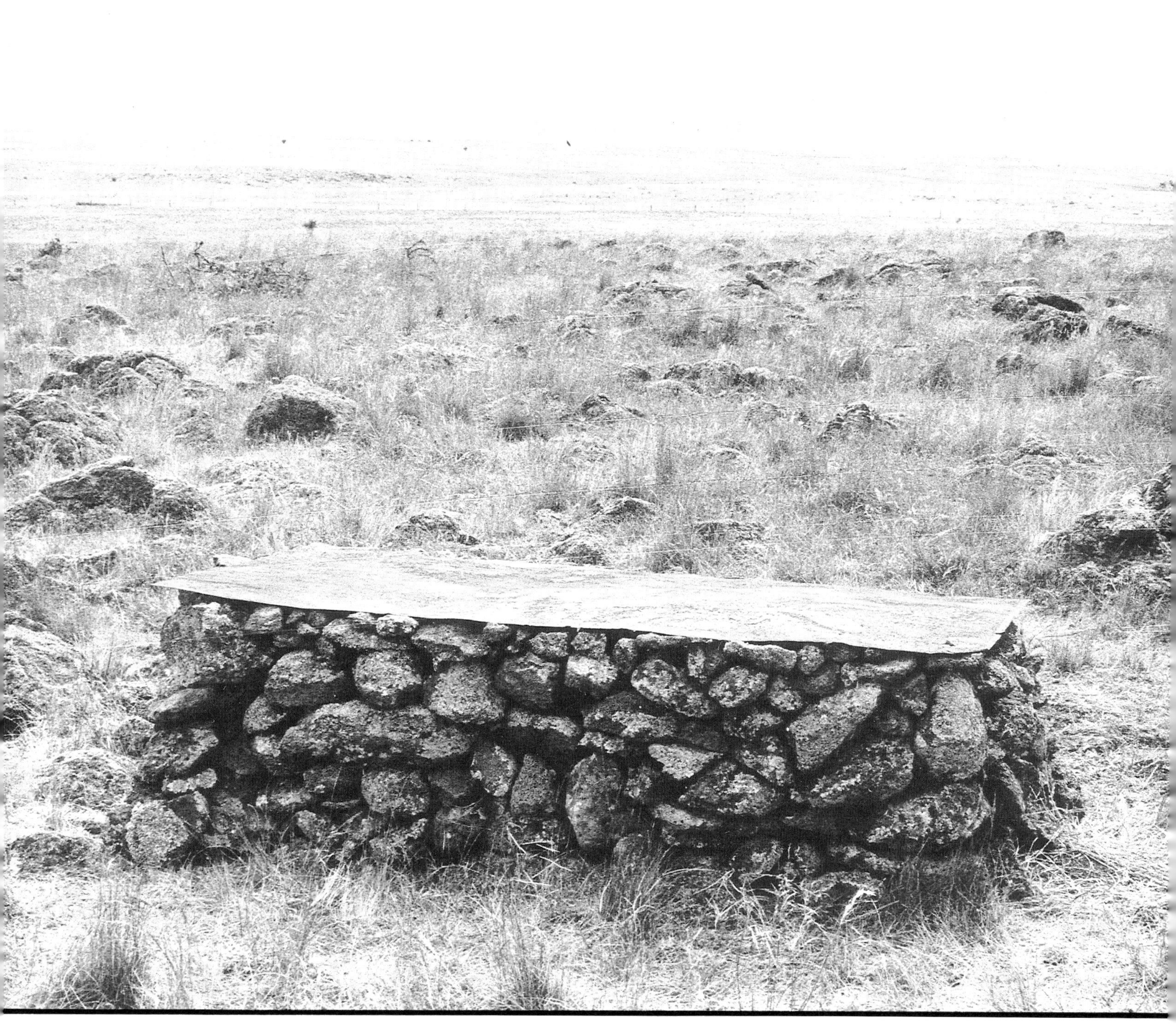

60 John Davis, 'Solar Piece' (1977). Installation near the You Yangs, Victoria, using rocks found on the site, plus a sheet of steel. Steel 2 x 1 m; rocks approximately 80 cm high; total dimensions 87 x 217 x 115 cm. Photograph by the artist.

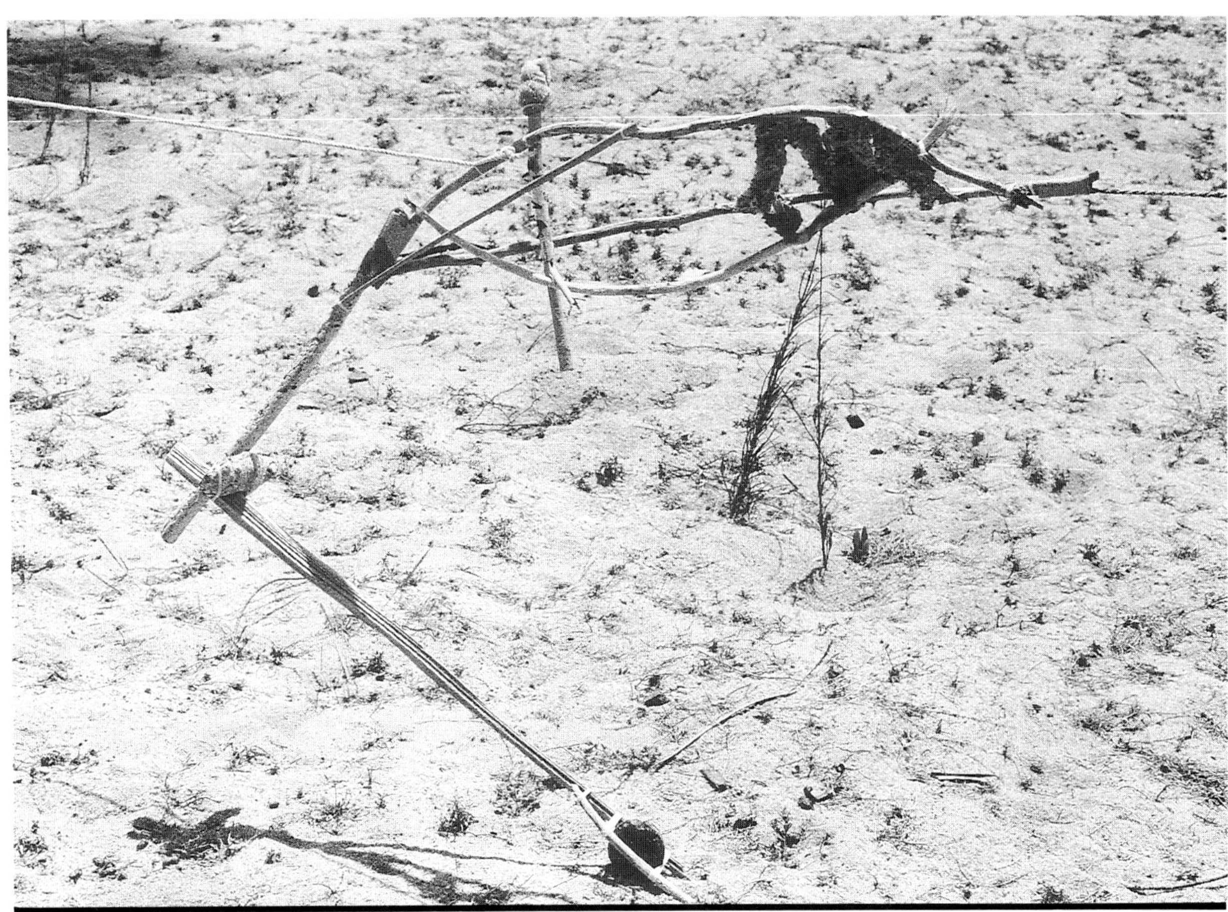

61 *John Davis, 'Relocation — Beach Work', installation on the beach at Cholamandal, India, February 1978. Made from materials collected on the beach — rope, driftwood, cloth, string, stone and paper, c. 2.5 m long. Temporary installation. Photograph by the artist (used on cover of catalogue Venice Biennale 1978 Australia).*

Venice Biennale and called *Marker*. Perhaps the pyramid was a favourite structure because of its elementary stability, when twigs and branches, merely tied together, could easily be unstable and difficult to control. On the other hand, the pyramid has been used widely in many cultures all over the world, from ancient Egypt to the Central American Pre-Columbian civilisations. Its simple form seems to have a mysterious significance.

This mysterious, ritualistic or semi-religious feeling was evident in another work which John Davis did at the You Yangs in Victoria in November 1977. Rocks were stacked to form a large, low rectangular prism, which was surmounted by a flat sheet of heavy steel plate. Called 'Solar Piece' (illus. 60), it seemed to suggest an altar for worship of the sun. One wonders if the altar is still there and whether casual picnickers at weekends discover it and ponder on its significance.

Another work of 1977, 'Kevington', has the distinction of being the only installation built in the bush and surviving to be shown in a gallery — Watters Gallery. From a piece of string, strung between two gum trees, five objects dangled in a loose arrangement, like objects on a clothes line. They were built from materials found on the site: twigs, stones and bark, assisted by some string. When shown at Watters Gallery a couple of vertical wooden poles replaced the two tree trunks.

When John Davis visited India in 1978, to exhibit in the Indian Triennale, he also had the opportunity to visit Madras, after the exhibition in New Delhi. While at the artists' village at Cholomandal, near Madras, he was able to make some installation works on the beach, one of which was reproduced in monochromatic colour on the cover of the 1978 Venice Biennale catalogue. 'Relocation — Beach Work' (illus. 61) was a sparse structure, with none of the intricacy or abundance of twigs found in some of Davis's work. The reason was simple — Indians don't leave quantities of usable fuel lying on the beach for the convenience of visiting sculptors.

The English sculptor, Nicholas Pope, visited Australia in 1979 and while in Melbourne had an exhibition of his work at the gallery of the Prahran School of Art. They were simple structures of split wood, stacked, piled and leaning together, without

62 John Davis, 'With Animal Trap' (1979). Constructed of materials found on the site — twigs, sticks and leaves, c. 210 x 90 x 150 cm. This work was built in the Grampians, while visiting the area with the English sculptor, Nicholas Pope. Photograph by the artist.

aid of adhesives, binding or traditional forms of jointing wood. The materials were permanent but the structures were temporary. While he was in Australia, John Davis took him and some sculpture students from Prahran for three or four days to the Grampians in Victoria. Pope didn't make any work in the area, but Davis made 'With Animal Trap' (illus. 62), a work which looked like a small temporary shelter in thick bush but which also had the implied qualities of an animal trap.

'Observatory' (illus. 63), built in 1979 in the Barmah Forest on the Murray River, near Echuca, Victoria, used two adjoining butts of trees which had been sawn off low to the ground, with the heavy twisting roots exposed above the ground. The location was on an earthy bank beside the Murray River. Using large sticks, Davis built two structures which leaned towards the centre from the two tree trunks, forming a large triangular arch. The intervening space was a well defined but slightly irregular triangle. Starting with the massive tree stumps and emerging roots, the structure became lighter, more transparent, as it went up: tree stumps, then twigs covered with mud, then

twigs forming a tracery that one could see through. It was an imaginative use of materials, uniting them into one simple composition, which looked natural as though it had been there for many years.

The Oxford Dictionary defines an observatory as a building from which natural, especially astronomical phenomena, may be observed. John Davis had visited the extraordinary Jantar Mantar, the eighteenth century observatories built by Sawai Jai Singh at Jaipur and Delhi in India; they are amongst the sculptural wonders of the world. As a casual tourist, one cannot grasp the astronomical significance of Jantar Mantar, but the structures are visually fascinating. One can walk within them, amongst hemispheres set into the earth, or climb sky high, up staircases that take one closer to the stars. All built precisely of stone and meant to last.

The 'Observatory' built by Davis was constructed of twigs, sticks and mud. When he revisited the area a year later the tree trunks were still there, but his structure had entirely disappeared.

Many people are annoyed by the transitory nature of some forms of contemporary art, believ-

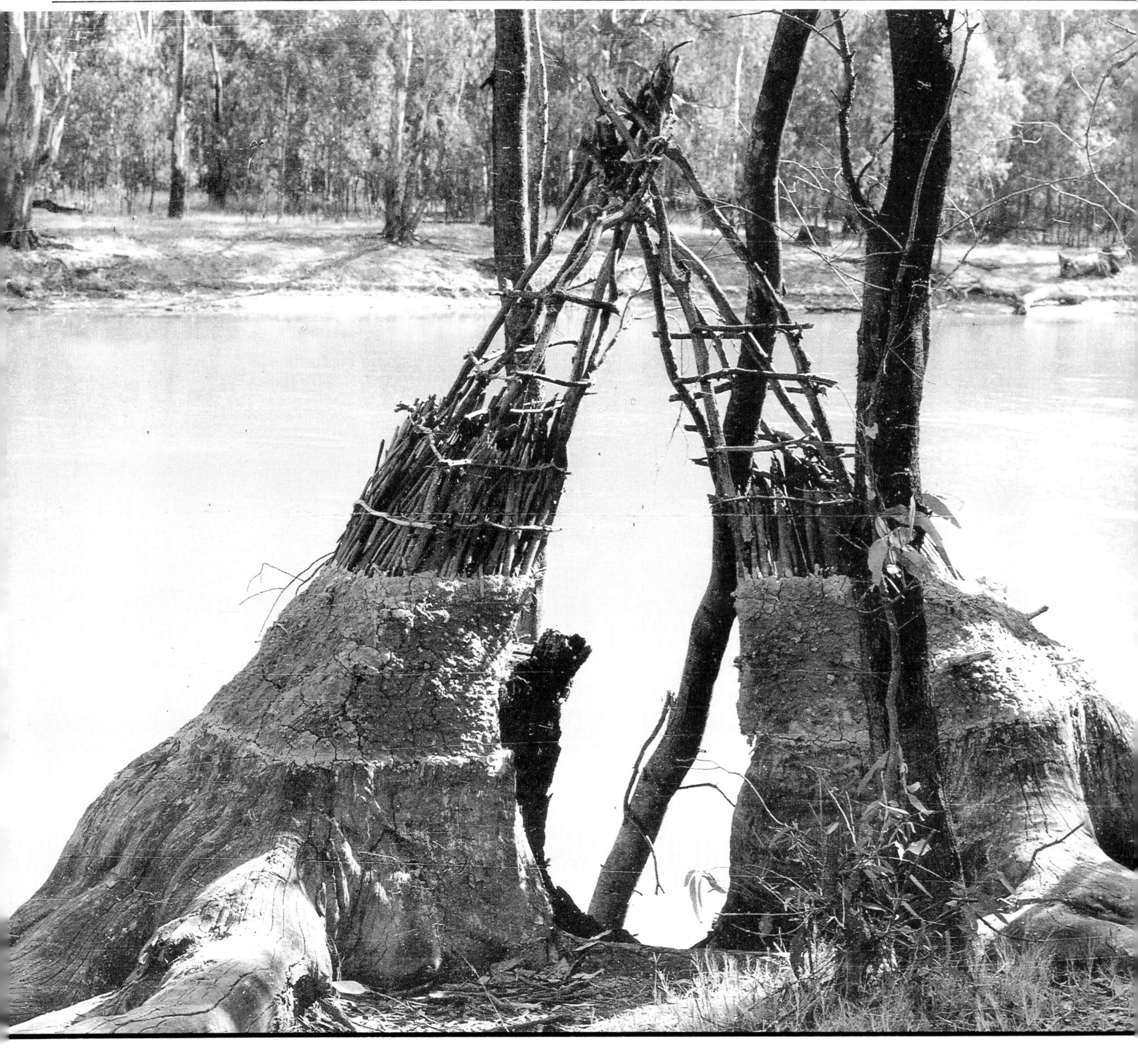

53 John Davis: 'Observatory' 1979). Constructed on the edge of the Murray River, at Barmah Forest, using an existing tree stump, to which was added branches, twigs, bark and mud, c. 240 cm high. This temporary installation was rebuilt in 1980 and called 'Observatory Revisited'. In June 1983 John Davis took the Japanese performance artist, Goji Hamada, to the same area and again rebuilt the work — though quite differently. This time it was entitled 'Goji's Bridge'. The dimensions for the third work were c. 50 cm high by c. 200 cm long with a variable width. Photograph by the artist.

ing that art is meant to last. They also believe that the reverse is true; that which does not last is not art. Of course, it is all a matter of time and differing attitudes towards the lapse of time. Not everything can last as long as the pyramids of Egypt (and many of them are showing decided signs of age). How many times have Giotto's frescos in the Church of St Francis in Assisi been repainted? But it is the short lapse of time before the inevitable decay and destruction that seems to irritate many viewers. Flowers in a vase may be decorative on the coffee table and their brief existence is accepted, but art should be in permanent materials.

Children make cities in the sand, creating buildings, roads, and of course using the water, as the tide comes in. Seaweed, shells and any timber washed up by the sea are prizes to be used in the construction and decoration of the imaginary city. At the end of the day they leave the work behind, proud of their efforts but not greatly worried by the fact that the tide, wind or other children will destroy it.

In 1981 Davis showed 'Place Two — An Installation' (illus. 64, 65, 66) at the First Australian Sculpture Triennial, which was situated at both La Trobe University and Preston Institute of Technology. His work was constructed of recycled wood, twigs, paper, tar, clay and earth, situated on a hill outside the ring road, near the Union Building at La Trobe University.

Davis's work at La Trobe brought back childhood memories. Located on the side of a small, gravelly hill, placed in a patch of bare ground and surrounded by scrubby trees the work meandered up the slope. The area had no special merit; it wasn't dramatic, wasn't centrally located, nor was it easy to find. But it did have a quiet seclusion, it was the sort of place that children would choose to build a cubby house — sufficiently hidden to make it somewhat secret, but commanding a good view of the surrounding territory. The work consisted of eight separate parts, informally arranged on the ground. The design was loose, almost formless in plan, but held together visually by similar materials, colours and textures for all of the parts. The general effect was as though one was looking down on a strange, primitive encampment. One wondered if a tribe of nomads had build a temporary resting place, before moving on, leaving all of the structures behind.

Mark Strizic, who came with me to photograph the work, had a similar reaction, but went further, identifying the various forms as part of an abandoned camp. The long low structures of twigs, covered in tarred paper, were shelters for the tribe, whereas the square tent-like form was the chief's hut. The partly carved log of wood was reminiscent of the boat which had brought them to the site. The square structure, built above a hole on the ground was a well, essential for water. The fragile, little leaning construction on the outskirts of the settlement was a device for communication. The largest of all the sculptural forms, pyramidal in shape, was basically constructed of weathered recycled timber, topped with a fragile structure of twigs, partly covered in paper. This was an object of veneration and worship, a symbol of their religion.

When I saw the work for the second time, a week after the official opening, the magic of the imagery was almost lost. A third visit, a fortnight after the first viewing proved how temporary the whole installation was. Not only had the rain had a marked effect upon the tarred paper, but wind had played havoc with some of the fragile construction. However, most of the destruction was deliberate, for it was easy to identify the shape of a boot placed on top of broken twigs, the 'well' had been kicked in, the 'boat' had its superstructure destroyed.

One was forced to question the sculptor's motives in building such an installation. Was the

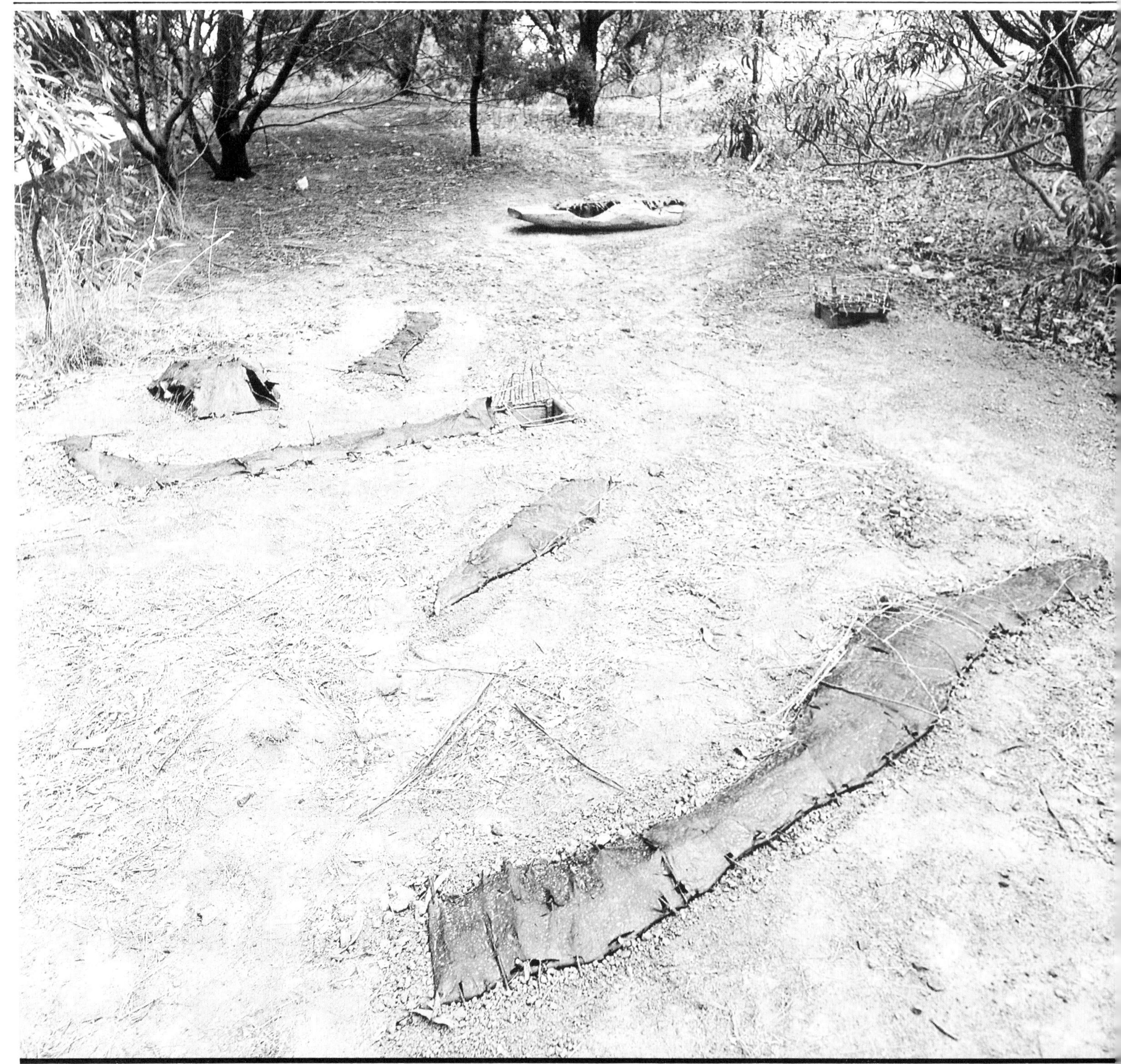

64 John Davis, general view of 'Place Two — An Installation' (1981). Wood, twigs, paper, tar, clay, earth. The work covered an area approximately 4 m wide by 12 m long. The installation was at La Trobe University, as part of the Australian Sculpture Triennial, 28 February–12 April 1981. Photograph by Mark Strizic.

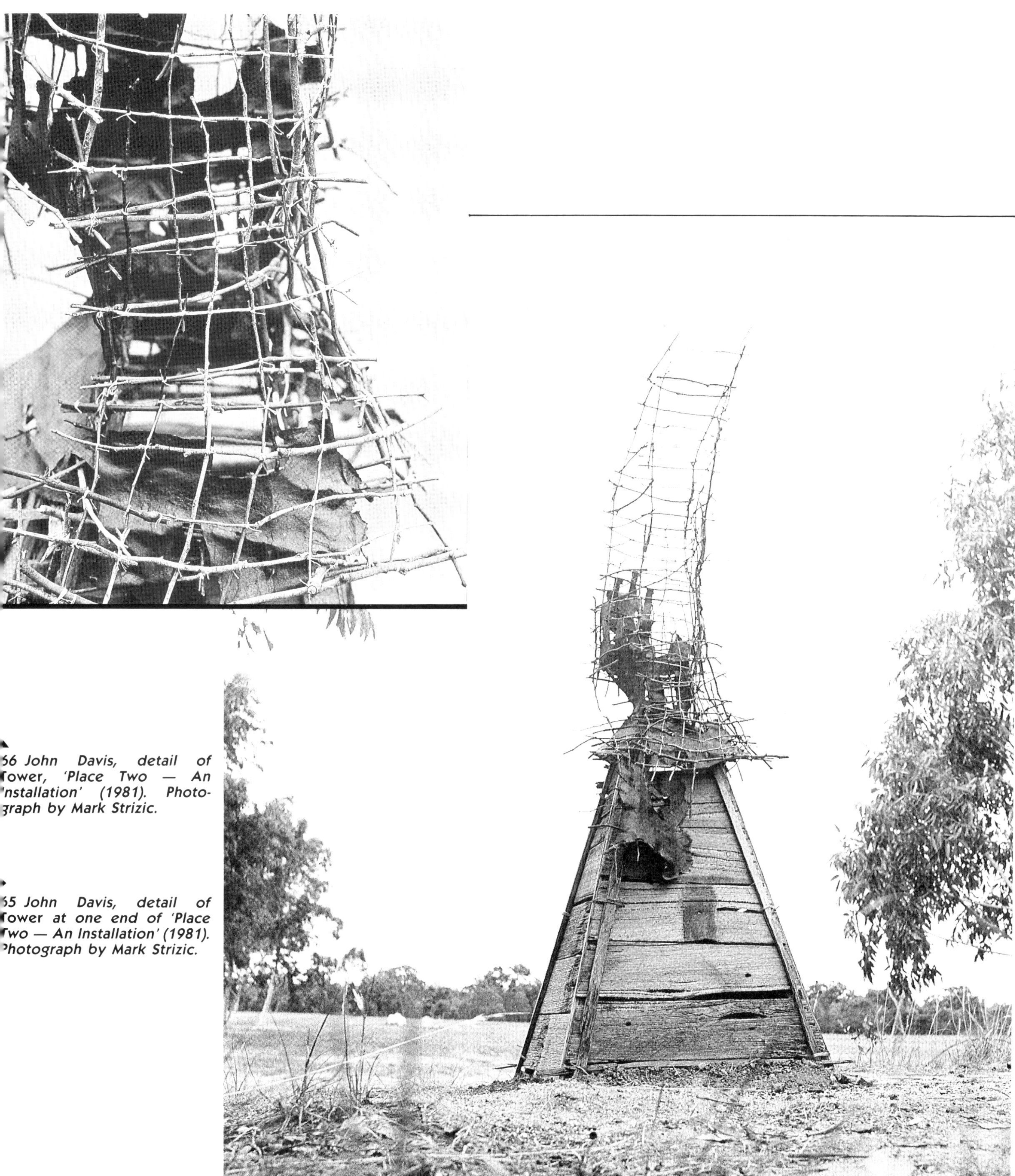

56 John Davis, detail of Tower, 'Place Two — An Installation' (1981). Photograph by Mark Strizic.

55 John Davis, detail of Tower at one end of 'Place Two — An Installation' (1981). Photograph by Mark Strizic.

main satisfaction for the artist gained in the process of construction? If the artist wished to communicate his ideas to other people, then how many spectators saw the work in the first week before it was destroyed? What opinion do visitors form when looking at a structure that is partly destroyed? When does the gallery director or artist remove the work, or is it still valid until it decays completely? Is the work produced to be viewed by the general public, or is it for a selected élite? Is it going to be known to posterity by a catalogue entry?

John Davis expressed his own thoughts on the ephemeral nature of some installations when he wrote:

■ *If my materials are temporal, it does not concern me. It's what they express at the time of their existence which matters, and if the materials deteriorate over time, then that becomes part of the work: the process continues as part of the content just the same as the space works in their installation. Therefore the materials embrace time and journey through their own history. Each exhibition is an event in my history.*[3]

John Davis has designed one installation that was meant to last and has in fact survived continual public exposure since 1980. About 1978 the City of Unley, a suburb of Adelaide, became engaged in an ambitious redevelopment scheme for the Unley Civic and Community Centre. They acquired a considerable number of nearby stone cottages, and by demolishing all the back fences and combining the backyards, created the Unley Village Green. The houses have since been used for a variety of art and craft activities such as ceramics and puppetry. The Council appointed a 'Civic and Community Centre Task Force . . . which in association with the Federal Visual Arts Board and the State Department for the Arts, held the competition to select an artist and sculpture for the Village Green'.[4] At the time the Adelaide sculptor, Tony Bishop, was both a member of the Visual Arts Board and on the Board of the Art Gallery of South Australia, so was a logical appointee to the Unley Committee. In a conversation with me he remembered that at first the Council had sought Visual Arts Board funding for a piece of sculpture to sit on a concrete slab near the Council offices — the slab was actually the remains of an old air raid shelter.[5] When the architects displayed plans for the redevelopment of the area, Tony Bishop asked why they were planning to add a piece of sculpture, like a brooch, as a decorative addition to the architecture. He suggested that any sculpture should be integrated with the landscape.

Eventually a total of $50,000 was raised from the Corporation of the City of Unley, the South Australian Department for the Arts, and the Visual Arts Board and artists were invited to submit proposals for the site. The judges (Stephen Nains, a representative of the Unley Council; Ian North, then Curator of Painting from the Art Gallery of South Australia; and Tony Bishop, representing the Visual Arts Board) gave the commission to John Davis. The symbolism of his work was understandable to the Council members, his concept permitted public use of the area without risk to children playing on the green, and it was unlikely to be attacked by vandals. All were practical points to be considered when locating a piece of public sculpture.

John Davis wrote a report on the concept of his environmental sculpture:

■ *The work is based on three factors:*
— *the four elements of air, water, fire, earth;*
— *the integration of these elements into the environment by using the existing spaces, common materials, topography of the Adelaide surroundings, and historical references;*
— *the potential of the space for public use.*

The landscape will be formed into three 'hills', each with a circular ground plan. Integrated into these are: rocks, representing earth; a steel disc, absorbing

▶ **67 John Davis, 'Environmental Sculpture' (detail), Village Green, Unley, South Australia (1980). The work consists of earth, stone, water, a steel disc and a windmill c. 10 m high with blades c. 4.25 m in diameter, in all covering an area approximately 40 x 21 m (Unley Council.) Photograph by the artist.**

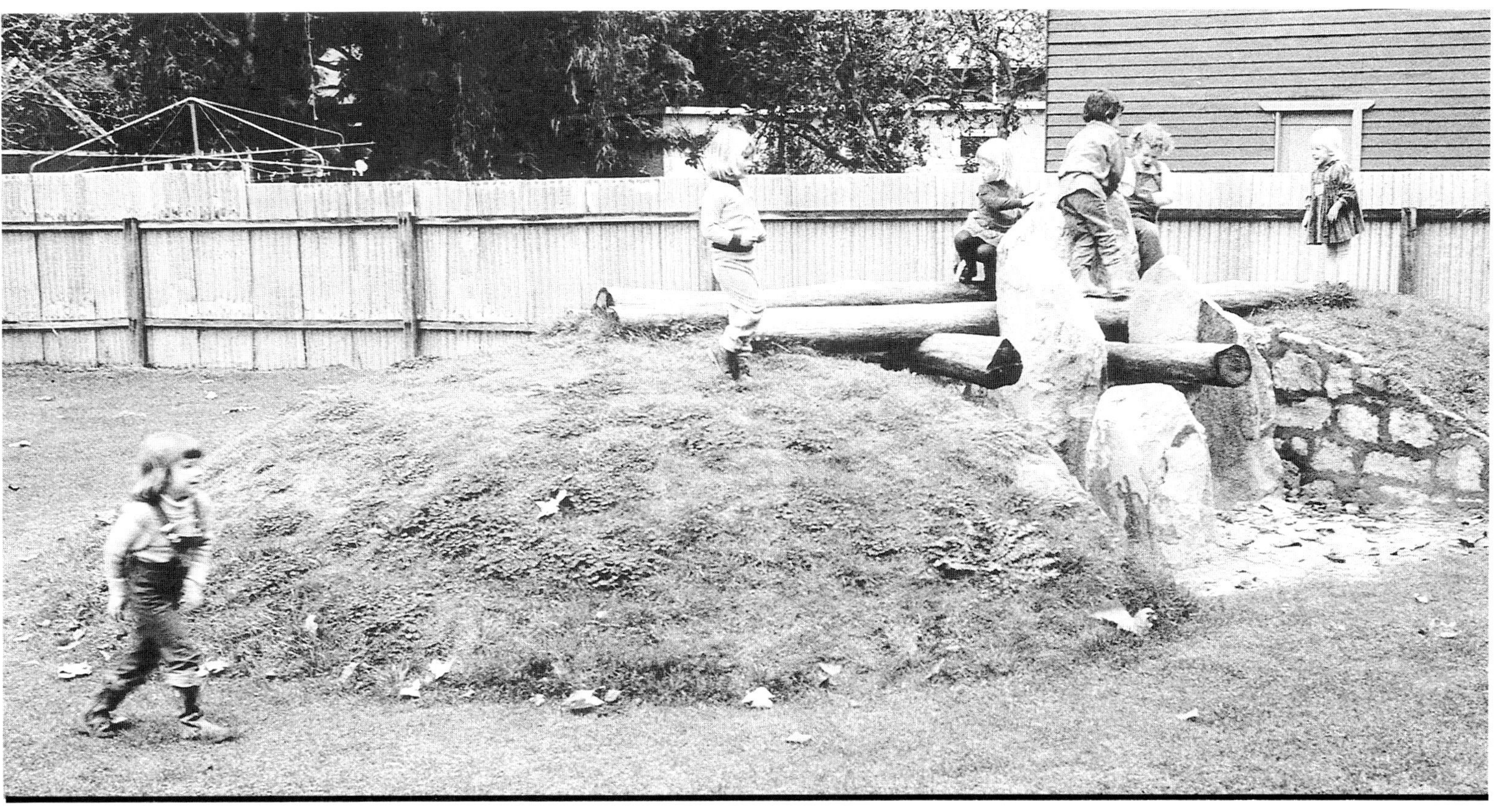

the heat of the sun, creating a 'column' of rising air and representing fire; a stone channel to contain water.

The 'hills' will vary in diameter and height.

Adjacent to the water segment will be an old windmill . . . which fulfills three roles:
— to indicate the air element through its use of wind;
— to draw water from the underlying watertable for use in the water piece nearby. The water will seep back into the earth to be re-used, thus establishing a cycle;
— an historic link to Adelaide and Unley's past when such a piece of machinery was commonplace and necessary to enable settlement to exist, and is a direct reference to the original Unley spring nearby.

On completion, the installation will visually reflect the Adelaide hills seen at the eastern end of the 'green', and to emphasise, through re-use, the stone used in the peripheral houses.

The 'green' itself caters for many activities including performers, entertainers and group activities. Physical aspects of the work may be of use in these activities; the 'fire' hill could be used as a stage, the gently rising hill for the water element could serve as a seating area, and the water itself — an attraction for children. The windmill, because of its height and movement, would be a landmark and create a feeling of happiness and activity in the district. On the other hand, the 'earth' piece will be placed in such a way as to create a feeling of contemplation and quiet, with a sense of its own separate presence, achieved through the arrangement of the forms and the space.

Consequently, the installation can be seen to work on different levels, some obvious and practical, others more subtle. It is my hope that the Community of Unley will recognise some aspect of the work which will have relevance and meaning to their experience of it.[6]

Grant Revell, Recreation Planner for the City of Unley, had been associated with the initial planning of the Unley Village Green Environmental Sculpture and with the art and craft activities in the nearby cottages. Talking with him in December 1982, two years after the work was completed, he was still enthusiastic about Davis's concept, which had been respected and enjoyed by the public. After only a couple of letters of protest, the work had been well received and the area frequently used as a public park. The 'fire' mound had occasionally been used as a small outdoor stage.

John Davis has only received three commissions

— the first was the result of winning the Comalco Prize in 1970, the second was the work for Unley in 1980 and the third was the installation at the Australian Embassy, Saudi Arabia in 1986. Comalco paid each of the invited artists a fee of $750 for their maquette and John Davis as the winner received $3000. The total cost of the Comalco Commission for the Hydro Electric Authority in Hobart, including casting, fabrication, transport, insurance and erection on the site was $12,534.

The allocation of money for the Unley work was eventually $30,000 (not $50,000 as originally planned),[7] but most of that sum went in materials such as earth, rocks, cement; equipment such as windmill and pump; hire of plumbers, stonemasons, front-end loader, crane and payment to student assistants. After paying obligatory fees to the two galleries that handled his work, Art Projects in Melbourne and Watters Gallery in Sydney, John Davis was left with $3000 from a fee of $4500 to cover his design and his physical participation on the site for ten days.

The installation at the Australian Embassy, Riyadh, Saudi Arabia was probably the most financially rewarding of the three commissions. John Davis was paid a fee of $10,000 and had his airfare and accommodation paid in order to supervise the installation of the work in the newly completed building. As the materials used were twigs, paper, canvas and synthetic bitumen his materials and production costs were low. Nevertheless, with only three commissions during a career of nearly thirty years it is little wonder that most sculptors in Australia have alternative jobs, mainly as lecturers in sculpture, or teachers of art, as the chance of earning sufficient money from their profession is very slight.

An article in an American art journal explored the problem:

■ *It is a simple fact that Australia has not yet bred a generation of artists who take it for granted, and even regard it as their natural right, to live from their art, measuring their success or failure by their ability to do so . . . Davis, for instance, only began occasionally selling his work in 1977. He feels that since he earns a comfortable living from teaching, he doesn't need to sell his art . . .*[8]

Having recognised this problem, one is then immediately aware of many more complex issues in our contemporary society. Who employs the sculptor and for what purpose? What is the role of the sculptor in a twentieth century capitalist society?

■ *Do our Australian sculptors wish to be commissioned by Australian firms? Do they wish to work for the multi-national corporations? That is where the money and power lies . . .*

The other alternative sources of power and money are the Federal and State Governments. Contemporary reasons for government involvement in funding the arts also appear to be more subtle than in the past as democratic governments do not wish to appear as though they have great wealth or power . . .

In all fairness, however, one must give praise to both Labor and Liberal parties for their continued support of the Australia Council, which has done much to stimulate the arts in Australia. It is an interesting reflection on our standard of living (notwithstanding current unemployment), that money can be spent on the arts. The recent inauguration of the Art Bank, set up as a lending authority for works of art (initially to Government organisations), is an interesting development, which may bring Australian contemporary art into areas at present living visually in the past.[9]

In realistic terms, Australian sculptors have a limited number of choices. They can continue to produce sculpture, hoping that when it is exhibited in commercial galleries some of it will sell. If they are young, or single, and prepared to accept a frugal lifestyle, they can exist precariously by taking unskilled manual labour jobs when money becomes short.

Alternatively, they can train to be an art/craft

▸ **69 Ron Robertson – Swann, Vault (1979–80). Steel, painted yellow, 615 x 1185 x 1003 cm. Originally designed for City Square, Melbourne, moved to Batman Park (City of Melbourne). Photograph by the author.**

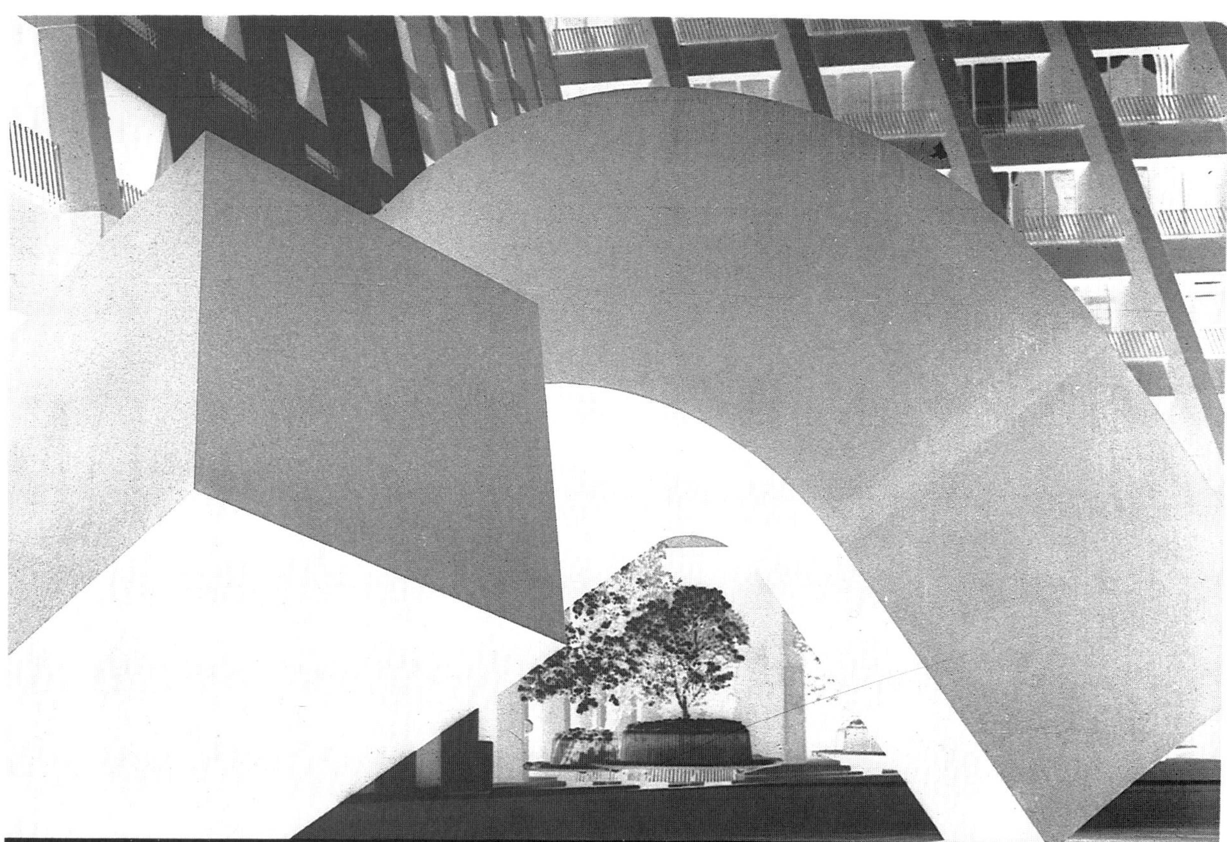

▶ *68 Clement Meadmore, Awakening, corten steel. 447 x 785 x 691 cm. AMP Square, Bourke Street, Melbourne. Photograph by the author.*

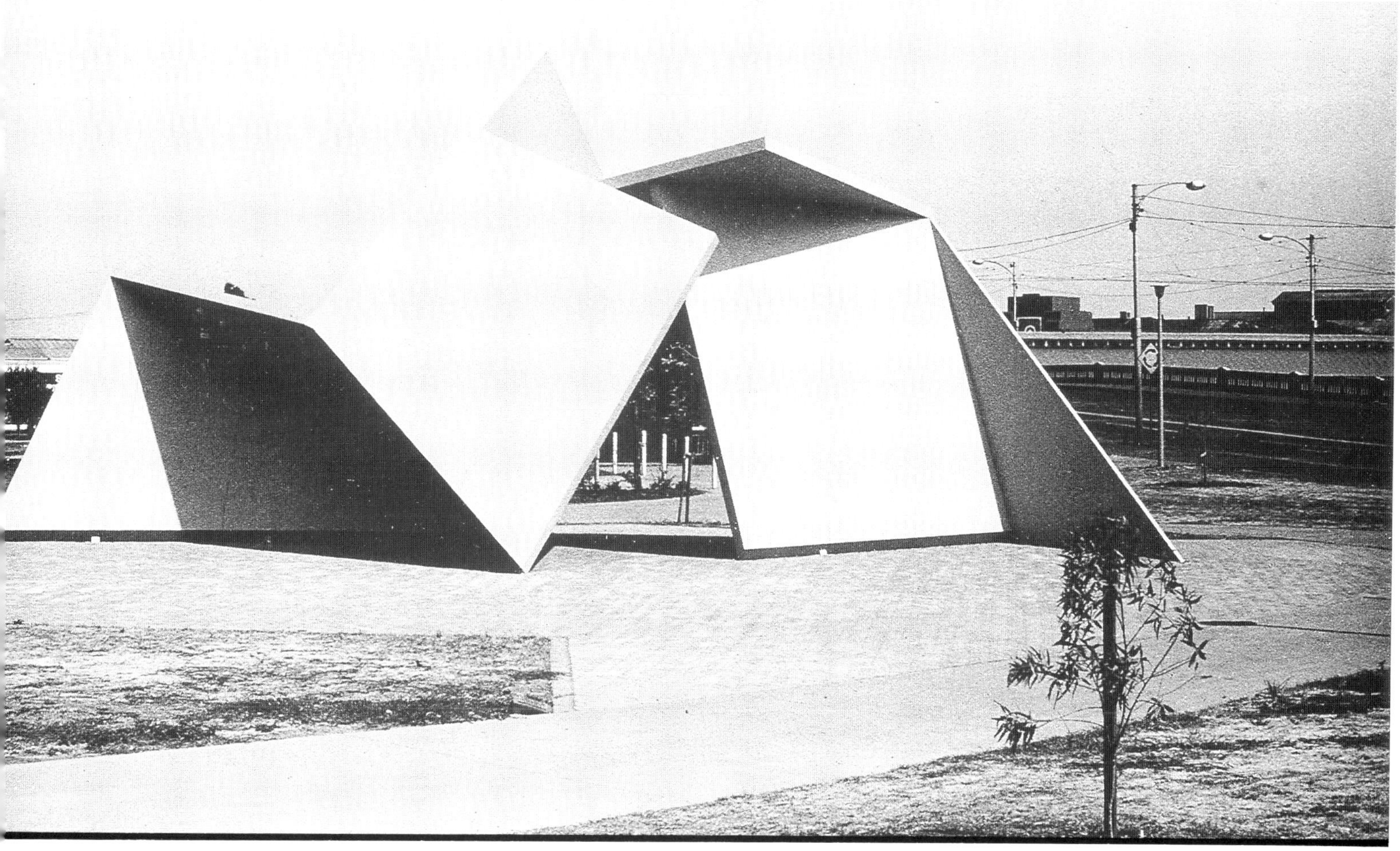

teacher in a secondary school. After some years of teaching and producing sculpture at weekends, they can try to get a position as lecturer in sculpture at a tertiary institute. Once on the staff of an art school they are in effect subsidised by the Federal Government. As the tertiary art school will only employ practising artists, it automatically follows that once having employed the artists to teach, they must also be given time in which to practise their art. A full-time lecturer will get one, or possibly two days a week, plus weekends, in which to concentrate on his work.

A limited number of sculptors have managed to build solid, professional reputations for themselves, often after many years of limited recognition and low income. They reach the stage where commissions can provide a sufficient, even if very irregular, income. Interestingly, a number of women artists could be placed in this category, such as Margel Hinder, Norma Redpath and Inge King.

It would be heartening to report that architects, town planners and landscape architects are encouraging artists by incorporating sculpture in their planning. Sadly this is not the case. There are isolated examples of enlightened patronage by architects and limited examples of co-operation between architect and sculptor, but they are all too few. Part of the 'Centre Five' programme in Melbourne during the 1960s (see Chapter 1) was to attempt to build links with architects. Even though some of the members, notably Inge King, eventually received some major architectural commissions, it cannot be said that 'Centre Five' managed to alter the overall situation.

The greatest potential for commissions for sculptors lies with State and Federal Governments. The Federal Government has been cautiously interested and particularly in Canberra, through the National Capital Development Commission, has purchased or commissioned a considerable quantity of sculpture, though one would have wished for more quality.

At least Canberra has sculpture of the twentieth century, whereas one could be forgiven for thinking that most of Melbourne's sculpture was produced in the nineteenth century. In the city of Melbourne there are two major works by Clement Meadmore (illus. 68), a sophisticated arrangement by Ken Reinhard, a banished Ron Robertson-Swann, and a group of contemporary works associated with the Arts Centre in St Kilda Road: not very many pieces of twentieth century sculpture in a city of three million people.

The predominance of nineteenth century figurative sculpture in Melbourne made the sudden arrival of Ron Robertson-Swann's *Vault* (illus. 69) more than the general public could accept. With a nineteenth century Gothic Revival cathedral at one end of the City Square and a nineteenth century Classical Revival Town Hall at the other end, how could the 'Yellow Peril' survive?[10] It was moved to a disused piece of land beside an elevated railway line, surrounded by roads and heavy traffic.

State and Federal Governments are cautious, city councils are conservative, and the general public is ill-informed, if not hostile, towards contemporary sculpture. If a sculptor is producing works in durable materials, such as bronze or steel, there is the chance that a major public company will purchase a work to add prestige to a plaza or foyer, but if the work is in fragile or impermanent materials, then sales are even more limited.

Most of Davis's work is in such materials. There is obviously no chance of sales for impermanent installations in the bush. A commission such as the work for Unley City Council is a once-in-a-lifetime possibility. Remarkably few private collectors purchase sculpture. Sculptors hope to see their work in the collections of the major State Galleries, but there are only seven, including Darwin, although there is now one privately funded public gallery in Brisbane.

At the time of writing, John Davis is represented in the following State Galleries: Australian National Gallery, Canberra; Art Gallery of New South Wales; National Gallery of Victoria; Tasmanian Museum and Art Gallery; Queensland Art Gallery; Art Gallery of Western Australia, and the recently established Museum of Contemporary Art, Brisbane, which has the most comprehensive collection of John Davis's sculpture.

The smaller Regional Galleries in the country cities and towns are usually operating on a very limited budget and the Directors are frequently obliged to accept the subtle restrictions of a conservative regional public. Surprisingly, three Regional Galleries in Victoria have works by John Davis in their collections: Geelong, Mildura and Shepparton. But none have purchased his fragile constructions of twigs and sticks.

Now in his late forties, producing mature works of originality and great sensitivity, with many productive years ahead, one can only wonder how many more works Davis will produce. And who will buy them? With approximately a hundred pieces of sculpture permanently in storage,[11] many given away to friends, others destroyed, some re-used in later works, one wonders what drives him to keep on producing — certainly not financial return.

■ NOTES

[1] John Davis, 'Some Brief Notes on Issues Which I Think are Raised in My Art', written in answer to questions from Kimio Akiyama, Editorial Department, *Ikebana Ohara*, November 1982.

[2] *John Davis: A Sculptural Installation*, Wollongong City Gallery, 10 September–12 October 1980.

[3] John Davis, 'Some Brief Notes on Issues Which I Think are Raised in My Art', op. cit.

[4] Andrea Young, Recreation Planner, City of Unley, letter to the author, 23 May 1983.

[5] Tony Bishop in conversation with the author, 19 March 1983.

[6] John Davis, 'Unley Environmental Sculpture Commission', *News from the Visual Arts Board*, Sydney, February 1981. Reprinted from Grant R. B. Revell, *Unley Civic and Community Centre, Environmental Project Schedule Report*, November 1980.

[7] Grant R. B. Revell, ibid.

[8] Suzi Gablik, 'Report from Australia', *Art in America* (New York), vol. 69, no. 1, January 1981.

[9] Ken Scarlett, 'Who Employs the Sculptor?', *The First Australian Sculpture Triennial*, Preston Institute of Technology and La Trobe University, 28 February–12 April 1981.

[10] 'Yellow Peril' was the name given to *Vault* by the media. The title suggests an alien philosophy, hints at invasion, trades on racial prejudice and skilfully sums up the reaction of many people who saw *Vault* as a direct threat.

[11] Some years ago John Davis purchased a block of land in the country and built a shed for storage of his sculpture.

It is fascinating to analyse the reasons for an artist's success. In Australia, the characteristics needed for success are varied, not always relying on the quality of the work produced. To be known is one basic prerequisite. This is achieved by producing work regularly, exhibiting frequently, and being seen and recognised at well patronised galleries, particularly on opening nights. The gallery chosen for exhibitions should have a policy of exhibiting contemporary art; have a clientele of wealthy professionals — doctors, dentists, solicitors, accountants; should have good contacts with the State Galleries and particularly with the Australian National Gallery. Good sales help to prove success, especially when they are to the State and Regional Galleries, for these are a stamp of approval. Furthermore, the various public collections can be listed in subsequent catalogues, giving an added impetus to sales.

As well as the State Galleries there is the Australia Council and its various Boards, giving approval in the form of cash grants for travel, study, equipment or simply time in which to work. The Australia Council, acting in association with the Department of Foreign Affairs, makes decisions as to which artists will represent Australia overseas at such prestigious exhibitions as San Paolo, Venice Biennale, Paris Triennale, or be included in government-sponsored exhibitions travelling in Asia or Europe.

It is a strange contradiction that in a capitalist society which has very little use for art and artists, it is the government bodies that give the stamp of approval.

Success is also promoted by articles in magazines, such as *Art and Australia*, or more recently *Art Network* or *Art and Text*. Interestingly these magazines, with relatively small circulation, do more to build artistic reputations than does the television, which seldom seriously concerns itself with the local contemporary artist. 'Art' on television is Robert Hughes or Sir Kenneth Clark, with a lavishly produced programme expensively promoted. The local contemporary artists have a very low television rating unless they can do something outrageous.

It is commonly assumed that the newspaper art critic has the power to promote artists and build reputations, though I believe this is exaggerated in artists' minds. One can remember Patrick McCaughey's championing of abstract expressionist art and the painters and sculptors who showed at the Chapman Powell Street Gallery in the 1970s in Melbourne, but in general it would appear that the art critic's power is negative rather than positive. Current art criticism tends to be cynical and destructive rather than optimistic, appreciative and positive. Certainly it is relatively easy to belittle an artist's reputation, to reduce attendance at exhibitions and lessen sales, but in general over the last decade collectors have become more sophisticated and willing to make up their own minds without such reliance on the critics' reviews.

One ingredient that the artist adds to the recipe for success is maturity — that nebulous quality, almost impossible to define. We have all known students with great talent, who have failed to develop. But we have also seen artists such as Brett Whiteley producing convincing, mature work in his mid-twenties. At the other end of the scale, an artist such as Roger Kemp produced his best work at the age of 70. For an artist, maturity is the rare moment when personal philosophy, concepts of art, style, media and technique all fuse to produce totally convincing work.

And beyond all of these characteristics of success is the crucial matter of timing. Sometimes the timing can be manipulated by a dealer, an art critic or by the skilful use of publicity in newspapers and art magazines, but timing is usually just a matter of

▶
70 John Davis, works which were shown at Fourth Indian Triennale, New Delhi, in February 1978. Rear left, Parts; centre, Marker; foreground, Wood/Stone, all produced in 1977. Twigs, branches, string, canvas, paper, papier mâché, latex, underfelt, rock. Photographed by Sue Vaughan in studio at Prahran College of Advanced Education prior to Indian Triennale.

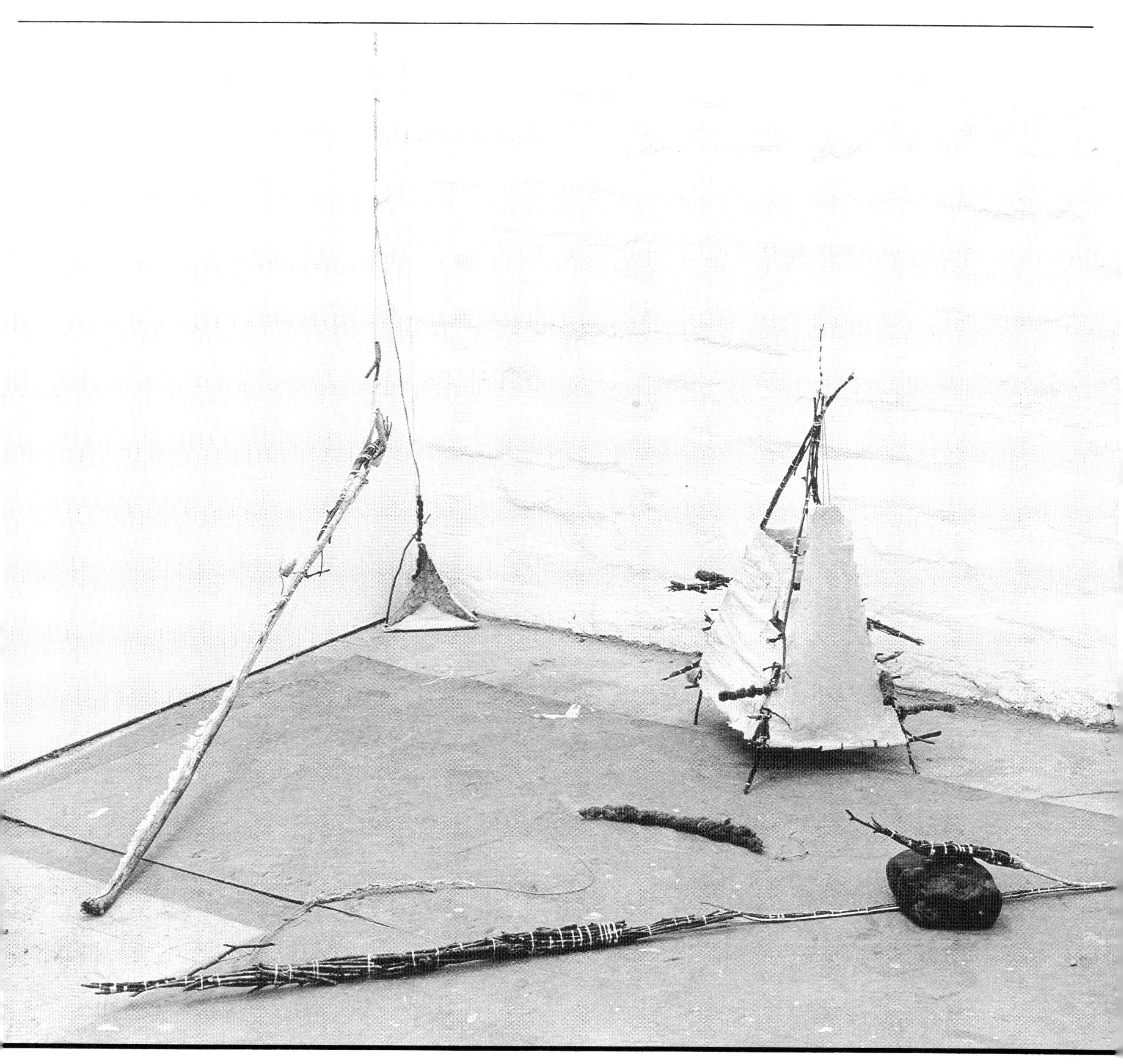

luck, of being in the right place at the right time and then being perceptive enough to realise the situation and make use of it.

For John Davis, 1978 was the culmination of his previous years of success. By that year he was well known as a sculptor, having shown at major galleries in Melbourne, Sydney, Brisbane and Adelaide, as well as exhibiting in important competitions and in the Mildura Triennial since its inception in 1961. He had received a great deal of publicity when he won the prestigious Comalco Prize and carried out the commission for the Hydro Electric Commission in Hobart. John Davis was much respected as a teacher and the Sculpture Department of Prahran College of Advanced Education was looked upon as a stimulating studio for the study of contemporary sculpture. His work was in important public collections in Victorian Regional Galleries, several Colleges of Advanced Education in Australia, though, at that time, in only one State Gallery — the Art Gallery of New South Wales. In 1976 he had been Artist-in-Residence at Monash University.

He began the year with a visit to India in late January, setting up his work in New Delhi for the Fourth Indian Triennale, which opened in February.

I suspect that the spectator can approach the work of John Davis visually with comparative ease, given a certain knowledge of sculpture and contemporary art forms, given also a degree of sophistication. But to read his titles sometimes results in an intellectual discussion with oneself, justifying, clarifying, ferretting out the meaning. The general title for his works shown in India was 'Location, Displacement, Transference and Installation and Exchange Work'. 'Location' referred to sites in Australia; 'Displacement, Transference', displaced from their original sites and transferred to India; 'Installation', installed within the confines of the pavilion of the Indian Triennale; 'Exchange Work',

small sculptures made specifically for exchange, particularly with other Indian artists.

The individual works had separate titles: *Parts*, *Wood/Stone*, *Mat*, *Marker*, *Journey 3*, *Lean-to*, and twenty Exchange Works (illus. 70). All of these titles would have been confusing for the average Indian, but then the 'average' Indian was even less likely to visit an exhibition of contemporary art than is the 'average' Australian. The audience in New Delhi was even more upper-middle class than it would be in the galleries of Australia. To visit an exhibition in India it was necessary to have wealth, education, time, and a sophisticated attitude capable of encompassing western art. The other group which visited the exhibition at New Delhi were the students from art schools, who were delighted to make first-hand contact with a contemporary western artist and be able to discuss his work. John Davis found the students at Baroda University anxious to talk with him, interested, sympathetic and intrigued by the sparse qualities and simple techniques of his sculpture.

In the large pavilion at New Delhi John Davis had one display area approximately 12 × 6 metres. *Parts* consisted of an open-sided, triangular pyramid, placed in a corner of the space. From this relatively small pyramid, a thin vertical went nervously upward. Coming down from the end of this vertical, like a line on a fishing rod, was a rough string. From the end of the string, sloping diagonally back to the floor, was a long straight branch of a tree. The whole structure was essentially linear and very sparse.

Wood/Stone lay casually on the floor. A long, fairly straight line, made up from a tied bundle of twigs to which a stone was attached. At the opposite end from the rock, a twiggy line meandered away from the straight line, petered out into a piece of string and then solidified into a thin cylinder made from underfelt.

Mat was also low-lying on the floor. The struc-

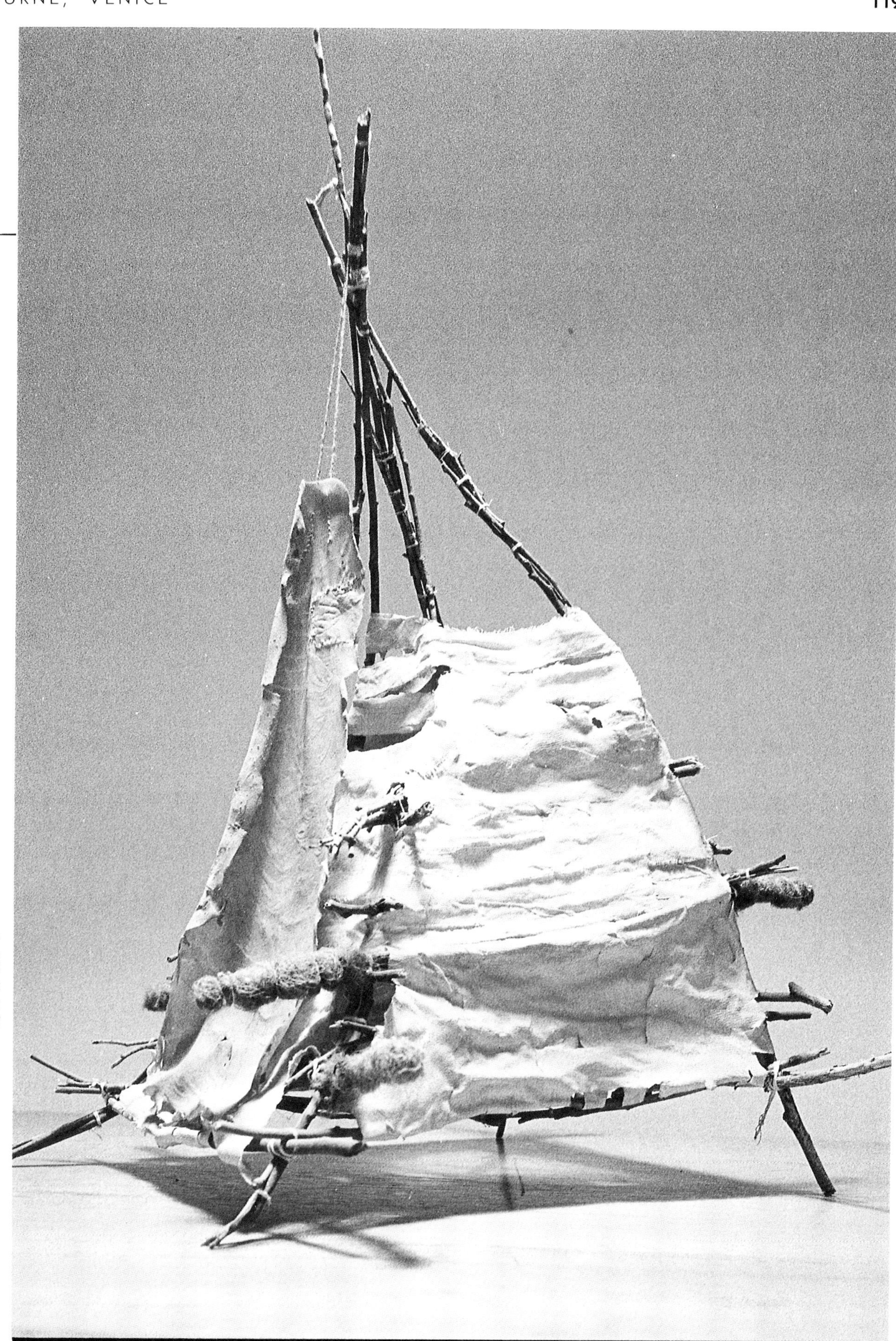

71 *John Davis, Marker (1977). Twigs, branches, string, paper, latex and underfelt. 63 x 43 x 46 cm (in the collection of Alun and Nola Leach Jones). Photograph by Mark Strizic.*

ture was obviously man-made, yet was reminiscent of an animal or bird's nest. One wondered if it were a ceremonial or symbolic recreation of a nest.

The whole installation appeared casual, though it had been carefully planned. In many ways it was similar to walking in the Australian bush — some objects were large and emphatic, as was *Marker* — but others, such as *Wood/Stone*, were the equivalent of the fallen branches and twigs that cover the ground in the Australian bush. Writing in the catalogue, Elwyn Lynn made note of Davis's use of space, which had the same dual quality, sometimes defined, other times deliberately vague: 'with Davis it is elusive, variable and undefined, both embracing and ignoring its environment — bringing to life an inert corner here or disregarding a formidable wall there'.[1]

Marker (illus. 71) was the most obviously sculptural object, being basically a square-based pyramid, with four feet on the ground. The construction was of twigs, tied together. The triangular sides were filled in with paper and latex. *Marker* reminded one of those pyramidal, wooden structures that inexplicably appear on tops of hills in the Australian countryside, or on promontories near the sea, presumably as guides to ships, planes or surveyors. Because one never sees anyone actually making use of these devices, they take on a strange, mysterious quality. They are always in good repair, freshly painted white, as though the practitioners of some secret religion tend them in the night.

Another work in the group at New Delhi was *Journey 3* (or *Journey III*). *Journey II*, which was shown at Watters Gallery in 1977, had been purchased by Patrick White and donated to the Art Gallery of New South Wales, so a new work *Journey 3*, was made for the Indian Exhibition.

Lean-to is now in the collection of Monash University.

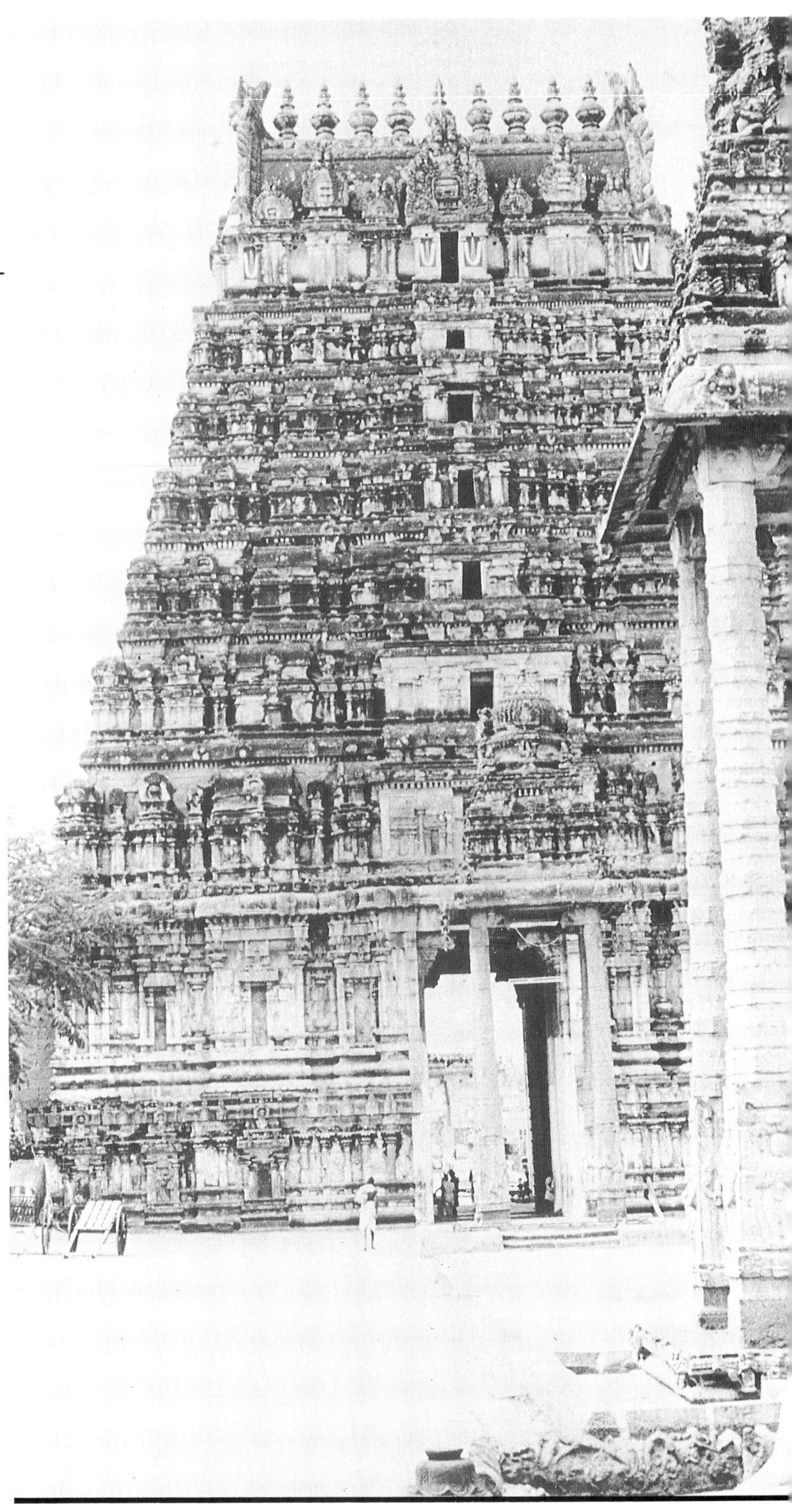

The twenty small Exchange Works must have been a source of puzzlement to the Indian viewers. John Davis had originally intended that the works would be available for immediate exchange, as he had done at Watters Gallery, but he was almost beaten by the Indian Customs officials, who ruled that everything he took into the country must also be taken out again. The exchange works were returned to Australia, then posted back to India as gifts.

John Davis was in India for seven weeks: three weeks setting up his own installation in New Delhi, acting as official commissioner for the Australian exhibition (which included the painter Keith Looby), then four weeks travelling. In a postcard to me dated 7 March 1978 he wrote:

■ *Liked Ellora better than Ajanta — more changes and variety — Buddhist, Hindu, Jain. So far I've been to Chandigarh, Simla, Lucknow, Varanasi, Jaipur, Aurangabad, Bombay — after Delhi. Tomorrow I go to Madras before staying at an artists' village on beach. The country is one huge living museum . . .*

The effects of India upon his work were neither immediate nor obvious. The cultural differences between Australia and India are so vast that in some ways it is extremely difficult for a short-term traveller to bridge the gap. Yet no one can go to India and be unaffected. The impact is too strong.

The Hindu architecture and religious mysticism intrigued Davis, rather than the clarity and logic of the Moslem architecture of northern India. The great temple complexes at Kancheepuram and Mahabalipuram south of Madras, and the huge rock-cut temples at Ellora, near Aurangabad, were the places that impressed. The basic structure of a Hindu temple is simple, an elementary post and beam system identical with that used by the Greeks. Yet, whereas the Parthenon has the pure joy of distilled logic, the Hindu temple has the mystery of the unknown, the unknowable. The struc-

ture of a Hindu temple almost ceases to be recognisable under a burden of decoration, which covers every surface, column, beam, ceiling and wall, only the floor being smooth, worn and polished by countless bare feet. The brilliant sunlight of India throws the exterior decoration into strong relief and makes the contrast with the dark interiors all the greater. The temples of Kancheepuram can have a strong impact, even on a non-believer. As one proceeds within the dark complex one is aware of a great stillness and strength, the cumulative power of endless prayers and offerings made by countless pilgrims over the centuries.

Davis's work already had an element of mystery, but his visit to India reinforced this aspect. His exhibition at Pinacotheca Gallery in 1974 had illustrated this latent mysticism. It could be found in his use of simple objects which gained a strange significance by being displayed in boxes, as though they were specimens worthy of preservation and inspection, and in the repetitious use of the numbers 3 and 9 which seemed to impart a magical significance to the objects, grouped in compartments.

The works shown at Watters Gallery in 1977 had also frequently hinted at the mysterious. *Journey II*, a large grid of sticks, string, latex, paper and underfelt hung from the ceiling, like a large and enigmatic map. What was shown on the map? Secret sites? Places for sacred rituals? Was *Journey II* only understandable to those already initiated into some secret religion?

Only in a work such as *Cape Schank* (illus. 73), made during 1978–79, both before and after his visit to India, does John Davis make the interest in ritual and mysticism appear obvious. The tower and the small platform of twigs take on a religious connotation, made all the more definite by the careful arrangement of rocks on the platform, like sacred objects on an altar. Even though the artist's statement, in the catalogue of 'Survey 15, Relics and Rituals', is deliberately cool and detached, John Davis nevertheless says '. . . the symbolism is much more apparent'.[2]

The influence of India upon John Davis and his work has generally been subtle and slow to emerge. His structures have become more complex, more intricate, but without losing the simple, almost geometric forms that underly them. It is as though the huge gopurams, the decorated temple gates of the Hindu complexes, reinforced his interest in tower forms and encouraged his love of complexity. Perhaps *Region*, shown at Watters Gallery in 1981, suggests the closely packed mud brick homes and the narrow streets of an Indian village rather than the characteristics of an Australian country town.

After travelling to other parts of India, particularly Madras, where he made contact with Indian artists, John Davis returned to Australia just in time for the opening of his exhibition at the National Gallery of Victoria. The plane from India was late, so he arrived an hour and a half after the opening. 'Survey 1 — John Davis', was the first of a series of exhibitions organised by Robert Lindsay to show the work of contemporary Australian artists. 'Survey 1 — John Davis' was later shown at the Art Gallery of New South Wales in May–June of the same year.

Robert Lindsay, the newly appointed Associate Curator of Australian Art — Contemporary (see Chapter 8) had experienced great difficulty in finding a space within the National Gallery of Victoria where the 'Survey' exhibitions could be shown. After twelve months of negotiating and planning, the narrow area to the left of the main foyer was allocated. As an exhibition space it was not entirely satisfactory — it was a main thoroughfare giving access to the Asian Collections, the Great Hall, and the cafeteria and one side was a wall of glass, looking out to an internal courtyard. Exhibitions had to

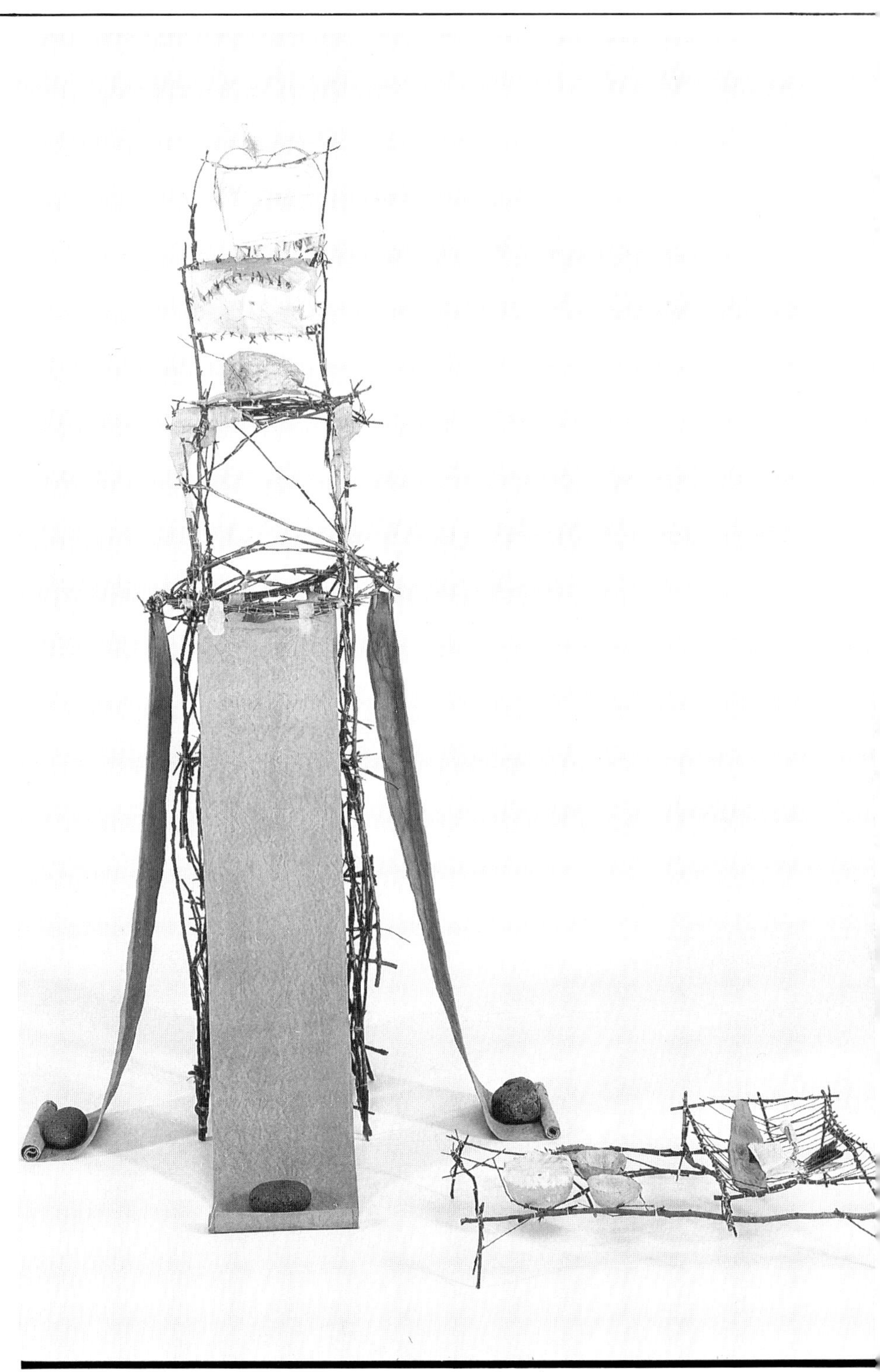

be displayed without impeding the flow of pedestrian traffic through the area. Nevertheless, the first 'Survey' exhibition was welcomed by Melbourne's art community as a public statement by the National Gallery of Victoria and the new Director, Eric Rowlison, that contemporary Australian art would be shown — not ignored, as some felt had been the case in the past.

No doubt one of the reasons why Robert Lindsay chose John Davis for the first 'Survey' exhibition was because his work had not been shown much in Melbourne, since his one person exhibition in September 1974, at Pinacotheca Gallery, and his small exhibition at the Exhibition Gallery, Monash University, in September 1975. His work had been chosen to represent Australia at the Indian Triennial and the Venice Biennale, yet it had not been seen in Melbourne where John Davis lived and worked. He had shown frequently in group exhibitions but it was four years since he had shown any quantity of work in Melbourne, and in that time his work had changed a great deal.

'Survey 1' set a pattern for subsequent 'Survey' exhibitions. Work was carefully selected to show the work of the particular artist, a colour video was made in which the artist talked about his work and a simple but authoritative catalogue was produced, available to visitors for a small donation.

The sculpture in 'Survey 1' ranged from early wood carvings of the mid-1960s such as *Abreaction* and *Bent on Mayhem*, to works in industrial materials, such as aluminium, fibreglass and car duco; from the individual object to the concern with repetitions systems; from the precious object to the use of cheap commonplace materials allied with low technology.

Of the thirty-one works shown, only the last four gave a hint of the new style that John Davis had developed. The exhibition at New Delhi, on display at the same time as 'Survey 1', clearly showed

the current style — informal structures built of twigs and sticks, covered in papier mâché, set in a loosely defined space. Only the last object in the 'Survey' exhibition, *Bicycle II*, had the characteristics of his latest work.[3] So though the exhibition was a survey of the work of John Davis, it did not point to his current and future style. John Davis had become well known throughout Australia, amongst artists and gallery directors in particular, but the public in Melbourne did not see a large body of his current work after he ceased exhibiting with the Pinacotheca Gallery in 1974 and the last of the theme shows were held at the Ewing Gallery in 1975. Admittedly John Davis did have a one person exhibition at Art Projects, Melbourne, in April 1979, but Art Projects had a small gallery space, and though the gallery was much respected by contemporary artists, one could not say that it had a mass following. (Art Projects closed in January 1985.) His next one person exhibitions were at Watters Gallery, Sydney in 1979; Institute of Modern Art, Brisbane in 1980; Wollongong City Art Gallery in 1980; Q Space Annex, Brisbane in 1980; and again at Watters in November 1981.

It may have been this lack of exposure in Melbourne, the fact that many people were unaware that John Davis had developed a mature and individual style, that caused Ronald Millar to write a strongly critical review of 'Survey 1'. He saw only the succession of styles that John Davis had worked in, without being aware of the body of recent work.

■ *The choice of John Davis, a sculptor, for the first show, is safe — too safe. If the curator had been casting about for someone on the local scene who could exemplify in one exhibition the successive modes of recent modern sculpture, he could have done no better than Davis. Nothing funky or ill-mannered or excessive, but tentative excursions into those areas where the ground has been cleared fairly well. Davis embraces (if that is not too passionate a word for his cool pro-*

ductions) multiples and conceptual art, art language and minimalism, organic forms and ecological art, video and the trendy democratising of art . . . in other words, the standard advance-guard conventions.

He is one of those artists whose progress (I will not say development) is marked by a gentle shifting from one academically acceptable manner to another. At each stage there is a neat and apparently effortless transition, with demonstration pieces to fit. These are expertly crafted, with an obvious sensitivity to the various properties of his materials, alloy, fibreglass, plastics, cloth, sticks, paper.

Davis is an enterprising technician. Some of the sculpture is better than much of its kind in and around Melbourne, but to see it all solemnly documented with a curatorial gloss worthy of some old master's retrospective, only exposes the artist's limits.

Two television screens at the entrance show the artist expounding his points of view in a long monologue: the catalogue makes every minor arrangement of twig and newsprint seem as portentous as Picasso's studies for Guernica. *Perhaps it is just the kind of exhibition curators like: it is 'educational', in the sense that it reflects historical and topical art currents, it is easy to mistake Davis's changes for gradual improvements, and it underlines the pernicious critical idea of the theory coming before the art.*

What the show really does is to prove that a creative attitude based on the display of processes (rather than upon compulsion) can be sterile. One would like to see a more personal Davis, less precious craft and more risk.

His later work seems to me the best, not because the style is more up-to-date but because the feeling begins to show . . .

As to the next few surveys, perhaps the management could go for something quite unfashionable or at least not quite so pompous in the treatment.[4]

On the other hand, when the exhibition transferred to Sydney, the critic, W. E. P. Pidgeon, who appeared to be more familiar with the work of Davis, saw the various styles in the context of his environment and paid due respect to him as a mature and significant sculptor.

■ *The Art Gallery of NSW presents 'Survey 1', a retrospective exhibition of works by Victorian sculptor John Davis.*

Sculptures and documentations trace the development of his art since 1964.

The 1977 works reveal the mature, self-realised artist, one who has already made a significant contribution to Australian culture.

The variations in style and technique made during those years can be understood only when we relate them to a common factor — the artist's constant involvement with his environment and period.

The materials he uses are representative of specific places and their appropriate technologies . . .

During the past few years he has reidentified himself with our bushland and expresses his response to it in materials of the simplest nature: twigs, fibres, strings and paper.

With these he has created a personalised and immediately recognisable artistic unity . . .

The assemblage Nomad, *which deals with the integration of man and the land, gives the key to the Aboriginal quality of his recent works.*

In these, space, time and organic processes are resolved with elemental simplicity.[5]

How fascinating that the same exhibition of works by the same artist could receive such different reviews in Melbourne and Sydney!

Later that year Davis's work was shown at the Australian exhibition at the Venice Biennale, which was open to the public for three months from July 1978. Australia showed for the first time at Venice in 1956 with a selection of paintings by Sidney Nolan, Russell Drysdale and William Dobell. In 1958 it was paintings from Arthur Boyd and the late Sir Arthur Streeton. Then there was a lapse of twenty years until 1978, when the works of John Davis, Robert Owen and Ken Unsworth were exhibited. The title chosen for the 1978 Venice Biennale was ideal for John Davis, 'From Nature to Art, From Art to Nature'. It was a happy coincidence, perfect timing.

The three Australian artists showing at the Venice Biennale in 1978 were a strangely diverse group. Ken Unsworth was a sculptor and performance artist, Robert Owen showed drawings and sculptural constructions, and John Davis exhibited an installation which filled a large room.

The room was a perfect exhibition space for John Davis, a characterless void in which he could establish an environment (illus. 74). The room was very simple, with a painted wooden floor and white walls, without any skirting board between floor and wall, without any moulding around the doorway — in fact no actual door, just a space. The light was diffused, coming through a glass roof below which a white cloth had been stretched. The usual gallery spotlights were absent.

Even though none of the objects amongst Davis's work were directly reminiscent of the structures of a country town, the parts nevertheless suggested the aerial view of an Australian township. A European town is compact and the division between city and country often quite decisive. An Australian town usually straggles in an uncertain manner, from the predictable main street to the outskirts, where country and town compete uneasily. Without actually suggesting any of the objects, John Davis wanted to create the casual, untidy feel of a country town — the isolated farm houses on the outskirts, the abandoned cars and outmoded farm equipment rusting in paddocks, sheds, barns, garages — and the irregular, undefined space between them.

Early settlers in Australia found the Australian bush very untidy and when compared with the regularity of a European birch or pine forest it is so. Few Australian trees grow straight and regular. The characteristics of the Australian bush and the Australian town are strangely similar. In both cases the relationship between objects is casual, tentative, a situation in which one is as much conscious of the space between objects as of the objects themselves.

An Australian, looking at the sculptures in the Venice installation, may have found references to known and observed objects. *Ridge* was actually in three parts, named after three beaches Davis had visited — Jan Juc, Green Cape and Mallacoota. In each case, a line of string which stretched irregularly along the floor suggested low hills, papier mâché rocks imitated the solid mass of boulders, fragments attached to the string were similar to the flotsam found at high-water line on the beach. But the references were deliberately vague — perhaps it wasn't debris on the sand but material left behind after floods, debris caught in wire fences, around posts or stranded in irregular heaps by receding water.

Tower was a tall structure built from short twigs, a wobbly square prism, moving upwards, looking as though construction had not finished. Again, one could find parallels in the Australian countryside — lookout towers for spotting bushfires, shark-watch towers on the beach. Or was *Tower* more reminiscent of childhood games, a weekend activity with a couple of mates, an improvised lookout tower at the bottom of the backyard?

Marker A and *Marker B* were similar to *Marker* shown at the Indian Triennale. Their verticality was needed in the installation to set up a relationship with *Tower*. The three works made a direct contrast with *Ridge*, *Device* and *Flag Renamed Place*, which were all essentially horizontal and sitting flat on the floor.

Observant Australians visiting the installation

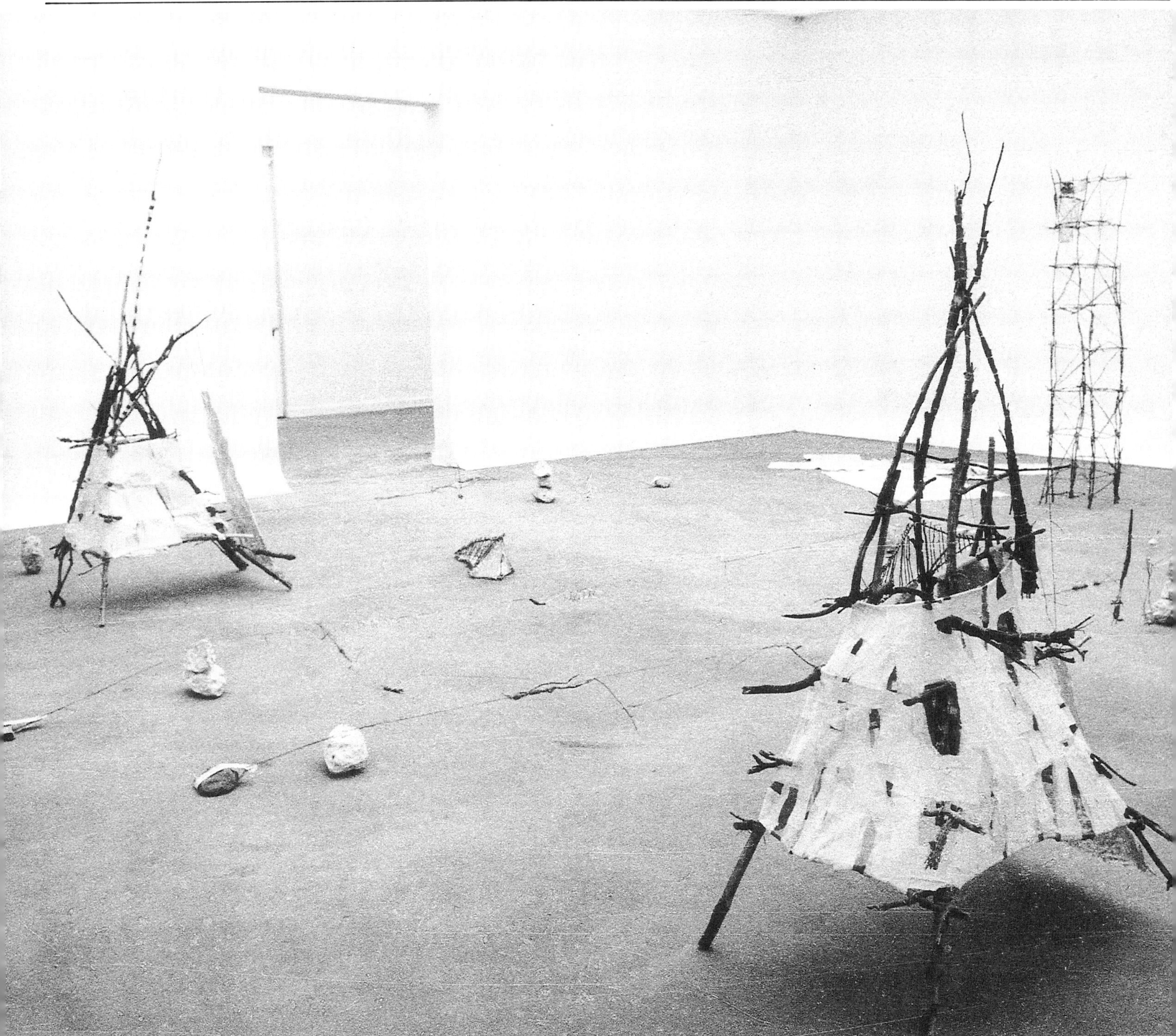

74 John Davis, 'Continuum and Transference', installation at Venice Biennale, 1978. *Rear:* Flag (1978), canvas and latex, string, twigs, feathers and cast paper stones; (later called Flag Renamed Place). *Rear right:* Tower (1978), twigs, string, papier mâché, stone, canvas and latex. Left and foreground Marker A and Marker B (1977), twigs, branches, string, papier mâché, latex and underfelt. On the floor: various parts of Ridge (1977) and Device (1978). *Photograph by the artist.*

may have noted the links with the Australian landscape, been aware of the general similarities, but a European visitor to the Venice Biennale would not have had these stored mental images. The European saw the installation firstly as art, then possibly generalised from this concerning the nature of Australia and Australians. Any visitor must have been aware of distance and space — distance being the actual physical separation of objects, the measurement between them, the isolation of parts, and space being that illusive three dimensional quality, the shape of the void. Even Australians living in cities are still very aware of distance in Australia, it is a factor to be contended with. For Europeans the scale is different. In Europe travel between cities never removes one from evidence of mankind and civilisation, but in Australia, the space between cities is often a great void. One goes out into the unknown and then returns. Time becomes a conscious thing.

Some of these illusive qualities were evident in the work of John Davis at Venice. One wonders if Europeans were able to make contact, or whether they merely saw the installation as sparse or empty.

Nature in Europe has been tamed, forced to conform to man's sense of order. The average Australian shelters in a large city and for most of the working year does not need to go beyond the suburbs. Nevertheless, the annual holidays give everyone an opportunity to escape the confines of the city when the reality of the Australian continent is made clear again. The traveller with air-conditioned caravan is forced to realise that in Australia, Nature is large and man is insignificant. Except for Botanical Gardens in some of the capital cities, Australians have few opportunities of observing the results of man forcing nature to conform. Australians are much more aware of the characteristics of the natural bush which, though invaded by campers, traversed by road, flown over by planes, desecrated by beer cans, is still an aspect of nature in which mankind is the intruder.

In a way, the spectator was the intruder in the installation in Venice. There was no obvious entrance, no path, no commanding view, no centre of interest or climax. It was like a walk in the Australian bush. One proceeded from object to object, with one eye on the floor in case one tripped over the smaller parts sitting on the floor. The whole layout was casual, the parts were separate, with few compositional devices used to hold the installation together. It had little more formal order than the Australian bush, but the installation also had as much visual unity as one presumes there is in the Australian landscape. The materials used were dried twigs and branches, to which were added string, papier mâché, latex, canvas and a few feathers. The colour was minimal, merely the faded brown of the twigs and the off-white of papier mâché, latex or canvas. Textures varied from the brittleness of dried twigs to the dough-like quality of papier mâché and the occasional softness of feather and underfelt.

The one part of the installation which had a tentative link with the whole was *Flag Renamed Place*. What began as a flag, made from white canvas, took on a different shape as John Davis worked on it. It has links with the canvas structure *Unrolled* (shown at Mildura in 1973), or the canvas *Asyntatic Work — Part III* (shown at Pinacotheca also in 1973). Whereas those works using canvas were complete, *Flag Renamed Place* (illus. 75) appeared to be incomplete and is still listed by the artist as a 'work in progress'. Relying heavily on intuition and the quiet joy of making the objects, Davis started with a general plan which changed direction, faltered and stopped. Yet it added another aspect to the installation. It seemed to suggest that

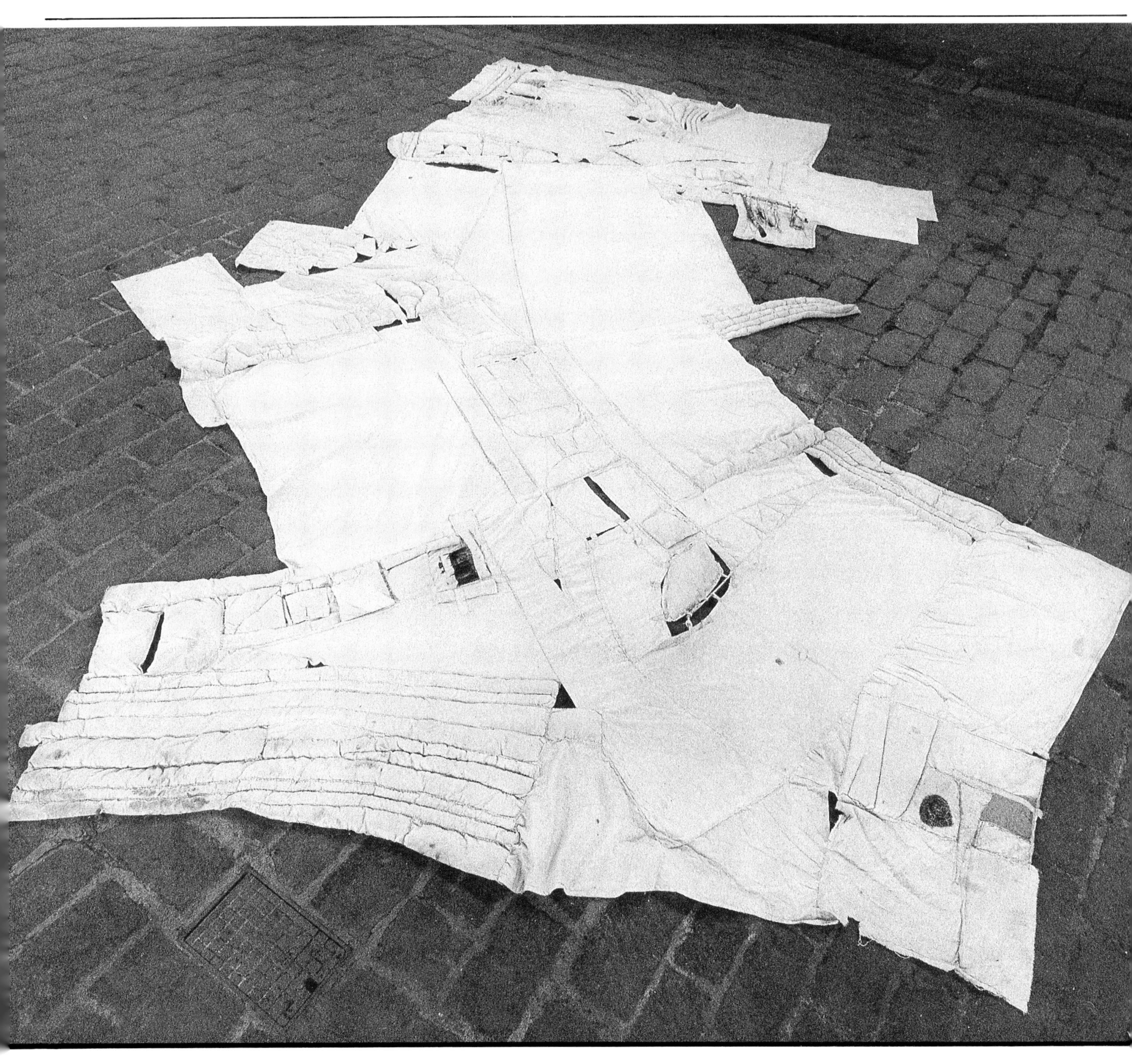

the artist was at work and the installation was capable of further development, it was not a static, completed structure.

Davis wrote four years later that it was still

■ *A work which I keep adding to or altering. It evokes the landscape from above distantly, and can be viewed from a distance generally, or very close, specifically. It is very portable (like a map) and because I have been working on the piece for some years, it also has the signs of its own evolution and history obviously built into it.*[6]

In view of the fact that Australia had not been represented at the Venice Biennale for twenty years (or possibly *because* of that fact) the three Australians received considerable press coverage. It was flattering that their work was noted amongst the vast number of exhibits and pleasing that all reports were favourable.

■ *The Australian representatives, John Davis, Ken Unsworth and Robert Owen, each in his own way produced work within the limits of the art and nature theme, with Davis and Unsworth at least proclaiming their Australian identity without obvious recourse to an overtly Australian subject choice.*

Davis, who earlier this year represented Australia at the 4th Indian Triennial, might best be described as a Romantic formalist (what could be more hopelessly romantic than carting a trunk full of bush twigs tied together with string all the way from Melbourne to Venice?). He produced a series of structures which made up an environment of great charm and fragile beauty.

To Australian eyes these works were unmistakably the product of the Australian environment, but judging from the response of visitors to the show they had a much wider relevance and were able to trigger memories and meanings which saw parallels with the work of many different primitive cultures.[7]

Other critics wrote appreciatively.

■ *An impressive entry [of Australian art], with*

traces of Aborigine-consciousness cultivated by John Davis. [8]

■ *The Australian pavilion (their first for 20 years) includes the poignant, sculptural installations of John Davies [sic], in which rocks real and artificial, string, and twigs paradoxically form remnants and souvenirs of rituals still to be invented.*[9]

■ *Davis builds constructions of woods, brick, cord, stones and feathers that strive for a sense of something magical and that may very well be inspired by an interest in the Aboriginal cultures of Australia.*[10]

■ *Australia's John Davis looked to another culture's perception of nature and its magic forces. He took the Aborigines' shamanistic way of assembling natural material into delicate mystery and meaning.*[11]

■ *Davis's work is nature seen with a tracker's eye: it involves small displacements, fragile connections, scarcely visible interferences — signs of passage of an ephemeral brush between imagination and environment.*[12]

This statement comes very close to the sculptor's own written comment, in which he reminisces about his childhood and the influence of the Australian landscape.

■ *In my younger formative years I spent a great deal of time living and learning from the natural environment; an environment which is very flat, no hills only gentle mounds of sand, a huge hot sky, clumps of trees which clung to waterholes or rivers or stood isolated in open space sometimes without apparent reason. I learnt to see the world, in general terms — miles of it at once — or specifically through its details, the things that I had to step over, to avoid as dangerous, or to admire in its state of completeness, beauty or fragility. I frequently experienced these moments alone, thus being aware, at an early age of the sense of isolation, of being like an isolated tree, in the vastness of that landscape and eventually through time and familiarity*

◀
75 John Davis, Flag Renamed Place (started in 1978 and added to at irregular intervals since then). Canvas, latex, string, twigs, feathers and cast paper stones. Irregular flat piece of canvas with twigs and feathers held in place by loops of canvas (in the artist's possession). Photograph by Mark Strizic.

recognising how I occupied part of that landscape. Superficially it appears empty and barren but it is full of small life systems surviving together offering only fragile evidence of their existence, or small moments of importance, or a story of some event that occurred.[13]

One review appeared in a Japanese magazine early in 1979, and in the light of subsequent developments it is interesting to note that it was an ikebana magazine that published the first article and photographs of John Davis's work in Japan. The links between Japan and Davis and between ikebana and his installations were to develop in the next few years.

■ *The idea of arrangement can already be seen as a recognizable trend in the world of contemporary art. Last year, Australia participated in the Biennale and presented some very interesting works. Among them, the works of the artist, John Davis, using branches, cloth, stones and thread — based on arrangement, restricting treatment to as little as possible they were memorable. I don't know much about the Australian Aborigines, but Davis's work could be seen as the primitive fetish of a hunting people. A logical connection could be made between the minimization of treatment, a feeling like fetishism, and universality, as an interrelated whole.*[14]

After he had installed his work at Venice and the formalities of the official opening were over, John Davis took the opportunity to look again at parts of Europe. In a letter written just after his return to Australia, he gives a brief summary of his impressions of the Venice Biennale and the highlights of his quick European tour.

■ *The trip was very good, enjoyed Venice very much and the show itself was pretty varied in seriousness, quality, resolve, etc. In brief we did very well and got a very good share of the press, T.V., radio. I'll have all the catalogues shortly so you can judge from them . . . After the opening I went to Milan, Florence, and then drove to Sienna, Arrezzo, Perugia and Assissi (marvellous Giottos) and Rome, then flew to London (Jasper Johns, Matisse, Bonnard) and Paris (Cézanne show tremendous). It was extremely busy but very satisfying indeed.*[15]

It had been a year of diverse travel for John Davis: firstly India, then Italy, London and Paris. During the Christmas vacation he and his family visited Mexico and the United States. The range in time was from the sixth and seventh century rock-cut temples of Ellora and Ajanta in India to the Space Centre, Houston, Texas, USA.

■ NOTES

[1] Elwyn Lynn, 'Preface', Australian section, *Fourth Triennale — India*, February 1978.
[2] John Davis, 'Artist's Statement', *Survey 15, Relics and Rituals*, National Gallery of Victoria, 17 July–13 September 1981.
[3] See Chapter 6, note 6. *Bicycle II* was listed in the 'Survey 1' catalogue as *Bicycle* (1977), and in the Watters catalogue of 1977 as *Bicycle I*. The work known as *Bicycle I* was actually produced in 1976 and is in the collection of the Art Gallery of New South Wales.
[4] Ronald Millar, 'The Safe Side', *The Australian*, 27 March 1978.
[5] W. E. P. Pidgeon, 'The Maturing of a Sculptor', *Sunday Telegraph*, 28 May 1978.
[6] John Davis, 'Some Brief Notes on Issues Which I Think Are Raised in My Art', written in answer to questions from Kimio Akiyama, Editorial Department, *Ikebana Ohara*, November 1982.
[7] Graeme Sturgeon, 'Taking Twigs to Venice', *The Australian*, 14 July 1978.
[8] William Feaver, 'The Biennale's Romp with Nature', *New York Times*, 6 August 1978.
[9] Marina Vaizey, 'Venice: Vast and Various', *Sunday Times*, 2 July 1978.
[10] Henry Martini, 'The Venice Biennale: Back to Nature', *Art International*, vol. 22, no. 6, October 1978.
[11] Caroline Tisdall, 'When the Avant Garde Goes for a Skate', *Guardian*, 8 July 1978.
[12] Robert Hughes, 'It's Biennale Time Again', *Time*, 17 July 1978.
[13] John Davis, 'Some Brief Notes on Issues Which I Think Are Raised in My Art', op. cit.
[14] Yusuke Nakahara, 'Invisible Aspects of Sculpture', *Ikebana Ryusei*, no. 227, March 1979.
[15] John Davis, letter to Frank Watters and Geoffrey Legge, 2 August 1978.

 1979–81
A PERSONAL STYLE

Although 1978 was a year of acclaim for Davis he failed to find a major commercial gallery to represent him in Melbourne, though he had Watters Gallery in Sydney.

From 1979 onwards, Davis showed work in Melbourne at Art Projects, a gallery for the determinedly avant-garde which opened in that year. Located in a tired area of Melbourne, not yet attacked by developers, the gallery was located on an upper floor reached after climbing endless grubby stairs. The gallery spaces were spartan — small rooms with the original worn lino on the floor, minimal lighting, sad views from the windows over anonymous buildings and a generally desolate atmosphere. It was difficult to locate, cold and unwelcoming, definitely not a gallery for the general public. Art Projects was a gallery mainly frequented by artists, art lecturers, curators and critics, who were aware of the limited opening hours — by 1983, the hours had been reduced to Friday and Saturday afternoons.

With no concessions to display techniques, no use of public relations to stimulate interest, no advertisements in daily newspapers, Art Projects relied entirely on the power of the work shown to generate interest. Anything exhibited at Art Projects had to be good to survive the bleak surroundings!

In April 1979, John Davis showed a number of new works at Art Projects, including *Cape Schank* (illus. 73). Robert Rooney, a Melbourne art critic, visited the exhibition and wrote a scathing attack upon Art Projects, *Cape Schank* and John Davis.

■ *Art Projects, Melbourne's 'Mausoleum of Conceptual Art' (566 Lonsdale Street, City), is showing several sculptures by John Davis ($750–3000) made from twigs, paper, latex, canvas, rocks, feathers, bones, and string. These materials were gathered during his recent expedition into the primitive wilds of darkest Cape Schank in search of a lost tribe of holiday campers.*

Cape Schank (1978–79) is a three-part work consisting of an altar-like construction of four cubes made from bound twigs, four strips of disposal green canvas held down by stones, and a crown of twigs and feathers; a long low structure of string and twigs stretched between two stones; and a primitive coffee-table with pseudo-primitive pottery and implements on it. It adds up to an absurd essay in sham Shamanism.

Davis has gone a long way since the days when he used to do reliefs of repeated duck's feet — he recently represented Australia at the Venice Biennale. But I can't help thinking that he is more of an odd-jobs man and adapter of other people's ideas than an originator. His sculptures rarely seem to come from inside his head.[1]

In spite of this adverse review, *Cape Schank* was purchased for the National Gallery of Victoria from the Art Projects' exhibition.

Flag Renamed Place, first displayed at Venice 1978, was shown again as part of the 1979 exhibition at Watters Gallery, Sydney, and later reappeared at the Ina Gallery in Tokyo in 1982. Over the years the irregular shape has spread, angular and gawky. The canvas doesn't sit flat; undulating and crinkling it looks like a partly completed relief map. Pockets and pouches contain twigs, sticks and feathers, resembling the stylised symbols that one finds on a map.

In the Watters Gallery exhibition of 1979 Davis showed *Nargen* (illus. 76), one of the largest single sculptural pieces he had made up till that time. In the form of an irregular pyramid constructed of branches and twigs, it appears much more solid than other work of a similar date. One can see into the structure, for there are many little crevices and cracks, but the general effect is of a large, solid form of white canvas stretched over the linear structure of branches.

One reviewer referred to it as 'The outstanding work . . .' (in the exhibition) and then went on to write:

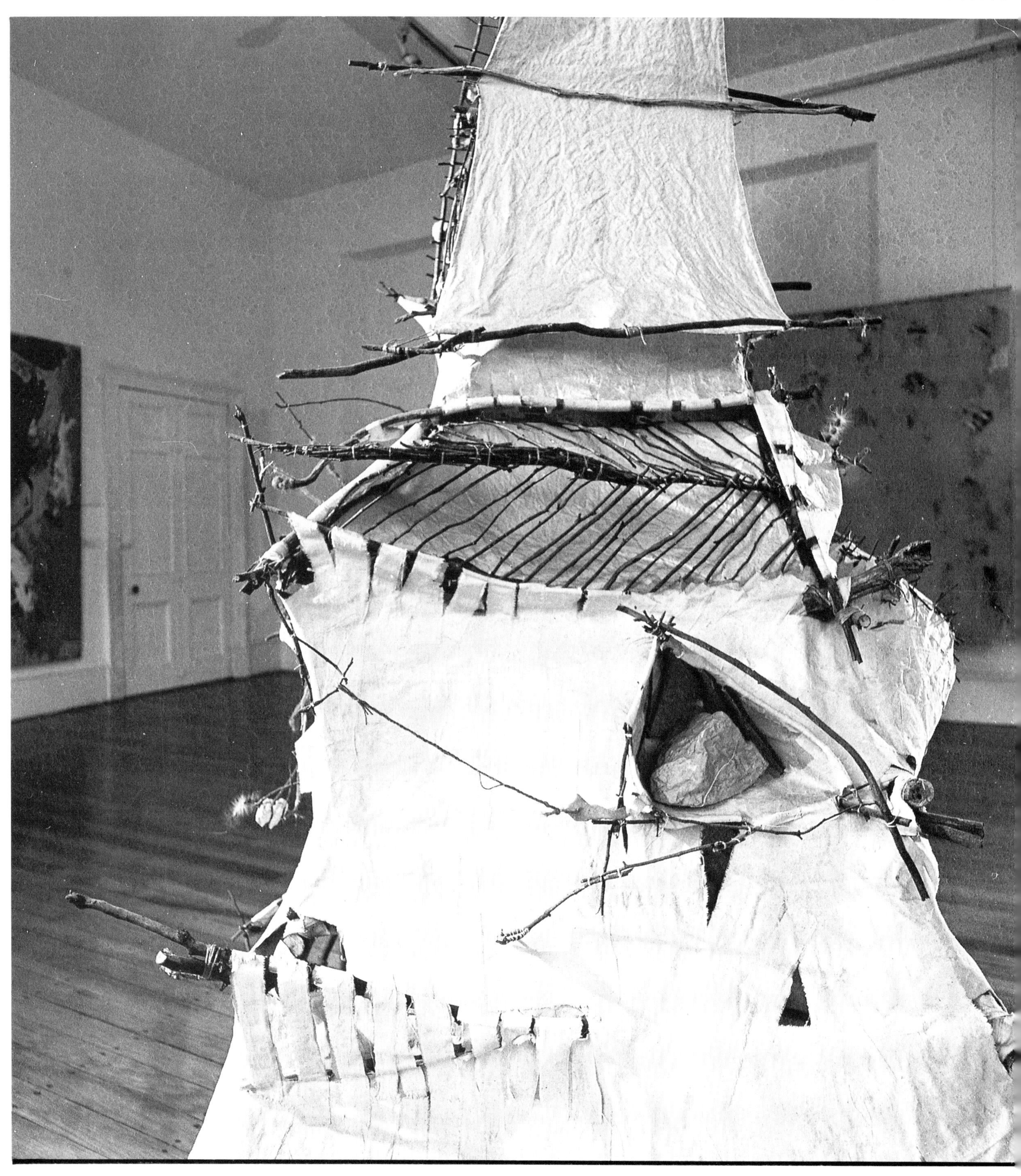

◄

76 John Davis, Nargen (1979). Branches, twigs, string, papier mâché stones, canvas, calico, felt. 230 x 180 x 140 cm. (Tasmanian Museum and Art Gallery). Photograph by Mark Strizic.

■ *Any description of its basic form tells nothing of the small works of intriguing sculptural ingenuity and refinement which this tree house contains or conceals from those of us not bent on discovering them. Reflecting a settled rather than a nomadic community, thus more Melanesian than Aboriginal, 'Nargen' stands as a wonderfully buoyant achievement.*[2]

Far from being 'buoyant', I found the work heavy to the point of being clumsy. Whereas John Davis had used the pyramidal form with great success in works such as *Marker, Marker A, Marker B, Marker Three, Place Two* and as the basic structure in *Cape Schank*, in *Nargen* the pyramid was very wide at the base, not giving the simple upward movement of the other works. A pyramid has one distinct characteristic, based on the fact that the diagonal is greater than the length of any side; what can appear as a satisfying proportion from the side suddenly becomes much wider and heavier as one moves around. This phenomenon, coupled with the fact that the simple linear structure was almost completely enclosed in strips of canvas and papier mâché, meant the delicacy of the twigs and sticks was lost and one was primarily aware of a large, heavy mass. On the other hand, the detail close up was fascinating.

Normally, Davis has a very good relationship between the detail and the whole. Even in such a complex work as *Region*, shown first at Art Projects in 1981 and then later in the year at Watters Gallery, he was able to relate the intricate to the overall structure. Possibly it was a matter of scale. In later works such as *Region* or *Incident*, the overall size was greater, but those works were made up of a considerable number of parts, each skilfully related to the other. There was a contrapuntal visual relationship, whereas *Nargen* was a monumental, isolated structure.

My bias in relation to *Nargen* is made all the stronger by a memory of the work badly displayed

at the Tasmanian Museum and Art Gallery, Hobart — by whom it was purchased. Sitting on a highly polished wooden floor, stained a strong reddish-brown, the work was protected by a glistening chrome metal barrier. *Nargen* looked out of place, artificial and overstated — not words I would normally use to describe the work of John Davis.

A Tasmanian magazine published some comments by Davis on the work:

■ *'Nargen' has evolved from two other works each called 'Marker' and shown at Watters Gallery in 1977 and the Venice Biennale in 1978. In each development the pyramidal form has grown in size and complexity of image, scale and material.*

I wanted 'Nargen' to express some aspects of Australian landscape in a specific and general sense, as well as establishing a dichotomy between the assertive and aggressive stance of the pyramidal form and the fragility, tenuousness and poetic qualities of the detail. The work on first glance primarily indicates external form, but the interior spaces should be glimpsed through subtle niches and crannies and allowed to play its part, negating to a certain extent the positiveness of the exterior.[3]

Nancy Borlase in her description of 'Nargen' made reference to both Melanesian and Aboriginal cultures as a possible influence on John Davis. The Brisbane art critic, Dr Langer wrote: 'Davis evokes arid land, nomadic life, and the ancient culture of our own Aboriginal people.'[4] It would be very easy however to over-emphasise the influence of Aboriginal culture on the work of John Davis. To varying degrees, Australians have a feeling of guilt towards the Aborigines. Having destroyed their way of life, stolen their land, undermined their beliefs, decimated their numbers with disease and alcohol, ignored their sacred sites and all but destroyed their culture, we have every reason to feel guilty. As the Aborigines have gathered strength and a sense of pride in their own cultural

77 John Davis, Another Place (1980). Sticks, canvas and paper. 42 x 72 x 187 cm. (In the possession of the artist.) Photograph by Mark Strizic.

background, making demands for land rights, sympathetic Australians have attempted to compensate for the past. There is a tendency, particularly amongst Australians who live in the cities and who have probably never talked with an Aborigine, to adopt a romantic attitude, more appropriate to the ideal of the 'noble savage' current in the eighteenth century. There is also a tendency to link current attitudes towards conservation of nature with a romantic view of the past. The Aborigine is seen as being in perfect harmony with his harsh surroundings, whereas in some desert areas the reality must have been a constant fight for survival.

White Australians find it difficult to adopt a balanced and realistic attitude towards Aborigines. Albert Namatjira received praise for paintings that proved he could paint like a western watercolourist. He deserted his culture and our extravagant praise and inflated monetary rewards destroyed him.

Our feelings of guilt continue and we attempt to give praise as some compensation for past neglect. John Davis is a major Australian sculptor. His work shows the influence of Aboriginal culture. Therefore we are not only praising Aboriginal art, we are also indirectly equating it with European culture.

John Davis has written: 'In 1976 I rediscovered an informal education in the Australian bush denied to me through urbanisation and formal education. It is as relevant to my understanding of what it is to be an Australian in 1982 as to my interpretation of European and Aboriginal histories'.[5] I can only read this as a generous gesture on the part of John Davis, by which he infers that both European and Aboriginal history have influenced his development. The sad reality is that most Australians are supremely ignorant of Aboriginal history and culture and the lives of the majority who live in the major cities are in no way influenced or affected by Aborigines, past or present.

The similarities between the work of John Davis and the Aborigines are based on two things: they both use the materials they find in the bush and they both have a great love and respect for the Australian landscape. Twigs, sticks, water-washed rocks, bark, mud and simple methods of construction by tying, give the finished products a superficial resemblance.

Tony Bond, writing about Davis's exhibition when he was Director of the Wollongong City Art Gallery, saw the Australian landscape as the common link, rather than John Davis being directly influenced by Aboriginal art.

■ *The sculptures [of John Davis] fit ideally into the landscape situation and also recall to mind the delicacy and sensitivity of Aboriginal ritual objects. Like the Aborigine, John Davis is in harmony with the Australian landscape and yet unlike so many of the artists who use informal media, the structural design and spatial organisation of his work are as strong as any sculptor using more conventional materials.*[6]

John Davis made his own attitude clear during a lecture he gave at the Institute of Modern Art in 1980:

■ *In overall looks and 'feeling' there could be said to be some correlation between John Davis' sculpture and Aboriginal artifacts. However the relationship is coincidental, as he [says he] 'never looked at Aboriginal art until after I started making this. I suppose I've got to realise I'm going to have a similar quality to Aboriginal art, because I'm using the same kind of materials that they do, by making things out of the landscape and twigs . . . But the motivations that I have in this are completely different, and I see a lot of 'western' attitudes coming through in the work. So the 'Aboriginal' attitude is not really that strong.*[7]

In a recorded interview with me in 1983 Davis again explained that his interest in Aboriginal art had developed after he began making his structures out of twigs and sticks and after people pointed out

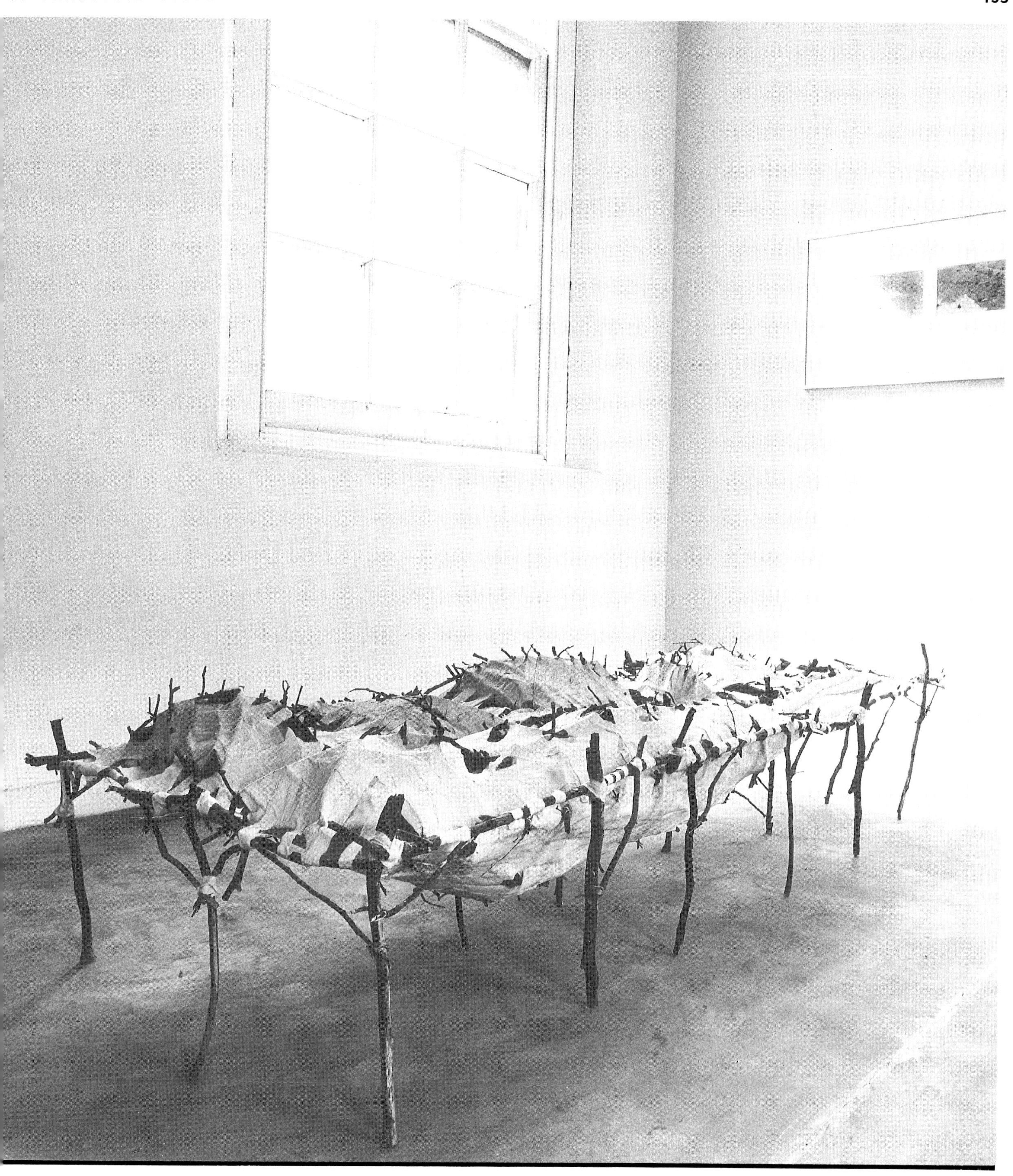

the apparent similarities. He also mentioned some fundamental differences, including the fact that he saw his work as 'more volumetric'. Obviously Davis's work flows from a western tradition: 'To me it's simply the problem of trying to make a piece of sculpture that works formally as well as expressively.'[8] There is none of the religious significance, none of the worship of natural phenomena, so fundamental to the Aborigines.

During discussion with John Davis, it became clear that he was aware of the dangers of being too closely involved with Aboriginal art. Through sheer lack of knowledge it is possible to trivialise another culture. The influence of Chinese architecture, painting, ceramics, furniture etc. was bastardised in the eighteenth century to give Europe a new style entitled Chinoiserie. In a similar manner Aboriginal patterns have been taken from bark paintings and shields and transferred to tablecloths and serviettes. The interview touched on the problem:

KS: 'I think basically most of us are ignorant of Aboriginal art — except for seeing a few things in museums and occasionally glancing at a book here or there, most of us have no knowledge of the real significance of Aboriginal art. Very limited knowledge.'

JD: 'I suppose I'm consciously separating myself from it anyhow. I'd like to get more involved in it, but in a way I daren't, because if I do, then — '

KS: 'Might end up like Margaret Preston?'

JD 'Yes! On the razor's edge and I might go the other way. Have to be very careful about that.'[9]

John Davis made his attitude clear in a written statement for the catalogue *Singular and Plural*: 'Some people feel . . . that I'm trying to make Abor-

iginal art; in fact I feel that I'm very much a Western artist and that the work I make is formal and structured like a Western artist's. It hasn't got that feeling of myth and ritual that Aboriginal art has'.[10]

In spite of his caution, the idea of a major Australian sculptor influenced by Aboriginal art is a story too good to be missed by some art critics and journalists. Take, for instance, the report that appeared in a Japanese newspaper in late 1982.

■ *Of course, since Davis himself was born in Australia, where migration from England was so numerous, he also started from the European [style of art] first. However, playing with the Aboriginal race (which has a history of 50,000 years), with whom he has mingled since childhood, spurred him towards art 'which is created in the midst of nature'.*[11]

This paragraph so confused the translator that she wrote to me: 'Did John Davis grow up somewhere where he associated with Aboriginals during his childhood? If not, either I have not understood the sentence or the reporter did not understand John.'[12] When Davis was at school in Swan Hill there were Aboriginal children in the classes, but the contact was limited and the knowledge gained of Aboriginal culture was probably non-existent.

If there has been an influence of Aboriginal art upon John Davis, then it is just as superficial as the influence of African sculpture upon the Cubists. The Cubists ignored the essential symbolic, religious, ceremonial and magical significance of African sculpture and accepted some of the visual mannerisms.

It is a characteristic of twentieth century western art that the art of previous cultures, of advanced societies or of tribal groups is all readily available to be viewed, assessed and absorbed. Brett Whitely uses Chinese calligraphy. Juan Davila depicts characters from comic strips. Peter Booth checks back to Brueghel and Bosch.

In his mature work, Davis has certainly been

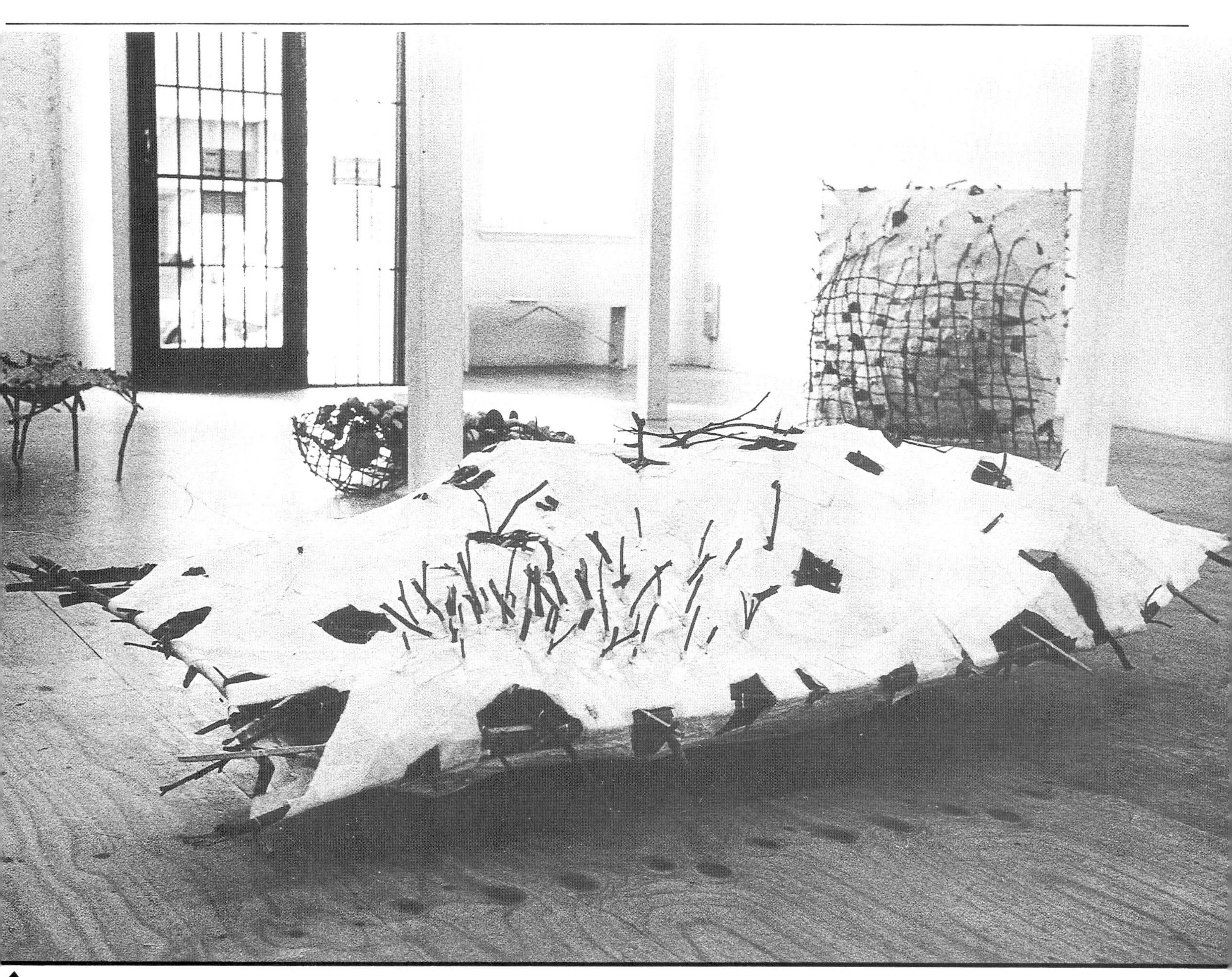

▲

78 *Another Time, Another Place was the title given to the exhibition by John Davis at the Institute of Modern Art, Brisbane, 5–30 August 1980. Far left (partly hidden), Another Place; centre (behind post), You Yangs; right, Moraine and in foreground Potkarok. (You Yangs — Queensland Art Gallery; Potkarok — James Baker Collection, Museum of Contemporary Art, Brisbane, and the other two works are in the artist's possession). Photograph by the artist.*

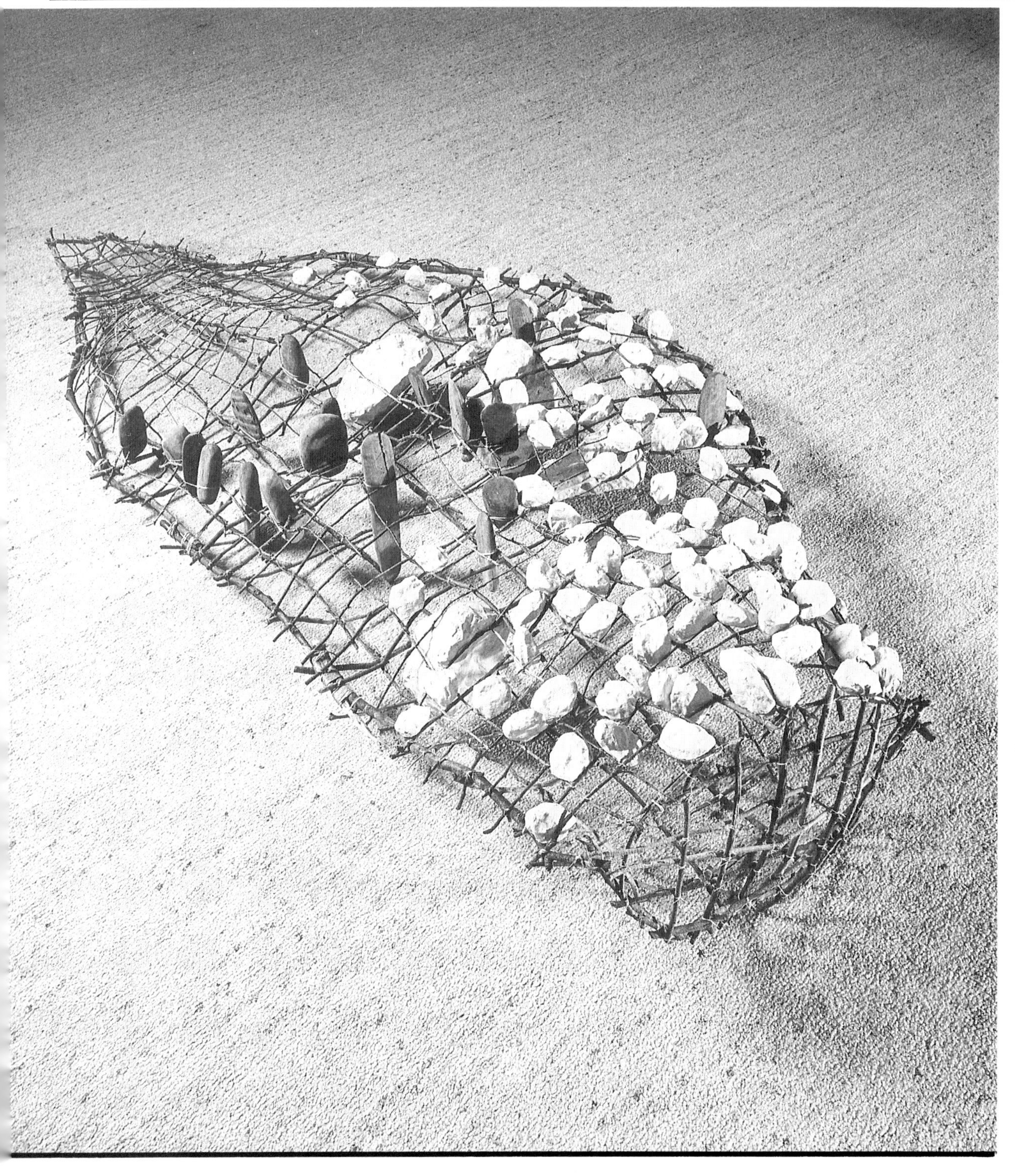

79 John Davis, You Yangs (1980). Twigs, cotton, papier mâché, paper cast 'stones' and small wooden 'rocks'. 196 x 90 x 30 cm. (Queensland Art Gallery.) Photograph by Mark Strizic.

influenced by Aboriginal art, but only as part of broader influences, which include tribal art, such as the woodcarvings and masks of New Guinea, the art of the Pacific Islands, American Indians and the folk art of Mexico, India and Bali. There are some cross-references and influences from fellow Australian sculptors such as Peter Cole or Marr Grounds and tentative links with a range of artists from Rosalie Gascoigne to Ann Thomson. From the international art magazines he would know the work of English artists, Richard Long and David Nash. When Nicholas Pope was in Australia in 1979, John Davis spent some days with him.

When Suzi Gablick visited Australia in 1980, she visited a number of artists, before writing her 'Report from Australia'. She was impressed by the work of John Davis and gave a large part of her article to a discussion of his career and recent work. But just prior to writing about his sculpture, she included an introductory paragraph that seems to sum up the influences that have shaped the work of John Davis:

■ *The artists I responded to in Australia seemed to be seeking something like a national identity, and expressed a commitment to local culture even while they remained open to influences from abroad and to modernist traditions; they saw their art as being dialectically determined, from local as well as international sources. To begin with, then, I shall address myself to three artists for whom landscape in particular has been a generative force: Tom Arthur from Sydney and John Davis from Melbourne... and farther afield, in remote Tasmania, Peter Taylor...*[13]

Europe, America, the Australian Aborigines, contemporary Australian artists, primitive art, folk art — in no previous culture have artists been able to absorb influences from such a wide range of sources, but by the late 1970s John Davis had welded these disparate influences into a personal style.

During 1980, in the months of August to October, John Davis exhibited at the Institute of Modern Art in Brisbane and then at the Wollongong City Gallery. It was basically the same exhibition with concessions to the particular spaces available at each gallery. In both locations he exhibited new works *Another Place*, *Unspoken*, *You Yangs* (illus. 79), *Potkarok* and *Moraine* (illus. 77, 78). At the Institute of Modern Art, Brisbane, he showed all of the works from the Venice Biennale in an upstairs gallery, while at Wollongong he only showed one part of the Venice Biennale installation, *Ridge*.

The four new works had a number of features in common. They were all essentially rectangular in shape, all either sitting directly on the floor or very low slung, and, of course, constructed of similar materials, twigs bound with cotton or string, partly covered with canvas and papier mâché.

Another Place was about the same size and proportions as an old-fashioned camp stretcher, a rectangular surface, complete with spindly legs, but instead of sagging as a camp stretcher would, the surface rose up like a gently undulating landscape. *Potkarok*, also rectangular, swelled up somewhat ominously. *Moraine* was emphatically sitting on the ground, but had more vertical movement than the other works, its origins being the irregular shapes that John had seen on the edge of the glaciers when he had visited New Zealand on holidays, early in 1980. *You Yangs* (illus. 79) appeared to be the result of carefully looking at the ground, examining the fallen twigs and sticks, the scatter of rocks, the gritty, sandy soil, rather than the monolithic grandeur of the range of hills between Melbourne and Geelong. Built of twigs, it had both 'rocks' made of wood and papier mâché casts of rocks, caught between the network of the twigs. This work was purchased for the Queensland Art Gallery, Brisbane.

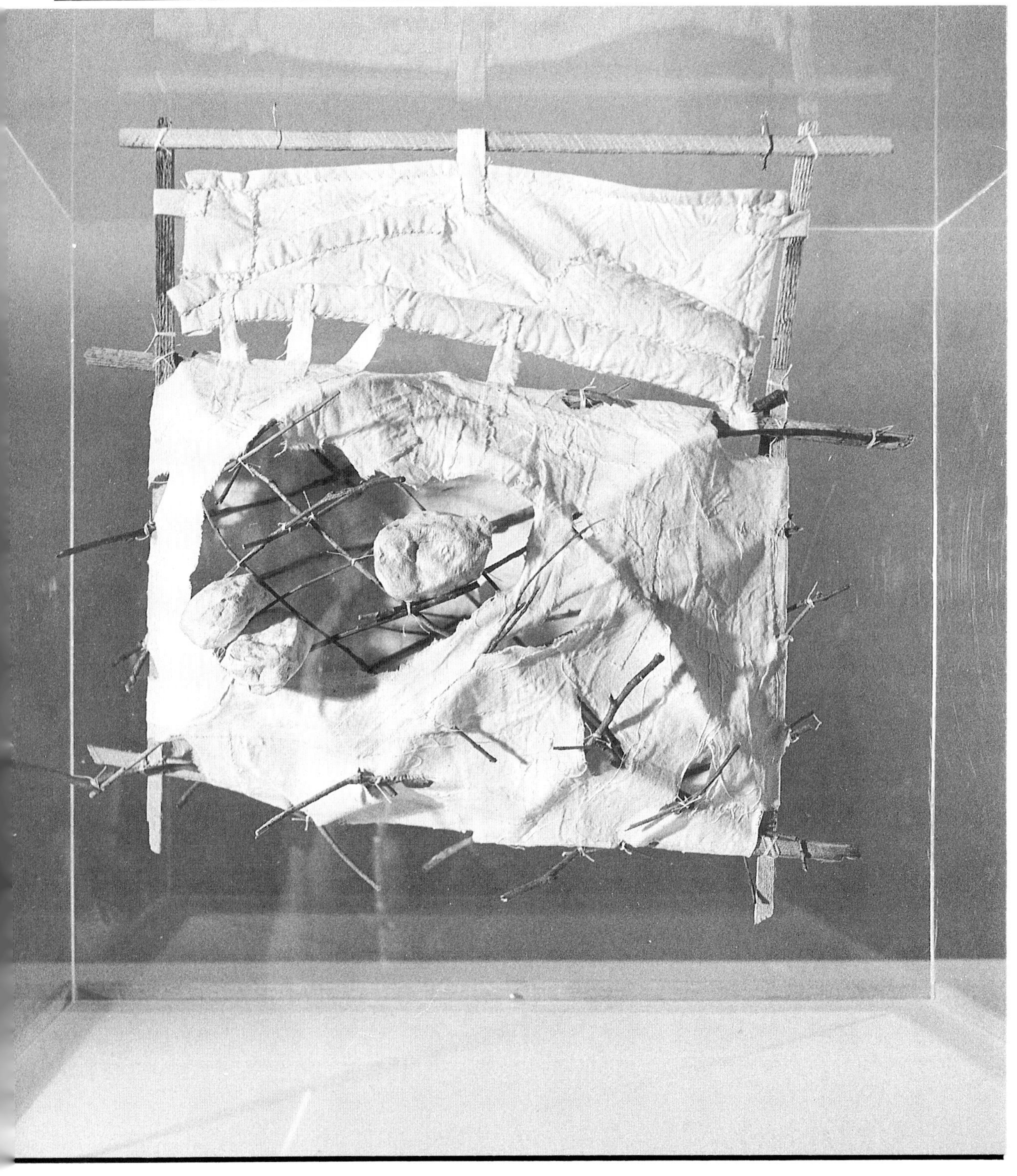

◄

80 John Davis, New England (1979). Sawn timber, twigs, cotton thread, cotton, calico, papier mâché stones cast from latex moulds, underfelt used as stuffing. Suspended from latex tabs within perspex box. Box: 48 x 53.5 x 26.5 cm; work within box c. 37 x 42 x 12 cm. (Wollongong City Gallery.) Photograph by Mark Strizic.

The works shown at Brisbane and Wollongong were not an installation as such, nor specifically planned for those exhibition spaces; nevertheless the artist was very concerned with their placement in space, the interrelationship of the objects within the space and the use of space as a component of the sculptural objects themselves. His lecture at the Institute of Modern Art, Brisbane, explained the link between his sense of space and the Australian landscape. 'Space is important to me. I like to think that the space in this exhibition is as important as the objects themselves. I think the objects themselves cut up and measure the space.'

This interest in space, and spaces, plays an important role: 'I ask myself, how do things actually operate in the space that I move in around Australia?' The essential 'meaning' of the work is derived from the country, the landscape.

■ *It's all about living in this country. I think we have a peculiar kind of space, and I didn't seem to recognise that until I went away from it, and came back again. Then it hit me like a cultural shock, and I saw how things grow in this country.*

You approach the work from a distance and see it as an object, and then you come in and almost press your nose up against parts of it, because some of the parts are very small. That's how I think Australia works . . . it's vast, but there's tiny little fragile things in it.[14]

In the years immediately after the Venice Biennale, John Davis exhibited constantly in Sydney, Melbourne, Wollongong and Canberra, including the Art Gallery of New South Wales, the National Gallery of Victoria, the Art Gallery of South Australia and several provincial galleries in country areas. He sold works to major public collections: National Gallery of Victoria, Tasmanian Museum and Art Gallery, Queensland Art Gallery and in 1981 was to sell one of his largest and most complex works to the Art Gallery of Western Aus-

tralia. His work was widely known and included in major national exhibitions such as 'Perspecta '81' at the Art Gallery of New South Wales. He had been invited to join several committees, including the Visual Arts Board of the Australia Council.

John Davis was not only producing mature work, he was accepted as a major Australian sculptor.

■ NOTES

1 Robert Rooney, 'Stringy Lines and Horrible Surfaces', *Age*, 12 April 1979.
2 Nancy Borlase, 'Transferences, Displacements', *Sydney Morning Herald*, 10 November 1979.
3 John Davis, 'Statement on "Nargen"', *Frieze* (Hobart), no. 5, c.1979.
4 Dr G. Langer, 'Boyd Reaches for the Past', *Courier Mail*, 14 August 1980.
5 John Davis 'A Sense of Place' *Sculpture*, Education Department of Victoria (Melbourne), 1983.
6 Tony Bond, 'Introduction', *John Davis: A Sculptural Installation*, Wollongong City Gallery, 10 September–12 October 1980.
7 Peter Anderson, unpublished notes from lecture given by John Davis at Institute of Modern Art, Brisbane, 5 August 1980.
8 John Davis, interview with the author, 16 March 1983.
9 Ibid.
10 John Davis, 'Statement', *Singular and Plural*, South Australian School of Art Gallery, 1–26 April 1985.
11 'Naked Faces '82. Mr John Davis: Australian Artist Known for his Bush Art', *Komei*, 17 October 1982.
12 Valerie McGowan in a note to the author, 19 May 1983.
13 Suzi Gablik, 'Report from Australia', *Art in America*, vol. 69, no. 1, January 1981.
14 Peter Anderson, op. cit.

1981
MAJOR EXHIBITIONS IN SYDNEY AND MELBOURNE

John Davis's early experiences in the Australian countryside, plus the great myth that is part of all Australians — the myth that Australians all have strong links with the outback — combined in his work to overwhelm the more obvious influence of the urban environment in which he lived from 1963 onwards.

Australia is a very young country and memories of the rigours of life in a new and harsh land are still strong. But they are secondhand memories for this generation, acquired from books, plays, works of art and, more recently, television. Sidney Nolan, the most skilful perpetuator of the myth of the outback, views the desert from a plane, or from the security of a four-wheel drive vehicle. He produces paintings which confirm the Australian myth: a land peopled by rugged individualists who can survive in the most difficult of environments — and if by chance they don't survive, then like Burke and Wills, they will become legendary heroes.

Yet there are some aspects of Australia's past that have continued into its urban life to influence actions and attitudes. Because of the isolation of the early settlers they were often unable to call upon blacksmiths, mechanics, veterinary surgeons or even doctors. They developed a wide range of skills that enabled them to do their own repairs, whether it was to the house, their farm equipment or a broken bone. Australian sculptors have suffered similar problems brought on by their isolation, their small numbers and the lack of specialised assistance. Whereas their European counterparts of the nineteenth century would have had assistants to build armatures, make plaster-moulds, carve stone and cast bronze, Australian sculptors have had to learn all of these skills and do the complete job. Charles Summers actually built his own foundry in Melbourne in 1864 in order to cast the Burke and Wills statues.

This ability to acquire skills and work in a wide range of materials is clearly obvious in the range of works that Davis has produced in wood, bronze, fibreglass, latex, papier mâché, terracotta, canvas, twigs and sticks. The influence of the past is also present in a more subtle way. The Australian farmer, through sheer necessity, learnt to fix anything, often with a piece of fencing wire. He was a master craftsman at improvisation. Accompanied by a declaration of 'It'll be right!' he could make anything go, hold anything together, prop up and prolong the life of car, tractor, gate or windmill.

One has only to look at the sculptures of Peter Cole, the work of the Canberra artist Rosalie Gascoigne, and the structures of John Davis, to see a continuation of this Australian attitude. Overseas artists are using similar found materials but the Australian works have an earthy directness which avoids obvious sophistication and refined craftsmanship. There is an acceptance of second-hand materials and a love of simple techniques such as nailing and tying. The general effect is rough and strong — a continuation of the 'It'll be right' attitude.

The size of Australia has had a continuing influence on the population. Even the contemporary Australian, living on his suburban block in the midst of a great city, is still aware of the vast distances. The average Australian is prepared to travel great distances for casual enjoyment. One automatically gets a feeling for space, which may help explain why the paintings of Fred Williams were so quickly accepted by the people of Australia. In spite of their conservative attitudes to the visual arts, Australians were able to relate to Fred Williams's concept of space. His empty, flat areas of colour, populated with small squiggles of paint, were so close to the empty Australian landscape dotted with tree stumps and rocks that they could be intuitively understood.

John Davis's sculpture is also very Australian

and strongly influenced by the characteristics of the bush.

■ *John Davis uses the irregular, asymmetrical growth of the eucalypt, incorporates the apparent untidiness and accepts the neutral colour of the vegetation.*

He uses twigs and branches of the Australian eucalypt for his basic constructions, though he is no purist and is quite willing to add other man-made materials such as paper and latex. He has not collected the prunings from city trees, forced to conform to preconceived shapes, but rather he goes into the bush and collects the fallen branches and twigs. These reflect the battle for survival, the twisted, irregular growth of trees living in a harsh climate.

John Davis is fascinated by the Australian bush — the space, the tentative links between objects within that space, the irregular and asymmetrical nature of objects in nature, or the temporary casual structures made by the people living within this environment. He is not intrigued by the order imposed by town planning, not impressed by the size and complexity of a city, but is fascinated by the simple, casual farm houses, sheds, windmills and other signs of man's tentative relationship to a harsh country.[1]

Anyone who has travelled by car throughout Australia soon becomes familiar with the pattern of Australian towns, particularly the smaller towns in the less populated areas. One can travel for hours through country that is overwhelming in its similarity. Time doesn't seem very important any more. Roads are generally straight, so that the traveller sees everything from a great distance and has ample time to examine any object as he slowly comes closer and closer. 'The landmarks on an Australian landscape, the structures that signify settlement, are usually practical buildings, such as water towers or wheat silos: later, closer to the town, one may see the church spires.'[2]

John Davis lived in a number of country towns during his childhood and then returned to the country in the early years of his teaching career — to Queenscliff, Numurkah, and Mildura. Nevertheless, he was not intrigued by the visual rawness of 'the self-serve petrol stations or the fast food shops of our country towns, where the signs of man are in opposition to the environment. He has absorbed the aspects of man's presence that have been quietly taken over and worked upon by nature.'[3]

Time can make a steel windmill and a corrugated iron tank appear distinctly Australian and at peace with the landscape. What was once a harsh geometric structure of tall pyramid and full circle, in direct contrast with a horizontal landscape, becomes rusted and decayed to become a romantic ruin — a typically Australian ruin associated with the search for water and the problems of survival.

Most of the structures of Australia's past, outside the limits of cities and large towns, were built without architects. There were no architects for the farm houses, the cow sheds, barns, shearing sheds, blacksmith's shop, hay barn, even some bridges. Often built of undressed timber, or simply split logs, the style was simple, sturdy and functional. Farm houses and sheds kept on growing, as families became larger, storage was needed or more equipment was purchased. Farm buildings had a tendency to grow sideways, whereas farm houses retreated backwards, each addition getting lower and lower, until eventually even the back veranda was covered in.

This casual attitude to structure is very much in keeping with John Davis's personality. There was a simple plan, a basic starting point, but after that things just kept on growing. Early in his career his wood carvings had emphasised an organic sense of growth; his recent works grow naturally in a manner that fuse man-made structures with the organic growth of nature.

Like the early builders in the bush, who used

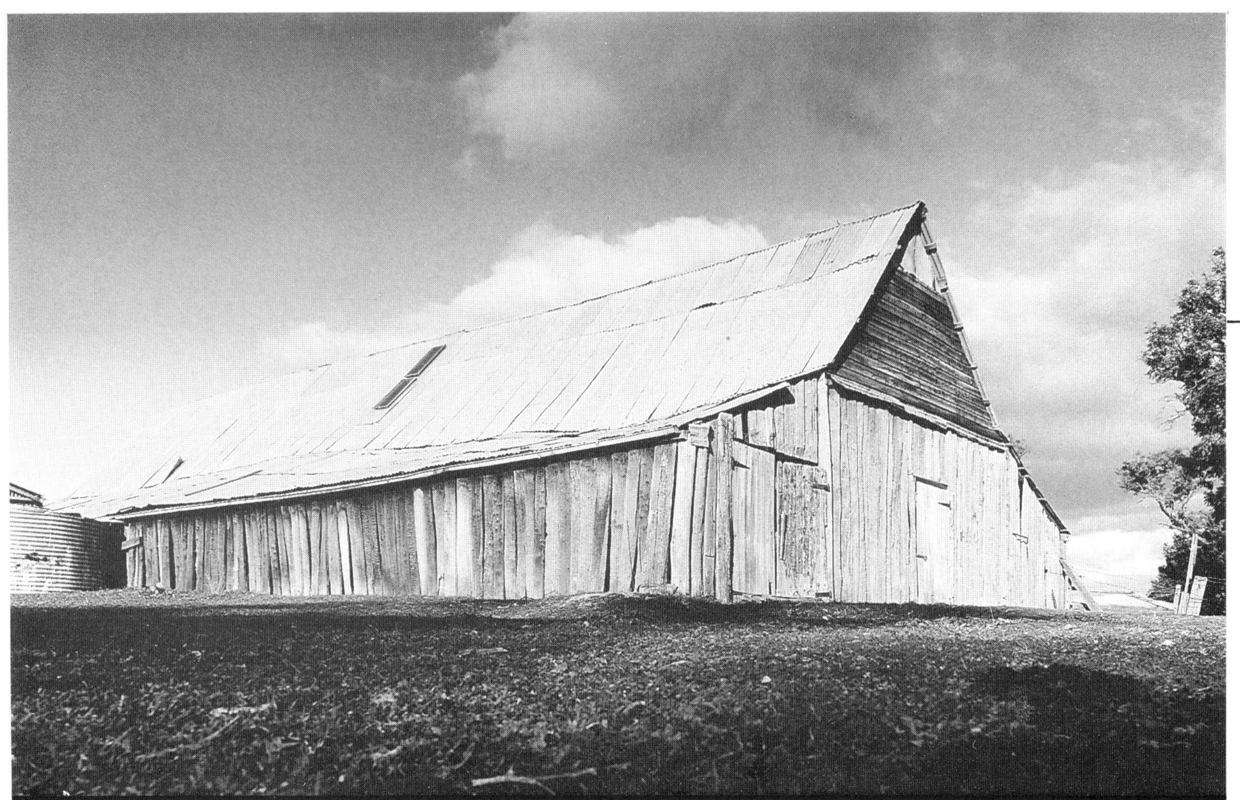

◄ 81 Shearing sheds, Morro-wolga, Yamble, NSW. Reproduced from Rude Timber Buildings in Australia, by Philip Cox, John Freeland, and photographer Wesley Stacey. Published by Angus and Robertson (Sydney), 1980.

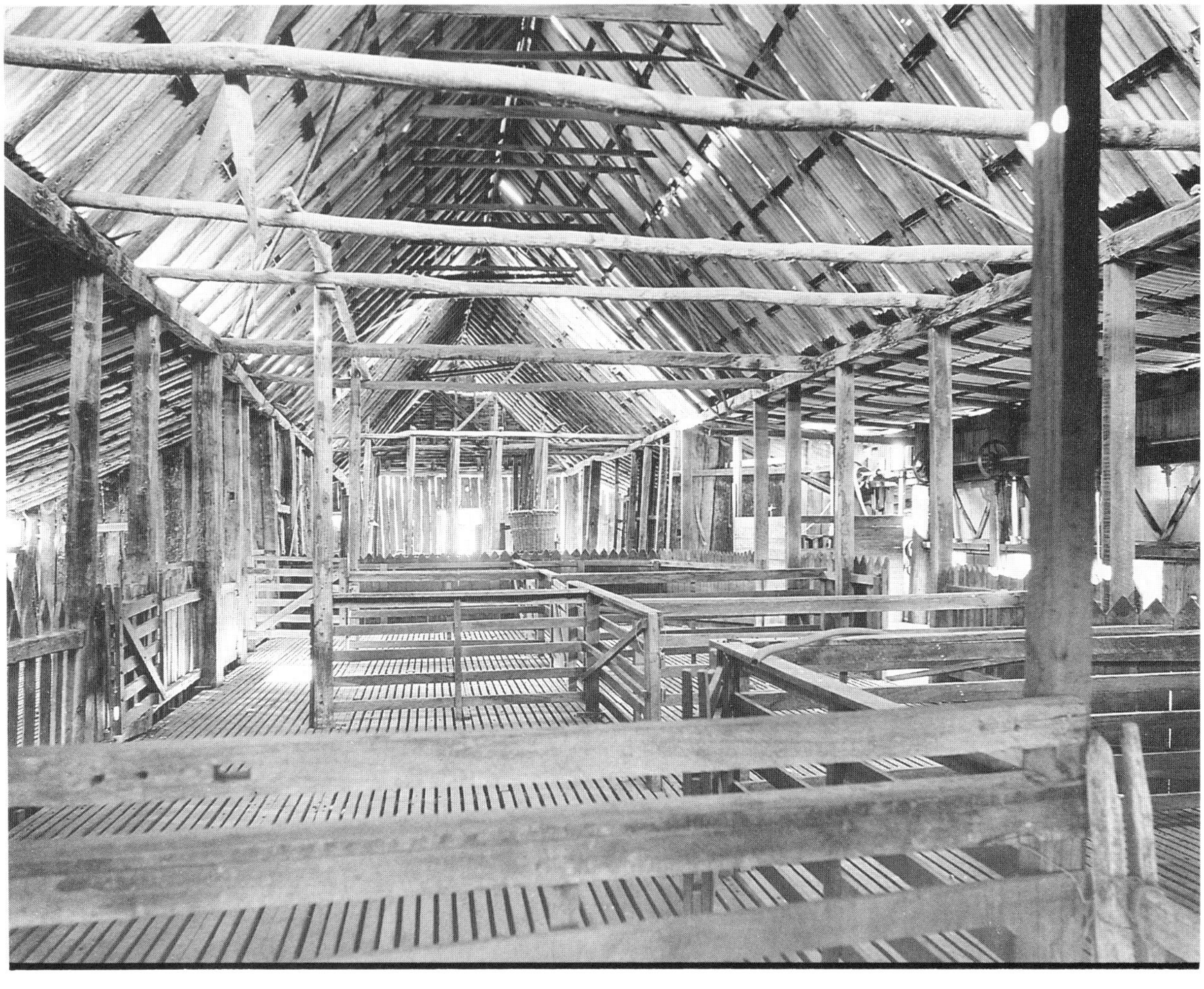

◄ 82 Interior of woolroom, shearing sheds, 'Morrowolga', Yamble, NSW. The rough wool bins are constructed from small saplings and sticks. Reproduced from Rude Timber Buildings in Australia, by Philip Cox, John Freeland, and photographer Wesley Stacey. Published by Angus and Robertson (Sydney), 1980.

natural timber and simple, often improvised methods of construction, Davis built his sculptures of partly sawn, but mainly undressed branches and twigs, bark and all. The scale was different, so instead of twists of fencing wire to give extra strength and stability, he used cotton or string.

Australian farmers were not aesthetic puritans, using all natural materials. Corrugated iron was to become one of the most commonly used materials for walls as well as the roof. Davis mixes sheets of latex rubber, papier mâché and tarred paper with the twigs. He does not accept the simplistic current reasoning that 'natural' is good and man-made materials are bad. His choice of materials, colour and texture, along with a deliberate weathering, gives a general feeling of structures that are in sympathy with nature.

■

It is ironic that John Davis, the neo-romantic ecological sculptor, should exhibit at Watters Gallery, for the streets around Watters Gallery, Sydney, are crowded with a conglomeration of factories, offices, pubs, houses, used-car yards, and restaurants. Watters Gallery is a building that defies a stylistic label. Inside, one is aware of grey concrete, new spaces within the shell of the old building.

John Davis showed three major works at Watters in November 1981. In spite of the surroundings, he established a mood of contemplation, a timeless quality, a serenity which affected people as soon as they stepped into the gallery. Spectators moved slowly, talked little.

Region (illus. 83) was one of the largest and most complex works yet produced by him. It almost covered the concrete floor making it difficult to move around the work. Immediately ahead of the main entrance door was a series of small works, also sitting directly on the grey floor, listed as *Region Extension 1* to *Region Extension 7*. By their

fragility and placement, the spectators' progress was impeded, so the view of *Long Journey* was reached after a quiet walk amongst fragile constructions. *Long Journey* stretched endlessly along the floor to the far end of the gallery. Propped against the wall, *Crossing* was partly overwhelmed by *Region*, partly unnoticed because one's attention was directed to the floor and it was the only work using the wall.

In spite of the general air of austerity, and almost total lack of colour, the visitor was at first overwhelmed by the visual complexity. *Region* was made up of perhaps twenty-five separate pieces, yet each piece was different. It took some time before the eye and the mind absorbed the obvious diversity and found the underlying structure, which was basic and simple. Each of the units had a rectangular or square base, so that the plan was a grid of shapes and lines always at right angles, like the map of a city. There was a complex uniformity. Each form began as a rectangle, built from lightweight, sawn, recycled timber, tied with cotton or string at the corners. From this rigid base grew a great variety of structures, all built with dried twigs and sticks, some covered with papier mâché. The diversity of the parts was quite extraordinary with a wide range of forms and barely any repetition of similar structures — there was one row of three truncated prisms, but all other forms were different from each other.

The longer one viewed *Region*, the more one became aware of the subtleties — a contrast of horizontal against vertical, a solid structure beside another that one could look into, black tarred paper near off-white papier mâché, linear structures contrasted with flat planes, twigs against paper. The possibilities were explored endlessly with great enthusiasm and no sense of boredom. Yet nothing dominated within the complex uniformity.

All of the forms were packed closely together,

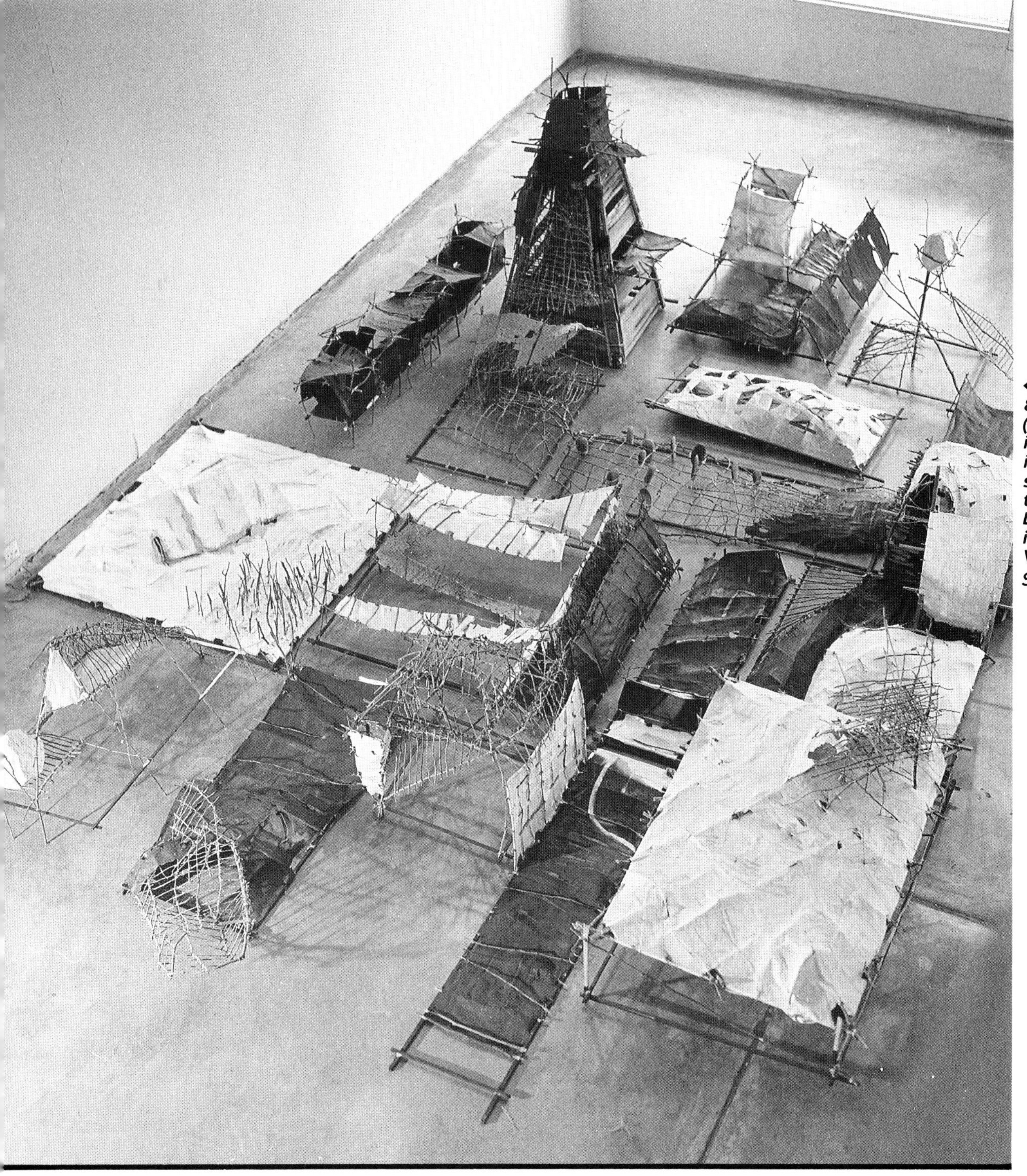

83 John Davis, Region (1980–81). General view of installation at Watters Gallery in 1981. Sawn timber, twigs, string, paper, calico, latex and tar. 110 x 355 x 305 cm. Dimensions vary with each installation. (Art Gallery of Western Australia.) Photograph by Mark Strizic.

with small paths of space between them. Paths, perhaps roads, streets? They suggested a link with buildings, houses, sheds, towns and settlements. There were obvious parallels between *Region* and the plan of a site.

Region is a generalisation about man and the pattern of his living. It is not Australian in particular, does not hint at Australian suburbia, has none of the brash newness of Australia. It ignores the harsh reality of an Australian country town. Davis's view is idealistic and romantic. *Region* is a generalisation which is timeless, a statement about man, the structures he builds and his relationship to his environment. It is a comment on man's individual relationship to the complex society in which he lives.

Region Extension 1 through to *Region Extension 7* (illus. 84, 85, 86, 87) were outposts from the main settlement. Linked by the same rectangular plan and an almost identical choice of materials, they were obviously made by representatives of the same society. Yet, they courageously expressed their individuality by moving away from the main settlement, placing themselves in a more vulnerable isolation. Individual forms from the main body of *Region* had been expanded so that they became separate items of sculpture.

Of the seven works, *Region Extension 7* was the largest — a tall, narrow pyramidal form, on a narrow rectangular base. The structure of twigs was almost completely covered in white papier mâché, though it was possible to see inside from the narrow triangular ends. It suggested a form of shelter, but the similarity in shape to an Indian temple gopuram gave it a symbolic religious character.

Crossing was another work which also showed the influence of Indian architecture on Davis — the simple post and beam structure of a Hindu temple was the basis of the work. It was reminiscent of a dark doorway, but in the Watters exhibition it was the odd one out, the only work leaning against the wall, when all others were directly on the floor. In scale it was also completely different, looking too much like a domestic mantelpiece. Nevertheless, *Crossing* is of interest, particularly as it was the beginning of a series of works to hang from or lean against the wall.

Long Journey stretched endlessly down the gallery, like a primitive boat carved from the log of a tree. It was actually made in a number of sections: solid wood, partly carved; an area constructed of twigs, mainly covered in white paper; a large section built of twigs, covered in black tarred paper and a final section covered in white papier mâché with some touches of pink. The whole structure was reminiscent of a boat, and the detail suggested storage holds, cabin compartments, whilst a large vertical screen hinted at a solar source of power. There was one small circular opening, which gave access to the interior of the structure.[4]

In her review of the 1981 Watters Gallery exhibition, Nancy Borlase gave the work of John Davis a most appreciative review.

■ *Relics of some primitive culture, an imaginary city, dislocations in space and time — these are the concerns of Melbourne sculptor John Davis . . . All the works are made with sticks, twigs, paper, canvas strips, or in the case of 'Region' and 'Long Journey' — partly with weathered wood.*

Balanced on fragile frameworks of sticks, laced together with fine cotton twine, they are coated with white paint or blackened with creosote to give them a scorched, abandoned look.

The works are all part of an interrelated theme — arrested time, in 'Region', and time without beginning or end, in 'Long Journey'.

'Region', the largest and most complex work, occupying a large area of floor space, can be viewed as a landscape — but a landscape bounded by a sense of locality. It is composed of many parts.

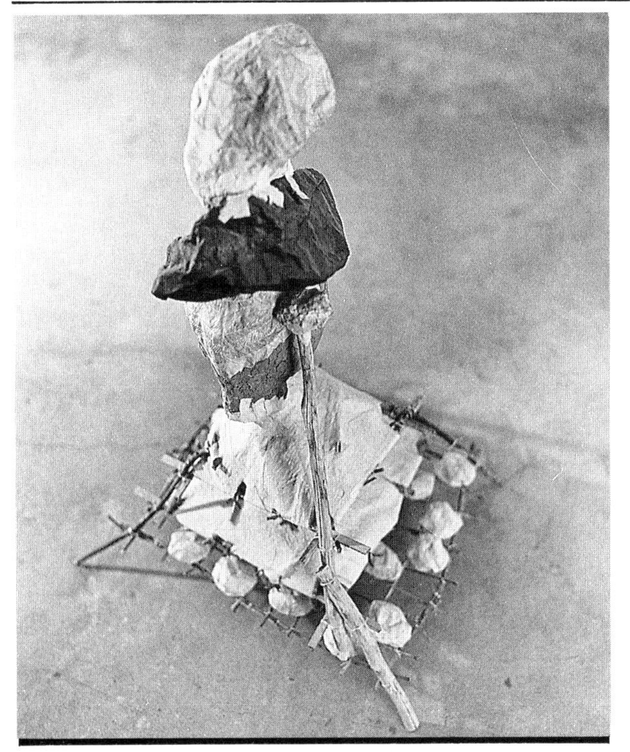

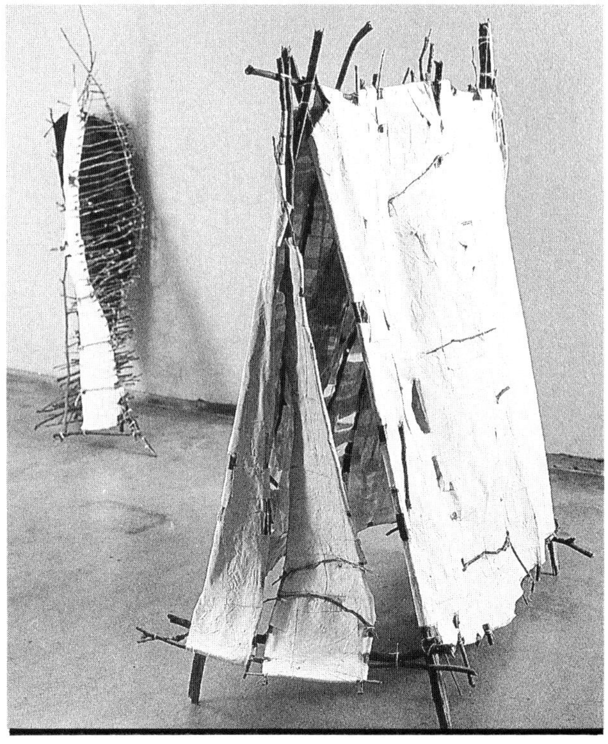

84 John Davis, Region Extension 1 (1980–81). Twigs, string, paper painted cream, green and pink with some paper left white. 62 x 39 x 33 cm. (In the Collection of Frank Watters.) Photograph by Mark Strizic.

85 John Davis, Region Extension 7 (1980–81). Twigs, string and paper left unpainted white. 89 x 84 x 43 cm. (In the possession of the artist.) Photograph by Mark Strizic.

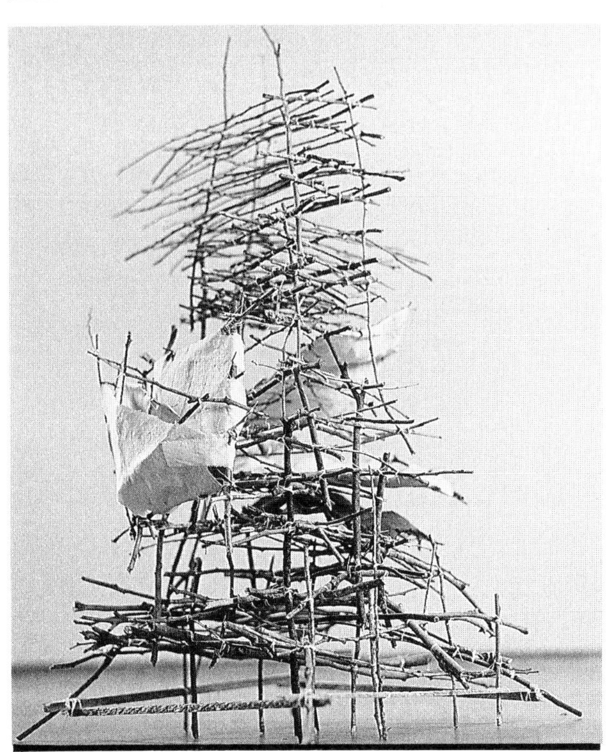

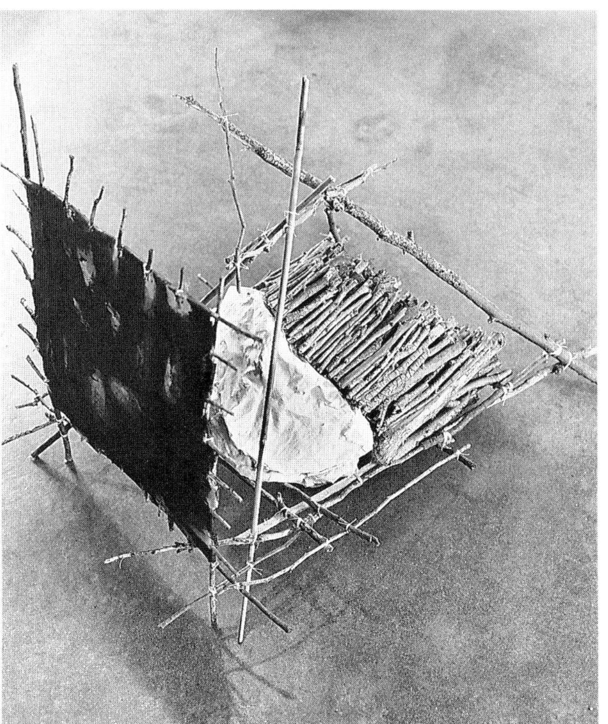

86 John Davis, Region Extension 5 (1980–81). Twigs, string and paper — some papier mâché painted pink, other areas left white. 66 x 38 x 38 cm. (In the Collection of Alex and Geoffrey Legge.) Photograph by Mark Strizic.

87 John Davis, Region Extension 4 (1980–81). Twigs, string and paper — area of white papier mâché painted yellow at bottom. Vertical area of paper painted with tar. 44 x 62 x 50 cm. (In possession of the artist.) Photograph by Mark Strizic.

Locked into a cohesive, conceptual frame are individual sculptures of fastidious refinement and inventiveness.

These works — communal meeting houses, topped with towers as light and airy as a bird on the wing, kilns like shattered shell cases, ramps and bridges, a commanding pyramidal structure — are the evidence of a once settled community.

Each of these separate parts bristles with a life of its own. Indeed, in this remarkable work, the parts and the connecting links — a languidly curving shape with a haul of lint stones caught in a net of finely meshed sticks — seem greater than the whole . . .

['Long Journey'] is Davis's most poetic work — a wonderfully mobile sculpture in the form of a long, low-slung boat, part Chinese hulk, part native canoe, with the grace and tail of a crocodile. An odyssey, a journey into the unknown — it is full of romantic connotations.

'The Crossing', a black, flame-licked wall installation, perhaps has Stygian references. Its meaning is more obscure.[5]

Geoffrey Legge sat at the desk at Watters Gallery during November 1981 when *Region* was on display. In a letter to me he discussed the qualities of *Journey II* and *Region* and draws a comparison with two other Australian sculptors.

■ *'Journey II' (1977) is a miracle of invention, prodigal of ideas, a myriad of intricacies which always surprise one with their intriguing but unassuming rightness. Nothing clamours for attention as the eye is beguiled here and there full of wonder.*

Such a description would fit his greatest work (of those I've seen) — 'Region' of 1980/81. Both works have an unemphatic grid to lend them cohesiveness but how has he developed between the two works. Both are about 'life' as expressed by its traces; the earlier work seems to investigate those signs that insects leave and cause one to marvel — webs, chrysalysis, etc. 'Region' however is about humans and their constructions in the fullest anthropological sense: not merely buildings as shelter, but as expression of beliefs and traditions, prime urgings and complex needs, all those intangible mysteries that add up to culture.

For me the Australian works closest to 'Region' are those of John Armstrong of which I wrote in the catalogue to Project 3 — Objects at the A.G.N.S.W. Armstrong's are more specific — religious awe, authority/compliance etc. Davis being less specific allows of interpretations at different levels, sheltering from the rain or the evil eye may require similar structures, the temples of temporal power stretch up to a heaven from which the gods look down.

I believe the searchings which result in Robert Klippel's sculpture are similar to those that prompt John Davis. But their approach to the discovery of the essence of life, the inner structure of things is quite different. Klippel, as it were, tries to delve into the secrets of the atom. Davis tries to read those secrets in their physical emanations. Both are accepted methods of research and on the surface Davis seems to be more 'modern' in that his broadness seems to give scope to the operations of the gestalt. However, this is where we discover an undeniable and unexpected characteristic of John's work, first brought to my attention by Nancy Borlase in her review in S.M.H. 14/11/81. She says 'Indeed in this remarkable work (Region) the parts and the connecting links . . . seem greater than the whole''. Can Davis be in contradiction to those great art maxims $1+1=3$, $2+2=5$? Is the critic's interpretation incorrect? Or is it that as we approach some basic aspects of life the rule is inverted and the parts become greater than the whole? The flower more than the shrub, the petal more than the flower? Can a person's exceptional qualities, expressed in every line of the body be yet more essentially found in the gaze of the eye, the lines round the mouth? But 'Region' is complex, like a forest for which we evolve a greater and greater love as we come to admire each tree, but the mysterious hold on our minds of the whole forest cannot really be *encompassed by us, so we return to the trees gaining a deeper insight into each and making the encompassing of the whole a more and more remote possibility as its mysterious hold on us grows stronger.*[6]

Since 1982 the work of John Davis has been immediately identifiable. The style and materials have been consistent, although experimentation has been continuous. His ideas, structures and materials have come from the Australian bush. Intuitively he has built his fragile sculptures, which reflect the irregular growth of Australian trees, the casual do-it-yourself structures of the Australian farmer. In common with many Australians, John Davis

■ *has a deep love, almost a need for the country. Perhaps he has inherited an attitude which has its origins in our early settlers. They had a very direct relationship with the environment, a relationship based on an elementary need for survival in a harsh country . . . Many of the ideas and attitudes of contemporary Australians have their origins in an earlier rural life — even if nowadays the average Australian only visits the country during his annual holiday — and then takes his transistor in case he finds nature too quiet.*[7]

■ NOTES

[1] Ken Scarlett, 'John Davis in Japan', *Ina — Art News*, Ina Gallery, 1–29 October 1982.

[2] Ken Scarlett, 'John Davis at Watters', *Art and Australia*, vol. 20, no. 2, 1982.

[3] Ibid.

[4] This description of the exhibition is based on Ken Scarlett, ibid.

[5] Nancy Borlase, 'Time, Space and Relics Dominate New Sculpture', *Sydney Morning Herald*, 14 November 1981.

[6] Geoffrey Legge, letter to the author, 16 March 1983.

[7] Comments by Ken Scarlett on the work of Richard Long and David Nash, made in November 1982 and extracted from article on work of John Davis, 'Bush Art of John Davis', *SOKA/ Ikebana Ohara*, no. 387, February 1983, pp. 19–35. (Also articles by John Davis and Goji Hamada.)

 1982–83
JAPAN

The fact that an Australian sculptor, living in the suburbs of Melbourne, formed close ties with Japan and exhibited there on a number of occasions is intriguing enough, but the set of circumstances that brought about this link is even more unusual. A series of chance encounters, contacts with friends, an ability to act when the opportunity seemed right, all helped to bring about a series of exhibitions of the work of John Davis in Tokyo, Tokoname, Kyoto and Nagoya.

During 1966–67 Stelarc was a student at Caulfield Technical College when John Davis and I were on the staff. After a few years teaching he left for Japan to see Expo '70, but stayed on and has lived in Japan ever since. Letters back and forth kept him in touch with Australian artists and gallery directors, as well as informing us of the development of his suspension events. The link with Stelarc eventually brought about a meeting with John Davis and a Japanese artist, which was to have interesting ramifications.

In a letter to me in September 1979, Stelarc mentioned that he might be able to help arrange an exhibition of recent Japanese art for the Gryphon Gallery (Melbourne) and in particular 'some artists might forward instructions for pieces to be constructed by students in Melbourne'. From this idea a very ambitious exhibition developed entitled 'Yo In: Ideas from Japan, Made in Australia', in which seven tertiary art schools in Victoria and some seventy art students worked on ideas sent to Australia by twenty-seven Japanese artists.

During the exhibition in August 1981 several Japanese artists, musicians and journalists visited Melbourne, including Goji Hamada, a performance artist. Goji Hamada had requested a wide range of materials and equipment for his performance on the lawns at the rear of the National Gallery of Victoria (illus. 88), logs of wood to form a high tripod, chains, block and tackle, a TV monitor, bales of hay

and a shark(!) As it was still winter, all the sharks had left Port Phillip Bay for warmer water and securing a shark became a major problem. This was solved by Paula Dawson, when she contacted a professional fisherman in Queensland who eventually caught a 3.6 metre shark. The most convenient way of getting this frozen giant to the lawns behind the National Gallery was to trolley it through the gallery and out the rear door, but the crate was too big and wouldn't fit through the opening. The only alternative was to take it up the back stairs from the Nolan Street entrance. Even here it proved extraordinarily difficult, as the huge crate had to be carried by hand and it then stuck halfway, on the turn in the stairs. John Davis, who was lecturing at the Victorian College of the Arts in the sculpture studios just across the road, had brought a group of students to assist. Four hours of hard work eventually got the shark on to the lawn area, but not before it began to thaw, dripping blood from the open crate.

Such dedication to art cemented a friendship between Goji Hamada and John Davis. The friendship was also based on the great interest shown by Goji Hamada in Davis's work, which he saw as being essentially Australian. On his return to Japan, Goji Hamada was instrumental in securing an invitation for Davis to exhibit at Ina Gallery in Tokyo in October 1982.

Davis took two older works, *Flag Renamed Place* and *Journey III*, as well as a partly completed structure called *Journey Extended*. After arriving in Tokyo, he travelled to the small town of Tokoname, which is on the coast south of Nagoya. There he moved into a large workspace (illus. 89), with part of the sculpture that had been built in Australia and after ten days completed *Journey Extended* (illus. 90), which grew to over 6 metres long.

Most of the commercial galleries in Tokyo are

remarkably small by Australian standards, and this great length was a cause of wonder. Some Japanese artists visited the Pinacotheca Gallery in Melbourne recently and were overwhelmed by the huge gallery display areas, vast storage rooms, high ceilings and the abundant space. It was like a visit to Ayers Rock in central Australia — to them, it confirmed that Australia was a land of vast, open spaces.

Davis had taken with him all the necessary materials and tools (including bundles of eucalypt sticks), ready to finish the work, but wished to incorporate some materials found in Japan. Rod O'Brien, an Australian journalist who has lived in Japan for several years, explains how Davis chose the materials he used:

■ *On the beach in Aichi Prefecture where he made 'Journey Extended', it would have been easier if he had chosen plastic instead of bamboo. In fact, he did start using it and then changed his mind. 'I became a bit nervous', he said. The way in which plastic has invaded modern society. Seeing the endless deluge and dumping of rubbish and the state of the pollution which has contaminated the coast, he probably decided that the use of plastic could be nothing more than a trite comment.*

Interested in Japanese disposable chop-sticks which are used in the same throw-away manner as plastic, he said with regret that if his stay in Japan had been longer, he would have made something with disposable chopsticks. If I imagine myself in his position, as a conservationist of nature, his aspirations could be seen as a powerful criticism of Japan, an industrial giant which single-mindedly expands its demands more and more and consumes resources in great gulps.[1]

In relation to *Journey III*, O'Brien commented,
■ *it conveys the feeling of the menace of nature in Australia which is turned to parched and blackened scorched earth by drought and bush fires. Is it the image of a sand dune which has been burnt almost to its peak, or perhaps a wild animal which has died in the scorching heat?*

By comparison, the piece which was made in Japan expresses clearly, using a very simple form, the shape of the undulations of a beach which have been traced by violent typhoons, or the appearance of tranquility and softness of a rain-soaked landscape after being drenched by heavy rain. The net of small stalks of bamboo . . . gives an appearance of uncertainty and fragility . . .[2]

It was intriguing that John Davis was able to take to Japan a long narrow structure, made of eucalyptus sticks covered in paper blackened with tar, and then build another section, equally long and narrow. The second half was constructed of short lengths of bamboo, again covered in paper, but left white. Tied to the bamboo or embedded in the papier mâché were fragments of weathered and water-washed timber, found on the beach at Tokoname. With only a few small verticals, the emphasis was emphatically on long, low horizontal lines, reminiscent of a native canoe. When displayed it rested on the carpeted floor of the Ina Gallery. Nearby, also on the floor, *Flag Renamed Place* sprawled erratically across the grey carpet. *Journey III* hung from the ceiling like a delicate net.

The reaction to the exhibition was very favourable. Not only was the work taken back to the studio at Tokoname, where it was on show for a month, but the exhibition was also displayed at Ryo Gallery in Kyoto. Davis returned to Australia delighted with the positive response to his work.

While in Japan, Davis was surprised by the great interest in his work shown by ikebana artists. Australians have a narrow image of ikebana, thinking of it as a gentle art form practised by bored housewives. Australians fail to recognise the strength of tradition in Japan and cannot comprehend someone studying the art of flower arrangement for many years. Nor are Australians familiar

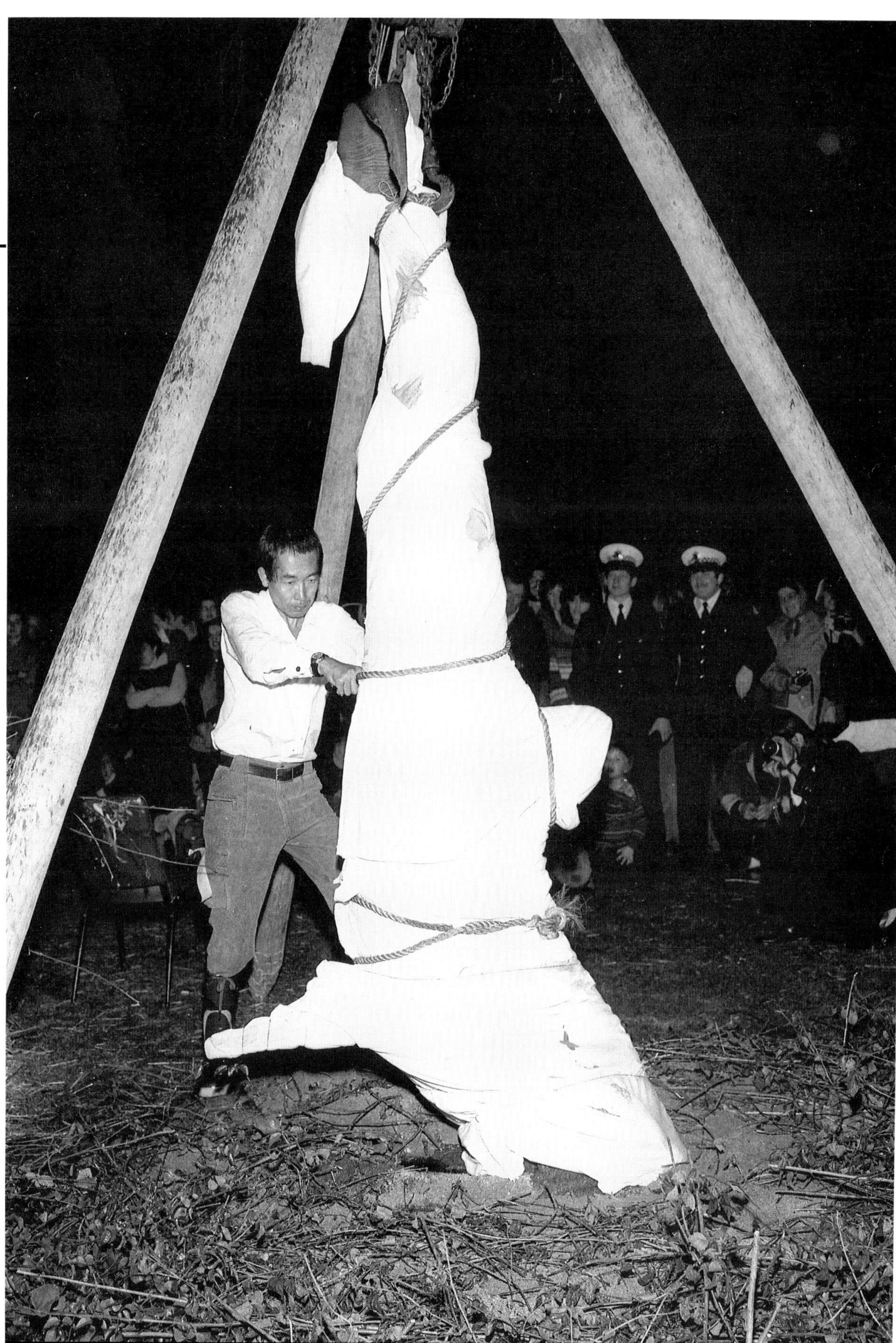

88 Goji Hamada, performance entitled 'Soft Language — Shark' on the lawns at the rear of the National Gallery of Victoria, during 'Yo In', 1981. Photograph by Tony Boyd.

with the contemporary developments in ikebana, where some experimental artists have moved their arrangements off the table or pedestal and used the floor and wall. Ikebana has increased in scale, being similar to what we might know as an installation.

John Davis had only just returned to Australia, when he and I received a letter from Kimio Akiyama, in the Editorial Department of Ikebana Ohara, the large institution in Tokyo that teaches ikebana and publishes an attractive monthly magazine. He wanted to know if we would prepare material for an article on John Davis to be published in their magazine.

■   *October 15, 1982*

Dear Mr. John Davis:

<u>*No. 1*</u>

In Mr. Ken Skerlet's manuscript titled "Australian view to the Nature", he said Mr. John Vavis was taken with Australian Bush; the connection of the things in the Bush Space or construction in the space.

Your works which were exhibited at the INA Gallery at Kyobashi were very much concerned with Australian Bush. So that we would like to know about your opinion about Bush Space and human being.

Also we would like to borrow your pictures and sketches for this.

<u>*No. 2*</u>

If possible, we would like to borrow your description of your thought of the procedure for your works in Japan.

<u>*No. 3*</u>

We also would like to know about your image concept for your works at INA Gallery.

<u>*About a talk with Mr. Ken Skerlet*</u>

I would like to ask you to have a discussion with Mr. Ken Skerlet about Australian nature or intention to the nature, and have a discussion with him about installation in the nature or about the occasion of the installation.

Then we would like to borrow the pictures or sketches of its talk if it is not trouble for you.

<u>*About the manuscript from Mr. Ken Skerlet*</u>

The manuscript we would like to have from Mr. Ken Skerlet is his thought of Mr. John Davis's concept of his work. I think Mr. Richard Long, Mr. Vavid Nash in England, they have same idea of their works. How about his opinion on this matter. If there are some affection from Ikebana on their concept of their works, we would like to know about your opinion for that. Thank you very much for your kind help on the above matter.

Sincerely,

Kimio Akiyama (Editorial Department)[3]

In answer to Kimio Akiyama's request, Davis wrote 'Some Brief Notes on Issues Which I Think Are Raised in My Art'. In the notes he sheds light on early influences of the Australian environment upon himself and his work and goes on to discuss a number of issues.

■ *In my younger formative years I spent a great deal of time living and learning from the natural environment; an environment which is very flat, no hills only gentle mounds of sand, a huge hot sky, clumps of trees which clung to waterholes or rivers or stood isolated in open space sometimes without apparent reason. I learnt to see the world, in general terms — miles of it at once — or specifically through its details, the things that I had to step over, to avoid as dangerous, or to admire in its state of completeness, beauty or fragility. I frequently experienced these moments alone, thus being aware, at an early age of the sense of isolation, of being like an isolated tree, in the vastness of that landscape and eventually through time and familiarity recognising how I occupied part of that landscape. Superficially it appears empty and barren but it is full of small life systems surviving together offering only fragile evidence of their existence, or small moments of importance, or a story of some event that occurred.*

This is all reflected in the work through the placement of the objects that make up the work through the

▶
89 John Davis in studio at Tokoname, Japan, in 1982 working on Journey Extended. Photograph by Goji Hamada.

▶
90 John Davis, Journey Extended (1982). The work taken from Melbourne consisted of twigs, string, canvas, paper, yellow paint and tar. The following materials were gathered on the beach at Tokoname, Japan and added: bamboo, parts of wrecked boat, water-washed timber fragments, Japanese rice paper, canvas and tar. 56 x 610 x 57 cm. (In the possession of the artist.) Photograph taken by the artist, showing work exhibited at Ina Gallery, Tokyo, Japan, 1982.

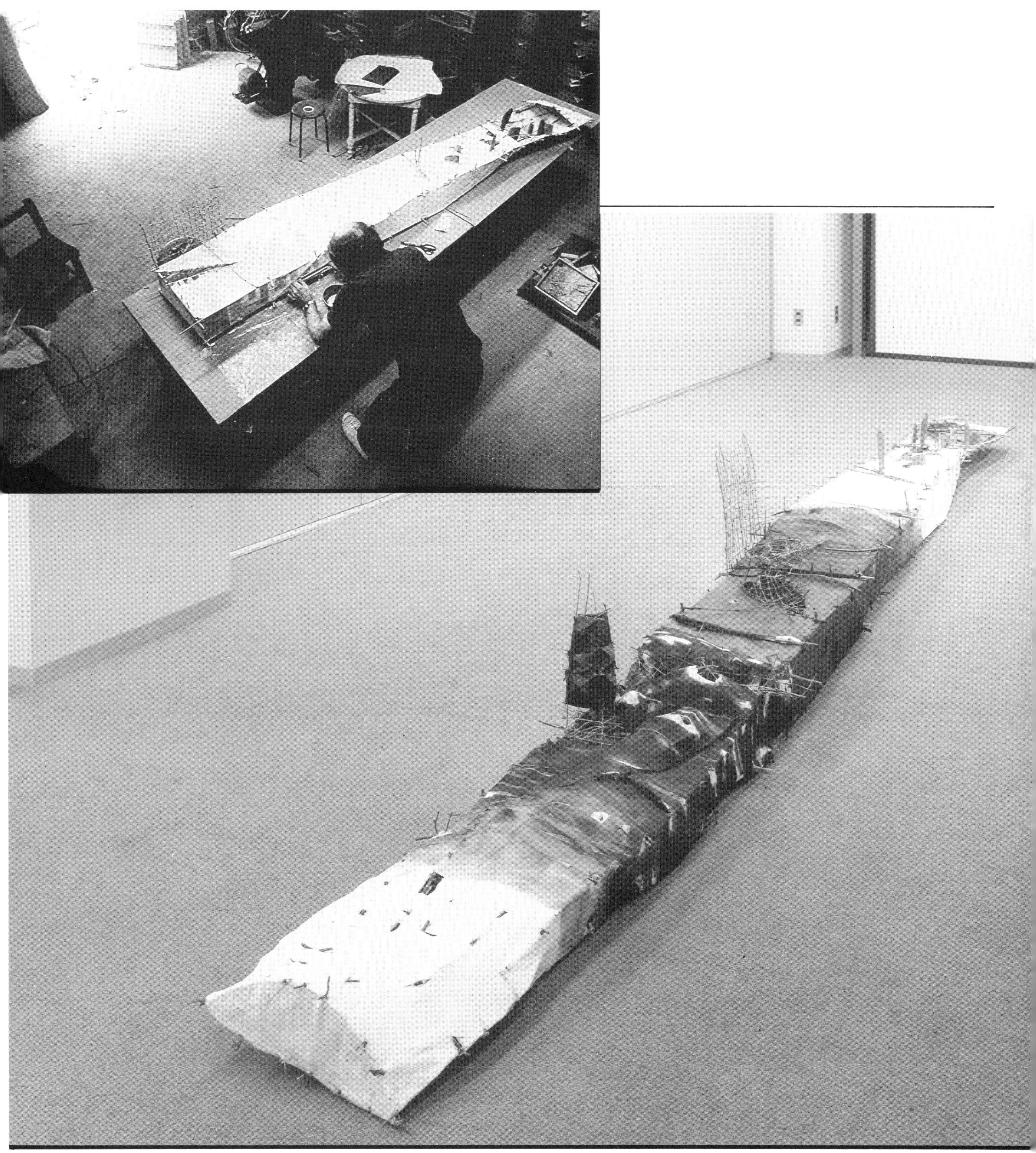

materials I use, and the methods I employ to construct the objects.

I want my work to evoke all of these sensations and situations, to create a strong sense of place, of identity and uniqueness either within the specifics of the objects, or within the spaces in which they are installed — a place which has general characteristics and specific details.

My selection of materials is also symbolic and metaphoric — tar as an aesthetic media, a traditional preserver of organic material in the natural environment, and because it gives the appearance of burnt surface, a vehicle of destruction. Herein lies a curious contradiction: the work may look negative and threatening but to compare it with the landscape it is interesting to note that parts of the Australian bush require fire to burn off accumulated natural debris in order to cleanse, and at the same time causing seeds to be freed from their pods by extreme heat as a necessary process in the release of these seeds for germination.

The piece 'Journey Extended' which I completed in Tokoname evolved through two needs or attitudes. The first was practical — how large was the space in which it was to be exhibited and how should the finished piece occupy this space? This determined its total length. What materials would be available in Japan for me to construct the second segment? This determined the expression and created the tensions within the work. The second was based on the problem of working on one idea in totally different environments and my responses to such things as space and scale which are important within my work. Would I bring enough of my 'Australianess' with me, or would I be markedly 'persuaded' by the Japanese environment to radically change my forms and concepts?

Thirdly the idea of making work in another country appeals to me, as it marginally removes me from being only a tourist. It means that I am drawing more deeply on the environment, making more than a superficial visitation, and on completion of the piece,

I offer something to the society which invited me to visit, something which I have obtained from within that society. When the two segments are put together, then I think it makes an interesting symbolic gesture about the dialogue which is developing between Japanese and Australian artists.

'Journey Extended' is based on a landscape evoking long distances, bare earth surfaces, dead animals dried out in the sun's heat, man-made objects which perch tenuously in the landscape, bright light, ancient remnants. The general form of the piece is like a log or plank of timber lying discarded in an open space.[4]

■ *'Journey Extended' is about something which has begun somewhere and then moves to another place and continues to move on, so it is extended in terms of actual dimension, but it also extended in terms of an idea, which began in Australia and was completed in Japan. So it works at a physical as well as an intellectual level in that sense.*[5]

Kimio Akiyama's questions brought about a response from both Davis and me. I wrote some thoughts on the work of Richard Long and David Nash, drawing comparisons with John Davis.

■ *The British sculptor, Richard Long, produced work in the late 60s, through the 70s and into the 80s which appear to be concerned with three aspects — walks in the country, sculptures constructed in the countryside of local materials, or sculptures installed in galleries, also using materials acquired nearby.*

Line was, and still is, a basic ingredient to all his works, whether they be walks or sculptural constructions. He tends to favour a straight line, the circle or the spiral, though he moved somewhat from geometric patterns to lines related to nature — such as the line of a river.

Richard Long has a deep respect for nature and even though his sculptures completed in the countryside are man-made, they are always in sympathy with nature. He presumes that nature will slowly over-

whelm his structures by the growth of plants and natural weathering caused by rain and wind.

As with the installations made by John Davis in the country

■ *Only photographs record and make permanent. On the other hand his circles of natural materials, placed carefully on art gallery floors, contrast rocks and wood with a geometric structure and display natural materials in a man made environment . . . John Davis is more conscious of his Australian origin rather than his European background. For him the linear patterns of Aboriginal bark painting or shield decoration are more relevant. He is intrigued by the Aborigines' respect for sacred stones and their use of feathers on decorative and symbolic objects.*

Richard Long is essentially an English artist, making gentle changes to a landscape he loves. John Davis shares a gentle humility with Richard Long, but relates to a harsher Australian environment. Both artists have visited far distant exotic places, yet when they get there, their commitment to their own known environment is so strong, that the work they produce abroad is essentially the same as work made in their own country . . . John Davis has made installations in India and Italy in 1978 and in Japan in 1982 (also in USA during 1984, '86 and '87) all works of a similar sensibility. Richard Long's 'A Line Made by Walking' in England in 1967 is basically the same as his 'Walking a Line in Peru', produced in 1972.

In spite of the great growth of urban civilisation and the rapid development of high technology, both artists are committed to the country rather than the city — they are romantics who prefer nature rather than the civilisation of man.

David Nash has lived for some years in an isolated Welsh village in Great Britain, where he has produced sculptures in two main forms. Either he has sawn, carved and assembled timber to produce objects which exploit the qualities of both natural logs of timber and the characteristics of sawn planks of timber, or he has

used growing trees to form sculptures in the nearby forest. He has actually planted trees, controlling their growth so as to get the desired arrangement over a period of years, taking into account the changes of the seasons . . .

David Nash relates many of his works directly to nature — they are set in forests, amongst trees, in clearings or even in a stream. He has used the ancient technique of espalier, long used to control the growth of fruit trees, to give a sculptural form to natural growth. David Nash appears to need a personal relationship to a particular place, so lives, works and makes his sculpture in the environment that is essential for him.[6]

When David Nash visited Australia in 1986 and made a number of works at Heide Park and Art Gallery, he tended to remake previous sculptures, or repeat ideas and techniques. By comparison, John Davis has been much more inventive when he has worked overseas. Even though the materials and techniques used by John Davis have been the same, the forms and installations have been varied, making imaginative use of the space available.

In the interview with Davis after his return from Japan, we began by talking about Goji Hamada and Emiko Namikawa's reaction to Davis's sculpture.

KS: 'When Goji Hamada and Emiko Namikawa visited Australia and looked at your work, they both saw your sculpture as Australian. Presumably this was the main reason you were invited to exhibit at Ina Gallery in October this year. Do you see your work as Australian?'

JD: 'I don't see my work as particularly Australian although there are Australian qualities about the work: the most obvious ones I suppose are the materials, but there are qualities which could relate to North American Indian or Melanesian art around

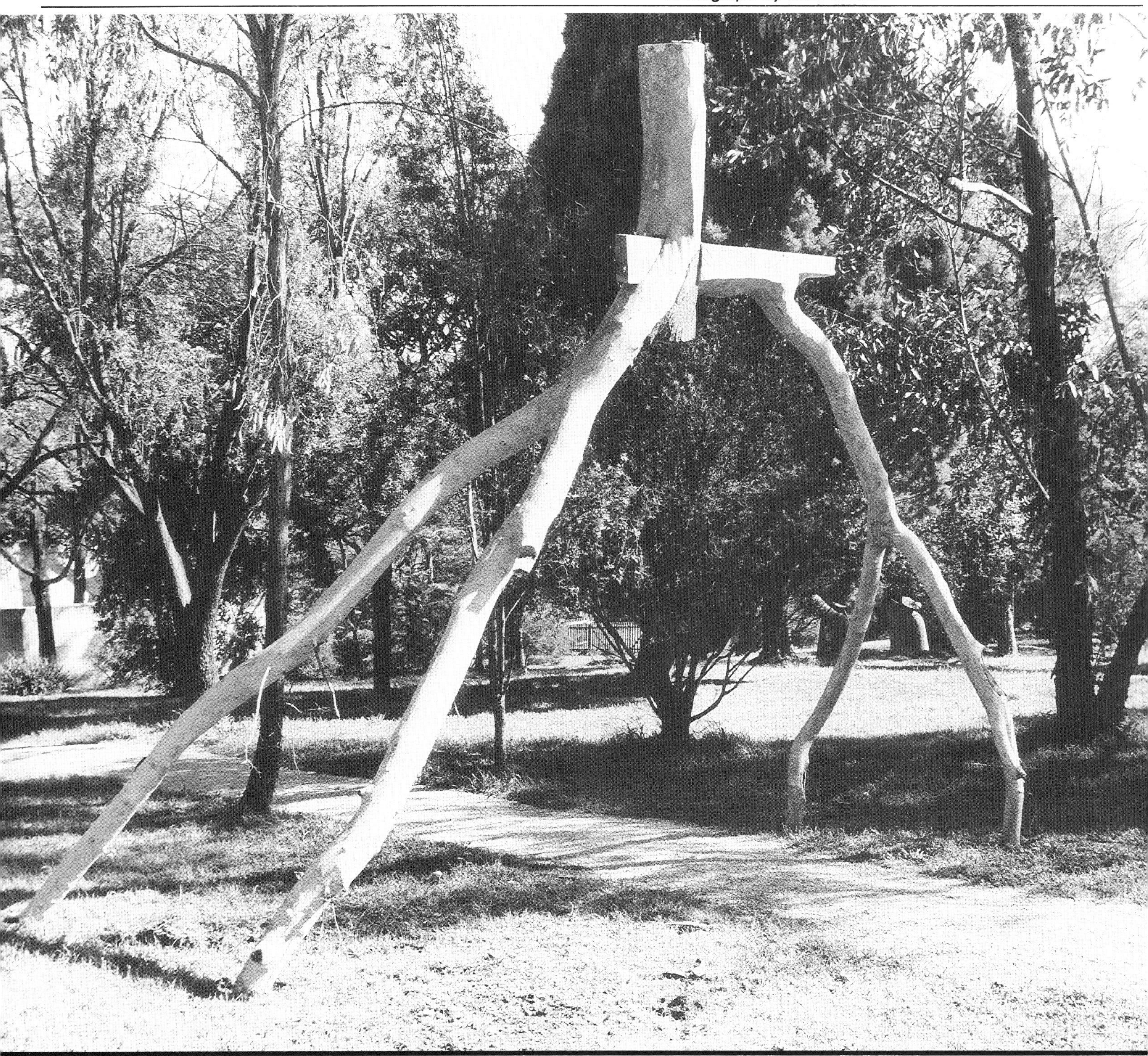

91 David Nash, Elm Arch (1985). Elm. 395 x 490 x 223 cm. Gift of the artist to Heide Park and Art Gallery. Photograph by John Brash.

the Pacific area. Perhaps the quality that's most Australian about it is the feeling of space that I try and create within the installation, so when I talk about my work, it's not only the object that I've made, but the installation of objects within a room. I suppose the Australian thing is the scattered nature of the installation and the space that exists between the objects. There is also a very dry sparse quality about the way I use the materials which reminds people, or evokes pictures in people's minds of the Australian landscape. The Australian landscape is a very varied thing which ranges from rain forests in the north of Australia (tropical areas) to the dry desert areas, so Australia has a variety of qualities, but I suppose the most famous aspect of Australian landscape is its dryness — people tend to always refer to that as typically Australian.'[7]

Davis also referred to the Australian qualities in his work in the notes he had written for Kimio Akiyama.

■ *Australia has two visual arts cultures, the original one used by the Aborigines in their ceremonies and rituals and dating back over 40,000 years, and the much more recent, European, which has existed for approximately 200 years in Australia. I am fourth generation Australian and consequently find it 'natural' to be Australian which is quite a different attitude to my parents, who still sub-consciously observe England as home. Australia's geographical position has unique advantages and disadvantages. In recent years more artists have been able to travel to other art centres and we have been frequently visited by artists from these centres so that the isolation which once existed, has now been broken down. This means that art is now made directly from other art, whereas the Australian artist in the past has relied on repro-ductions from postcards, magazines, or books to develop art through 'second hand' means and subsequently subject to misinterpretation through the normal distortions of reproduction. However because of our distance from the power centres of art, Australian artists are not as heavily subjected to art imperialism if they wish to separate themselves from that influence. Canada (which is comparable in many ways to Australia) I think, is an example of this cultural dilemma. We are also situated in a region of rich cultural backgrounds other than European, plus Aboriginal culture, so that the opportunity to expand and invent concepts which directly reflect our cultural geographic region is immense and dynamic.*

I would hope to make art which is Australian in its 'feel' — to reflect the issues which we are facing at present, but at the same time coming from a personal basis, offering the spectator my view of the world, my obsessions, and my concerns about art.[8]

The interview also explored Davis's choice of materials.

KS: 'You've used a wide range of materials in your career — everything from carving wood to working in polyester resin and fibreglass, spraying things with duco, but how have you reached the point of wanting to work in fairly unorthodox materials such as twigs and sticks, string, papier mâché etc? . . .'

JD: 'By working directly with materials such as twigs, one could move much faster, so that when the twig was tied to another twig, the work was evolving at that point — and not having to go through a distant process — so the work was evolving quickly before me, which I found much more exciting. The second reason is that I was drawn to humble materials because it seemed like a good way of introducing people to the work without alienating them initially by the sheer weight of technique, or process that many sculpture pieces incorporate. If people were familiar with things like twigs and string and paper, they would immediately be drawn into the piece because they felt they understood those materials and they were quite familiar to them . . .'

KS: 'Is this a romantic notion to have in the twentieth century: in view of the fact that the twentieth century is chiefly characterised by rapid increase in technology, are you deliberately going in the opposite direction in which you ignore high technology and wish to work out simple procedures using cheap, commonplace materials?'

JD: 'I suppose I've never really thought about it like that because I am preoccupied and obsessed with my own interests. In a sense I suppose you could say that I am working against a general trend now for work to be passed around and people to lose contact with the finished product — I'm thinking of assembly lines and motor car building lines and so on. There's a certain amount of disillusionment and unhappiness because people don't have the satisfaction of following something through from the beginning to the end in their normal lives. They see themselves as part of a system having very little to do with any real major decision making within that system. With my own work perhaps it's my way of coping with living in that kind of society. I can make certain decisions and follow them through myself which gives me an enormous amount of satisfaction . . .'

KS: 'I think you and I have noticed a change that has occurred in Australia over the last few years: whereas in the nineteenth century and the earlier twentieth century Australian artists always went to Europe or in particular to Great Britain, I suppose since 1945 — in the 50s and the 60s in particular, Australian artists started going to America — what we've also noticed in more recent times is that Australian artists are fascinated by Oriental cultures and more and more Australian artists have gone to Japan. It's going to be interesting to see whether influences start to appear in Australian art. Do you think your link with Japan — as short as it was — is likely to have any influence upon your attitudes and your style of work?'

JD: 'I'm sure it will, but it takes some time for these sorts of factors to filter through. It may not be a physical form which will evolve in time. It might be more to do with metaphysical things, or evocative things. I don't think I'll be changing my materials or anything like that because I went to Japan, but this is all supposition. I sometimes think back to when I went to India and how that has influenced my work. Certainly the work has become more complex in its combination of forms. But the thing that suddenly struck me, when I was in Japan, why I enjoy the temples of both India and Japan very much, is because they both have an incredibly strong sense of place. The thing that's important about my work is the sense of place that I want to create — either within a room or, if I make a piece out in the open, then it reinforces that sense of place. So when I visited the temples in India and the shrines in Japan, I became very aware of this strong sense of a special place, within a forest or on the side of a hill, or even out on an open beach, depending where it was, of this special kind of place. That's the thing that is being reinforced in my work from my visits to India and Japan.'

▶
92 Professor Ko Morishita working on his ikebana installation of rocks and paper in the Gryphon Gallery, during the visit of the Japanese group from Soka Ikebana Ohara, in March 1983. Photograph by Mark Strizic.

▶
93 Professor Atsuko Kosaku arranging strips of bark and paper on the floor of the Gryphon Gallery as preparation for the three day exhibition by the Soka Ikebana Ohara group, 6–8 March 1983. Photograph by Mark Strizic.

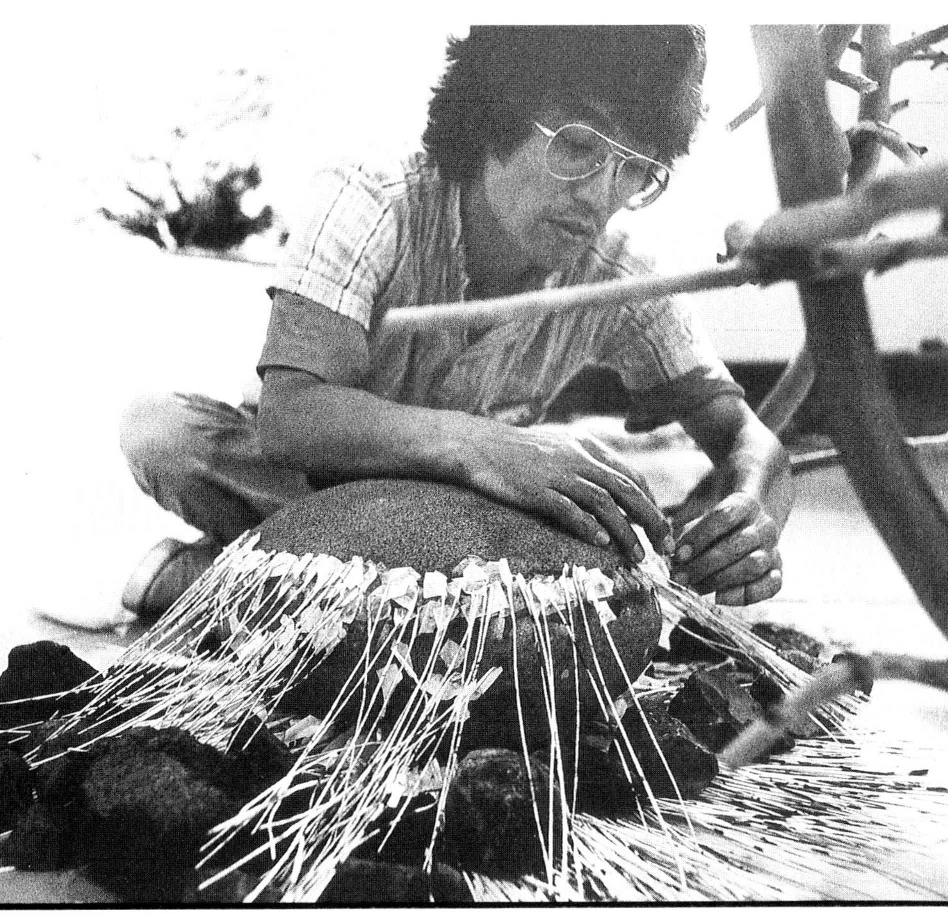

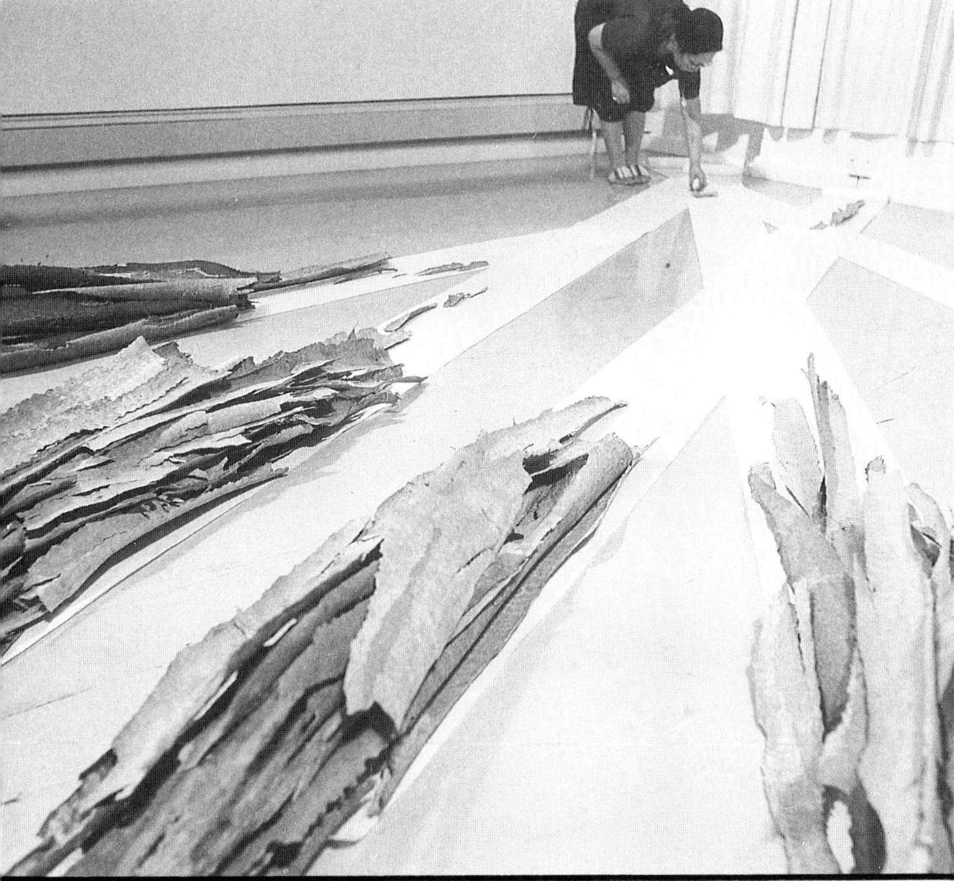

KS: 'In Australia, some natural forms have a strong sense of place — you mentioned Ayers Rock earlier — but very few architectural structures have a real sense of identity. Possibly the Sydney Opera House has become a national symbol. What one can find in India and Japan are man-made forms which have a very beautiful serenity, or a timeless quality, which we do not have in Australia. We're all too new here — we haven't got architectural forms which have this strong sense of identity.'

JD: 'Perhaps that's what I'm trying to create, since we don't have that kind of man-made symbolism in our landscape such as one finds in other parts of the world. It might be a need within my psychology to create some kind of a special place that we lack in this country. I know it's not to do with controlling the landscape — that doesn't worry me at all. I enjoy the way Australia spreads and spreads. I try to establish an area in that vast space, that will work within the existing space, as well as attempting to catch the sense of time and character of the locality.'[9]

Once set in motion, an almost inevitable process seemed to continue, linking Australian and Japanese artists. The official opening of the new Concert Hall in the Victorian Arts Centre on 6 November 1982 brought a galaxy of visitors to Melbourne, including two Japanese, Mr Sakai and Mr Sugawara, who were also interested in contemporary Australian art. They gathered material for articles back in Japan.

Towards the end of February 1983, another group arrived in Melbourne, as a direct result of having seen John Davis's exhibition in Tokyo. *Ikebana Ohara* had published a seventeen-page article on the 'Bush Art of John Davis', and the management was so impressed by the work and intrigued by the country that it sent four staff members to Australia to look at the bush.[10] Having seen photographs of his installations at the Hattah Lakes in the Mallee, they wanted to go there and see it for themselves. Hiring a car they set off for the Mallee, where in spite of the 45°C heat, they proceeded to make installations in the bush, duly recorded for later publication.[11] They arrived in Australia only a few days after the terrifying destruction of the bushfires on Ash Wednesday, 16 February 1983, when nearly seventy people had been killed and 2,000 homes destroyed. Ikebana teaches an observation of nature in all its moods, but this was an aspect of nature with which they were not familiar. Both the destruction and the miraculous regeneration of the bush fascinated them. They drove along the Great Ocean Road, seeing vast expanses of blackened trees and burnt houses.

Coming back to Melbourne the two ikebana artists, Professor Ko Morishita and Professor Atsuko Kosaku, installed an exhibition of their work in the Gryphon Gallery for a brief three-day period (illus. 92, 93). The work ranged from traditional arrangements (even if with Australian plants) to experimental, contemporary ikebana, such as a white plastic bag full of incinerated apples, black and hard, like burnt potatoes.

For me, the visit of the four representatives of Ikebana Ohara was a wonderful opportunity to secure first hand the reaction of Japanese to the Australian landscape and to the work of John Davis. Their replies to my questions conveyed their impressions. Kimio Akiyama said

■ *The light of the sun and the colour of the earth left a very strong impression on me.*

Professor Ko Morishita replied to my questions

■ *the vastness of nature is completely different from that in Japan. I discovered both the terror and the warmth of nature in the midst of the bush fires. I felt the undisguised awfulness of the energy which can bring back life, even after the death of nature.*

The bush fires on the way to Hattah Lakes made a very strong impression on me. Human beings looked small against the cycle of nature.

Mindful of the constraints of living in a densely populated urban society, the space and loneliness of the Australian landscape was a revelation to Professor Atsuko Kosaku. She wrote

■ *It was a truly marvellous and mysterious experience. In particular, the fact that there were no people, that we met no one, made me feel anew that in so far as human beings 'live', it means only that each individual, each person lives. If possible, I want to go 'alone' again.*

Many of these characteristics of the Australian landscape are to be found in the works of John Davis — colours bleached by the sun, or blackened by fire, forms loosely related in space, an ageless quality in which time is suspended, an environment in which the structures of man are fragile and vulnerable against the forces of nature. Yet the Japanese visitors such as Professor Atsuko Kosaku, who had only seen one exhibition of work by Davis, were able to discern underlying qualities. She wrote 'I feel emotions such as fragility, mutability, tenderness, loneliness, futility . . .'

Professor Ko Morishita possibly gave an important reason for the acceptance of John Davis's installations in Japan:

■ *From his works in Japan at the Ina Gallery and from photographs, there seem to be points in common with ikebana, so I feel a sense of familiarity.*

John Davis was virtually unaware of ikebana until he visited Japan, when Japanese noted the similarities between his work and experimental ikebana. His knowledge of larger scale, ikebana installations could only have been gained through magazines, and during two visits to Japan when he saw some contemporary ikebana. As with the effect of Aboriginal art on his work, referred to by many critics, I see ikebana as a parallel of ideas, attitudes and materials, rather than an influence. The visual

94 John Davis, Raft (1983). Sawn timber, twigs, papier mâché, canvas, synthetic bitumen, pigment and shells. 90 x 248 x 300 cm. Dimensions variable according to installation. Photographed in the artist's studio at the Victorian College of the Arts, prior to being shown at Gallery Lunami, Tokyo, as part of 'Continuum '83'. (In the possession of the artist.) Photograph by Mark Strizic.

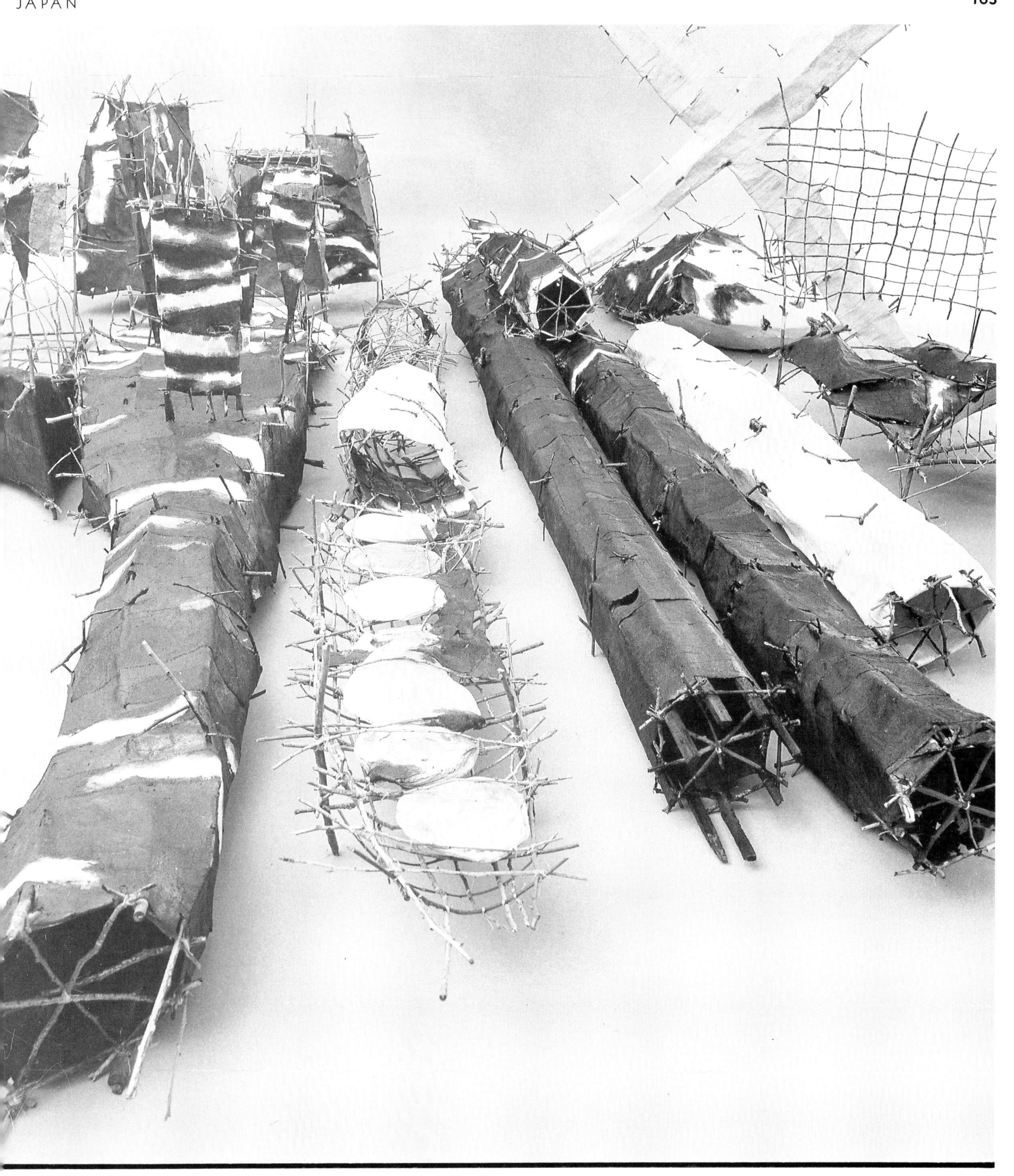

similarity existed before the influence. Ikebana can vary from the traditional flower arrangement to large-scale installations, which westerners would know as sculpture. The jump to the work of John Davis is not as great as one would have imagined. In both cases there is a modified version of 'truth to material', perhaps better stated as 'truth to nature'. The materials and forms of nature are used with respect, but allowing freedom for the artist to impose his will. As with bonsai, nature is revered, but the result is controlled by man.

Of the many visitors from Japan, probably one of the most influential was Emiko Namikawa, Director of Lunami Gallery in Tokyo, who visited Sydney and Melbourne in May 1982. She had formed a friendship with Maryrose Sinn, a young Australian artist who had been resident in Tokyo during most of 1981, and through her became greatly interested in contemporary Australian art. Two other Australians in Japan, Stelarc and Peter Callas, plus the first-hand knowledge of Goji Hamada, helped formulate an ambitious idea.

Emiko Namikawa came to Australia to talk with artists and gallery directors and to select artists for a major exhibition of contemporary Australian art in Tokyo during 1983. After her return to Tokyo, Emiko Namikawa persuaded fifteen commercial gallery directors to show Australian contemporary art in their galleries from 22 August–3 September 1983 — a major act of diplomacy and organisational skill! This important series of exhibitions was organised by artists and gallery directors, the initiative did not begin at a government or Australia Council level, though at a later stage the Visual Arts Board, the Japan Foundation and the Australia-Japan Foundation helped with funding.

I was deeply involved with the organisation of these exhibitions which John Davis had aptly named 'Continuum '83', and eventually travelled to Japan, along with about twenty-five Australian art-

ists, tertiary art lecturers, art teachers, curators and friends.

The Japanese had selected most of the Australian artists. They were fascinated by the Australian landscape, but avoided the obvious — they did not invite any painters to contribute. The emphasis was on sculpture, installations, photography and performance, with additional sections devoted to video, film, artists' books, posters, sound and a photographic record of women's performance work in Australia. Eighteen artists contributed (including the expatriate Stelarc, who was living in Yokohama), but nearly seventy artists were linked with some of the group exhibitions. The Japanese publicised 'Continuum '83' as 'The first exhibition of contemporary Australian Art in Japan'.

In August 1983, Davis returned to Japan to exhibit *Raft* (illus. 94), this time at the Lunami Gallery, as part of 'Continuum '83'. *Raft* was simple and direct in composition, consisting basically of five long narrow, cylindrical forms, placed parallel to each other on the gallery floor. Even though they were packed closely together, they almost filled one end of the small Japanese gallery — it was difficult to walk down either side, so one viewed it mainly from the front. The long cylinders suggested the structure of a raft, though the total shape of the work was irregular and not like one's image of a rectangular raft. Links with the sea were suggested by the inclusion of seven large water washed flat shells, attached to the twigs of one of the long forms. The other cylinders were mostly covered in calico, some left white, others partly painted black and two almost completely black. A few small vertical forms broke the possible monotony of the numerous horizontals. A large cross reared up dramatically in one corner, the diagonals attracting a lot of attention amongst the repetitious horizontals. In a strange alteration of its normal significance, the equiarmed, square cross suggested movement, compared with the static quality of the parallel cylinders. Without in any way looking like mast or sails it hinted at a structure for sailing.

Again, Davis's work was very well received in Japan. I visited the Lunami Gallery many times during the fortnight I was in Tokyo and on each occasion I observed a constant flow of Japanese visiting the gallery, quietly contemplating *Raft*, and no doubt, puzzling over the translation of *Is a Foolish Dog Barks at a Flying Bird* by Peter Cole, exhibited at the other end of the gallery. When he exhibited *Incident* in Melbourne in June 1983, John Davis received one review and not a mention in any other magazine or newspaper. When he showed in Tokyo he gained a great number of reviews, photographs and listings in newspapers and magazines. A quick check of the bibliography for John Davis reveals at least twenty separate references for Japanese publications during 1983 compared with about eight in Australia, yet during 1983 he exhibited in Perth, Melbourne and Sydney. In Tokyo he had a certain advantage by exhibiting at Lunami Gallery, as the Director, Emiko Namikawa, was the centre of the organisation for 'Continuum '83'. Any newspaper reporter, journalist or art critic tended to start at Lunami and then visit other galleries in the Ginza. But he was also entertained by the publishers of *SOKA Ikebana Ohara* and *Ikebana Ryusei* and it was his work, rather than the work of any other of the eighteen major artists exhibiting, that was chosen to be exhibited at a second gallery in Nagoya.

The reaction to his work not only raises the question of why Davis is appreciated in Japan, but why do the Japanese appear to have a great curiosity about contemporary Australian art? 'Continuum '83' was a major series of exhibitions, which brought together fifteen separate galleries, plus other venues for film, video and sound. Why was there such an emphasis on Australian art in Tokyo? I would have thought that Japanese wanting to know something of contemporary western art would have gone to Europe or America, after all, there are reputed to be up to 1,500 Japanese artists in New York.[12] But America in particular may be seen as a threat to Japan economically and culturally. Australia is neither an economic nor cultural threat and can therefore be observed with interest, with little antagonism.

When Japanese society and culture are tied so securely to tradition, the Japanese probably find a great sense of freedom in Australian art, particularly in the 1980s when there is no discernable mainstream. Compared with the restraint and antiquity of their own culture, no doubt Australians appear youthful and vigorous, if not aggressive and brash. When even shop assistants wrap up a parcel in a department store with exquisite skill, John Davis's twigs wrapped in strips of canvas or papier mâché must appear to be trenchant. In writing in general about 'Continuum '83', Memory Holloway headed her article 'A Clash of Culture', which infers an encounter, with conflict, or at the least, she suggested, a basic misunderstanding.[13] Rod O'Brien, writing after seven years' residence in Japan, seemed to be more in touch with Japanese opinion. He quoted a Japanese critic who had taken a particular interest in Australian art shown at 'Continuum '83': 'One Tabashi Akatsu has already decided the work of Melbourne sculptor, John Davis, has given the Japanese "culture shock" '.[14]

If anything the visual shock increased Japanese curiosity to see the Australian work. Rod O'Brien wrote in his article

■ *I regularly visit galleries, but in seven years I have never seen so many people in these spaces, which are mostly not as big as a suburban Australian living room.*

Streams of local artists, students, even foreigners,

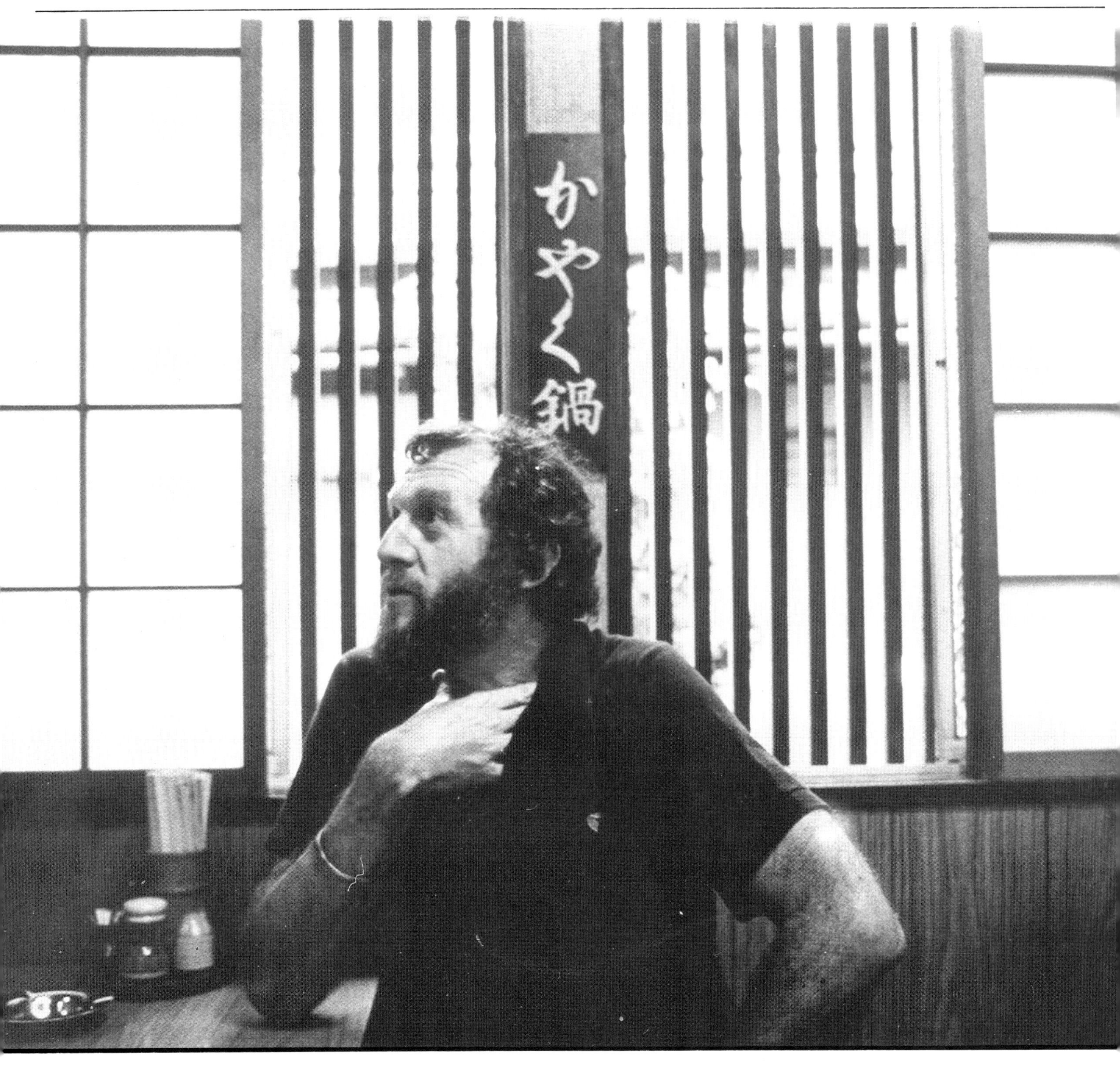
かやく鍋

◀
95 John Davis in a restaurant at Tokoname, Japan, 1982. Photograph by Ikebana Ryusei. Photographer, Koichi Taniguchi.

are sampling the new energy and sensitivity of how Australians see and feel about their landscape and society, its conflicts and their conflicts, in themes stretching from the stone age to high technology.[15]

Again, Rod O'Brien quotes the Japanese critic:

■ *Mr Akatsu says that the Japanese are 'very familiar with European art, also American (art), almost too much so . . . This is the first time for Australia and our task is to discover the unique characteristics of Australian art'.*

The influence of Asia on Australian artists has been obvious for some time — one has only to think of composers Peter Sculthorpe, '. . . Anne Boyd and Richard Meale, painters John Olsen, Fred Williams, Brett Whiteley, Donald Friend, Royston Harpur, potters Peter Rushforth, Ivan McMeekin, Col Levy, architects, playwrights, novelists, choreographers, puppeteers, fashion designers and chefs.'[16] 'Continuum '83' ensured that Australian art received respectful attention in Asia. What is more, Japanese artists wanted to exhibit in Australia and several have already made visits.

Performance artist, Goji Hamada, who first came to Australia for Yo In, made five visits to Australia between 1981 and 1987, giving performances and holding exhibitions in Melbourne, Sydney, Adelaide, Perth and Mildura. Yoji Haijima, who wrote on the work of John Davis in 1979, has visited Australia twice, exhibiting his own drawings in colour at the Gryphon Gallery, Melbourne.

'Continuum '85' was the obverse of 'Continuum '83' — not Australian art in Tokyo, but contemporary Japanese art in Melbourne. Eight galleries worked together to show painting, installations, graphics, sculpture, video, performances and architecture for a three-week period. A great number of Japanese artists, gallery directors, art critics and friends came to Australia, and even though they only saw the country on the journey to visit the penguins at Phillip Island, or on the road to Healesville to see the kangaroos, they did stay with Australian artists, students and gallery directors. The contact was personal and direct, and friendships were made. Performance artist, Akio Suzuki, and his wife, the dancer Junko Wada, stayed with John Davis; when Davis next visited Japan he and his wife stayed with the Suzukis.

A dialogue is occurring between Japanese and Australian artists. Only the next few years will tell whether this will become significant for both countries. Traditional Japanese culture has had some influence on Australian artists, but will contemporary Japanese art also influence them? Will there be a time when an Australian influence will be discerned on some aspects of Japanese art? As for the present, John Davis can only observe, with a note of surprise in his voice, 'I have more friends in Tokyo than I have in Sydney!'

■ NOTES

[1] Rod O'Brien, 'Journey Extended, or Meeting of Eucalyptus and Bamboo', *Ikebana Ryusei*, no. 273, January 1983.

[2] Ibid.

[3] I make no apology for publishing Kimio Akiyama's quaint English, which is so much better than my non-existent Japanese!

[4] John Davis, 'Some Brief Notes on Issues Which I Think are Raised in My Art', November 1982.

[5] John Davis, interview with author following Davis's return from Japan, 26 October 1982.

[6] Comments made by Ken Scarlett on the work of Richard Long and David Nash, made in November 1982 and extracted from article on work of John Davis, 'Bush Art of John Davis', *SOKA Ikebana Ohara*, no. 287, February 1983, 19–35.

[7] John Davis, interview with the author, 26 October 1982.

[8] John Davis, 'Some Brief Notes on Issues Which I Think are Raised in My Art', written in answer to questions from Kimio Akiyama, Editorial Department, *SOKA Ikebana Ohara*, November 1982.

[9] John Davis, interview with author, 26 October 1982.

[10] John Davis, Goji Hamada, Ken Scarlett, *SOKA Ikebana Ohara*, no. 387, February 1983.

[11] Goji Hamada, 'Australian Contemporary Art Assembled in Tokyo. Fascinating Art in a State of Growth', *SOKA Ikebana Ohara*, no. 393, August 1983.

[12] Rosemary Warburton, 'Enduring Images', *Asahi Evening News* (Tokyo), 26 August 1983.

[13] Memory Holloway, 'A Clash of Culture', *Age*, 25 August 1983.

[14] Rod O'Brien, 'A Whiff of Eucalypts Along the Ginza', *Sydney Morning Herald*, 6 September 1983.

[15] Ibid.

[16] Janet Hawley, 'Australia and the Asian Connection . . .', *Age*, 24 September 1983.

Chapter 14

1984–87
USA, JAPAN, SAUDI ARABIA

For the first time a sculptor resident in Australia was exhibiting abroad regularly and building a reputation overseas, particularly in Japan and USA.[1] Australian painters such as Boyd, Tucker, Nolan, Whiteley and Williams had all exhibited widely overseas and had established major reputations, but for Australian sculptors there were grave problems of weight, size, cost of transport and insurance, which restricted their exhibitions. Possibly the only sculptor to show his work abroad with any frequency during a similar period was Ken Unsworth, who was included in a number of major international exhibitions, but he is as much a performance artist as he is a sculptor.

In the three-year period 1984–87 Davis exhibited in Los Angeles, Seoul, Tokyo, Osaka, Melbourne, Sydney, Hobart, and installed a large work in Saudi Arabia. He was Artist in Residence at the University of Southern California in Los Angeles in 1984 and Resident Fellow at the Djerassi Foundation, near San Francisco, in 1986 and again in 1987.

It was an intriguing development for a boy who spent his early youth making things, merely because he liked working with his hands; a young boy who graduated from constructing billy carts to thinking of becoming an architect, but grew to dislike the necessary mathematics. His early interest in drawing led him to the point where he thought he would become a painter, so he trained as an art teacher as a means of securing tertiary art instruction. Sculpture emerged as his basic interest while he was at Mildura in 1961. Yet it was to be many years, virtually not until 1978–79, before John Davis evolved a personal style on which he has been able to build a major reputation.

The word 'synchronicity' seems to sum up the linking of the apparently unrelated facts, disconnected processes, chance meetings and apparent coincidences that have combined to bring Davis to his present position. His growing reliance on intuition as a means of producing sculpture has probably enabled him to retain a fluid state of mind, allowing him to welcome opportunities when they have appeared. As he stated: 'The beginning is in the tying of two twigs. Then it takes its own direction . . .'[2]

There is a range of apparently irrelevant points that have assisted Davis to become known in Japan and USA. Australia's growing economic and political links, firstly with USA and more recently with Japan, have brought about an increasing interest in Australia. Paul Hogan's unorthodox TV commercials in the USA came at a time when Americans were cancelling travel plans for Europe because of hijacking and bomb scares and were receptive to the possibility of holidays in Australia. The devaluation of the Australian dollar has made Australia an extremely cheap holiday resort for Japanese tourists and honeymoon couples. Paul Hogan's film 'Crocodile Dundee' was impossible to translate for Japanese audiences, but it was a huge success in America. Japanese have collected Australian two-cent coins because the frilled necked lizard, depicted in low relief, seems an extraordinary creature. Japanese newspapers announce the arrival of koalas at local zoos and give daily reports on their health. It is a list of apparently trivial points, but illustrates a growing interest in those countries of things Australian. The general notion has been established in the minds of many Americans and Japanese that Australia is a fascinating place, and by implication the work of Australian artists is equally fascinating. With the growing urbanisation of life in USA and particularly in Japan, Australia is seen as one of the few western countries in which the vast countryside is dominant. Whether this is a fact, or an exaggeration of the truth is another matter.

John Davis certainly has the ability to convey a

▶ *96 John Davis, 'Traveller', an installation consisting of four parts, left, L.A. Marker III; centre, L.A. Marker I; right, L.A. Marker II; foreground, Midden. Respective dimensions, left 117 x 262 x 81 cm; centre 193 x 147 x 158 cm; right 249 x 152 x 147 cm; foreground; height 66 cm; diameter 272 cm. Photograph by Cindi McCain taken at exhibition shown at University of Southern California Atelier, 18 April–20 May 1984.*

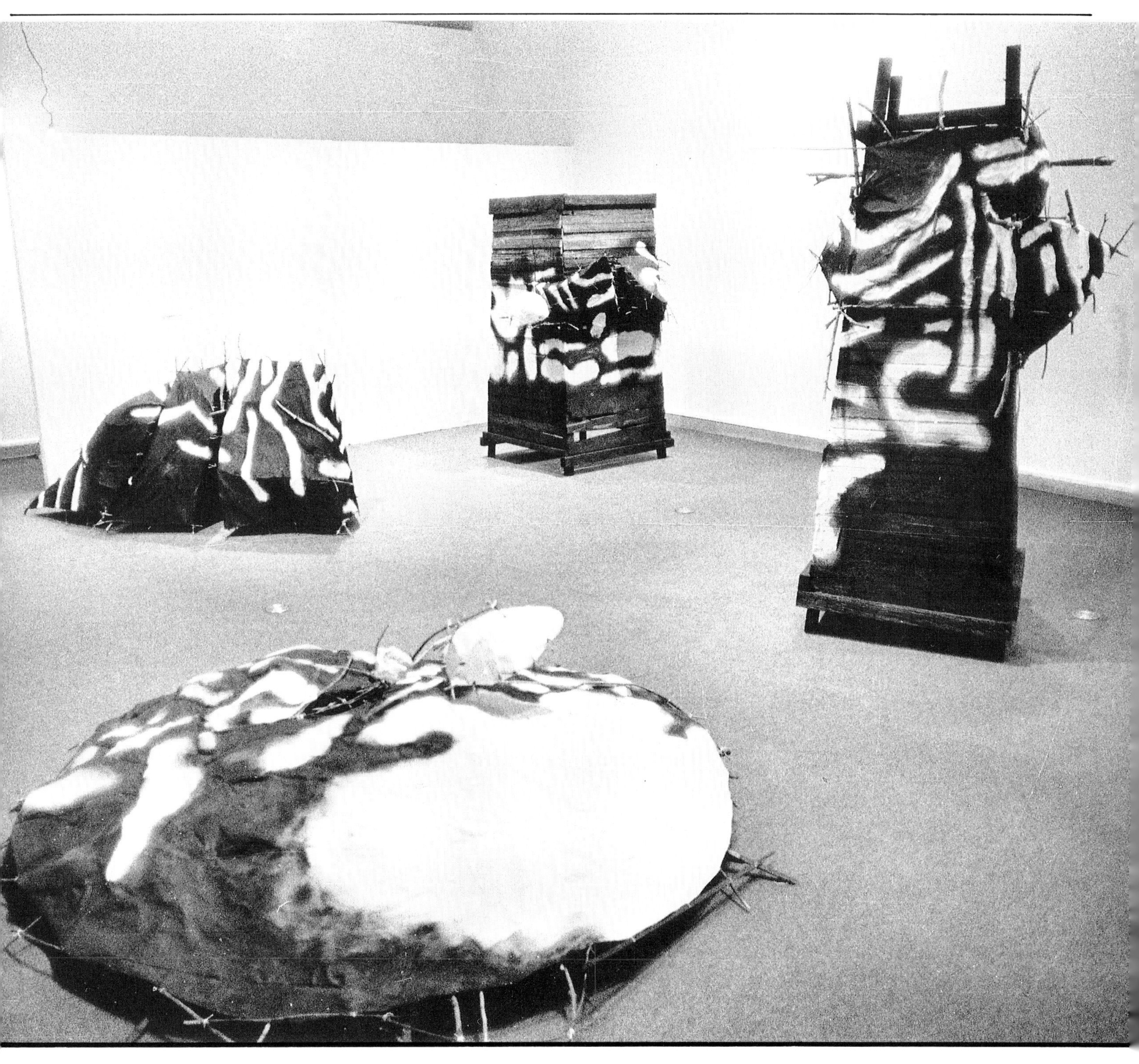

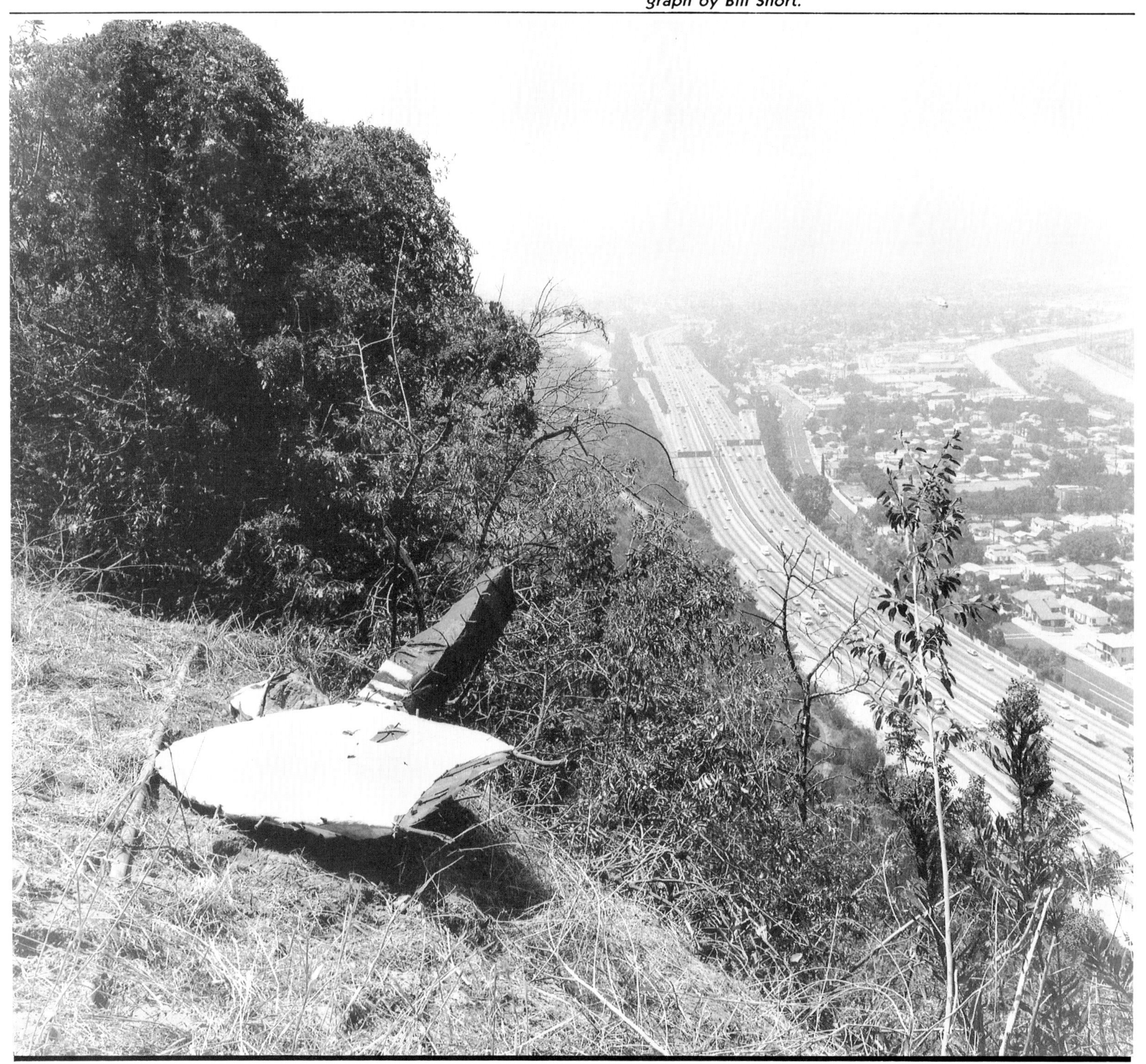

97 John Davis, 'Elysian Park Installation' (1984). Twigs, paper, calico and synthetic bitumen. 85.5 x 51 x 23 cm. Left on the site, Elysian Park, Los Angeles, USA. Photograph by Bill Short.

sense of space, both by the placing of his works within an installation and by the very nature of the objects themselves — they often look as though they have been temporarily placed in a gallery and really belong 'in the vast stretches of Australia's flatlands'.[3]

Compared with the dominance of technology in Japan and USA, the increased sophistication of the art market and the extreme refinement of craftsmanship in Japan, Davis's work must appear as from another age, another place. Reviewing his exhibition at the University of Southern California Atelier, Robert L. Pincus used the heading 'Primitivism from Australia'. The readily available, natural materials, simple methods of construction and a hint of ritual or shamanism can lead observers to believe that Davis's work is indeed primitive and in particular, strongly influenced by the Australian Aborigines. But Pincus rightly observed that 'It is simultaneously indigenous and international'.[4]

The works reviewed by Pincus were collectively entitled 'Traveller' (illus. 96) consisting of four parts, *L.A. Marker I* and *L.A. Marker II* which were square, tower like structures, *L.A. Marker III* which was an earth bound, heavy form, and *Midden* a slightly domed, circular structure, resting on twigs just above the floor. The works were the result of two weeks as Artist in Residence, at the University of Southern California, assisted by USC art students and later shown at the Atelier, the University's gallery from 17 April–20 May 1984.

The four works were also placed in an outdoor setting in Elysian Park, Los Angeles, where *Midden* in particular related to the landscape extremely well. The black and white pattern on the surface appeared to repeat the broken patches of light and dark on the forest floor. *Midden* really did suggest the character of an abandoned Aboriginal kitchen without actually depicting bones and shells, though the surfaces, painted with tar, certainly hinted at charcoal.

Another work was placed at Elysian Park, high on a hill, with a precipitous drop to the Golden State Freeway directly below (illus. 97). The view was from the strange primitive object in the foreground, across the multi-laned freeway, to endless rows of suburban houses in Los Angeles. The contrast was extraordinary. It was as though some primitive tribe had emerged from the parklands, seen the view of suburban USA and been terrified by the sight. The work by Davis seemed like an object to placate the Gods, left behind by unseen people. It was one of the very few cases when John Davis has made a statement in opposition to the environment.

Following his brief two-week period as Artist in Resident at the University of Southern California, John Davis again visited USA. He was invited to exhibit as one of the artists in 'Australia: Nine Contemporary Artists', which was part of the Olympic Arts Festival held in Los Angeles, 30 June–14 August. This was a unique situation for John Davis, he was able to use a derelict urban situation for the first time. He is quoted as saying I responded immediately to the site'.[5]

The site was a 77-year-old public building designed in Spanish Mission style, empty inside, except for broken flooring and the accumulated debris of years. John Davis found that someone had done a large circular drawing on the concrete floor — a drawing that could have been a symbolic work by an American Indian. It had no apparent meaning, but took on a ritualistic character when he cleared away the rubbish and placed five of his small sculptures in the centre (illus. 98). Another work was placed inside a boarded-up window, projecting out into the internal space (illus. 99). 'I placed them in this niche because they seemed to float outward from the wall and my colours matched those of the ageing background . . . I don't want my sculpture to look like real art or museum art. Here they resemble the junk that surrounds them.'[6]

Back in Australia, John Davis had shown his contribution to 'Austausch/Exchange', a collaborative installation by Marr Grounds and eight other artists.[7] Marr Grounds had spent a year in Berlin and had been deeply affected by the forbidding presence of the Berlin Wall, finding a parallel with the dingo fence in Australia. In both cases, the unnatural restrictions of the wall and the fence imposed unacceptable limitations on freedom. On 25 December 1981, Marr Grounds sent a letter to the eight artists telling them of the project. He subsequently sent to each artist a 5 metre length of white canvas, which was to be placed with 3 metres vertically on a wall and the rest horizontally on the floor. On the canvas was a standing half-figure, arm and leg outstretched, as an image of Renaissance man. On the floor, not a simple shadow, but an outline of a fallen figure, with obvious references to the many who had died at the Berlin Wall. A mirror, placed at head height on the figure, enabled spectators to visually link with another mirror at the top of the canvas, forming a periscope and giving a view over the Berlin Wall. In each case the left-hand side of the canvas was blank, available for the particular artist to make their contribution. In addition, each participant received a small wooden box full of mysterious, but apparently meaningful objects.

Aleks Danko, Kevin Mortensen and Tony Trembath all made statements that captured the bleak political mood, reinforced by Marr Grounds's video. Aleks Danko topped his structure of bricks with a reference to the concentration camps of the Second World War — 'Work Liberates Us All'. In Kevin Mortensen's work a solitary, anonymous

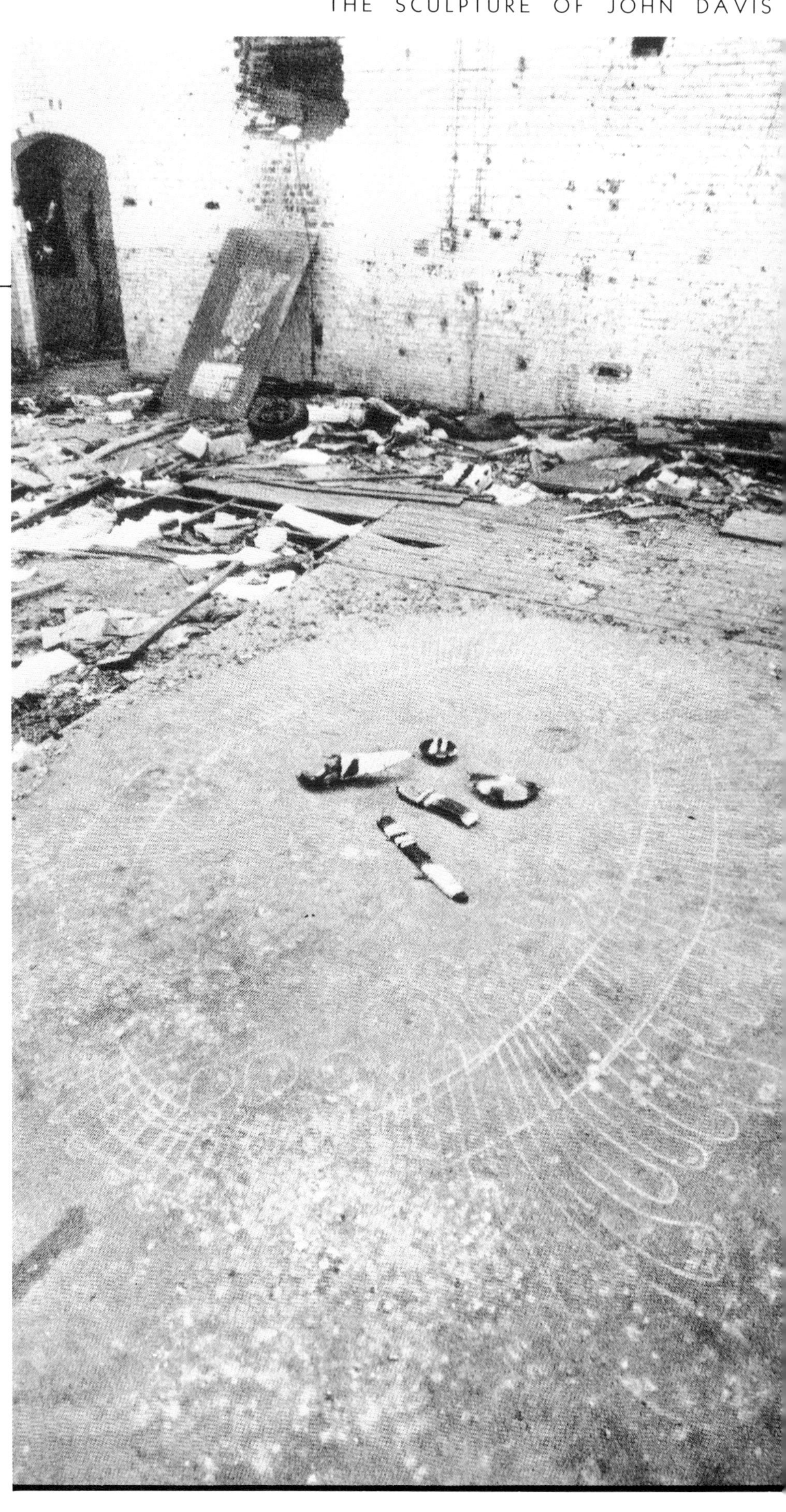

◄
98 John Davis, 'Ivy Station Installation' (1984). Twigs, paper, calico, synthetic bitumen and objects collected on the site, such as timber, plastic, cardboard, plus existing drawing in white paint, found on the concrete floor. Oval shape on the floor about 244 x 366 cm. Installed at Ivy Station, as part of the LAICA Exhibition, in Los Angeles, USA. Left on the site. Photograph by Bill Short.

▶
99 John Davis, 'Ivy Station Installation, Niche' (1984). Twigs, paper, calico, bamboo and synthetic bitumen. 107 x 112 x 35 cm. Left on the site, Ivy Station, one of the venues for the LAICA Exhibition, Los Angeles, USA. Photograph by Bill Short.

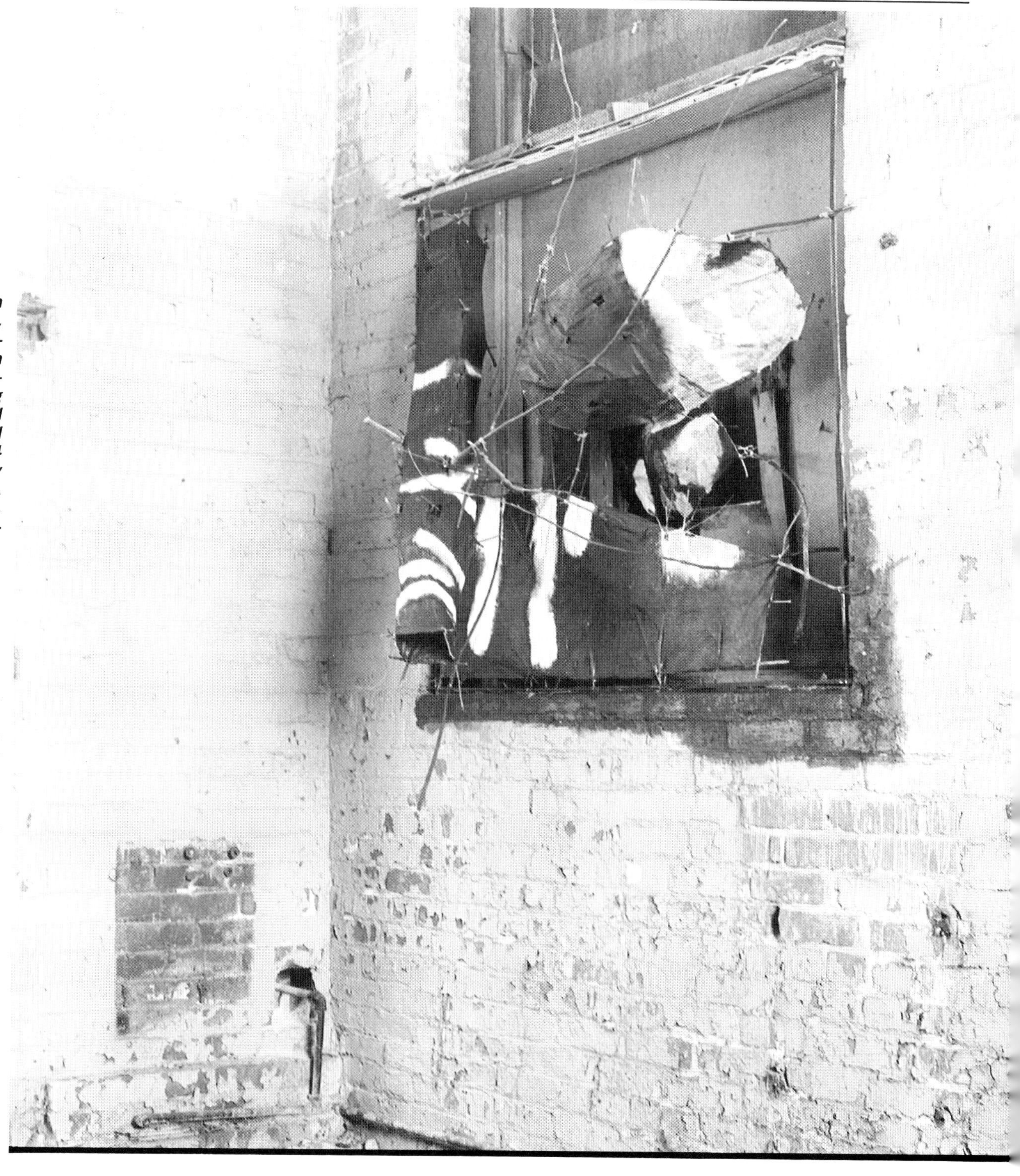

figure at the top of a steep set of steps, was both a threatening figure of power and also a figure overwhelmed by the menacing grey structure of the steps. Tony Trembath made the greatest change to the basic items provided by Marr Grounds. He added a complete hospital bed of iron, painted white, covered with three hoops of iron, from which hung electric light globes. A small hand-operated generator provided electric current. The implication of human torture was conveyed very strongly.

Such political statements were out of character with the work normally produced by John Davis, who attempted to overwhelm the parts provided by Marr Grounds, to encapsulate them in his normal structure of twigs and sticks. The mysterious box was almost lost in a papier mâché structure, which was then elevated on spindly sticks. Some objects from the box were barely visible inside a long, irregular cylinder of twigs covered in canvas. But there were interesting developments from the exercise. Davis was introduced to the idea of using canvas on a large scale and placing it on the wall. A later work, *Cloud and Pebbles*, consisted entirely of canvas (no twigs!) partly stuffed with underfelt and then painted with synthetic bitumen. Whereas for the past six years John Davis had placed all his works on the gallery floor, or on the earth in outdoor installations, he now began to realise the possibilities of working in relief on the wall.

Incident (illus. 100), which was produced 1982–83, at about the same time as 'Austausch/ Exchange', shows some links — the spindly structures on long twiggy legs to the left of the complex arrangements are very similar to the two structures in 'Austausch/Exchange'. *Incident* illustrates another positive development — John Davis started working on a much larger scale, and did it with confidence. It is all the more remarkable when *Incident* is so complex. A series of verticals dominate the cluster of forms against the far wall, the twiggy structures walk unsteadily forward on the left and a diverse arrangement of forms sweep around in an arc from the right. Like *Region* of 1980–81, it is a *tour de force* of sculptural invention, with a wide range of forms held together visually by a simple sweeping curve, the repetition of similar materials (twigs, paper and calico), and by the repetition of similar colours, off-white and black.

Another Place (1984), shown at the National Gallery of Victoria, during the Second Australian Sculpture Triennial, and later at Watters Gallery in March 1985 (illus. 101), illustrated Davis's new interest in the wall. Nevertheless, *Cloud and Pebbles* brought some adverse criticism from the critic, Terence Maloon. When reviewing the Watters exhibition he wrote:

■ *Davis's sculptures no longer slouch casually against the wall, and only one work in this exhibition consists of unattached or partially attached pieces informally distributed across the floor. The other works are wall reliefs or wall hangings suitable for domestic adornment. 'Cloud and Pebbles', a large picture made in quilted calico, is so apologetically decorative, it wouldn't scare off even the most conservative interior decorator.*[8]

But Maloon's long review of the Watters exhibition was essentially full of praise and perceptive analysis.

■ *... Davis's work still retains a power to shock. The wonky, ramshackle structures of his sculptures seem incongruous products of a modern, technologically advanced, affluent western society. They seem to come from another world. Indeed they compel us to recognise that there is another world — one not so far from our doorsteps.*[9]

He went on to discuss links with Pacific cultures — the paper lanterns and kites made in Japan and the black and white patterns on Fijian tapa cloths — which are apparent underlying influences on Davis's work.

During 1985 Professor Albert Elsen from

▶
100 John Davis, Incident (1982–83). Twigs, paper, calico, pigment and tar. Illustration shows the work set up at the Art Gallery of Western Australia, when the dimensions were 3540 x 5070 x 5500 cm — width and depth are variable. (In the possession of the artist.) Photograph by the artist.

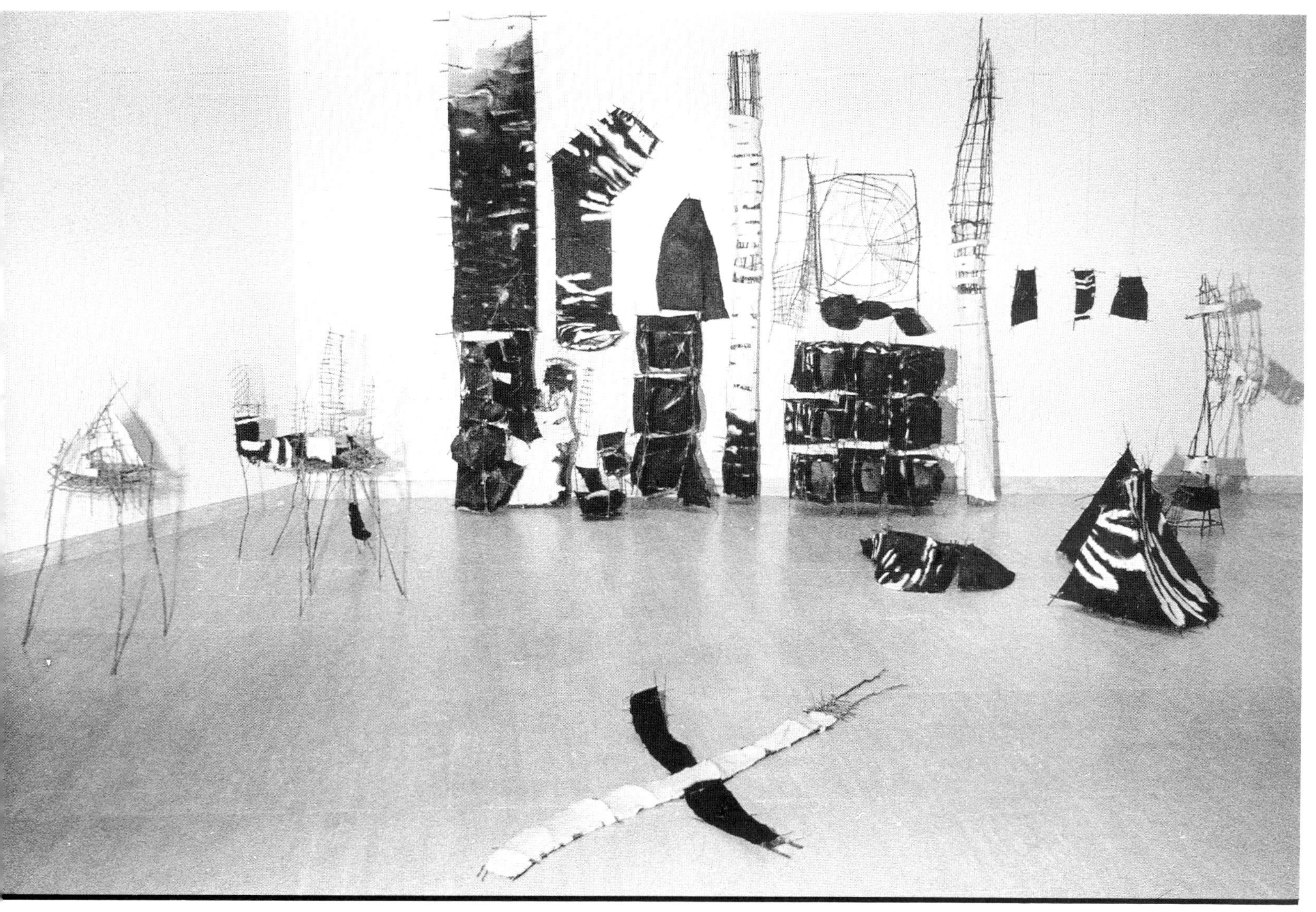

Stanford University visited Australia, giving a series of lectures on Rodin. At an informal dinner at the home of Noel Hutchison, sculptor and lecturer in fine art, Davis met Professor Elsen. In casual conversation Davis mentioned how he would like to return to the USA, stay for some time and work there. Professor Elsen mentioned the Djerassi Foundation, which provided accommodation and working facilities for a wide range of composers, painters, sculptors, and writers, enabling them to devote themselves full-time to their particular work while staying at the Djerassi ranch. John Davis's application to the Djerassi Foundation was supported by Professor Elsen, and he was invited to go to USA for two months, March and April 1986. The Djerassi cattle ranch (rather inexplicably entitled SMIP) was set in rolling hills with patches of redwood forest within the Santa Cruz mountains. The Pacific Ocean was in the distance, the nearest

small town was Woodside about 15 km away and San Francisco was an hour's drive. The isolation was conducive to long hours of work. Ten people were in occupation — five writers, a painter, a composer, two dancers/choreographers and Davis. Each had their own motel-like accommodation and a basic studio, but ate together every night as a group. Working 14–16 hours a day, with no telephone and no interruptions. Davis produced twenty-three works in four weeks. Except for one installation, predictably entitled *SMIP* (illus. 102), all of the works were single objects. When installed at Space Gallery, Los Angeles, in April–May most of them were hung on the wall, with only a few sitting directly on the floor. It appears Davis used the time to explore new forms, rather than make one major piece.

One can only judge *SMIP* from photographs and slides, but it appears to have been ideally located in

▼
101 Works by John Davis, Watters Gallery, Sydney, 19 March–13 April 1985. Far left (partly behind staircase), Another Place (1984); far right, Location Piece (1984–85); foreground, Second Incident (1984). All three works contained twigs, calico, canvas, paper and synthetic bitumen, Another Place also included timber and stones. (All works in the possession of the artist.) Photograph by the artist.

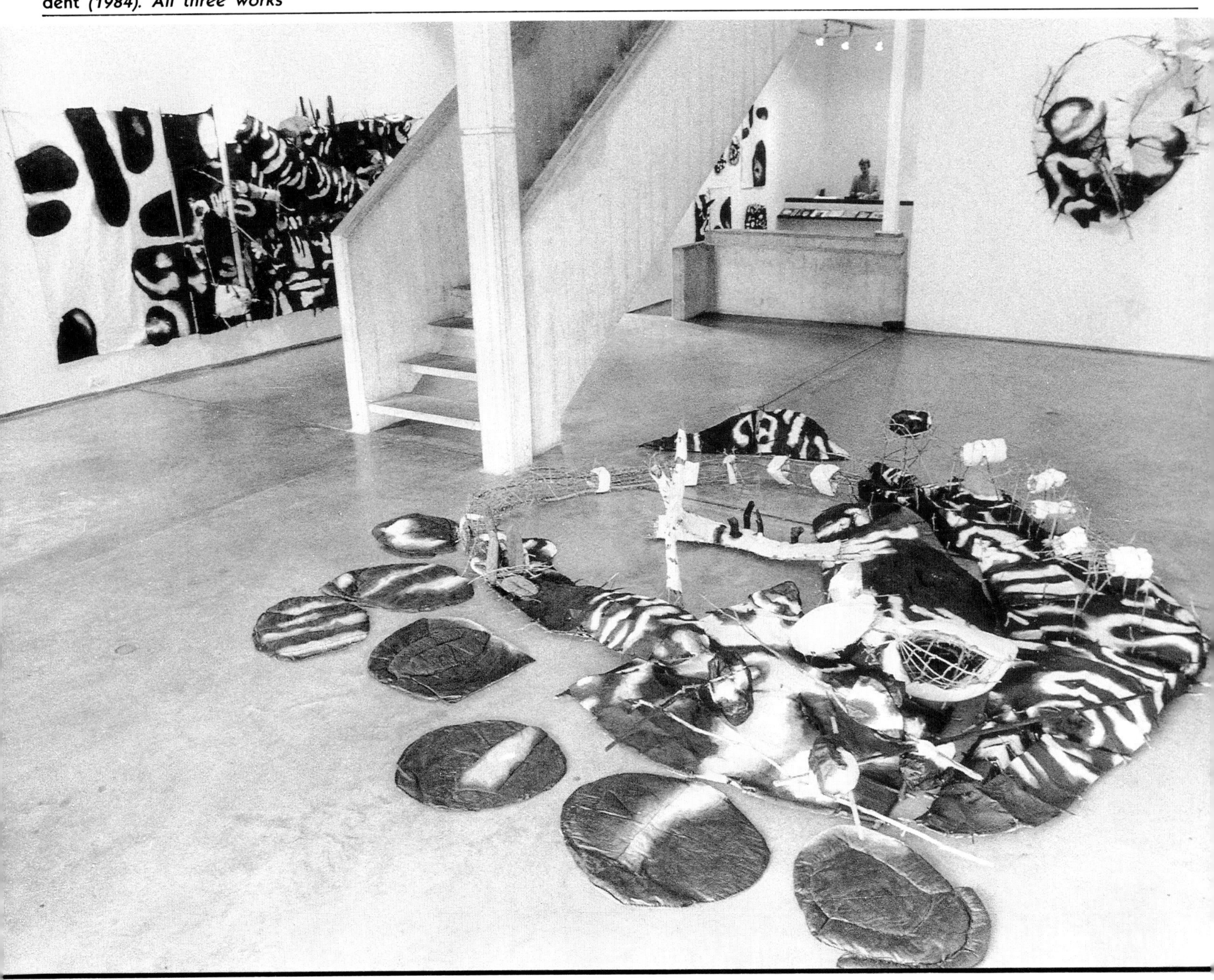

102 John Davis, 'SMIP', an installation in nine parts (1986). Twigs, paper, canvas, synthetic bitumen. Approximately 4.5 x 4.5 m. Produced while the artist was Invited Resident at the Djerassi Foundation USA, installed and left on the site. Photograph by the artist.

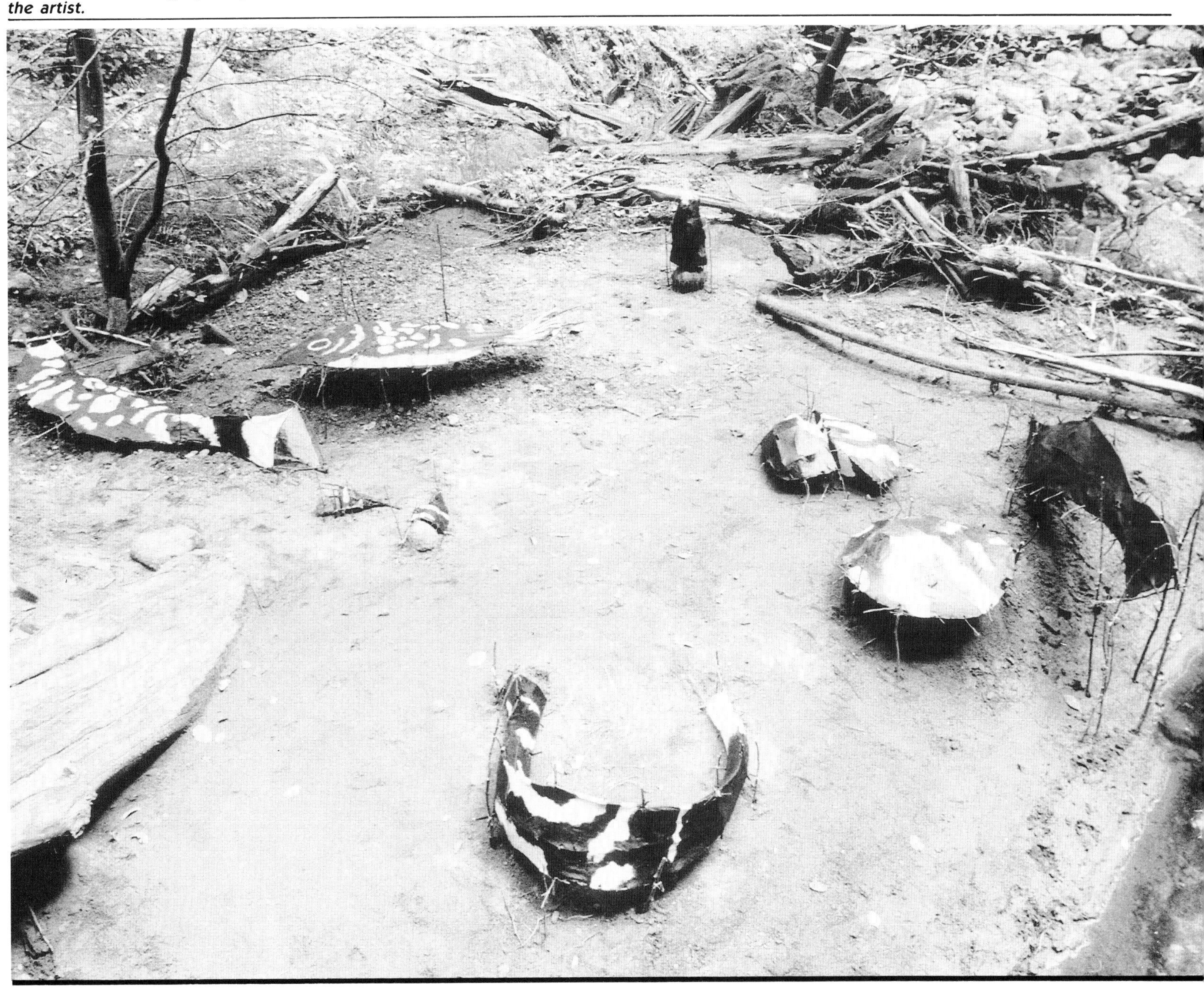

an area of bare earth, surrounded by forest trees and bordered on one side by a small stream. The nine parts, all painted black on white calico, sat on the ground on short sticks projecting underneath the forms. The arrangement was casual, on a loosely square plan, looking as though the parts had been left behind by an unseen group of people who had been engaged in some secret rites.

Leaving the Djerassi Foundation and his exhibition at Space Gallery, Los Angeles, John Davis travelled to Japan for his exhibition at the Inax Gallery in Tokyo, which was also shown later at the Inax Gallery in Osaka. He showed three large works *Another Place* (1984), and the two works from the 'Drought Series' (1985), *Off Beaumaris* (illus. 103) and *Lean-to, Two*, as well as a number of small works on the walls.

Off Beaumaris, displayed at the far end of the gallery, carried very well, as the forms are strong and direct. The Japanese audience would not have known that Beaumaris was a seaside suburb, but the large fish on the edge of the work would have given a clue to the other forms, which suggest rocks, shells, and the patterns of water on sand. Indeed, the fish may have been a welcome point of identification for the Japanese, as it resembled the inflatable flags in the form of fish that the Japanese fly from their roof tops for the Boys' Festival, prior to 5 May each year.

Lean-to, Two was a very complex work, of innumerable parts, which presented some difficulties of installation in Osaka after Davis had returned to Australia.

While Davis was resident at the Djerassi Foundation he met two young American choreographer/dancers, the husband and wife team, Duncan MacFarland and Clare Whistler, who were the driving force in the MacFarland/Whistler Dance Art Company. They were interested in innovative dance, contemporary music and collaborative performance events, and were fascinated by Davis's sculpture. Conversations between the three artists about dance and sculpture grew to include David Rosenboom, a composer/performer interested in electronics, computer science, music and performance areas.

When Davis was back in Australia, letters were exchanged and eventually the three Americans came to Australia. Facilities were made available at the Victorian College of the Arts, culminating, not in a 'performance', but in 'a work in progress'[10] on 20 February 1987, in the Studio at the VCA. As Davis pointed out to the small audience of invited guests, only the objects on the far wall were actually finished and other sculptural forms on the floor were exploratory ideas, mocked up in cardboard. The finished works were mainly made in California, five or six weeks later.

'Systems of Judgement' was described on a hand-out sheet as 'an evening length work concerned with tracing the development of thought, discerning and choice from the unformed through to the complexities of existence'. The performance began with a Prologue of music only, sombre, timeless, with a feeling of great space. The two dancers were seated cross-legged on the floor, motionless. As the music grew in volume, barely perceptible movement of arms, then torsos gave a mood of tentative exploration. Eventually the two bodies began to roll vigorously on the floor, before rising unsteadily to their feet, then cautiously using different forms of movement they became aware of each other. After some time they began to pick up Davis's sculpture, passing it from one to the other, exploring the several small works, repositioning them around the stage. At one time they moved with great speed, locating the sculpture almost at random with a futile restless movement. But towards the end of the performance they had changed to a slow ritualistic walk around the stage,

▶ *103 John Davis,* **Off Beaumaris** *(1985). Twigs, paper, calico, synthetic bitumen. 2.24 m x 4 m x 76 cm. (In the possession of the artist.) Photograph by Garry Shirley in sculpture studio of the Victorian College of the Arts.*

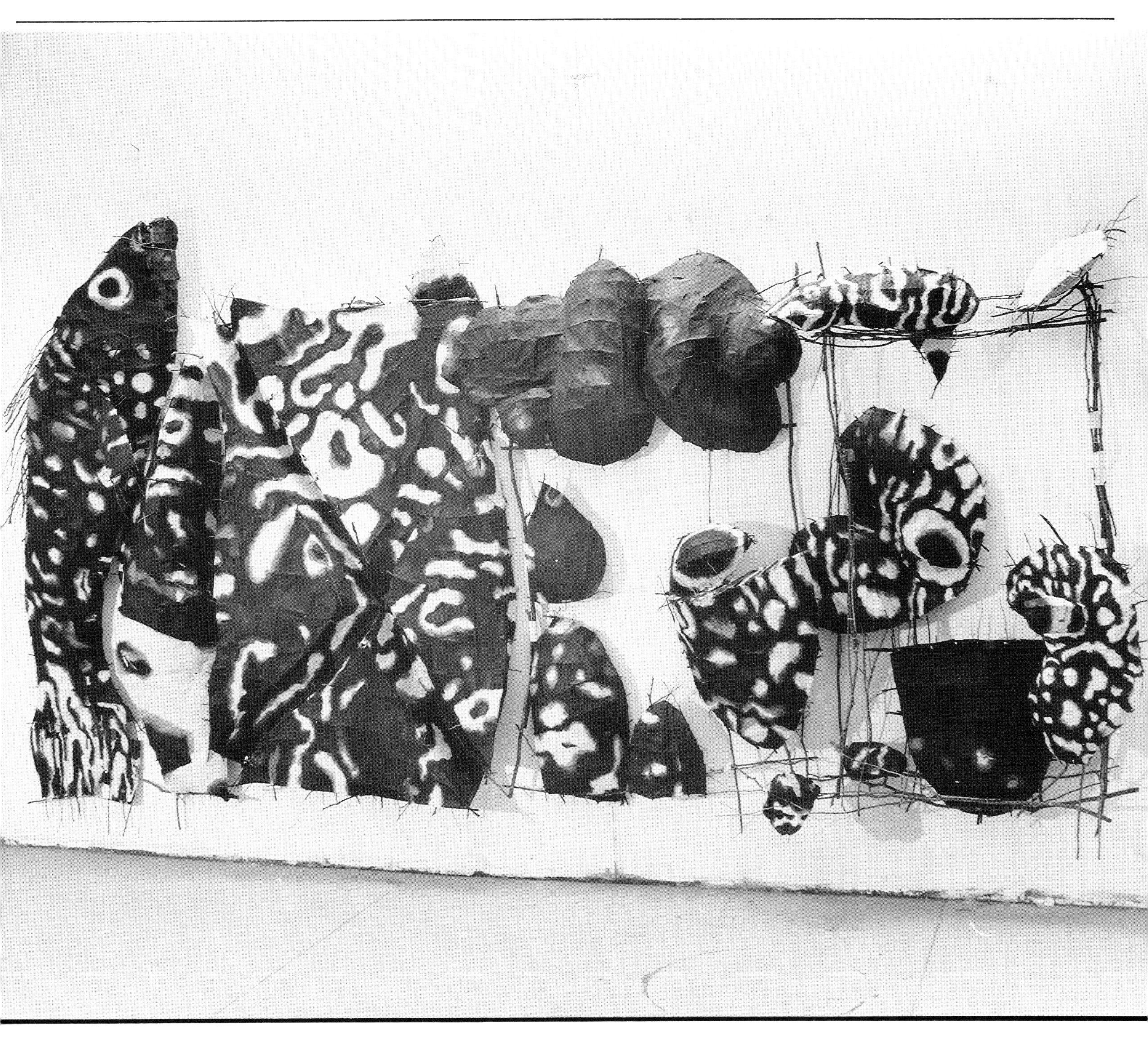

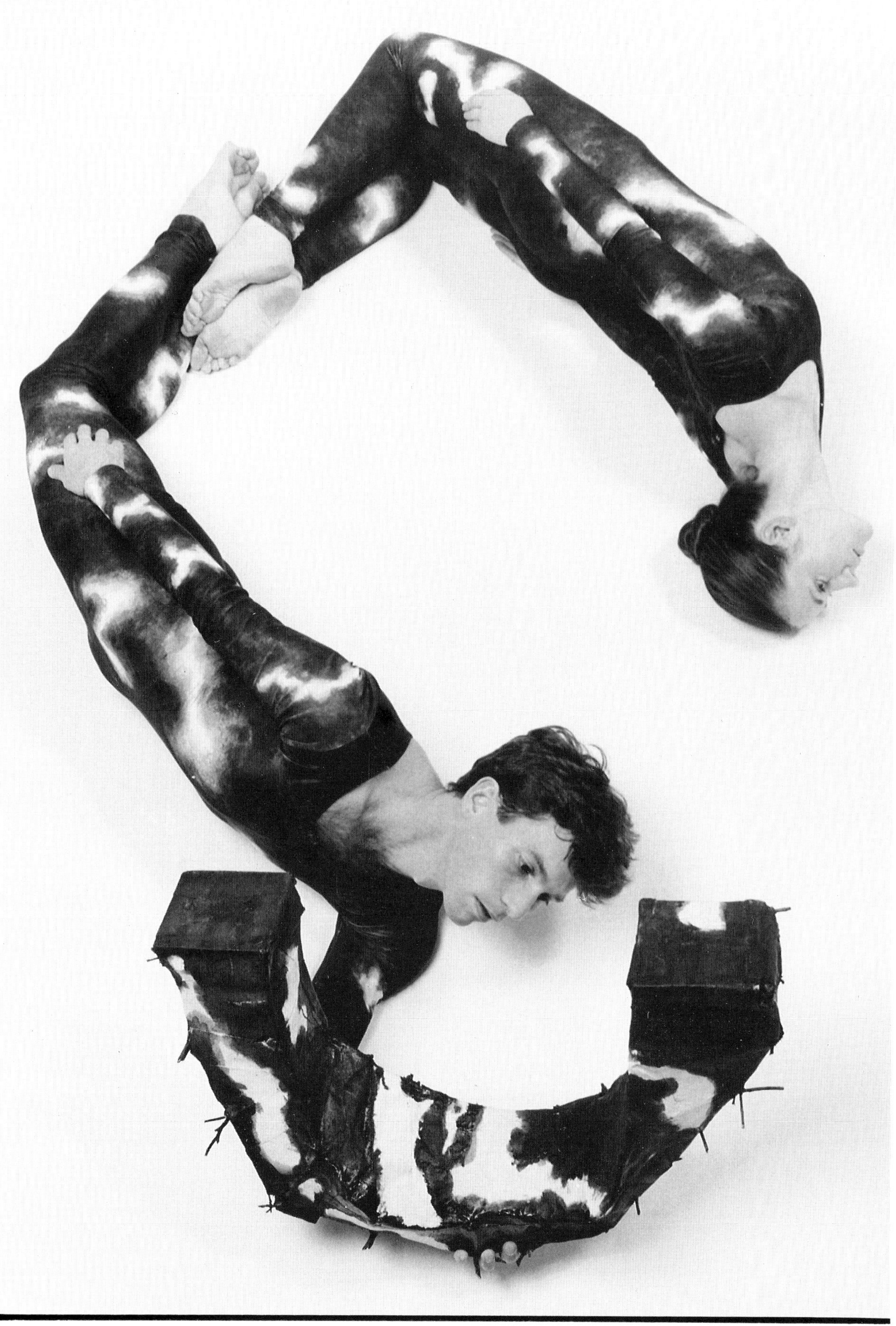

◄ *104 Duncan MacFarland and Clare Whistler in dance performance, 'Systems of Judgement'. Costumes painted by John Davis, who also made the sculpture at the bottom of the illustration. Photograph by Arne Folkedal.*

placing individual twigs on the floor. The work ceased with the two dancers motionless, with their backs to the audience.

Some of the sculptures made for the VCA performance were taken back to the USA, but Davis returned to the Djerassi Foundation and made three more large forms. He also painted the leotards worn by the dancers, in his characteristic pattern of bitumous black on white cloth (illus. 104). While in the USA he saw two performances of *Systems of Judgement* in the 'New Performance Space' at San Francisco, a small theatre capable of seating 200 people. At the end of each of the four nights, the two dancers symbolically presented a bundle of twigs to the audience, and then invited the people present to view the sculpture. The audiences seemed intrigued, but the critics apparently did not like the dance, the music or the sculptures.

One other event culminated that year when Davis installed his work in the new Australian Embassy building at Riyadh, Saudi Arabia. Produced during 1985–86, Davis supervised the hanging of the many parts during January 1987. The project had begun with a telephone call from the architect Daryl Jackson, and this was followed up by a visit from Bob Sinclair, who became the liaison between the architects[11] and Davis. Plans, elevations and a model of the new embassy building were provided for Davis, but it was difficult to envisage the spaces in what was a fairly complex buiding.

Bob Sinclair said in a conversation with me: 'We selected John Davis because his forms suggest a certain naturalness, an Australian quality, which we were trying to incorporate into the building — particularly in view of the restrictions placed upon building in Saudi Arabia.' It was an act of considerable imagination and courage on behalf of the architect, for as Bob Sinclair mentioned, 'We didn't know what he would do — but we thought it was a nice opportunity for John Davis to get his work off the ground and into the air.'

Davis proceeded on a very simple basis. He made a considerable number of forms, big, medium and small, to occupy the space he had envisaged, but he did not attempt to visualise the relationship of all the parts. On arrival in Riyadh he first placed the biggest form, actually allowing it to project from a wall, then proceeded to the next largest part, a long snake-like piece, which he hung from the ceiling. He had instructed the architects to have fittings for possible suspension points, 1 metre apart, over the whole ceiling, so he had a flexible system, which allowed him to work out the relationship of the parts on the job. He had first thought that his work would be in the entrance foyer, but on viewing the building he found this area visually too busy. The installation is not immediately visible from the entrance foyer, but a part can be glimpsed and that is enough to lead the visitor around the corner to a long narrow space, which is two storeys high. There is also another view of the installation from the large window of the Ambassador's office on the first floor, looking down inside the building on the suspended forms.

Davis has only had two architectural commissions: the one for the Hydro Electric Commission in Hobart (1971), and this one for the Australian Embassy in Saudi Arabia. The difference between the two works is extreme. One is almost anonymous in style, minimal in form and very much a symbol of a sophisticated, industrial society. The other is highly personal in style, diverse and varied in form and makes a statement about nature in the midst of an obviously man-made environment.

Was the first work produced accepting the reality of our capitalist society? And is the later work out of touch with reality, a form of romantic nationalism that cannot survive?

Perhaps one of the conceits of the minimalist

period of sculpture in the 1960s (of which Davis's Hobart commission is a by-product), was the thought that those simple forms could be entirely self-sufficient. It was implied that art could exist without reference to nature. The ecologists have taught us that all living things are interdependent. In fact, the industrial society needs nature for survival. So Davis's point of view is a contemporary one that endeavours to achieve a balance by emphasising natural materials in an age of plastics, using hand processes in a time of mass production, of stressing the simple solution when computers appear to have made life more complex. At first thought, it seems an entirely obsolete activity to be producing works of twigs, paper and calico, in an age that can produce rockets for space travel. Davis's art quietly restates the importance of the human being; the fragility and the ephemeral nature of the objects is not unrelated to the vulnerability of the human being.

Stelarc can write, 'It may no longer be an advantage to evolve as a species or even remain human in form . . . It is now time to redesign human beings to make them more compatible to machines.'[12] Davis, in contradiction to hi-tech, makes us more aware of our far-reaching past. At the same time that research is taking Aboriginal occupation in Australia further and further back in time, he is making Australians aware of their primitive past. It is not a simple borrowing (or stealing) from Aboriginal sources, but rather a suggestion that all of us still have links with our origins, not yet forgotten or lost in the midst of an industrial society.

Even though some of the works produced by Davis during his visit to the Hattah Lakes in May 1976 were not of great individual significance, they did illustrate a new attitude. He simply made the structures in the trees, or the patterns of sticks on the ground, then moved on and left them. He has since been involved in similar activities in India, Japan, United States and Saudi Arabia. A couple of the forms that he took to Riyadh were not used within the Embassy building, so they were taken out into the desert, carried up the rugged escarpment and left there. Like a latter-day nomad, he visits countries, makes his art and departs — not on foot, but by jet.

Davis is a committed artist but he does not see the final object as precious. The Australian Embassy in Saudi Arabia was the biggest installation, his most remunerative commission, and he could have regarded the two left-over pieces as marketable commodities, but he preferred to see them against the desert backdrop and left them for unknown travellers to discover.

He hopes he has evolved a visual language of forms that communicate with people, regardless of nationality and cultural background. He certainly seems to have built up an audience in Japan, ranging from contemporary artists to practitioners of ikebana, and an audience of the artistically-informed in USA and Australia. Unfortunately the general public, particularly in Melbourne, has not seen enough of his work. The new phenomenon, the Australian sculptor, acknowledged overseas, has now to be fully recognised at home.

When Australia's links with Great Britain were very strong, both visual and performing artists left Australia for further training and experience in London (or Paris), hoping to make their name abroad and return with a greatly enhanced reputation. But after the Second World War changes occurred. Not only did Great Britain's position of political and economic eminence decline and British influence on the Australian arts weaken, but air travel greatly reduced the time and cost of voyages abroad and Australian artists began to travel widely. Whereas in the past, art movements had arrived in Australia already filtered through British eyes — Impressionism, Art Nouveau or Art Deco

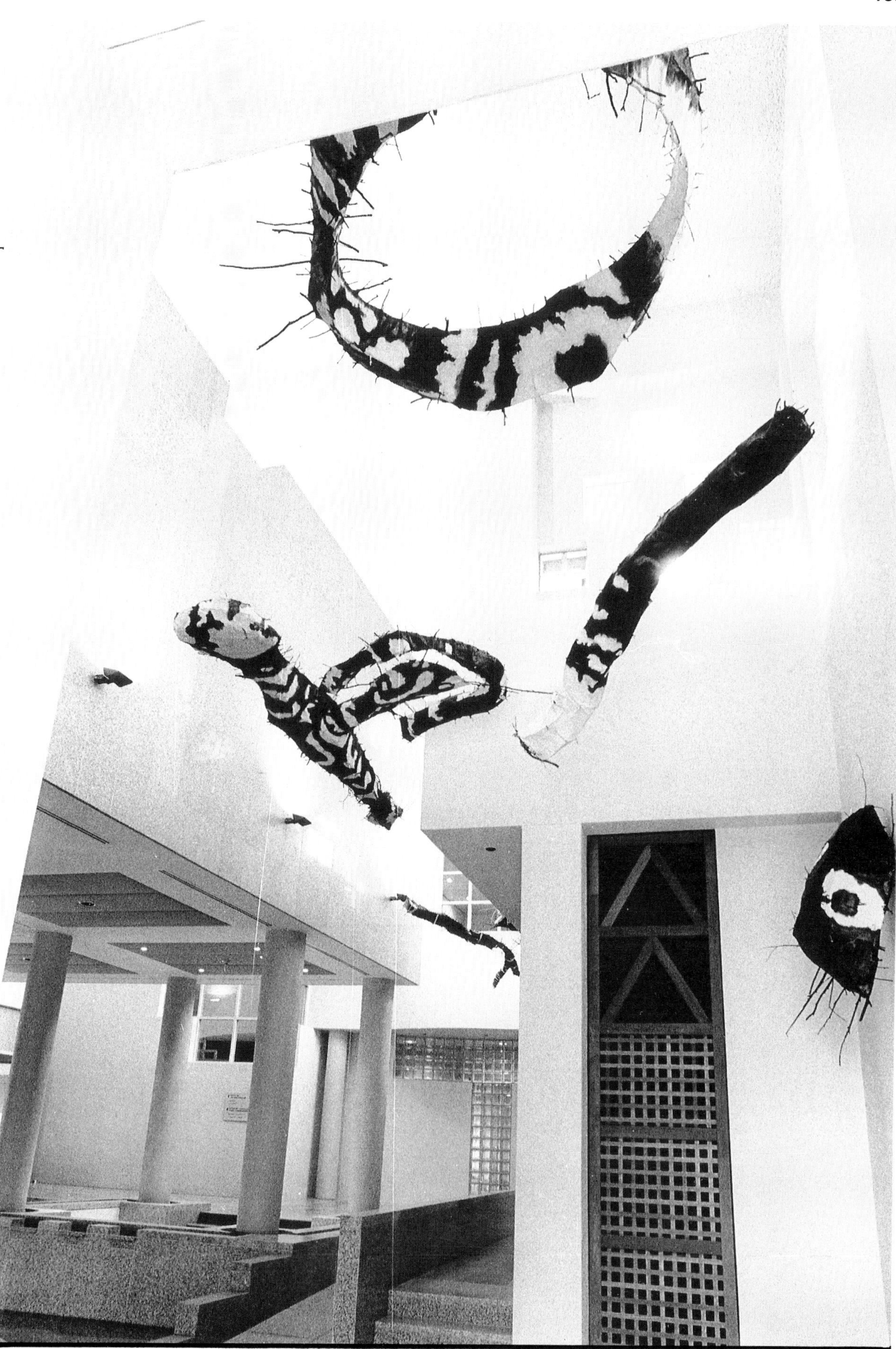

▶ 105 John Davis, installation at Australian Embassy, Riyadh, Saudi Arabia. Various parts made in Australia 1985–86, taken to Saudi Arabia and hung in place by the artist in January 1987. Materials used were twigs, paper, calico, synthetic bitumen and stainless steel wires for suspension. The embassy building was designed by Daryl Jackson, Meldrum, Burrows Collaboratives Pty Ltd. Photograph by the artist.

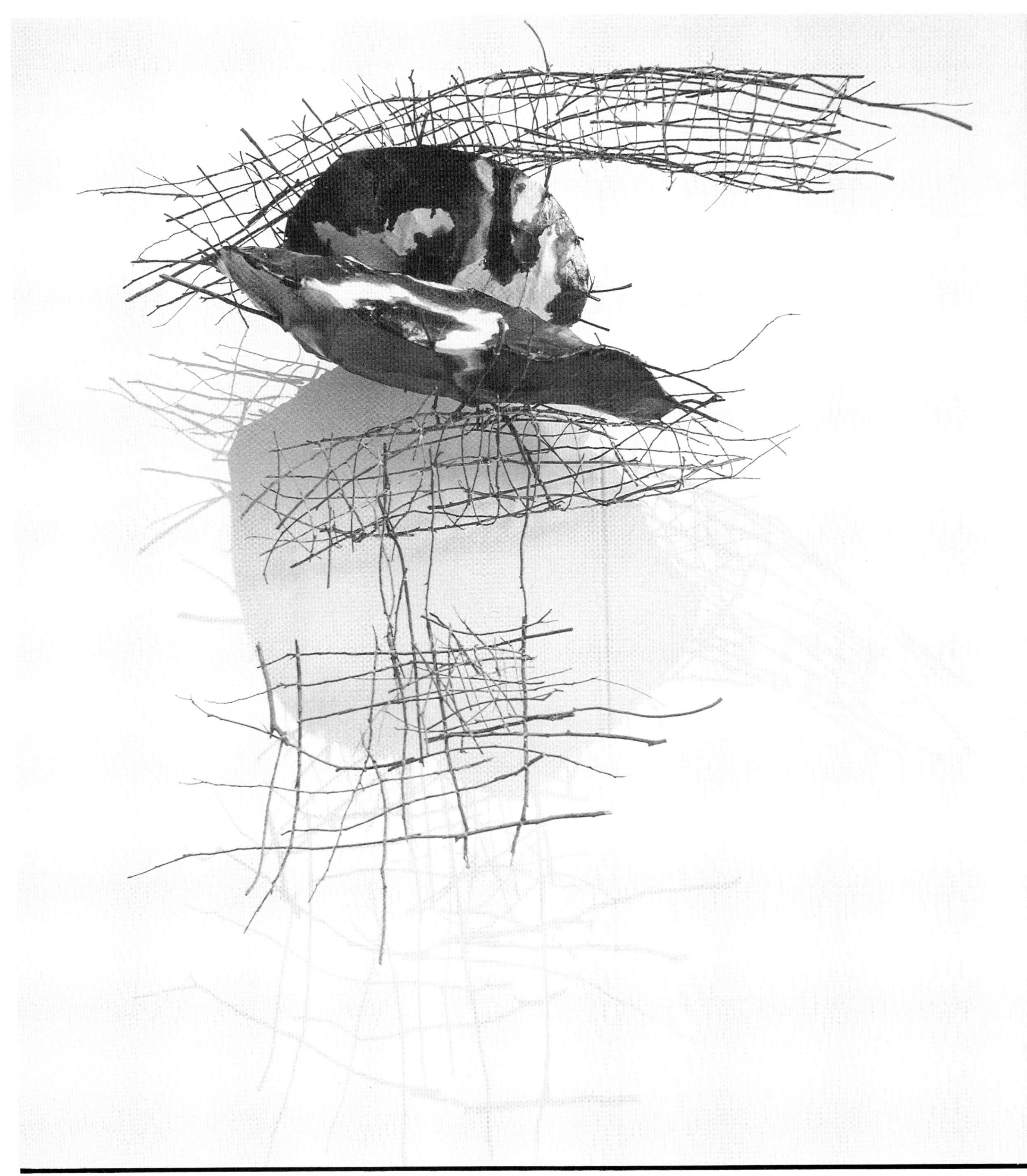

with a British flavour — now Australian artists were visiting the centres of art as the new movements became known. Those artists who stayed home in Australia subscribed to the art magazines, which kept them up to date with latest developments.

International movements which had their origins in New York, such as Minimal Art or Abstract Expressionism, were taken up by Australian artists in the 1960s and 1970s. More recently Australian painters have embraced Neo-Expressionism, Post-Modernism and the new interest in Romanticism. An exhibition such as 'Perspecta', held in Sydney in 1987, revealed to the critics how strong were the influences of international art movements on Australian artists, particularly the painters. Sadly, this exhibition was shown in Germany, merely revealing that the work of Australian artists looks the same as that of European artists. So in a way it is no longer necessary for Australian visual artists to go abroad for recognition. If they follow the latest international developments they can be given a stamp of approval by the galleries and curators in Australia.

In the case of Davis, overseas praise has been based on a perceptive understanding of his Australian qualities — and in the current situation this has not necessarily meant greater prestige at home. For a brief time in the mid-1970s, Regionalism looked like being an acceptable alternative to Internationalism, but it was a short lived phenomenon in Australia.

John Davis, without any sense of nationalistic opportunism will continue to produce work that has strong links with the landscape, sculpture that has an identifiable sense of place, work which has Australian characteristics. Perhaps overseas observers see these aspects more clearly from a distance. Given time, we will understand the unique qualities of John Davis's contribution.

106 John Davis, Traveller (1987). Twigs, paper, calico, bondcrete, bituminous paint. 117 x 130 x 56 cm. (In the possession of the artist.) Photograph by Mark Strizic.

■ NOTES

1 This may seem an exaggerated claim but lists of exhibitions abroad by Australian sculptors seem to prove its correctness. Sir Bertram Mackennal was certainly known in Great Britain and Europe, but he was resident in London for a large part of his life. Tina Wentsher exhibited in Europe and Asia before she became a resident of Australia. Robert Klippel showed his early work in London and Paris in 1948–49 and later in 1958–62 he exhibited in the USA, but has rarely exhibited overseas since. In more recent times, Clement Meadmore left Australia in 1963 and has lived in New York ever since. Colin Lanceley exhibited in London, New York and Europe, but more frequently as a printmaker or painter. Guy Boyd lived in Canada for a few years and has exhibited in Canada, USA and London and has since returned to Australia. Ken Unsworth has shown overseas frequently during recent years, but he is as much a performance artist as he is sculptor. Stelarc, as an expatriate Australian living in Japan, certainly has an international reputation, but, of course, he is a performance artist.

2 Campus newspaper, University of Southern California, 12 April 1984.

3 Robert L. Pincus, 'Primitivism from Australia', *Los Angeles Times*, April 1984.

4 Ibid.

5 Robert L. Pincus, 'Olympic Arts Festival. Nine Australians Offer Art that Fits the Gallery', *Los Angeles Times*, 19 July 1984.

6 Ibid.

7 Aleks Danko, John Davis, Bonita Ely, Kevin Mortensen, Bruce McLean, Tony Coleing, Stephen Turpie and Tony Trembath.

8 Terence Maloon, 'Bridges of Imagination Span Different Minds and Cultures', *Sydney Morning Herald*, 30 March 1985.

9 Ibid.

10 Verbal description by Duncan MacFarland prior to the dance 20 February 1987.

11 Daryl Jackson, Meldrum, Burrows Collaboratives Pty Ltd.

12 Stelarc, 'High Technology and Art 1986', catalogue of exhibition in Tokyo, 1986.

APPENDICES

COLLECTIONS

Works by John Davis are in the following public
collections
Art Gallery of New South Wales, Sydney
Art Gallery of Western Australia, Perth
Australian National Gallery, Canberra
Brisbane College of Advanced Education,
    Queensland
Djerassi Foundation, USA
Flinders University Art Museum, South Australia
Geelong Art Gallery, Victoria
Hydro-Electric Commission, Hobart, Tasmania
Melbourne College of Advanced Education,
    Victoria
Mildura Arts Centre, Victoria
MOCA — Museum of Contemporary Art, Brisbane
Monash University, Victoria
National Gallery of Victoria, Melbourne
Newcastle Region Art Gallery, New South Wales
Queensland Art Gallery, Brisbane
Shepparton Art Gallery, Victoria
Tasmanian College of Advanced Education, Hobart
    (work destroyed in fire)
Tasmanian Museum and Art Gallery, Hobart
Unley City Council, South Australia
Wollongong City Gallery, New South Wales

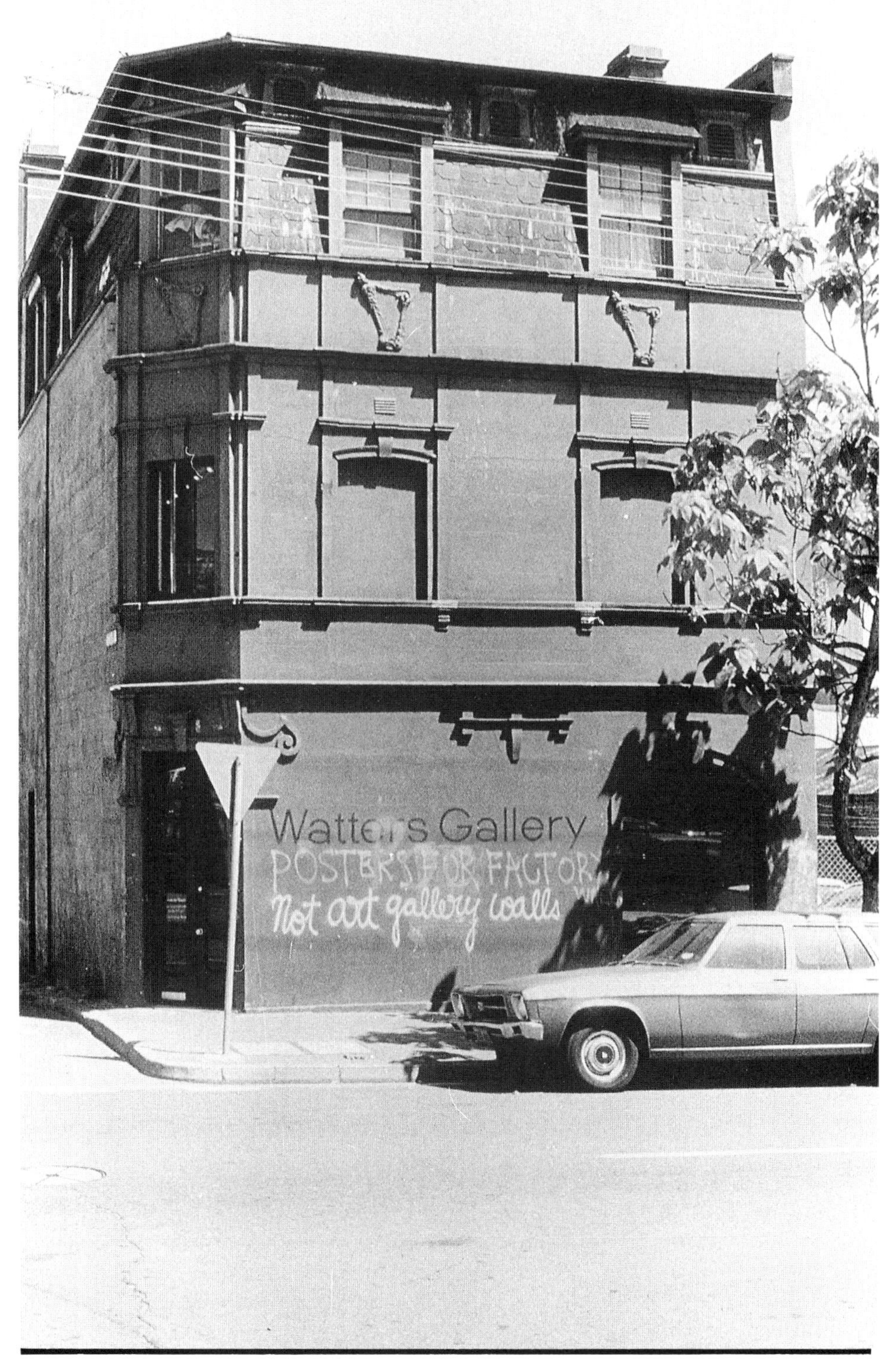

EXHIBITIONS

1960	Council of Adult Education, prize for Sculpture	
1961 22 April–21 May	Mildura Art Gallery, Mildara Prize for Sculpture	
1963 1–11 March	Treasury Gardens, Melbourne, *Herald* Outdoor Art Show	
1965 20 September– 1 October	Victorian Artists Society Galleries, Melbourne, Victorian Sculptors Society Annual Exhibition	
1966 5 June–(?)	Australian Sculpture Centre, Canberra, opening exhibition	
27 July–28 August	Art Gallery of NSW, Sydney, Alcorso Sekers Travelling Scholarship for Sculpture	
26 September– 7 October	Victorian Artists Society Galleries, Melbourne, Victorian Sculptors Society Annual Exhibition	
	Various Provincial Galleries in Victoria, Council of Adult Education, Travelling Sculpture Exhibition	
1967 7 April–(?)	Victorian Sculptors' Society, National Gallery of Victoria, Melbourne and Council of Adult Education, Victorian Travelling Exhibition, 'Sculpture '67', first shown at the Art School, RMIT, Melbourne	
14–30 April	Atheneum Hall, Doncaster, Doncaster & Templestowe Festival of Arts	
22 April–30 May	Mildura Arts Centre, Mildura Sculpture Triennial	
September	Victorian Artists Society Galleries, Melbourne, Victorian Sculptors Society	
1968 18 November– 29 December	National Gallery of Victoria, Melbourne, Alcorso Sekers Travelling Scholarship Award for Sculpture	
Month unknown	Pinacotheca Gallery, Melbourne Rental Exhibition	
1969 5–17 October	Strines, Melbourne, first one man exhibition	
15–23 November	Eltham Shire Hall, Eltham Awards	
1970 28 February–18 April	Mildura Arts Centre, Fourth Mildura Sculpture Triennial	
17 June–3 July	Sydney, Captain Cook Bicentenary Sculpture Exhibition	
September	National Gallery of Victoria, Melbourne, Comalco Invitation Award for Sculpture in Aluminium, 'Sculpture for Architectural Environments'	
19–26 October	Monash University, Law School, Sculpture Award Exhibition	
20 November– 6 December	Von Bertouch Gallery, Newcastle, 'Collectors' Choice', group exhibition	
Months unknown	Shepparton Gallery & Ballarat Fine Art Gallery, Victoria, two man exhibition with Ti Parks	
1971 19 May–5 June	Watters Gallery, Sydney, one man exhibition	
June	Age Gallery, Melbourne, Marland House Invitation Competition	
29 October– 14 November	Von Bertouch Gallery, Newcastle, group exhibition	
November	Pinacotheca Gallery, Melbourne	
7 November–(?)	'Heide', John Reed's property, Bulleen, 'Process Work'	
December	Bonython Galleries, Sydney, Transfield Art Prize	
1972 5 March–(?)	Gallery I Eleven, Brisbane, one man exhibition	
September (?)	Installation, Scottish highlands	
September	Geelong Art Gallery, 'Victorian Contemporary Sculpture', group exhibition	
1973 1 April (only)	'The Birches', Elsternwick, Melbourne, 'Balaclava Art Exhibition', Australian Labor Party	
April–7 July	Mildura Arts Centre, 'Sculpturscape '73'	
5–27 June	Latrobe Valley Arts Centre, Morwell, Ronald Awards	
18 October– 18 November	Art Gallery of NSW, Sydney, 'Recent Australian Art'	
30 October–(?)	St Paul's Cathedral, Melbourne, 'Spring Festival', exhibited with Kevin Mortensen	
16 November– 9 December	Queen Victoria Museum and Art Gallery, Launceston, 'Launceston Art Purchase'	
1974 5 March–14 April	Latrobe Valley Arts Centre, Morwell, 'Works with Paper'	
6–26 May	Ewing Gallery, University of Melbourne, 'Works with Paper'	
13–18 May	Sweeney Reed Gallery, Melbourne, 'Artists for Labor'	
1–12 July	Ewing Gallery, University of Melbourne, 'Letter Show'	
4–14 September	Pinacotheca Gallery, Melbourne, one man exhibition	
12–29 November	Latrobe Valley Arts Centre, Morwell, 1974 Purchase Award	
21 November	Art Gallery Theaterette, National Gallery of Victoria, programme 'Artist Film Makers'	
Month unknown	Ewing Gallery, University of Melbourne, 'Box Show'	
Month unknown	Art Gallery of NSW, Sydney, and Ewing Gallery, University of Melbourne, 'Artist Film Makers'	
1975 29 March–1 June	Mildura Arts Centre, Mildura Biennial	

13 May–15 June	National Gallery of Victoria, Melbourne, 'Artists' Artists — Sculpture'
27 June–27 July	National Gallery of Victoria, Melbourne, 'Artists' Artists — Recent Drawings'
11–22 August	Ewing Gallery, University of Melbourne, 'The Grid Show. A Structured Space'
2–26 September	Exhibition Gallery, Department of Visual Arts, Monash University, 'Place', one man exhibition
14 September–2 October	Contemporary Art Society Gallery, Adelaide, 'Substance-cause-number-relation', one man exhibition
26–28 November	Toorak Art Gallery, South Yarra, 'Artists for Labor and Democracy'
1–3 December	Paddington Town Hall, Sydney, Festival of Art, held by Committee of Artists
1976 5–29 March	Mildura Arts Centre, 'The Mask Show' (JD listed in catalogue, but did not exhibit)
May	Experimental Art Foundation, Adelaide, 'Post-Object Art: a Survey from Australia and New Zealand'
May (?)	Hattah Lakes, Victoria, installation
September (?)	Ovens River, Myrtleford, Victoria, installation
October	University of New England, NSW, 'Coventry Collection'
13 November–19 December	Art Gallery of NSW, Sydney, 'Second Biennale 1976'
17 November–4 December	Watters Gallery, Sydney, 'Small Sculptures', group exhibition
Month unknown	New Orleans, USA, Ninth Annual Sculpture Conference
Month unknown	Institute of Modern Art, Brisbane, 'Post-Object Art: a Survey from Australia and New Zealand'
1977 March	Kevington, Victoria, installation
13–30 July	Watters Gallery, Sydney, 'Location, Displacement, Transference', installation and exchange work
November	You Yangs, Victoria, installation 'Solar Piece'
1978 February	Lalit Kala Akademi, Fourth Indian Triennial, New Delhi, India
March	Cholamandhal, India, installation 'Beach Work'
17 March–23 April	National Gallery of Victoria, 'Survey I — John Davis', one man retrospective exhibition
25 March–28 May	Mildura Arts Centre, Mildura Sculpture Triennial
13 May–18 June	Art Gallery of NSW, Sydney, 'Survey I — John Davis', one man retrospective exhibition
2 July–(?)	Venice Biennale, Italy, John Davis, Robert Owen and Ken Unsworth
August (?)	Bay Wharf, London, installations with Ti Parks
4–12 November	Australian National University, 'ACT One', performance and participatory art, Commonwealth Gardens and Civic Centre, Canberra
1979 1–30 April	Arts Projects, Melbourne, one man exhibition
23–29 April	Metalworkers Auditorium, Melbourne, 'Paintings and Sculpture for Labor'
August	Art Projects, Melbourne, 'Region' on display, also work by Greg Ades
September (?)	Barmah Forest, Victoria, installation 'Observatory'
October	The Grampians, Victoria, installation 'With Animal Trap'
31 October–17 November	Watters Gallery, Sydney, one man exhibition
4–15 December	Art Projects, Melbourne, group exhibition
1980 January	Lake Wakatipu, New Zealand, installation
February	National Gallery of Victoria and other galleries in Victoria, South Australia and New South Wales, 'Fifteen Sculptors' travelling exhibition
March (?)	Piamena, Tasmania, installation 'Markers One, Two, Three'
21–28 May	Coventry Gallery, Sydney, 'Australian Artists Pay Tribute to Howard Hinton'
5–30 August	Institute of Modern Art, Brisbane, one man exhibition 'Another Time, Another Place'
10 September–12 October	Wollongong City Art Gallery, one man exhibition 'Another Place'
September (?)	Barmah Forest, Victoria, installation 'Observatory Revisited'
21 October only	Q Space Annex, Brisbane, exhibited one work, *Connection*
December	Village Green, Unley Civic and Community Centre, Unley, Adelaide, Environmental Installation constructed on site
1980–81 15 December–12 March	Australian National Gallery, shown at Australian National University, Canberra, 'Landscape ⇆ Art, Two Way Reaction', organised by the Australian National Gallery, photographs displayed
1981 4–20 February	Art Projects, Melbourne, group exhibition
28 February–12 April	Australian Sculpture Triennial, La

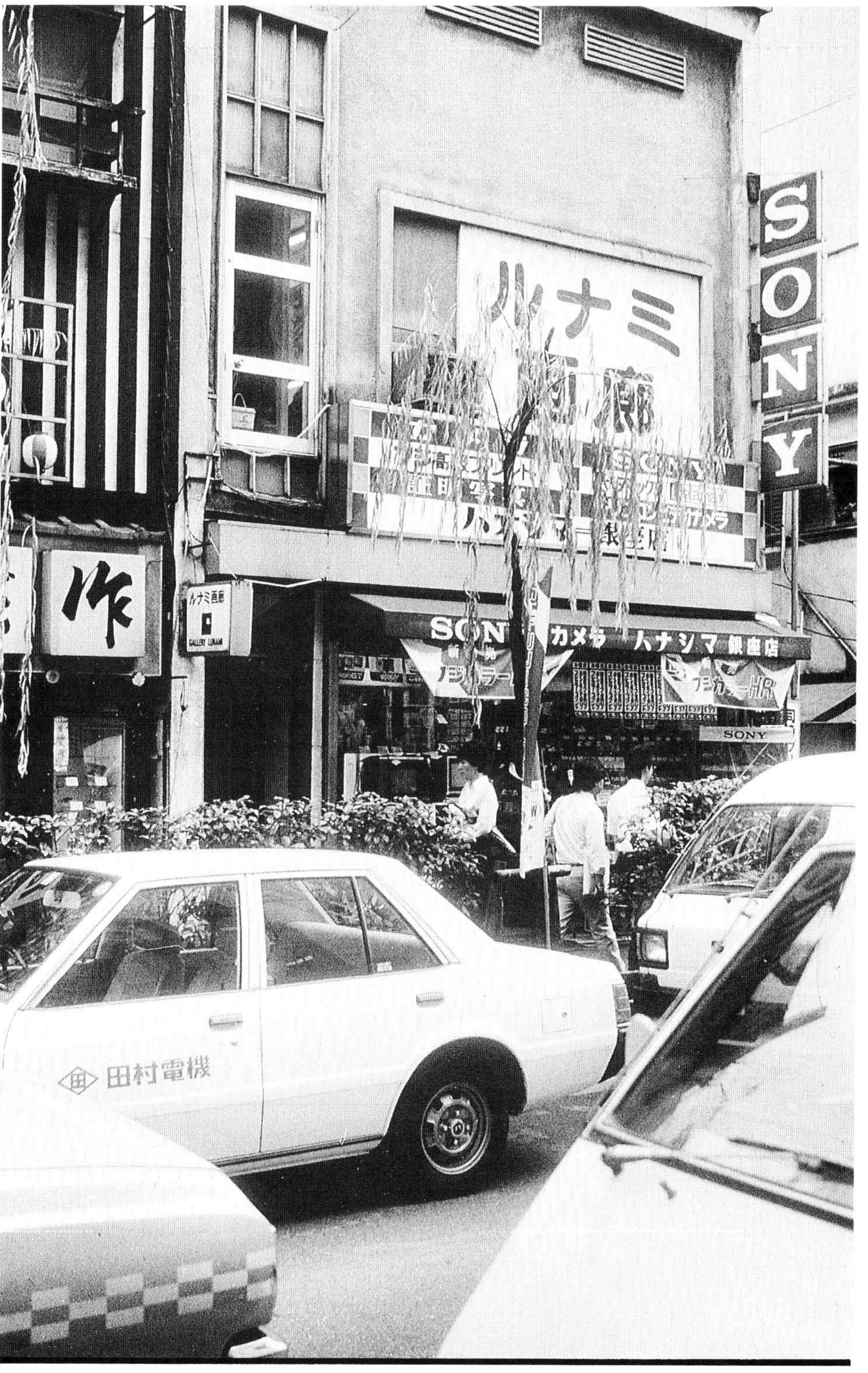

▼
108 Entrance to Gallery Lunami, Tokyo, site of two man exhibition by John Davis and Peter Cole, held as part of 'Continuum '83', August–September 1983. Photograph by John Davis.

	Trobe University, Melbourne, exhibited 'Place Two — An Installation'
8–25 April	Watters Gallery, Sydney, 'Sculptural Work at Watters', group exhibition
28 May–21 June	Art Gallery of NSW, Sydney, 'Australian Perspecta 1981'
17 July–13 September	National Gallery of Victoria, Melbourne, 'Survey 15. Relics and Rituals'
1–31 August	Art Projects, Melbourne, one man exhibition
9–30 September	George Paton and Ewing Galleries, University of Melbourne, 'Ten Years'
27 October–18 November	Victorian College of the Arts Gallery, Melbourne, 'Land Marks', group exhibition, exhibited photographs
October or November (?)	Paddington Town Hall, Sydney, 'Apmira' (exhibition in aid of Aboriginal land rights)
10–28 November	Watters Gallery, Sydney, 'First Expedition — Region — Long Journey — The Crossing', one person exhibition
21 December–(?)	Art Gallery of NSW, Sydney, 'Patrick White's Choice'
1982 23 February–5 March	Prahran School of Art Gallery, Victoria College, Prahran Campus, group exhibition
September	Tokoname Studio, Japan
1–27 October	Ina Gallery, Tokyo, Japan, one man exhibition
November (?)	Ryo Gallery, Kyoto, Japan, one man exhibition
1983 17 February–27 March	Art Gallery of Western Australia, Perth, 'Presence and Absence'
1–30 June	Art Projects, Melbourne, one man exhibition
15–17 June	Barmah Forest, Victoria, installation: 'Goji's Bridge'
13 August–18 September	Crafts Councils Centre Gallery, Sydney, 'Asian Interface: Australia-Japan', John Davis, Akio Makigawa, Carlier Makigawa, Mitsuo Shoji
22 August–3 September	Lunami Gallery, Tokyo, Japan, 'Continuum '83', two man exhibition with Peter Cole
9–27 October	Anri Gallery, Nagoya, Japan, one man exhibition
1984 9 February–10 April	Art Gallery of Western Australia, Perth, 'Australian Sculpture from the Collection'
17 March–17 April	Ivan Dougherty Gallery, City Art Institute, Sydney, 'Austausch/Exchange. The Dingo Fence. The Berlin Wall', Marr Grounds with Tony Coleing, Aleks Danko, John Davis, Bonita Ely, Kevin Mortensen, Bruce McLean, Tony Trembath, Stephen Turpie

17 April–20 May	University of Southern California Atelier, Santa Monica, Los Angeles, USA, one man exhibition
30 June–14 August	Los Angeles Institute of Contemporary Art, USA, 'Australia: Nine Contemporary Artists'
29 October–23 November	Gryphon Gallery, Melbourne, 'Austausch/Exchange . The Dingo Fence. The Berlin Wall', Marr Grounds with Tony Coleing, Aleks Danko, John Davis, Bonita Ely, Kevin Mortensen, Bruce McLean, Tony Trembath, Stephen Turpie
1–30 November	Monash University Gallery, Melbourne, 'Acquisitions and Alternatives'
Month unknown	Barmah Forest, Victoria, 'Barmah Installation'
1984–85 6 November–28 January	National Gallery of Victoria, 'Second Australian Sculpture Triennial'
19 November–13 January	Meat Market Craft Centre, Melbourne, 'Sculptors as Craftsmen'
1985 19 March–13 April	Watters Gallery, Sydney, one man exhibition
1–26 April	South Australian School of Art Gallery, Underdale, SA, 'Singular and Plural. A Look at Australian Sculpture, 1975–1985'
4 June–5 July	Fine Arts Gallery, University Centre, Hobart, 'Common Earth. Alive and Unfired', seven artists showing 'Works of Art in Unfired Clay'
August–September (?)	Avago Gallery, Sydney
30 November–7 December	Choubuk Art Centre, Institute of Contemporary Arts, Kunsan University, Seoul, Korea, 'Kis '85', Kunsan International Show
1985–86 16 November–16 March	Art Gallery of Western Australia, Perth 'Regions, Beaches, Interiors'
1986 22 March–4 May	Art Gallery of Western Australia, Perth 'Wood Works'
March–April	Djerassi Foundation, Woodside, USA. Installation, SMIP
12 April–10 May	Space Gallery, Los Angeles, USA, 'John Davis — Sculptures' and 'Minoru Ohira — Recent Work', two person exhibition
May	Inax Gallery, Tokyo, one man exhibition
6–31 August	Inax Gallery, Osaka, Japan, one man exhibition
1986–87 16 December–31 January	Watters Gallery, Sydney, group exhibition
1987 January	Australian Embassy, Riyadh, Saudi Arabia

21 February–29 March	National Gallery of Victoria, Melbourne, 'Field to Figuration, Australian Art 1960–1986'
11 March–5 April	Wollongong City Gallery, 'Sculpture: Wollongong City Gallery Collection'
6–9 May	New Performance Space, San Francisco, USA, 'Systems of Judgement'. Collaborative work with Dance Art Company and composer David Rosenboom
8–24 September	Charles Nodrum Gallery, Melbourne, 'From Texture to Sculpture', group exhibition
16 September–22 October	National Gallery of Victoria, Melbourne, Third Australian Sculpture Triennial
5–16 October	Victorian College of the Arts Gallery, Melbourne, one person sculpture installation

▶

109 Ina Gallery (later renamed Inax Gallery), Tokyo. John Davis's first exhibition in Japan was held at the Ina Gallery in October 1982. Photograph by John Davis.

PRIZES, COMMISSIONS, AWARDS

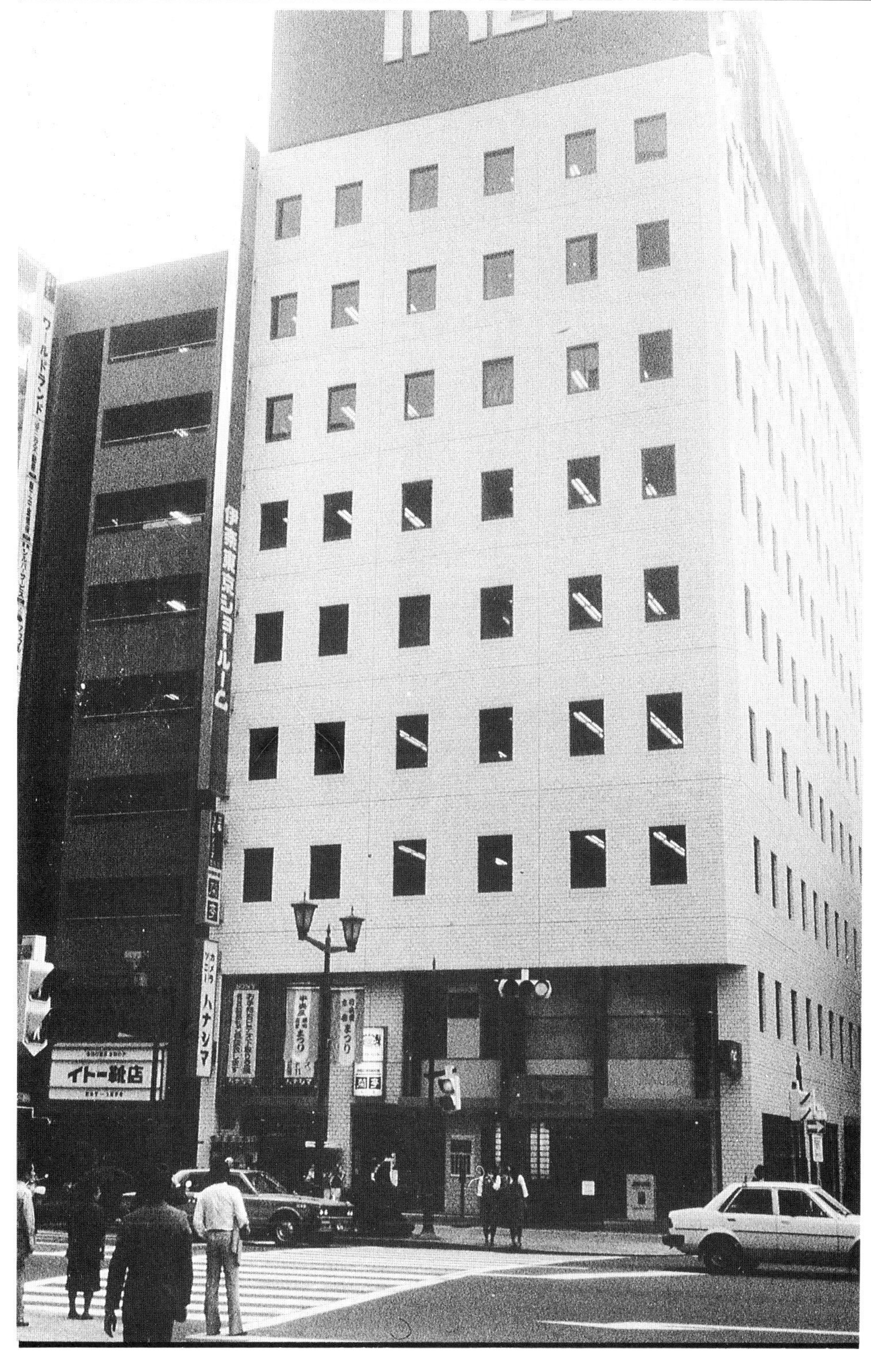

1960	Council of Adult Education Prize for Sculpture
1967	First Prize in Sculpture Section, Doncaster and Templestowe Festival of Arts
1967	Shared non-acquisitive awards, Mildura Prize for Sculpture
1969	Sculpture Prize, 1969 Eltham Awards
1970	Comalco Invitation Award for Sculpture in Aluminium
1971	Hydro-Electric Commission, Hobart, (following Comalco Prize)
1973	Purchase Award Mildura Triennial
1973	Visual Arts Board Grant
1975	Visual Arts Board Grant
1976	Artist in Residence, Monash University
1978	Represented Australia at the Fourth Indian Triennale in New Delhi and at the Venice Biennale
1980	Environmental Installation Village Green, Unley, SA
1984	Artist in Residence, University of Southern California
1986	Invited Resident, Djerassi Foundation near San Francisco, USA
1987	Installation at Australian Embassy, Riyadh, Saudi Arabia. Returned to Djerassi Foundation

LIST OF WORKS

In many instances the sculptor has supplied media description and dimensions, particularly for those works that have been made overseas or destroyed, but wherever possible sculptures have been viewed by the author. For those objects made from twigs, Davis has not listed cotton as the material actually used to tie the sticks together. In 1980 the sculptor used 'tar', but by 1983 he was describing the material as 'synthetic bitumen' and occasionally he used the trade name of the product 'Ormonoid'. When exhibiting in the USA Davis has described calico as muslin in catalogue entries. Calico is often used over twigs, but in the past Davis has sometimes listed it as canvas.

Davis first used the word 'installation', in relation to his work, in the catalogue of his exhibition at Watters Gallery in 1977. Subsequently he used the term to describe earlier works, such as 'Installation, Scottish Highlands' (1972). The word is used in the sense that a sculptural work, or group of works, have a total cohesion and relate to each other within a given space. Nevertheless, Davis uses the term somewhat loosely, as an installation may be made up of a number of objects, each titled individually, and available for sale separately.

John Davis has quite rightly presumed that the production of his sculpture is more important than the keeping of records on his work. The fact that many of his installations are ephemeral and the materials fragile may provide difficulties for the researcher, but are simply statements about the artist's character. John Davis has a casual attitude towards his sculpture — early works were sometimes given two or three variations of the one title, he leaves sculpture overseas, gives some to friends and forgets which ones are in storage. All of which is a preamble to saying that the following list of works is as accurate as possible, but is probably incomplete.

In accordance with normal practice, unless otherwise indicated multiple dimensions are given in the following order: height, width, length or depth in cm.

TITLE OF WORK	YEAR	MEDIA	DIMENSIONS	PRESENT LOCATION
Standing Figure I	1956	Wood, waxed, on wooden base, stained black.	122 (includes base) × 17.8 × 9 cm	In collection of Elaine Greene
Cry Out	1958	Wood.	c. 60 cm (h)	Was in private collection — person unknown
Standing Figure II	1960	Wood.	c. 60 cm (h)	Destroyed
Mallee Form	1961	Murray red gum.	22 × 19 × 35 cm	In private collection
Murray Form I	1962	Murray pine on wooden base.	c. 137 cm (h)	Either *I* or *II* sold at *Herald* exhibition. Neither works can be located.
Murray Form II	1962	Murray pine on wooden base, painted black.	c. 137 cm (h)	As above
Murray Form III	1962	Originally Murray pine lightly stained and waxed on red gum base. Was badly damaged and then restored by John Davis who restained it brown with some areas of green, on oregon base.	Sculpture: 137 × 20 × 16 cm; base: 14 × 26 × 26 cm	In collection of Pat & Ray Raison
Crucifix	1963	Bronze on wooden cross.	Wooden cross: 123 (h) × 70.4 cm (w); figure: 61 (h) × 38 cm (w)	In private collection
Pregnant Torso	1964	Murray pine.	c. 45 cm (h)	Destroyed
Abreaction	1964–66	Carved laminated wood, stained black, signed at bottom 'Davis 66'.	Sculpture: 127 × 74 × 36 cm; base: 4.5 × 45 × 42.5 cm	In collection of National Gallery of Victoria
Bird and Fish	1965	Cold cast solder with bronze patina.	73.5 (h) × 89 cm (w)	Destroyed
Wood Sculpture or *Totem*	1965	Stained jarrah.	145 (h) × 35 cm (w)	Was in private collection — destroyed
Small Bronze	1966	Bronze on wooden base.	Not known	Was in private collection — whereabouts unknown
Metamorphosis I and *II* (originally one work on slab base, later separated)	1966	Kauri stained green.	*I:* c.147 cm (h) *II:* 123 × 20 × 16 cm (without base)	*Metamorphosis I* was in private collection — whereabouts unknown *Metamorphosis II* in collection of Bev. & Ian Thomas

TITLE OF WORK	YEAR	MEDIA	DIMENSIONS	PRESENT LOCATION
Mandala	1966	Welded steel, jarrah and plastic. Four separate parts mounted on white board.	c. 150 cm (sq)	Was in private collection — cannot trace owners
Bent on Mayhem	1967	Carved and laminated kauri, stained black, with some areas painted red on hardboard structure painted white.	122 × 212 × 43 cm	In James Baker Collection, Museum of Contemporary Art, Brisbane
Relief Image	1967	Oregon, stained black on hardboard, painted white.	112 cm (h)	Destroyed
Suspended	1967	Wooden organic forms dowelled through a sheet of transparent acrylic resting on an aluminium frame keyed into top of pedestal. Work and pedestal stained black except for terminating planes on the forms which are stained orange red. This colour is repeated on the top of the pedestal and carried over into a semicircle at the top of one side. Aluminium polished self colour which is repeated in a narrow band around the bottom of the pedestal.	Total height 171 cm; pedestal 81 (h) × 46.5 cm (sq); construction above pedestal 90 (h) × 66 × 46.5 cm	In collection of Pat & Ray Raison
Prise	1967	The pedestal painted black and white, cut and displaced with red wooden sculpture placed between the two sections.	c. 260 cm (h)	Whereabouts unknown
Anvil	1968	Pedestal of hardboard covered in vinyl. Sculpture of bronze, chrome plated.	c. 55 × 27 × 12 cm.	Whereabouts unknown.
Drop Out	1968	White square prism with cube on top, covered in polyester resin and fibreglass. Top cube sprayed with blue automotive duco. Polished aluminium form emerging from circle on side of blue cube.	28 × 24 × 12.5 cm	In possession of the artist
Cruciform	1968	Upper section of wood stained black with some areas of red paint. Mounted on black vinyl. Lower section hardboard construction painted white.	124 cm (sq)	Originally in private collection — cannot locate work
Engine	1968	Horizontal 'T' shaped form with a rectangular prism projecting upwards at the intersection of the 'T'. Hardboard structure covered in vinyl. Five separate bronze forms chrome plated.	c. 25 × 38 × 45 cm	Cannot locate
Poised	1968	Vertical form with a projecting horizontal part at the top, covered in vinyl. Cast bronze, chrome plated form resting on top.	c. 60 × 38 × 15 cm	Cannot locate
Maquette for Prise (produced after *Prise*)	1968	Two vertical rectangular prisms, the smaller supported by the larger, separated by aluminium forms. 'Pedestals' painted black over fibreglass, red laminex on sides.	50 × 58 × 17.5 cm; on pedestal: 107 cm (h)	In collection of June English
Thru or *Through*	1969	Aluminium form penetrating vertical rectangle of cardboard or ply, covered with polyester resin and fibreglass. Sprayed with deep purple duco.	c. 37 × 50 × 50 cm	Was in collection of Tim Storrier — stolen
Loop	1969	Polished aluminium, polyester resin and fibreglass over hardboard, sprayed with blue-green automotive duco.	21.5 × 45 × 30 cm	In James Baker Collection, Museum of Contemporary Art, Brisbane
Wrapped Around (in catalogue of Shepparton Art Gallery as *Assembled*, but title incorrect)	1969	Cardboard construction covered in fibreglass and polyester resin, sprayed with red automotive duco. Cast bronze form chrome plated and polished.	39 × 46.1 × 25.5 cm	In collection of Shepparton Art Gallery
Sixteen or *16* or *Multiple — Sixteen*	1969	White fibreglass and polyester resin on hardboard and timber structure, painted white.	103 × 99 × 25 cm	In collection of Geelong Art Gallery; purchased in 1970 with funds from the Miss G. Bell and J. H. McPhillimy Bequest.
Hanging Three	1969	White fibreglass and polyester resin on hardboard and timber structure, painted white.	c. 122 cm (sq) projecting c. 90 cm	Destroyed

TITLE OF WORK	YEAR	MEDIA	DIMENSIONS	PRESENT LOCATION
Three Thirds or *3/3*	1969	Three forms in polished aluminium on white fibreglass, polyester resin and hardboard backing painted white.	$76.6 \times 78 \times 26$ cm	In collection of Brisbane College of Advanced Education
Linked	1969	—	—	No information available
Multiples	1970	Six black fibreglass and polyester resin squares with polished aluminium forms emerging.	6 units each $18.5 \times 31 \times 30.5$ cm	Three in collection of Bronwen & Geoff la Gerche; three in collection of Clive Murray-White
Multiple 1, 2 and 3 (different from above)	1970	Three square box forms, each with four projecting spatulate shapes. Box of pine and masonite covered with white fibreglass and resin. Projecting forms of white fibreglass and resin.	$250 \times 250 \times 120$ cm	Nos. *1* & *3* in collection of Jack Wyatt; no *2* in collection of David Mather
Multiples 1, 2 and 3 (shown at Balaclava Art Exhibition 1 April 1973, three years after works listed above, which were purchased in 1970. These works have not been identified. They can only be presumed as different from both the above works)		—	—	No information available
Untitled (theme for Comalco competition was 'Energy')	1970	Aluminium, cast and fabricated.	$109 \times 76.2 \times 24$ cm	In collection of Comalco Ltd
100	1970–71	White fibreglass and polyester resin on white hardboard.	250×250 projecting c. 38 cm	Destroyed
Opposing, also called *Confrontation* or *Confront*	1971	Fibreglass and polyester resin. Each piece a vertical board with one form coming out and down. Fibreglass and resin on hardboard and timber board, painted white.	Each work c. 122 (h) $\times$ c. 60 (w), projecting c. 23 cm. Shown as 16 separate pieces, 8 on either side of gallery	Destroyed
Commission, following Comalco Award	1971	Aluminium, cast and fabricated.	$533 \times 293 \times 100$ cm	Hydro-Electric Commission, Hobart
Transfield Sculpture	1971	Nine welded steel cubes, each with cast iron forms inside.	Each box $12 \times 12 \times 12$ cm	In collection of Frank Watters
9 Through 5 or *Nine Through Five*	1971	Five chipboard boxes, painted white inside and black outside. White forms of fibreglass and polyester resin, inside boxes.	Five boxes each $30.8 \times 33.3 \times 40.3$ cm	In collection of Newcastle Region Art Gallery
Untitled (shown Marland House Competition, Melbourne, June/July 1971	1971	A work consisting of three groups which included: 1 *Scooped* 3 long thin forms with spatulate endings; 2 9 circular shapes with spatulate forms emerging upwards; 3 2 long thin forms with numerous spatulate forms White polyester resin and fibreglass, dowelling painted white.	Variable size on floor, c. 455×215 cm	1 *Scooped* was in private collection — since destroyed 2 9 circular shapes became 2 separate works 3 Destroyed
Scooped 1 *Scooped* shown at Watters Gallery, 1 May–5 June 1971 2 Shown as 3 rods in Marland House Exhibition, June/July 1971, as part of work in three sections, listed as 'Untitled' 3 Also shown at Gallery 1 Eleven, 1971, as 5 rods entitled *Variable*	1971	Five white fibreglass and resin forms: the long sections, fibreglass and resin over wooden dowelling.	Each work c. 244 cm long	Was in private collection — accidentally destroyed
Untitled sculpture	1971	Nine circular shapes with spatulate form arising from each circle. White polyester resin and fibreglass. Separated from 'Untitled' (Marland House).	c. 15 cm (diam.) c. 15 cm (h)	3 used in following entry; subsequently all destroyed

TITLE OF WORK	YEAR	MEDIA	DIMENSIONS	PRESENT LOCATION
Untitled	1971	Three cylindrical pedestal-like forms with a single spatulate form emerging from the top of each cylinder. White fibreglass and polyester resin on top of cardboard cylinder. Painted white. Constructed from three parts of 'Untitled' (Marland House).	c. 60 cm (h)	Destroyed
'Grass Process Work — Part I'	1971	See list of Installations, Documentation.		
'Grass Process Work — Part II'	1971	See list of Installations, Documentation.		
'Boxed Process'	1971	See list of Documentation.		
'Black Disc Process'	1971	See list of Documentation.		
Redaction	1971	Wooden box with hinged lid. Nine divisions in box with nine ceramic cylinders, each wrapped in latex.	Box: $10 \times 58 \times 38$ cm; cylinders: 4 cm (diam.) 35 cm (l)	In collection of Kevin Mortensen
'Drawing — New York'	1972–74	Nine cardboard cylinders covered in papier mâché. Pencil marks on surface.	c. 15 cm (h) c. 6 cm (diam.)	In the collection of Robert Jacks
'Greene Street Piece'	1972–73	See list of Documentation.		
Installation, Scottish Highlands	1972	See list of Installations.		
Tree Piece	1973	See list of Installations and Documentation.		
Unrolled or *Unrolled Piece*	1973	Long length of canvas with pockets for 49 fired clay cylinders, partly glazed in opaque white.	Canvas: 1525 cm (l); 49 ceramic cylinders, each 40 cm (l); total dimensions 4 (h) $\times 45$ (w) $\times 1525$ cm (l), capable of being rolled into a large cylindrical bundle Original canvas damaged while displayed outside at 'Sculpturscape '73': new canvas 1574×43 cm	Purchased for collection of City of Mildura Arts Centre with a grant from the Visual Arts Board, Australia Council
Installation with Kevin Mortensen	1973	See list of Installations.		
Three Wax Pieces, Three Bronze Pieces	1973	Three wax cylinders, three bronze cylinders in wooden box.	Box: $7.6 \times 38 \times 30.4$ cm	Parts re-used. Work no longer exists.
Untitled	1973	Latex skin over ceramic.	c. $7 \times 7 \times 11$ cm	In possession of the artist
Untitled	1973	Latex skin over ceramic.	c. $5 \times 5 \times 8$ cm	In possession of the artist
Untitled	1973	Latex skin over ceramic.	c. $3.5 \times 3.5 \times 24$ cm	In possession of the artist
Asyntatic or *Asyntactic* (listed in 'Survey I, catalogue as *Asyntatic Work — Part I*)	1973	Cardboard box containing four paper bundles with each bundle consisting of 27 paper sheets of 1 Torn newsprint 2 Cut newsprint 3 Torn paper towel 4 Torn wrapping paper Each bundle tied with string.	Box: $7 \times 28 \times 38$ cm	In James Baker Collection, Museum of Contemporary Art, Brisbane
Asyntatic Part I (listed in 'Survey I catalogue as *Asyntatic Work — Part II*)	1973	Sixteen ceramic cylinders contained in pockets in length of white canvas. Capable of being rolled up and tied in a cylindrical bundle.	Maximum length unrolled 120×37 cm (w); when rolled, c. 9.5 cm (diam.)	In James Baker Collection, Museum of Contemporary Art, Brisbane
Asyntatic Part II	1973	Four rectangular sheets (lead, latex, polyester resin and papier mâché), plus white canvas bag with pocket capable of holding four sheets.	$2 \times 28 \times 38$ cm	In James Baker Collection, Museum of Contemporary Art, Brisbane
Asyntatic Part III	1973	Canvas rectangle with nine pockets, containing nine sheets of papier mâché. Capable of being folded up and tied into a square package.	92×71.5 cm	In collection of Melbourne College of Advanced Education

TITLE OF WORK	YEAR	MEDIA	DIMENSIONS	PRESENT LOCATION
Analectic	1973	Cardboard box containing five paper pieces. Newspaper cut, pulped, torn and woven, with pencil markings.	Each paper piece: c. 37 × 26 cm	Was in possession of the artist. Present whereabouts unknown
Anagramic, Anagramatic or *Anagramic Drawing Piece* (catalogued by National Gallery of Victoria as *Anagramic* Drawing *Piece*)	1973	Cardboard box containing 1 Three cardboard cylinders covered with newsprint; 2 Nine torn and pasted newsprint sheets. The newsprint sheets have drawn areas to define specific positions on the surface.	Box: 7 × 38 × 53.2 cm; newsprint sheets: 37 × 32 cm	In collection of the National Gallery of Victoria
Drawing Work	c. 1973	See list of Drawings.		
Ingots	1974	Long narrow wooden box with 27 divisions, 9 filled with papier mâché ingots, 9 with terracotta and 9 with lead.	Box: 5.5 × 103 × 14.5 cm	In James Baker Collection, Museum of Contemporary Art, Brisbane
Analogy	1974	Ten cylinders in latex, ceramic, canvas, wax, plaster, bronze, papier mâché and resin plus two lead moulds.	Each cylinder 39 cm (l)	In possession of the artist
About Space	1974	Construction consisting of lead tray, ten vertical papier mâché rods, plaited string and two long plaster cylinders. In addition a bundle of papier mâché rods wrapped in white canvas and a small canvas container for string.	Lead tray: c. 275 × 275 cm; total size c. 400 (w) × c. 1220 (l) × c. 150 cm (h)	Temporary structure — since destroyed
Untitled or *Cloth and Hanging Rods*	1974	Three papier mâché cylinders with plaited string. White canvas strip with six pockets for cylinders. Capable of being rolled up and tied.	When displayed on wall 150 × 43 × 2 cm	In collection of Mickie Wilson
Ti-ed Piece	1974	Twelve or more papier mâché rods made from newspaper leaning against wall with connecting plaited string at top with small bundle of paper tied to each piece of string.	c. 150 (h) × c. 457 cm (w) (width variable)	Was in collection of the artist — since destroyed
Drawing 1 — Diagonal	1974	See list of Drawings.		
Drawing 2 — Diagram A	1974	See list of Drawings.		
Drawing 3 — Grids	1974	See list of Drawings.		
'The Artist's Dream'	1974	See list of Documentation.		
'Inching'	1974	See list of Documentation.		
'When You Think About Art What Do You Think About?'	1974	See list of Documentation.		
'Ingots'	1974	See list of Documentation.		
'A Tearing Work' or 'Tearing'	1974	See list of Documentation.		
'Box Project'	1974	See list of Documentation.		
'Plaiting'	1975	See list of Documentation.		
'Place'	1975	See list of Installations and Documentation.		
Untitled	1975	Nine ceramic rods all wrapped with latex and stitched. Plaited string attached to each rod. In addition some cylinders also wrapped in strips of cloth or paper, or both.	Nine ceramic rods each c. 36 (l) × 1.5 cm (diam.); attached string varies from c. 20–c. 30 cm (l); grid: c. 70 cm (sq); latex hung down c. 22 cm	In the collection of Frank Watters
Ewing Work	1975	Ceramic rods, latex sheet with eyelet holes, string. Cardboard cylinder covered with canvas strips and ceramic rods (tied on with string)		Temporary installation — since destroyed
'Place'	1975	See list of Installations.		
Art as a time-consuming activity — time passes fast and slow	1975	Washer and length of plaited string.	915 cm	Not known

TITLE OF WORK	YEAR	MEDIA	DIMENSIONS	PRESENT LOCATION
Device for delineating a distance and to feel a space, while experiencing difficulty in controlling gravity	1975	Two identical forms, one in wood and the other in lead, separated by string.	One form to be held in each hand	Not known
Monad (appears to be a general title given to two earlier works *Anagramic*, 1973, and 'Greene Street Piece', 1972–73, when both shown at Contemporary Art Society, Adelaide, 1975)	1975			
On the need for a proper delineation in a moment	1975	From left to right: 1 Thirty-six small photographs on wall showing a latex cube getting smaller and smaller; 2 Rectangle of transparent plastic sheeting on floor, containing envelope, which also contained a rectangle of resin and fibreglass; 3 Square shallow tray of lead leaning against wall vertically; 4 Two vertical cardboard cylinders, covered with canvas, filled with sand, linked with two lines of string; 5 Sitting on floor — small flat latex form with four ceramic rods attached to top; 6 Square bundle, covered in white canvas and tied up with white canvas cords; 7 Small, flat square of solid cast papier mâché; 8 Stack of many large sheets of papier mâché with drawing on top sheet.	c. 180 cm (h) 16.5 × 31 × 31 cm 86 × 62 cm	Temporary installation; some parts in possession of the artist; two sections in other collections In collection of Marlee Creaser In collection of Monash University
'Space Definition'	1975	See list of Documentation.		
'Substance, Cause, Number, Relation'	1975	See list of Documentation.		
'Passage, Part I, Scan, The You Yangs'	1976	See list of Documentation.		
'Hattah Installations'	1976	See lists of Installations and Documentation.		
'Ovens River Installation'	1976	See list of Installations.		
Exchange Pieces — at least six works	1976	See list of Exchange Works.		
Nomad	1976	Grid of fibreglass and polyester resin rods tied together with cotton, held by loops of latex, suspended by string from ceiling. One sheet of latex attached and hanging from rods. Square of knitted string on floor. Thin bundle of twigs on floor attached to knitting. Three small structures on floor made from twigs, carved wood, fibreglass and latex. Twenty-six photographs on wall of installations at Hattah Lakes.	Grid: c. 215 cm above floor — 183 × 250 × 30 cm	Temporary installation — since destroyed
Bicycle I	1976	Sawn timber, sticks, papier mâché, string, cotton thread, knitted string.	In two parts: 77 × 51 × 2 cm (left), 24 × 62 × 3 cm (right); distance between parts variable	Donated by Marr Grounds to Art Gallery of NSW
Mat	1976	Sawn timber, twigs, string, latex and calico.	9.5 × 81 × 69 cm (meant to be viewed on floor)	In collection of Dr and Mrs Douglas Callister

TITLE OF WORK	YEAR	MEDIA	DIMENSIONS	PRESENT LOCATION
1. 2 and 3 all one work 1 *Table*	1977	left to right, hung in order 1, 2 and 3 Twigs, sawn timber, matches, papier mâché, calico, string, cotton thread, latex, knitted string, pencil marks on some papier mâché. Mounted on acrylic inside wooden frame.	$122 \times 122 \times 6$ cm	In collection of Chandler Coventry
2 *Journey I*	1976	Twigs, cotton thread, latex, paper, pencil marks on paper. Mounted on acrylic, inside wooden frame.	$122 \times 122 \times 6$ cm	In collection of Chandler Coventry
3 *Kite*	1976	Sawn timber, papier mâché, latex, string, cotton thread. Mounted on acrylic, inside wooden frame.	$122 \times 122 \times 6$ cm	In collection of Chandler Coventry
Bicycle II (listed in Watters catalogue 1977 as *Bicycle I* and in 'Survey I' catalogue 1978 as *Bicycle*, 1977)	1976	Sawn timber, latex, paper, string, twigs.	In two parts: section on right 251×5 cm (diam.); section on left $112 \times 60 \times 2$ cm; distance between parts variable; c. 240 cm (w)	In collection of Australian National Gallery, Canberra
Articles	1976–77	Number of small objects (branches, twigs, string, paper), sitting on small table made from chipboard and wood.	—	Location unknown
'Kevington'	1977	Five objects hanging from string line between two vertical wooden poles. Objects made from twigs, stones, string and bark. See also list of Installations.	Dimensions variable. Largest object c. 45 cm (l)	In possession of the artist
Exchange Pieces — Twenty-four shown at Watters Gallery	1977	See list of Exchange Works.		
'Solar Piece'	1977	See lists of Installations and Documentation.		
Parts	1977	Twigs, canvas, branches, string, latex and paper.	$280 \times 20 \times 150$ cm (variable)	In possession of the artist
Marker (listed as *Icon* in Watters catalogue, 1977)	1977	Twigs, branches, string, paper, latex and underfelt.	$63 \times 43 \times 46$ cm	In collection of Nola and Alun Leach Jones
Wood/Stone	1977	Twigs, string, rock and underfelt.	$20 \times 18 \times 145$ cm	In possession of the artist
Suspended Stone	1977 (?)	Listed in Watters catalogue as 1977, but possibly this work was not completed (or produced). Appears not to have been shown.	—	—
Sack	1977	Twigs, branches, latex and canvas.	c. 140 cm (h)	Location unknown
Journey II	1977	Sticks, string, latex, paper and underfelt, hanging from ceiling.	217×204.5 cm (irregular)	Donated to Art Gallery of NSW by Patrick White
Collection A *Collection B*	1977	Hanging on wall in glazed pine frame. Two identical groups of objects, but made of different materials: hardboard back. *Collection A* — limestone fragments, eucalyptus twig; *Collection B* — papier mâché.	$45.5 \times 95 \times 6.5$ cm	In collection of Rex Irwin
Lean-to	1977	String, twigs, wood, paper, latex, felt and underfelt.	$140 \times 108 \times 10$ cm	In collection of Monash University
Exchange Pieces — nineteen shown at Indian Triennial	1977	See list of Exchange Works.		
Journey III or *Journey 3*	1977–78	String, twigs, latex, paper, felt and underfelt.	$178 \times 218 \times 30$ cm	In possession of the artist
'Relocation — Beach Work'	1978	See list of Installations.		

TITLE OF WORK	YEAR	MEDIA	DIMENSIONS	PRESENT LOCATION
Venice Biennale, 'Continuum and Transference, Installation' (1–5):		Media listed in Venice Biennale catalogue varies from information given below.		
1 *Ridge* (consists of three parts: (a) 'Jan Juc'; (b) 'Green Cape; (c) 'Mallacoota')	1977–78	Twigs, string, papier mâché, rocks, cast paper rocks and feathers.	Dimensions variable according to installation	In possession of the artist
2 *Device* (consists of three parts: (a) an animal-like section; (b) a tent-like part; (c) a long whip-like section)	1978	Twigs, string, paper, underfelt, bark.	(a) c. $7.5 \times 22.5 \times 7.5$ cm (b) c. $18 \times 76 \times 20$ cm (c) c. 3 (diam.) $\times$ 140 cm (l)	In possession of the artist
3 *Tower*	1978	Twigs, string, papier mâché, stone, canvas, latex.	c. $230 \times 45 \times 45$ cm	In possession of the artist
4 *Flag Renamed Place* (listed as *Flag* in Venice Biennale catalogue)	1978–	Canvas, latex, string, twigs, feathers and cast paper stones; irregular, flat piece of canvas with twigs and feathers held in place by loops of canvas.	Work in progress — dimensions variable	In possession of the artist
5 *Marker A*	1977	Twigs, branches, string, papier mâché, latex and underfelt.	c. $180 \times 106 \times 76$ cm	In possession of the artist
Marker B	1977	Twigs, branches, string, papier mâché, latex and underfelt.	c. $215 \times 90 \times 90$ cm	In possession of the artist
Installation with Ti Parks	1978	See list of Installations.		
Nomad II or *Nomad Two*	1978	Wood, twigs, string, latex, paper, calico and rocks.	c. $150 \times$ c. $150 \times$ c. 300 cm. (width and depth variable)	In possession of the artist
Marker Three	1978	Twigs, string.	c. $60 \times 30 \times 75$ cm	No longer exists — incorporated as part of *Incident* (1982–83)
Untitled sculpture	1978 (?)	Twigs, papier mâché, string, mounted on chipboard.	Chipboard: c. 45×50 cm	Cannot be located — was in collection of School of Art, Tasmanian College of Advanced Education, Launceston. Presumed stolen
'Installation and Exchange Work No. 3'	1978	See list of Installations and Exchange Works.		
Cape Schank	1978-79	Twigs, cotton, canvas, rocks, paper, twine, bones, feathers.	In three parts: Tower: $220 \times 52 \times 52$ cm; table: $24 \times 58 \times 86$ cm; landscape line: length variable	In collection of the National Gallery of Victoria
New England	1979	Sawn timber, twigs, cotton thread, calico, papier mâché 'stones' cast from latex moulds, underfelt used as stuffing. Suspended from latex tabs. Enclosed in perspex box.	Box: $48 \times 53.5 \times 26.5$ cm; work within box: c. $37 \times 42 \times 12$ cm	In collection of Wollongong City Gallery
Nargen	1979	Branches, twigs, string, papier mâché stones, canvas, calico, felt.	$230 \times 180 \times 140$ cm	In collection of Tasmanian Museum and Art Gallery, Hobart
'With Animal Trap'	1979	See list of Installations.		
'Observatory'	1979	See list of Installations.		
'Lake Wakatipu Installation'	1980	See list of Installations.		
'Markers One, Two and Three'	1980	See list of Installations.		
'Observatory Revisited'	1980	See list of Installations.		
Another Place	1980	Sticks, calico and paper.	$42 \times 72 \times 187$ cm	In possession of the artist
Unspoken	1980	Twigs, carved timber, papier mâché, calico, wooden 'stones', and some pink pigment.	$13 \times 22 \times 184$ cm	In possession of the artist
You Yangs	1980	Twigs, string, paper cast 'stones' and small 'rocks' made from wood.	$196 \times 90 \times 30$ cm	In collection of Queensland Art Gallery
Potkarok	1980	Sawn timber, papier mâché and calico.	$52 \times 117 \times 220$ cm	In James Baker Collection, Museum of Contemporary Art, Brisbane

TITLE OF WORK	YEAR	MEDIA	DIMENSIONS	PRESENT LOCATION
Moraine	1980	Twigs, sawn timber, canvas, papier mâché and driftwood from New Zealand.	112 cm (h)	In possession of the artist
Connection	1980	Papier mâché, sticks, paper bag, dirt, plastic, stone, bottletops.	c. 7.5 × 45 × 45 cm	Temporary installation
'Environmental Installation'	1980	See list of Installations.		
Region	1980–81	Sawn timber, twigs, string, calico, latex, paper, tar (note: after 1983 used term synthetic bitumen).	110 × 355 × 305 cm (irregular shape, variable)	In collection of the Art Gallery of Western Australia
Region Extension 1	Works 1 to 7 produced in 1980–81	Twigs, string, paper (painted cream, green and pink with some paper left white).	62 × 39 × 33 cm	In collection of Frank Watters
Region Extension 2		Twigs, string, paper (painted with tar with small areas of yellow).	74 × 52 × 41 cm	In possession of the artist
Region Extension 3		Twigs, string, paper (painted with tar).	70 × 70 × 48 cm	In possession of the artist
Region Extension 4		Twigs, string, paper — area of white papier mâché painted yellow at bottom. Vertical area of paper painted with tar.	44 × 62 × 50 cm	In possession of the artist
Region Extension 5		Twigs, string and paper — some papier mâché painted pink, other areas left white.	66 × 38 × 38 cm	In collection of Alex and Geoffrey Legge
Region Extension 6		Twigs, string and paper — some papier mâché left white, other area painted with tar.	106 × 33 × 56 cm	In possession of the artist
Region Extension 7		Twigs, string and paper — paper left white.	89 × 84 × 43 cm	In possession of the artist
Long Journey	1980–81	Partly carved wood, twigs, string, paper, tarred paper.	50 × 549 × 68 cm	In James Baker Collection, Museum of Contemporary Art, Brisbane
Crossing	1981	Sawn timber, twigs, string, tarred paper.	178 × 193 × 43 cm	In possession of the artist
Exchange Pieces — six works	1981	See list of Exchange Works.		
'Place Two — An Installation'	1981	See list of Installations.		
Animal	1982	Twigs, paper, underfelt.	c. 61 × 76 × 23 cm	Destroyed
Journey Extended	1982–83	Work taken from Melbourne: twigs, string, calico, paper, yellow paint and tar; gathered on beach in Japan: bamboo, parts of wrecked boat, water-washed timber fragments plus Japanese rice paper, calico and tar.	56 × 610 × 57 cm	In possession of the artist
Incident	1982–83	See list of Installations.		
'Raft'	1983	See list of Installations.		
Myth	1983	Twigs, paper, paper collage, calico, underfelt, synthetic bitumen.	110 × 135 × 27 cm	In collection of Anthony Bond
Alice Springs Maquette	1983	Corrugated cardboard, twigs, timber, styrene foam, pigment.	c. 36 cm (h)	Whereabouts unknown
Exchange Pieces — seventeen works	1983	See list of Exchange Works.		
'Goji's Bridge'	1983	See list of Installations.		
Austausch/Exchange	1983–84	Exchange begun by Marr Grounds 25 December 1981. Parts supplied by Marr Grounds in 1982: canvas, wooden box with small construction inside, two structures with glass, mirror, b/w photographs; materials used by John Davis: twigs, sticks, canvas, papier mâché, black synthetic bitumen. Exhibited 1984.	324 × 208 × 207 cm	In possession of the artist
Second Incident	1984	Twigs, paper, calico, underfelt, synthetic bitumen.	60 × 370 × 370 cm (width and depth variable)	In possession of the artist
Exchange Pieces — seventeen works	1984	See list of Exchange Works.		

TITLE OF WORK	YEAR	MEDIA	DIMENSIONS	PRESENT LOCATION
Traveller — consists of 4 parts: 1 *LA Marker I*	1984	Timber, twigs, lathes, calico, paper, synthetic bitumen.	193 × 147 × 158 cm	Left in Los Angeles
2 *LA Marker II*	1984	As above.	249 × 152 × 147 cm	Left in Los Angeles
3 *LA Marker III*	1984	Twigs, paper, calico, synthetic bitumen.	117 × 262 × 81 cm	Left in Los Angeles
4 *Midden*	1984	Timber, twigs, paper, canvas, synthetic bitumen.	66 (h), 272 cm (diam.) (has been exhibited on floor or on wall)	In the possession of artist
'Elysian Park Installation'	1984	See list of Installations.		
Nine untitled works	1984	See list of Installations.		
'Ivy Station Installation' (in LAICA catalogue listed as *Ivy Station Location*)	1984	See list of Installations.		
Cloud and Pebbles	1984	Canvas, calico, underfelt and synthetic bitumen.	244 × 366 × 2.5 cm	In possession of the artist
Another Place	1984	Twigs, timber, paper, calico, canvas, underfelt, stones, synthetic bitumen.	178 × 374 × 28 cm	In possession of the artist
Conversation about India	1984	Twigs, sawn timber, paper, calico, synthetic bitumen.	Two parts: (1) 200 × 110 × 35 cm; (2) 210 × 130 × 65 cm	(1) In collection of Max Watters; (2) In possession of the artist
Face 1	1984	Twigs, paper, calico, synthetic bitumen.	49 × 46 × 12 cm	In possession of the artist
Face 11	1984	As above.	43 × 30 × 7 cm	In possession of the artist
Duo	1984	Twigs, paper, calico, canvas, underfelt, synthetic bitumen.	96 × 122 × 25 cm	In James Baker Collection, Museum of Contemporary Art, Brisbane

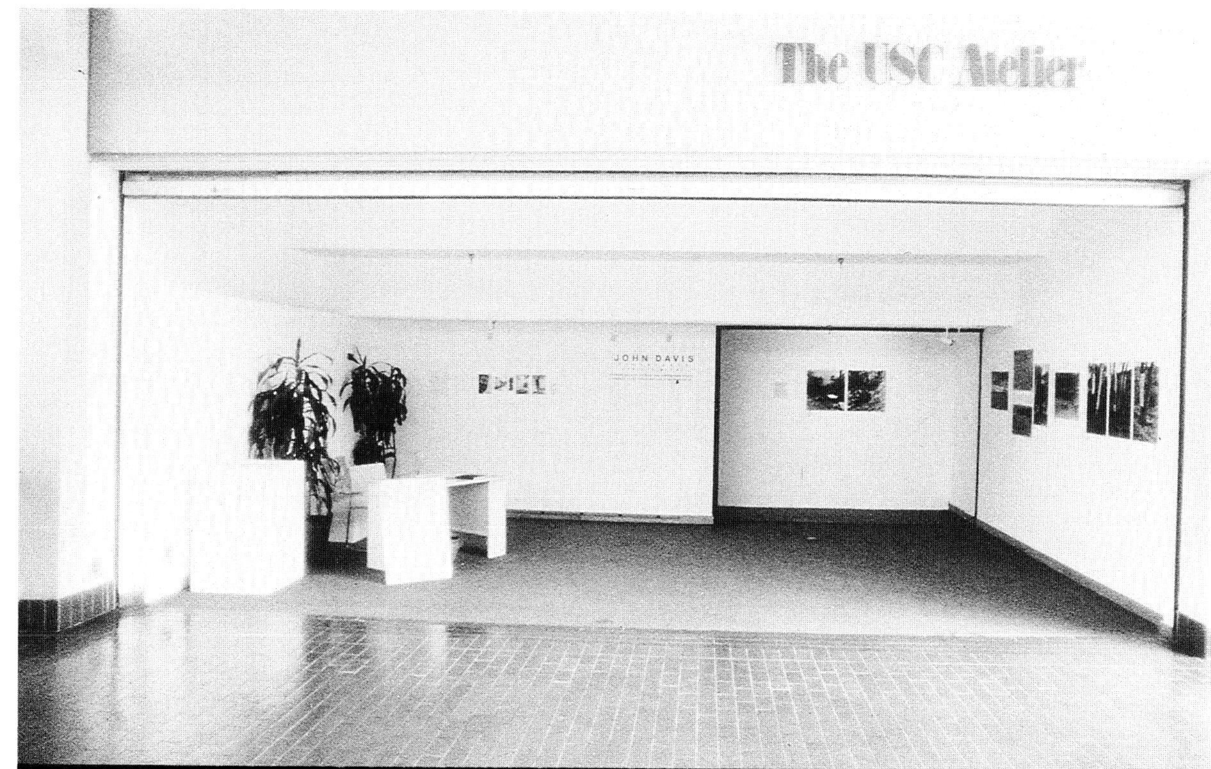

◀ *110 University of Southern California Atelier, Santa Monica, Los Angeles, U.S.A., where John Davis had a one person exhibition in April-May 1984. Photograph by John Davis.*

TITLE OF WORK	YEAR	MEDIA	DIMENSIONS	PRESENT LOCATION
Cross	1984–85	Twigs, paper, canvas, synthetic bitumen.	$59 \times 47 \times 33$ cm	In possession of the artist
Location Piece	1984–85	Twigs, calico, canvas, paper, synthetic bitumen, underfelt, sawn timber.	$150 \times 130 \times 45$ cm	In possession of the artist
Site	1984–85	Calico, underfelt, twigs, paper, synthetic bitumen.	$118 \times 92 \times 7$ cm	In possession of the artist
Earlier Incident	1985	Twigs, calico, paper, synthetic bitumen.	$165 \times 180 \times 40$ cm	In James Baker Collection, Museum of Contemporary Art, Brisbane
Cloud	1985	Calico, underfelt, synthetic bitumen.	$56 \times 66 \times 4$ cm	In possession of the artist
'Conversation'	1985	See list of Installations.		
'Drought Series' (including 'Off Beaumaris' and 'Lean-to, Two')	1985	See list of Installations		
Untitled	1985	Twigs, paper, calico, synthetic bitumen.	c. $54 \times 58 \times 6$ cm	Exhibited in Korea, but destroyed on return; remade into a work now owned by Gareth Sansom
Commission for Australian Embassy	1985–86 (installed 1987)	See list of Installations.		Australian Embassy, Saudi Arabia
Little Rock	1986	Twigs, paper, calico, synthetic bitumen.	c. $23 \times 16 \times 20$ cm	In collection of Professor Albert Elsen
Untitled	1986	Twigs, paper, calico, synthetic bitumen and stone.	$24 \times 46 \times 11$ cm	In collection of Carl Djerassi
Departure (in four parts)	1986	Twigs, paper, calico, synthetic bitumen.	Variable, according to installation	Produced at Djerassi Foundation. Works left in USA
Midden Two	1986	As above.	$33 \times 21.5 \times 8.9$ cm	As above
Midden Three	1986	As above.	$48 \times 30.4 \times 16.5$ cm	As above
Midden Four	1986	As above.	$33 \times 48 \times 23$ cm	As above
Prescence	1986	As above.	$42 \times 78.7 \times 17.8$ cm	As above
Another Thing	1986	As above.	$53 \times 38 \times 16.5$ cm	As above
Thing Found	1986	As above.	$35.5 \times 38 \times 22.7$ cm	As above
Further Events	1986	As above.	$96.5 \times 86.3 \times 99$ cm	As above
Billabong	1986	As above.	$177.8 \times 157.5 \times 48$ cm	As above
Northern	1986	As above.	$86.3 \times 101.6 \times 33$ cm	As above
Hattah	1986	As above.	$246.4 \times 266.7 \times 5$ cm	As above
Tyntyder	1986	As above.	$63.5 \times 71 \times 21.6$ cm	As above
Incident Two	1986	As above.	$127 \times 116.8 \times 40.6$ cm	As above
Along The Way	1986	As above.	$106.6 \times 79 \times 43$ cm	As above
Nyah	1986	As above.	$172.6 \times 158 \times 38$ cm	As above
Third Incident	1986	As above.	$121.8 \times 119.3 \times 50.8$ cm	As above
Drought	1986	As above.	$76.2 \times 78.7 \times 30$ cm	As above
Drought Two	1986	As above.	$96.5 \times 79 \times 30$ cm	As above
Conversations	1986	As above.	$119.3 \times 104 \times 20.3$ cm	As above
Nargen Two	1986	As above.	$152.4 \times 165 \times 106.6$ cm	As above
Habitat	1986	As above.	$94 \times 88.8 \times 38$ cm	As above
'SMIP'	1986	See list of Installations.		
Fish Basket	1986	Twigs, paper, calico, duraseal, bondcrete.	$68 \times 83 \times 22$ cm	In collection of Jane Allen
Traveller	1987	Twigs, paper, calico, bondcrete, bitumous paint.	$117 \times 130 \times 56$ cm	In possession of the artist
Further Conversations	1987	As above.	c. $102 \times 116 \times 26$ cm, (height variable)	In possession of the artist
SMIP 1	1987	As above.	c. $237 \times 227 \times 57$ cm, (height variable)	In possession of the artist
Mojave	1987	As above.	$224 \times 232 \times 38$ cm	In possession of the artist

LIST OF DRAWINGS

DRAWING	YEAR	MEDIA	DIMENSIONS	PRESENT LOCATION
Drawing — New York	1972	See list of Works.		
Drawing Work	c. 1973	Pencil on paper.	Unknown	Unknown
Anagramic Drawing Piece	1973	See list of Works.		
* Four Drawings (titles not recorded)	c. 1974	Pencil on paper.	Unknown	Could not be located. Was in collection of School of Art, Tasmanian College of Advanced Education, Launceston — presumed stolen
* *Drawing 1 — Diagonal*	1974	Pencil on paper.	In four parts, each image size 27.5 × 27.5 cm	Was in possession of the artist but can no longer be found
Drawing 2 — Diagram A	1974	Pencil on paper.	In three parts, each image size 40.6 × 40.6 cm	In private collection
Drawing 3 — Grids	1974	Pencil on paper.	In three parts, each image size 30 × 30 cm; total c. 54 × 138 cm	In collection of Chandler Coventry

* It is possible that *Drawing 1 — Diagonal* and Four Drawings are the same works.

LIST OF INSTALLATIONS

INSTALLATION	LOCATION	YEAR	MEDIA	DIMENSIONS	PRESENT SITUATION
'Grass Process Work — Part I'	'Heide' (John Reed's property at Bulleen, Melbourne), 7 November 1971	1971	Square of transparent plastic with circles cut out placed on top of grass.	c. 460 × 460 cm	Temporary installation. Photographs 30 × 38 cm in collection of Flinders University Art Museum
'Grass Process Work — Part II'	As above	1971	Bags of transparent plastic placed in a meandering line, on top of grass.	Plastic bags c. 45 cm (h) × c. 27 m (total l)	Temporary installation. Photographs 30 × 38 cm in collection of Flinders University Art Museum
					Total of 22 photographs for both 'Grass Process' works
Installation, Scottish Highlands	Scotland, September (?) 1972	1972	Approximately nine stacks of stones plus timber and string in a line in open country.	c. 6 m (l)	Temporary installation
'Tree Piece'	'Sculpturscape '73', Mildura Arts Centre, 7 April–7 July 1973	1973	A group of six eucalypt trees at Mildura each with materials wrapped cylindrically around trunks. The six tree trunks were covered in: — Papier mâché from newspapers — Green baling twine — Polythene sheeting with pockets containing grass clippings — Latex sheet — 4 rows of small sticks tied together — Canvas	6 tree trunks each c. 40 cm (diam.); materials began c. 40 cm above ground and continued to a height of c. 150 cm	Temporary installation
'Unrolled'	'Sculpturscape '73', Mildura Arts Centre, 7 April–7 July 1973	1973	Long length of canvas with pockets containing 49 ceramic cylinders partly glazed with opaque white.	Canvas: 1525 cm (l); 49 ceramic cylinders each 40 cm (l); total dimensions 4 (h) × 45 (w) × 1525 cm (l). Original canvas damaged while outside at 'Sculpturscape '73'. New canvas 1574 × 43 cm	In collection of Mildura Arts Centre
Installation with Kevin Mortensen	St Pauls Cathedral, Melbourne — 'Spring Festival', 30 October 1973	1973	Seven sheets of latex hanging over font. Four vertical structures, wrapped in white fabric, one at each corner of sunken basin for baptisms. On the top of the four columns a fox head, a fish head, a crow and a parrot. Floating on the water, in bottom of sunken baptismal font, a series of polyurethene islands with lighted candles on top. Baptismal area surrounded by white calico cushions filled with sand. Behind last row of pews four bundles of sticks tied together, surmounted by four candles. Sitting in one of the pews a male figure bare from waist, wearing large goat's head as mask (head had large horns).	—	Temporary installation
'Place'	Mildura Arts Centre and three locations on roads leading out of Mildura to Melbourne, Sydney and Adelaide. Mildura Sculpture Triennial, 29 March–1 June 1975	1975	In small room at Mildura Arts Centre — three photographs of the three 120 × 120 cm masonite panels on side of roads leading out of Mildura, plus one sheet of 120 × 120 cm masonite in room. TV monitor showing b/w video 'Plaiting' (John Davis plaiting nine	—	Temporary installation

INSTALLATION	LOCATION	YEAR	MEDIA	DIMENSIONS	PRESENT SITUATION
	Later, with some slight modifications at Exhibition Gallery, Dept of Visual Arts, Monash University, 2–26 September 1975		lengths of string). Ten b/w photographs of John Davis tying nine lengths of plaited string together.		
'Hattah Installations' (approximately 7 installations over period of 5 days, plus one small installation on banks of Murray River, near Mildura)	Hattah Lakes, Victoria, May (?) 1976	1976	Dead trees, branches, twigs, sand, sedimentary deposits.	—	Temporary installations
'Ovens River Installation'	Ovens River, Victoria, September (?) 1976	1976	Rocks, branches, twigs, reeds.	c. 120 cm (h)	Temporary installation
'Kevington'	Kevington, Victoria, March 1977, shown at Watters Gallery 13–30 July 1977	1977	String between two gum trees with five constructed objects hanging from string. Objects made from twigs, stones, string and bark.	Total work c. 240 cm (w); largest object c. 45 cm (l)	In possession of the artist
'Solar Piece'	You Yangs, Victoria, November; photo shown Mildura 1978	1977	Stacked rocks and steel.	Steel: 2 × 1 m; rocks: 80 cm (h); 87 × 217 × 115 cm (total)	Temporary installation
'Location, Displacement, Transference and Installations and Exchange Work'	Fourth Indian Triennale, New Delhi, February 1978	1978	See list of Works for details of individual works.		See list of Works
'Relocation — Beach Work'	Cholamandal, India, March 1978	1978	Rope, driftwood, cloth, string, stone, paper.	c. 2.5 m (l)	Temporary installation
'Continuum and Transference'	Venice Biennale, Italy, July–(?) 1978	1978	See list of Works for details of individual works.		See list of Works
Two installations with Ti Parks	Bay Wharf, London, August (?) 1978	1978	1 Canvas and dyes;	c. 1 m (l)	Temporary installation
			2 Twigs and paper.	c. 40 cm (l)	Temporary installation
'Installation & Exchange Work No 3' (one work plus 10 exchange pieces)	Canberra, 4–12 November 1978	1978	Twigs, string, paper, latex, rock, calico. See also list of Exchange Works.	c. 122 × 137 cm plus projecting part (variable)	In possession of the artist
'With Animal Trap'	The Grampians, Victoria, October 1979	1979	Sticks, twigs, leaves.	c. 210 × 90 × 150 cm	Temporary installation
'Observatory'	Murray River at Barmah Forest, Victoria, September (?) 1979	1979	Existing tree stump to which was added branches, twigs, bark and mud.	c. 240 cm (h)	Temporary installation
'Lake Wakatipu Installation'	Lake Wakatipu, New Zealand, January 1980	1980	Arrangement of driftwood in small excavated area in black sand on shore of lake.	c. 6 cm (h), c. 250 cm (w), c. 35 cm (d)	Temporary installation
'Markers One, Two, Three'	Piamena, Tasmania, March (?) 1980	1980	'Marker One': leaning tower constructed of twigs, sticks, bark and stones.	c. 200 cm (h), c. 15 cm (w), c. 15 cm (d)	Temporary installation
			'Marker Two': conical stack of small stones amongst larger boulders.	c. 36 cm (h), 36 cm (diam.)	Temporary installation
			'Marker Three': construction of twigs, timber, leaning against very large rock.	Rock: c. 140 cm (h); construction: c. 140 cm (w)	Temporary installation
'Observatory Revisited'	Murray River at Barmah Forest, Victoria, September (?) 1980	1980	Same tree stump as for 'Observatory' plus grid of sticks and off-cut of mill timber.	c. 140 cm (w)	Temporary installation

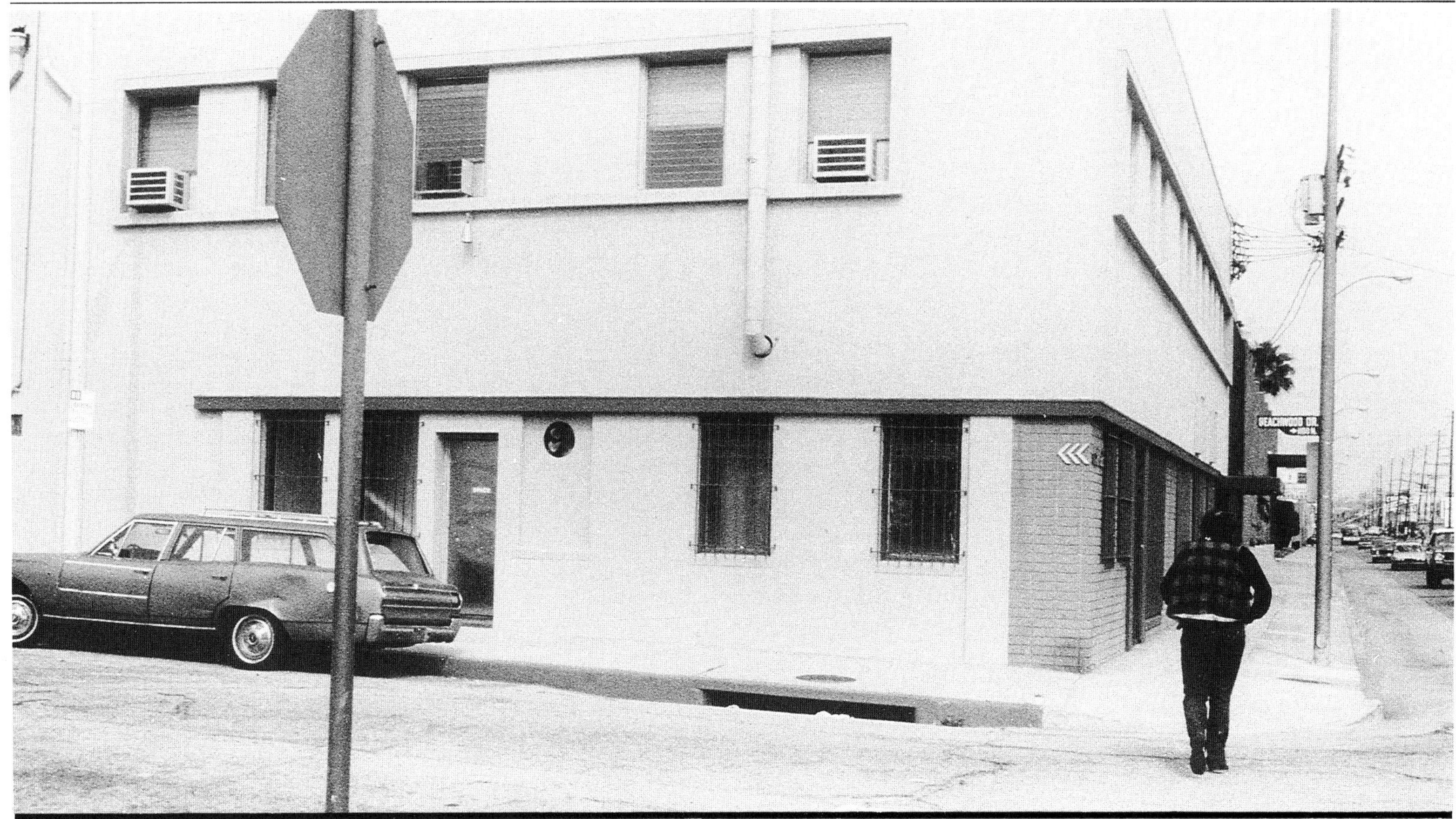

111 Space Gallery, Santa Monica Boulevard, Los Angeles, U.S.A Two person exhibition held by John Davis and Japanese artist Minoru Ohira, April-May 1986. Photograph by John Davis.

INSTALLATION	LOCATION	YEAR	MEDIA	DIMENSIONS	PRESENT SITUATION
'Environmental Installation'	Village Green, Unley, SA. Installed December 1980	1980	Earth, stone, water, steel disc and windmill.	Approximate area: 40 × 21 m; total area of Village Green: 120 × 28 m; windmill: c. 10 m (h); blades: c. 4.25 m (diam.)	Village Green, Unley, SA. Permanent installation
'Place Two — An Installation'	La Trobe University, Australian Sculpture Triennial, 28 Feb.–12 Apr. 1981	1981	Wood, twigs, paper, tar, clay, earth.	Area approx. 4 m (w) × 12 m (l)	Temporary installation
'Incident'	Art Gallery of Western Australia, 'Presence & Absence', Feb. 1983	1982–83	Twigs, paper, calico, pigment, and tar.	When set up Art Gallery of Western Australia, dimensions were: 3540 cm (h), 5070 cm (w), 5500 cm (d) (width and depth variable)	In possession of the artist
'Goji's Bridge'	Murray River at Barmah Forest, Victoria, June 1983	1983	Same tree stump as for 'Observatory', plus twigs, bark and clay.	c. 50 cm (h), c. 200 cm (l)	Temporary installation

INSTALLATION	LOCATION	YEAR	MEDIA	DIMENSIONS	PRESENT SITUATION
'Raft'	Lunami Gallery, Tokyo, Japan, 22 Aug.–3 Sept. 1983	1983	Sawn timber, twigs, papier mâché, calico, synthetic bitumen, pigment and shells.	90 × 248 × 300 cm (dimensions variable)	In possession of the artist
'Raft'	Anri Gallery, Nagoya, Japan, 9–27 October 1983	1983			
'Traveller' (in four parts)	USC Atelier, Santa Monica, Los Angeles, USA, 17 April–20 May 1984	1984	Twigs, paper, calico, wood, stone, synthetic bitumen.	366 × 457 × 549 cm	In possession of the artist
'Elysian Park Installation'	Los Angeles, USA, April 1984	1984	Twigs, paper, calico and synthetic bitumen.	35.5 × 51 × 23 cm	Left on site
'Austausch/Exchange'	Ivan Dougherty Gallery, Sydney, March–April; Gryphon Gallery, Melbourne, October–November 1984	1984	Following supplied by Marr Grounds in 1982: canvas, mirrors, two structures with glass, wooden box with small construction inside, b/w photographs; added by John Davis: twigs, papier mâché, canvas, synthetic bitumen.		In possession of the artist
'Second Incident'	Watters Gallery, Sydney , 19 March–13 April 1985	1984	Calico, twigs, paper, synthetic bitumen.	c. 370 cm (variable diam.), 60 cm (h)	In possession of the artist
'Barmah Installation'	Murray River at Barmah Forest, Vic.	1984	Same tree stump as for 'Observatory', plus twigs, sticks etc.		Temporary installation
'Ivy Station Installation' (in two parts) — Untitled Work	LAICA, Los Angeles, USA, 30 June–14 August 1984	1984	Twigs, paper, calico, synthetic bitumen and objects collected on the site, such as timber, plastic, cardboard plus drawing with white paint on concrete floor.	Oval shape on floor c. 244 × c. 366 cm	Left on site
'Ivy Station Installation' 'Niche'	As above	1984	Twigs, paper, calico, bamboo and synthetic bitumen.	107 × 112 × 35 cm	Left on site
Nine untitled works	As above	1984	Twigs, paper, rocks etc.	Variable	Seven sold in Los Angeles to collectors in Japan; two sold to American collectors
'Drought Series'	Inax Galleries, Tokyo, May and Osaka, August, Japan	1986	(Actually consisted of 'Off Beaumaris' and 'Lean-to, Two'. See below.)		
'Off Beaumaris'	As above	1985	Twigs, paper, calico, synthetic bitumen.	2.24 m × 4 m × 76 cm	In possession of the artist
'Lean-to, Two'	As above	1985	Twigs, paper, calico, synthetic bitumen.	Consists of approx. 35 parts; dimensions variable according to installation — c. 1.24 × c. 1.14 × c. 4.16 m	In possession of the artist
'Conversation'	School of Art, University of Tasmania, Hobart, 14 June–5 July 1985	1985	Mat, timber, branches, twigs, paper, calico, synthetic bitumen, adobe.	c. 3 × c. 1.25 × c. 1.25 m	Left on site, since destroyed
'SMIP' (in nine parts)	Woodside, Djerassi Foundation, USA, March 1986	1986	Twigs, paper, calico, synthetic bitumen.	c. 4.5 × c. 4.5 m	Produced at and left at Djerassi Foundation
Commission for Australian Embassy	Riyadh, Saudi Arabia. Installed January 1987	1985–86	Twigs, paper, calico, synthetic bitumen, suspended by stainless steel wires.		Australian Embassy, Saudi Arabia
Installation, Old Camel Trail	Saudi Arabia, January 1987	1987	Twigs, paper, calico, synthetic bitumen.	Not recorded	Left on site

LIST OF DOCUMENTATION

During discussion with the author in February, 1983, John Davis defined his attitude towards documentation as, ''The systematic visual and literal description of how a work functions.''

TITLE OF WORK	YEAR	MEDIA/DIMENSIONS	PRESENT LOCATION
Note: photographs by John Davis unless otherwise stated			
'Process One'	1971	b/w photographs.	Location unknown
'Process Two'	1971	As above.	Location unknown
'Process One Summary' (referred to in letter to Frank Watters as 'Black Disc Process' but listed in 1971 Watters' catalogue as above)	1971	As above.	Location unknown
'Black Disc Process'	1971	As above.	In possession of the artist
'Grass Process, Part I' and extension to various sites	1971	Four b/w photographs, each 14.6 × 20.3 cm, of process work, using polythene sheeting, and grass, at artist's home, plus seven b/w photographs, each 10 × 14.8 cm of various possible sites.	One copy in collection of Vic Majzner and another in collection of Gary Catalano
'Grass Process Part II'	1971	Twenty-two b/w photographs, each 30.2 × 38 cm of process work at 'Heide' using polythene sheeting, rocks, grass and plastic bags.	In collection Flinders University Art Museum
Box of photographs of 'Grass Process Part I and Part II'	1971	b/w photographs.	Given to John Reed after 'Grass Process' at 'Heide'
'John Reed's Process' shown at Gallery 1 Eleven, Brisbane, 5 March 1972–(?)	1971	b/w photographs.	Location unknown
* 'Boxed Process' (listed in letter to Gallery 1 Eleven, 1971)	1971	b/w photographs and typed information displayed in wooden box painted white.	In possession of the artist
* 'Photographic Documentation' (shown at Geelong Art Gallery, 'Victorian Contemporary Sculpture Exhibition', 1972)	1971	Chipboard box with lid, painted white, containing b/w photographs mounted on card.	In possession of the artist
* 'Boxed Work' (shown at National Gallery of Victoria, 'Survey I — John Davis', 1978)	1971 In 'Survey I' catalogue the date is given as 1972, but John Davis was overseas all of 1972	Chipboard, enamel paint, photographs, cards, 16 × 28 × 23 cm.	In possession of the artist
'Greene Street Piece'	1972–73	Four b/w photographs, each 47.5 × 32.5 cm. Three cardboard cylinders photographed in Greene Street, New York, 1972. Pencil marks added to four photographs 1973.	In collection of the National Gallery of Victoria
'Drawing — New York'	1972–74	Nine cardboard cylinders covered in papier mâché. Pencil marks on surface, produced 1972. Photographed 1972. Assembled 3 × 3 b/w photographs, mounted, framed 1974.	Original cylinders in collection of Robert Jacks; photographic documentation in possession of the artist
'Tree Piece'	1973	Three b/w photographs each 61 × 50.8 cm	In possession of the artist
'The Artist's Dream' (title given by John Davis in 1983, which may or may not be same as original title)	1974	Fifteen cylinders and fifteen b/w photographs of a ceramic cylinder (bronze for National Gallery of Victoria) outside fifteen Melbourne galleries: Munster Arms, Tolarno, Toorak, Joseph Brown, Victorian Artists Society, Chapman Powell Street, Leveson Street, South Yarra, Sweeney Reed, Realities, Stuart Gerstman, Andrew Ivanyi, Pinacotheca, Australian Galleries and National Gallery of Victoria.	One in collection of Noel Hutchison; Fourteen in possession of the artist.

*It seems that these are various titles for the same work.

TITLE OF WORK	YEAR	MEDIA/DIMENSIONS	PRESENT LOCATION
'Inching'	1974	Sixteen b/w photographs, each 18×28 cm, photographer not known.	In collection Flinders University Art Museum
'When You Think About Art What Do You Think About?'	1974	Written reply to question sent to 400 personalities by Ewing Gallery.	Location unknown
'Ingots'	1974	Eight pages of typed material, including one illustration, displayed unmounted, unframed on gallery wall, Pinacotheca, 4–14 September 1974.	Six pages in possession of the artist
'A Tearing Work' or 'Tearing' 'A Tearing Work' (similar, almost identical works, one video, the other Super 8 film)	1974	b/w video (27 minutes) made by a student at Prahran CAE. b/w Super-8 film by John Gardener.	In possession of the artist In possession of the artist
''Box Project'	1974	Kiffy Carter (Rubbo), Director, Ewing Gallery sent identical cardboard boxes to artists. John Davis returned the following two panels: 1 Primary Information — photograph of box $25.4 \times 29.2 \times 33$ cm 2 Secondary Information — Presentation — Perception. Part one — Dimension (drawing); Part two — Surface (drawing); Part three — Material (reduced to pulp on flat surface).	Location unknown
'Place' which included 'Plaiting' and thirteen b/w photographs	1975	1 'Plaiting' — b/w video, 45 minutes; photographer not known; 2 Three b/w photographs of 1.2×1.2 m sheets of hardboard on three roads leading from Mildura (or Monash University); 3 Ten b/w photographs by Susan Vaughan of John Davis tying nine lengths of plaited string together.	In possession of the artist
'Space Definition'	1975	Seventy-nine b/w transparencies.	In possession of the artist
'Substance, Cause, Number, Relation'	1975	Fourteen typed quotations from various philosophers defining space and time.	In possession of the artist
'Passage, Part One, Scan, the You Yangs'	1976	b/w video, 23 minutes.	In possession of the artist
'Passage. Part One. Scan'	1976	Two pages of typed notes, displayed in relation to video of 'Passage'.	In possession of the artist
'Passage. Part Two. Time-Table'	1976	Page of typed notes, displayed in relation to spectator watching video of 'Passage'.	In possession of the artist
'Hattah Installations'	1976	Twenty-six b/w photographs, shown as part of *Nomad*.	In possession of the artist
'Solar Piece, You Yangs'	1977	b/w photograph.	In possession of the artist
Photographs shown at Victorian College of the Arts Gallery, Melbourne, 'Land Marks', 27 Oct.–18 Nov. 1981.	1977–81	b/w photographs: 1 'Solar Piece' and 'With Animal Trap' by John Davis 2 'Place Two — An Installation', photographs by Mark Strizic.	In possession of the artist
'Place Two — An Installation' — photographs shown at Art Gallery of NSW, 'Perspecta 1981', 28 May–21 June 1981	1981	b/w photographs by Mark Strizic.	In possession of the artist

LIST OF EXCHANGE WORKS

These small objects were not offered for sale, but 'in exchange for other art, services or anything the recipient wishes to offer' (John Davis). They varied in size, but were often about 30–50 cm long. The materials were basically twigs tied with cotton, papier mâché and other media such as string, feathers, calico etc.

The first Exchange Works were made in 1976 and were given to students at Prahran College of Advanced Education. Since then large groups of exchange works have been shown on at least seven separate occasions, from which lists of names of owners are available, but other works were given to friends and visitors. The following list is presumed to be incomplete:

■ Exchanges with staff and students at Prahran College of Advanced Education 1976–77 — at least six works.
Mickie Wilson owns one — 27.5 × 12.5 × 5.5 cm

■ Watters Gallery, Sydney, 13–30 July 1977 — twenty-four works.

1 James Pilgrim	13 Geoffrey Proud
2 Robert Owen	14 Michael Rolfe
3 Tony Coleing	15 Richard Maude
4 John McInerny	16 Bernice Murphy
5 Alun & Nola Leach Jones	17 Frank Watters
6 George Mora	18 Marr Grounds
7 Marlee Creaser	19 Mark Koludrovic
8 Michael Hobbs	20 Annie Minchin
9 Geoffrey Legge	21 Colin Offord
10 Anne Cress	22 Michael McKillen
11 Tony Mortimer	23 Tomaso Trini
12 Rosalie Gascoigne	24 Peter Thorn

■ Fourth Indian Triennial, New Delhi, India, February 1978 — nineteen works.

1 S. S. Chadha	11 Amitava Das
2 Mulk Raj Anand	12 Sudha
3 Arti Gupta	13 Umesh Verma
4 Kala Saikia	14 Dilip Choudhury
5 Madhu Gupta	15 Geeta Kapur
6 Suresh Sharma	16 Dharma Ratnam
7 Arati Saikia	17 Kishori Kaul
8 Kishor Umarekar	18 Vivan Sundaram
9 Moti Zharotia	19 Manjit Bawa
10 Jagdish Chander	

■ 'ACT One', Australian National University, Canberra, 4–12 November 1978 — ten works

1 Penny Hunt	6 Mike Wardell
2 Margaret Benyon	7 Jennifer Phipps
3 Sam Ioannou	8 Don Walters
4 Ian Hamilton	9 Rosalie Gascoigne
5 Ingo Kleinert	10 Liz Honybun

■ 'Survey 15. Relics & Rituals', National Gallery of Victoria, 17 July–13 September 1981 — six works were exhibited, but in this case they were not for exchange. These are the only exchange works for which dimensions were kept.

1 48 × 8 × 12 cm	4 30 × 19 × 6 cm
2 29 × 24 × 10 cm	5 57 × 10 × 10 cm
3 14 × 31 × 2 cm	6 46 × 17 × 6 cm

■ 'Continuum '83', Lunami Gallery, Tokyo, Japan, 22 August–3 September 1983 — eleven works.

1 Emiko Namikawa	7 Akira Suzuki
2 Kanae Hagiwara	8 Stelarc
3 Masuki Nakayama	9 Shigeo Tomita
4 Goji Hamada	10 Shigeo Toya
5 Hiroko Yamada	11 S. Anzai
6 Toshikatsu Endo	

■ Anri Gallery, Nagoya, Japan, 9–27 October 1983 — six works.
Names not recorded

■ In addition, similar small works have been given to a number of people, including:
Three artists in Tokanami, Japan
Suzi Gablick, USA
Ken Scarlett — 33 × 14 × 12.5 cm

■ University of Southern California Atelier, Santa Monica, Los Angeles, USA, 17 April–20 May 1984 (also labelled LAICA Exchange Works) — seventeen works.

1 Sheila Elias	10 Joyce Kohl
2 Michael McMillan	11 John M. Miller
3 Dan	12 Giovanna Zamboni
4 Lane Relyea	13 Jerry Wellman
5 Faith Ham	14 Bob Smith
6 Cal Kerr	15 Carol Colin
7 Noel Korten	16 Ellen Freeman
8 Betye Soer	17 Regan Kibbee
9 Irene Freti	

BIBLIOGRAPHY

The following is a list of writings which refer to John Davis or his work. It is arranged in chronological order according to date of publication.

Alan Warren, 'Nolan Brilliant but Baffling', review, *Sun* (Melbourne), 21 September 1965, p. 18.

Charles Bush, 'Whiteley in Depth', review, *The Australian* (national), 1 October 1966, p. 12.

Alan McCulloch, 'Parade of Black Rhythms', review, *Herald* (Melbourne), 5 October 1966, p. 29.

Alan McCulloch, 'Sculpture That Can Breathe', *Herald* (Melbourne), 20 September 1967.

Elwyn Lynn, (unsigned), 'Sculpture', *Broadsheet of the Contemporary Art Society of Australia* (NSW branch), March 1969.

Alan Warren, 'Young Artists Enliven Scene', review, *Sun* (Melbourne), 8 October 1969, p. 28.

Alan McCulloch, 'A Sculptor's Skill', review, *Herald* (Melbourne), 15 October 1969.

Alan McCulloch, 'Prizes for All', review, *Herald* (Melbourne), 30 September 1970.

Elwyn Lynn, 'How to Stimulate Sculptors', review, *Bulletin* (Sydney), 3 October 1970.

Ross Lansell, 'Polished Plumbing', review, *Nation Review* (Sydney), 17 October 1970.

Alan McCulloch, 'Letter from Australia', *Art International* (Zurich), vol. XIV, December 1970, p. 40.

Donald Brook, art review, *Sydney Morning Herald* (Sydney), 20 May 1971.

Daniel Thomas, 'Art Review', *Sunday Telegraph* (Sydney), 23 May 1971.

James Gleeson, 'Art Review', *Sun* (Sydney), 19 May 1971.

Elwyn Lynn, 'Monuments to Boredom', review, *Bulletin* (Sydney), 11 December 1971, p. 45.

Noel Hutchison, 'Sculpturscape '73', *Art and Australia* (Sydney), vol. II, no. 1, July–September 1973.

Maureen Gilchrist, art review, *Age* (Melbourne), 4 September 1974, p. 2.

Alan McCulloch, 'The Inspired Larrikin', *Herald* (Melbourne), 11 September 1974.

Clive Murray-White with John Davis and David Wilson, 'Some Questions and Beliefs', *Art Almanac*, Ewing and George Paton Galleries (Melbourne), June–September 1975.

John Davis, *Place*, catalogue of exhibition at Monash University, 2–26 September 1975.

Noel Hutchison, 'Introduction' to *Place* (ibid).

Stephanie Britton, 'In Search of a Key to Time and Space', review, *News* (Adelaide), 18 September 1975.

Maureen Gilchrist, 'Prints Move into the Limelight', *Age* (Melbourne), 19 September 1975.

David Dolan, 'Art', review, *Sunday Mail* (Adelaide), 28 September 1975.

Noel Sheridan, 'Australia: il possibile è una scelta' (English summary), *Data Arte* (Milan), no. 19, November/December 1975.

Noel Sheridan, 'Part 2, Notes by NS, Mildura 1975', typed notes printed by Mildura Arts Centre.

John Davis, statement in catalogue, *Post Object Art: A Survey of Australia and New Zealand*, Experimental Art Foundation, Adelaide, May 1976.

Alycia Watson, 'Monash Sculptor Experiments with Latex and Fibreglass', *Monash Reporter* (Melbourne), 7 July 1976.

Gary Catalano, 'Non-Mimetic Realism', *Arts Melbourne 1*, Ewing and George Paton Galleries (Melbourne), vol. 1, no. 1, 1976.

Tommaso Trini, 'Domani 1 — Australia' (English summary, 'Australia Next'), *Data* (Milan), no. 26, April–June 1977.

Arthur McIntyre, 'Warmth and Passion in Sticks and Stones', review, *The Australian* (national), 'The Weekend Australian Magazine', 23 July 1977, p. 9.

Nancy Borlase, 'Two Aspects of Nature', review, *Sydney Morning Herald* (Sydney), 23 July 1977.

Margaret Geddes, 'It's a Case of Tit for Tat', interview, *Age* (Melbourne), 18 November 1977.

Norbert Loeffler, 'John Davis', introduction to catalogue, *Two Australian Artists — Fourth Triennale, India*, New Delhi, (printed in Australia), February 1978.

Elwyn Lynn, 'Preface', Australian section *Fourth Triennale — India*, (printed in New Delhi, India), February 1978.

Robert Lindsay, 'Introduction', *Survey 1 — John Davis*, National Gallery of Victoria, Melbourne, 18 March–23 April 1978. Also printed for exhibition at Art Gallery of New South Wales, Sydney, 13 May–18 June 1978.

John Davis, 'Artist's Statement', *Survey 1 — John Davis* (ibid.).

__________ 'Survey 1', colour video, made by National Gallery of Victoria and Media Resource Centre (Melbourne).

Mary Eagle, 'Sculptor of Environment', review, *Age* (Melbourne), 22 March 1978, p. 2.

Ronald Millar, 'The Safe Side', review, *The Australian* (national), 27 March 1978.

Memory Holloway, 'John Davis' Unique Australian Sculpture', review, *Melbourne Times* (Melbourne), 5 April 1978.

Rod Carmichael, 'Teachers Can Do', review, *Sun* (Melbourne), 29 March 1978.

Nancy Borlase, 'From the "sticks and twigs" school', review, *Sydney Morning Herald* (Sydney), 20 May 1978.

W. E. Pidgeon, 'The Maturing of a Sculptor', review, *Sunday Telegraph* (Sydney), 28 May 1978.

Suzanna Short, 'Back to Venice with Sticks and Stones', review, *National Times* (Sydney), week ending 1 July 1978.

Marina Vaizey, 'Venice: Vast and Various', review, *Sunday Times* (London), 2 July 1978.

William Feaver, 'Carnival of the Animals', review, *The Observer* (London), 9 July 1978.

Caroline Tisdall, 'When the Avant Garde goes for a Skate', review, *The Guardian* (London), 8 July 1978.

Graeme Sturgeon, 'Taking Twigs to Venice', review, *The Australian* (national), 14 July 1978.

Robert Hughes, 'It's Biennale Time Again', review, *Time* (Melbourne ed.), 17 July 1978, pp. 48–9.

William Feaver, 'The Biennale's Romp with Nature', review, *New York Times*, 6 August 1978.

Janine Burke, 'Survey Spotlights the New Faces in Art', *National Times* (Sydney), week ending 14 October 1978.

Elwyn Lynn, 'The Venice Biennale', review, *Quadrant* (Sydney), no. 135, October 1978.

Henry Martin, 'The Venice Biennale: Back to Nature', review, *Art International* (Zurich), vol. 22, no. 6, October 1978.

Suzanne Hampel, 'Biennale 1978 Venice', review, *Light Vision* (Sth Yarra, Melbourne), no. 8, November/December 1978.

Elwyn Lynn, 'Letter from Australia', *Art International* (Zurich), vol. XXII, nos. 5–6, Summer 1978.

Graeme Sturgeon, *The Development of Australian Sculpture 1788–1975*, Thames and Hudson (London), 1978.

Daniel Thomas, 'Australia', *General Catalogue, 38th Biennale of Venice: From Art to Nature/From Nature to Art*, Venice 1978.

Elwyn Lynn, 'Introduction', *Venice Biennale 1978: Australia*, Australian catalogue produced by Visual Arts Board, Australia Council, 1978.

Norbert Loeffler, 'John Davis', *Venice Biennale 1978: Australia* (ibid.).

Yusuke Nakahara, 'Invisible Aspects of Sculpture', *Ikebana Ryusei* (Japan), no. 227, March 1979, pp. 16–19.

Robert Rooney, 'Stringy Lines and Horrible Surfaces', review, *Age* (Melbourne), 12 April 1979.

Pierre Restany, 'Restany Forum', *Domus*, no. 596, July 1979.

Akira Moriguchi, 'Original Expression out of Natural Environment — The 3rd Sydney Biennial and Australian Artists', *Mizue* (Tokyo), August 1979.

Nancy Borlase, 'Transferences, Displacements', review, *Sydney Morning Herald* (Sydney), 10 November 1979.

John Davis, Statement on 'Nargen' in *Frieze* (ed. Matt Piscioneri), no. 5, Hobart, 1979.

__________ 'Model of History', *Art Actuel: Skira Annual 79*, Skira (Geneva), 1979.

Ken Scarlett, *Australian Sculptors: Exhibition Lists*, Melbourne State College (Melbourne), 1979, pp. 56–7.

Jeffrey Makin, 'Sculptors Test New Frontiers',

review, *Sun* (Melbourne), 20 February 1980, p. 26.

Robert Rooney, 'Bower-Bird Sculpture', review, *Age* (Melbourne), 21 February 1980.

__________ 'Green Light for Sculpture', *Sunday Mail* Adelaide, 8 June 1980, p. 22.

Peter Anderson, 'John Davis', unpublished notes of lecture given by John Davis at Institute of Modern Art, Brisbane, 5 August 1980.

Dr G. Langer, 'Boyd Reaches for the Past', review, *Courier Mail* (Brisbane), 14 August 1980.

Tony Bond, 'Introduction', *John Davis: A Sculptural Installation*, Wollongong City Gallery, 10 September–12 October 1980.

Tonia Zanetti, 'Sculptors Share Purpose and Idea', *Illawarra Mercury* (Wollongong), 3 October 1980.

Neville Weston, 'Shaping Up', *Advertiser* (Adelaide), 4 October 1980, p. 24.

Gladys Little, 'Art — The Local Scene', *Illawarra District News* (Wollongong), vol. 1, no. 28, November 1980.

Mike Burnett, 'John Sculpts All Elements', *News* (Adelaide), 8 December 1980, p. 8.

__________ 'Village Creation To Go On Display', *Courier* (Adelaide), 17 December 1980.

Ken Scarlett, *Australian Sculptors*, Thomas Nelson (Melbourne), 1980, pp. 161–4.

__________ *Art Actuel: Skira Annual*, special issue, 1970–1980, Skira (Geneva), 1980.

Suzi Gablik, 'Report from Australia', *Art in America* (New York), vol. 69, no. 1, January 1981, pp. 29–37.

Suzi Gablik, 'Report from Australia, Part 1', *Art and Australia* (Sydney), vol. 18, no. 3, Autumn 1981.

Rosemarie Brooks, 'Common Culture Community Sculpture', *Artlink* (Adelaide), vol. 1, no. 2, May 1981, pp. 6–7.

Bernice Murphy, untitled, *Australian Perspecta 1981*, catalogue of 'A Biennial Survey of Contemporary Australian Art', Art Gallery of New South Wales, 29 May–21 June 1981, p. 69.

Robert Lindsay, 'Relics and Rituals', introduction to *Survey 15: Relics and Rituals*, National Gallery of Victoria, 17 July–13 September 1981.

John Davis, 'Artist's Statement', *Relics and Rituals* (ibid.).

Janine Burke, 'Relics and Rituals', review, *National Times* (Sydney), 26 July 1981.

Janine Burke, 'John Davis', review, *National Times* (Sydney), 16–22 August 1981, p. 34.

Nancy Borlase, 'Time, Space and Relics Dominate New Sculpture', review, *Sydney Morning Herald* (Sydney), 14 November 1981.

Sandra McGrath, 'Vegetate or Bust', review, *The Australian* (national), The 'Weekend Australian Magazine', 21 November 1981.

Tim McLachlan, 'Sydney', review, *National Times* (Sydney), 22 November 1981.

Janet Hawley, 'Art Patrick White Admires', *Age* (Melbourne), 22 December 1981, p. 11.

__________ 'Exchange of Contemporary Work', *In* (Tokyo), no. 19, December 1981.

Graeme Sturgeon, 'Mildura Rides Again', *Art and Australia* (Sydney), Summer 1981.

Ken Scarlett, 'John Davis in Japan', *Ina — Art News*, catalogue of exhibition at Ina Gallery (Tokyo), 1–29 October 1982.

Ken Scarlett, 'John Davis at Watters', *Art and Australia* (Sydney), vol. 20, no. 2, Summer 1982, pp. 237–40.

__________ 'Naked Faces '82. Mr John Davis: Australian Artist Known for his Bush Art', *Komei* newspaper (Tokyo), 17 October 1982, p. 3.

John Davis, 'Some Brief Notes on Issues Which I Think are Raised in My Art', originally written for *Ikebana Ohara* magazine (Tokyo) 1982, later published in *Presence and Absence* (ibid.).

__________ 'Exhibitions', *Mainichi Shimbun*, evening edn (Tokyo), 28 October 1982.

__________ 'Modelling a Rich but Alienated World', *Asahi* newspaper (Tokyo), 23 October 1982, p. 5.

__________ 'Art News', *Geijutsu Shincho* (Japan), November 1982, p. 14.

__________ 'Outdoor Work by Davis', *Ikebana Sogetsu* (Japan), no. 145, December 1982, p. 104.

Leon Paroissien, 'Provincialism, Pluralism and Professionalism', *Australian Art Review*, Warner Associates, (Sydney) 1982, pp. 7–10.

Graeme Sturgeon, 'Sculpture', *Australian Art Review* (ibid.), p. 22.

Nancy Borlase, 'A Time of Uncertainty. The Visual Arts in Sydney', *Australian Art Review*, (ibid.), p. 51.

Goji Hamada, 'Art Focus: Performance. John Davis: Long Journey', *Bijutsu Techo* (Japan), vol. 35, no. 505, January 1983, pp. 216–17.

Rod O'Brien, 'Journey Extended, or Meeting of Eucalypt and Bamboo', *Ikebana Ryusei* (Tokyo), no. 273, January 1983, pp. 34–9.

John Davis, 'A Sense of Place', *Presence and Absence*, Art Gallery of Western Australia, 17 February–27 March 1983.

John Davis, 'A Sense of Place', *Sculpture* (ed. by Max Darby, Barbara Dover and Reimunde Zunde), Education Department of Victoria (Melbourne), 1983.

John Davis, Goji Hamada, Ken Scarlett, 'Bush Art of John Davis', *SOKA Ikebana Ohara* (Tokyo), no. 387, February 1983.

Memory Holloway, 'The Mid-Career Backroom Boys', review, *Age* (Melbourne), 23 June 1983, p. 14.

Bruce Adams, 'Presence and Absence: The Gallery as Other Place', *Art and Text* (Melbourne), no. 10, Winter 1983.

__________ 'Plans to Open Australian Contemporary Art Exhibition', *Asahi* newspaper (Tokyo), 25 July 1983, p. 21.

__________ 'Express. Noteworthy New Trends in Australian Contemporary Art, *Q* (Tokyo), 29 July 1983, p. 16.

__________ 'What's On Next Week', *The Japan Times* (Tokyo), 20 August 1983, p. 10.

Kaoru Tanaka, 'Australian Contemporary Art Exhibition '83', *Mainichi Grafh* (Tokyo), 29 August 1983, p. 40.

Rosemary Warburton, 'Enduring Images', *Asahi Evening News* (Tokyo), 26 August 1983, p. 10.

__________ 'Art From Down Under Shows up in Tokyo', *Japan Times Weekly* (Tokyo), 27 August 1983, p. 4.

Barbara Thoren, 'The Week in Art', *Japan Times* (Tokyo), 28 August 1983, p. 9.

John Davis, 'Continuum '83', *Lunami Journal* (Tokyo), August 1983.

__________ *Continuum '83*. Lunami Gallery and fifteen other galleries in Tokyo, 22 August–3 September 1983, includes statement by John Davis.

Robert Lindsay, 'An Assembled View of Sculpture', *Australian Art Review*, Warner Associates (Sydney), 1983, pp. 67–8.

Neville Weston, *In the Public Eye. Public Art in Australia*, Visual Arts Board, Australia Council (Sydney), 1983.

Ken Scarlett, 'Continuum '83', *Art and Australia* (Sydney), vol. 21, no. 2, Summer 1983, pp. 178, 179.

Dr Peter Emmett, 'Foreword', *Asian Interface: Australia-Japan*, Crafts Councils Centre Gallery, Sydney, 13 August–18 September 1983.

(Assistance with collection of material — Freda Freiberg and Rod O'Brien), '1. Ginza Galleries Go All Australian. Unique Art Which Continues to Ask the Question of Identity, Introduced Through the Works of 71 Artists', *Pia* (Tokyo), PIA News network, 12 August 1983.

Memory Holloway, 'A Clash of Culture', *Age* (Melbourne), 25 August 1983, p. 14.

Goji Hamada, 'Australian Contemporary Art Assembled in Tokyo. Fascinating Art in a State of Growth', *SOKA Ikebana Ohara* (Tokyo), no. 393, August 1983, pp. 22–41.

__________ 'Summer 1983. The Hot Wind of Art Blows Up from the South. ''Continuum, '83' Australian Contemporary Art Exhibition', (Art) *Elle Japon* (Tokyo), September 1983.

__________ 'Australian Contemporary Art Exhibition — Continuum '83', (Current Exhibitions), *Kateigaho* (Tokyo), September 1983.

Emiko Namikawa, 'The First Privately Organised International Exhibition Ends', *Sankei* newspaper (evening edn) (Tokyo), 9 September 1983, p. 9.

Rod O'Brien, 'A Whiff of Eucalypts Along the Ginza', *Sydney Morning Herald* (Sydney), 6 September 1983.

Janet Hawley, 'Australia and the Asian Connection: how Ginger Meggs turned Japanese', *Age*, 'Saturday Extra' (Melbourne), 24 September 1983.

Memory Holloway, 'Sculpture Comes in from the Cold', *Age* (Melbourne), 19 October 1983, p. 14.

Tadashi Akafude, 'Australian Contemporary Art '83. Departure and Return/From Living Aboriginal Art/And a Pitiless Nature', *Ikebana Ryusei* (Tokyo), no. 283, November 1983, pp. 30–5.

Hisao Matsuura, Exhibitions, 'Continuum '83/Australian Contemporary Art Exhibition. A Traveller's Notebook', *Bijutsu Techo* (Tokyo), vol. 35, no. 517, November 1983, pp. 174–9.

Kojin Tanaka, 'From Contemporary Australian Art — Change of Idiom', *SOKA Ikebana Ohara* (Tokyo), no. 396, November 1983.

Goji Hamada, 'Long Hot Summer — Exchange of Feeling', *SOKA Ikebana Ohara* (Tokyo), no. 396, November 1983.

__________ 'Sculpture on the Increase', *Goulburn Post* (NSW), 23 January 1984, p. 9.

Suzi Gablic, *Has Modernism Failed?*, Thames and Hudson (New York), c. 1984.

John Davis, 'Catalogue Statement', for exhibition 'Austausch/Exchange', organised by Marr Grounds, with eight artists, Ivan Dougherty Gallery, Sydney, 17 March–17 April 1984 and Gryphon Gallery, Melbourne, 29 October–23 November 1984.

Susanna Short, 'Art Work Has Strong Political Overtones', *Sydney Morning Herald* (Sydney), 29 March 1984, p. 10.

Josine Ianco-Starrels, 'A "Triple" for LA Contemporary', review, *Los Angeles Times* (USA), 22 April 1984.

Robert L. Pincus, 'Primitivism from Australia', review, *Los Angeles Times* (USA), 27 April 1984.

Tadashi Akatsu, 'Continuum '83 Review', *Art-Network* (Sydney), Spring 1984, pp. 43-5.

Peter Callas, 'Continuum Midstream', *Art-Network* (ibid.), pp. 46–8.

Lyndal Jones, 'The Continuum Symposium on Australian Art', *Art-Network* (ibid.), p. 49.

Susanna Short, Campus newspaper (name unknown), 'USC Atelier', University of Southern California, 12 April 1984, p. 11.

Peter Haynes, 'David Jensz/Wendy Teakel', introduction to catalogue, Canberra School of Art Gallery, 12 May–10 June 1984.

Paul Taylor, 'A Culture of Temporary Culture', *Australia: Nine Contemporary Artists*, Los Angeles Institute of Contemporary Art, 30 June–14 August 1984, pp. 11–14.

Daniel Alexander Wasil, 'Summary', *Australia: Nine Contemporary Artists* (ibid.), p. 15.

John Davis, 'A Sense of Place', plus photographs of work, *Australia: Nine Contemporary artists* (ibid.), pp. 16–23.

John Davis, Biography, Exhibitions, Bibliography, *Australia: Nine Contemporary Artists* (ibid.), p. 82.

Robert L. Pincus, 'Olympic Arts Festival. Nine Australians Offer Art that Fits the Gallery', *Los Angeles Times* (USA), 19 July 1984, part VI.

Robert L. Pincus, 'A Different Perspective from Australian Artists', *Los Angeles Times* (USA), 24 July 1984.

Jenepher Duncan, *Acquisitions and Alternatives, Sculpture*, in an exhibition of the same name, Monash University Gallery, 1–30 November 1984.

Graeme Sturgeon, 'Australian Sculpture Now', in catalogue of Second Australian Sculpture Triennial, National Gallery of Victoria, 6 November 1984–28 January 1985, p. 30, pp. 84–5, p. 204.

Janina Green, 'From the Walls of Misunderstanding', review, *Melbourne Times* (Melbourne), 7 November 1984, p. 14.

Sue Cramer, 'Seduced by the Clenched Fist of the Mass Media', review, *Age* (Melbourne), 14 November 1984, p. 14.

Sue Cramer, 'Chance to Assess Work of the Eighties', review, *Age* (Melbourne), 17 November 1984.

Sue Cramer, 'Teasing Images and Emblems into a Painted Tapestry', review, *Age* (Melbourne), 21 November 1984, p. 14.

Kim Martin, 'Artistic Creation, Thought Fuse in Sculptural Unity', review, *Age* (Melbourne), 20 December 1984, p. 14.

Graeme Sturgeon, *Sculpture at Mildura*, Mildura City Council (Mildura), 1985.

Gary Catalano, *An Intimate Australia. The Landscape and Recent Australian Art*, Hale and Iremonger (Sydney), 1985.

Terence Maloon, 'Bridges of Imagination Span Different Minds and Cultures', review, *Sydney Morning Herald* (Sydney), 30 March 1985.

Elwyn Lynn, 'A Palette of Harmony', review, *The Australian* (national), '*Weekend Australian Magazine*', 30–31 March 1985.

Ken Scarlett, 'Japanese Ceramists and Sculptors in Australia', *Pottery in Australia* (Sydney), vol. 24, no. 2, May 1985.

Mary Dineen, 'Is There Still Life With Earth?' *Mercury* (Hobart), 29 June 1985.

K. M., untitled article, *Los Angeles Times* (USA), part VI, 18 April 1986, p. 16.

__________ 'John Davis', *West Hollywood Paper* (USA), vol. 1, no. 37, 8 May 1986.

Kojin Tanaka, 'Harmony of Concrete and Abstract', *Mainichi* (Tokyo), 13 May 1986, p. 3.

__________ 'Art', *Asahi Journal* (Tokyo), 30 May 1986, p. 37.

Merle Schipper, 'Shapes of the Spirit', *Art Week* (USA), 31 May 1986.

Noriaki Kitazawa, 'Art and/or Installation', review, *Ikebana Ryusei* (Tokyo), no. 316, August 1986.

John Davis, 'Seiji Kunishima', Introduction to catalogue of Seiji Kunishima exhibition, Victorian College of the Arts, 20 August–3 September 1987.

INDEX

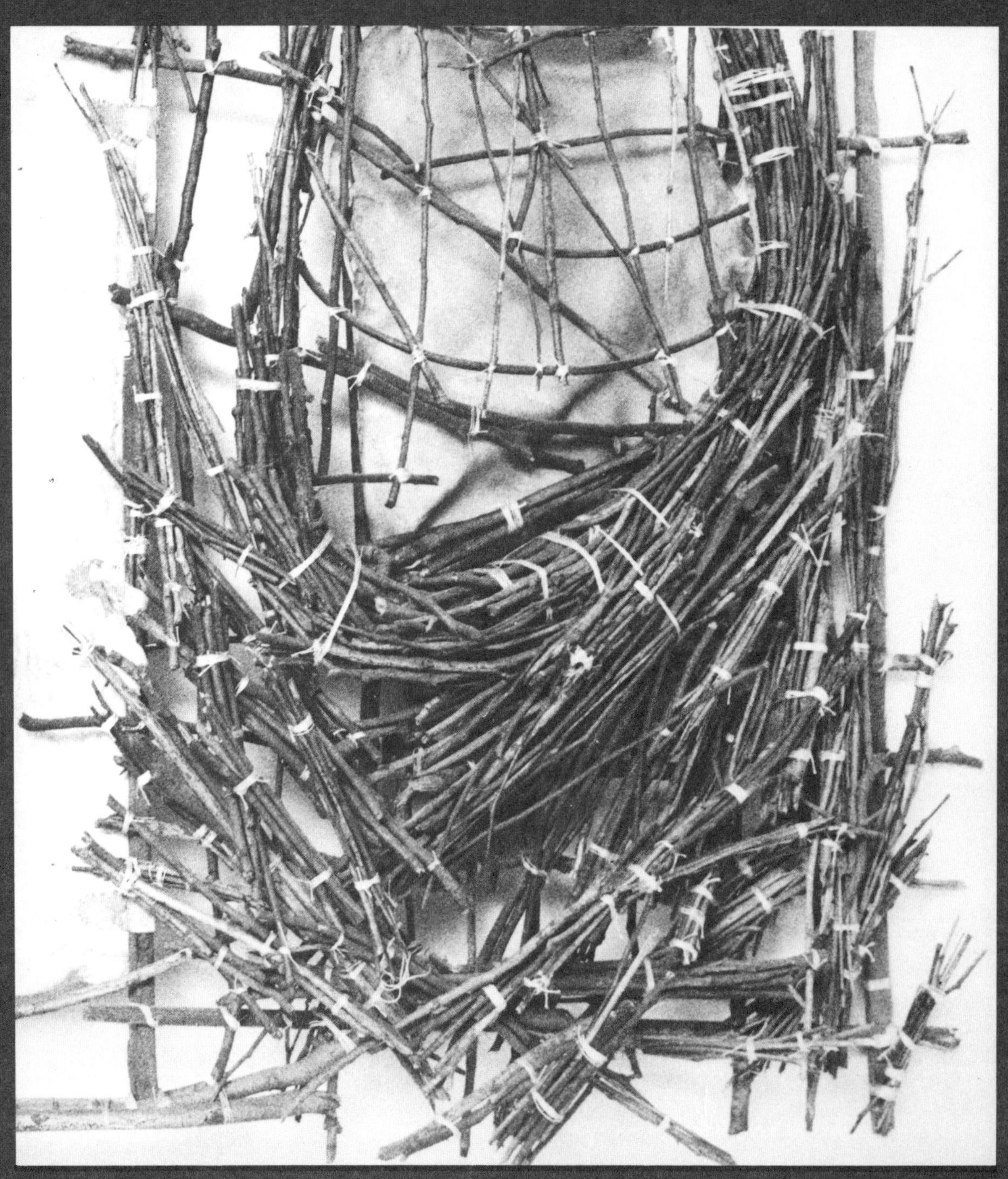